# LETHAL
# FRONTIERS

# LETHAL FRONTIERS

## A Soviet View of Nuclear Strategy, Weapons, and Negotiations

**Alexei G. Arbatov**

Translated by Kent D. Lee

Foreword by William G. Hyland

PRAEGER        New York
Westport, Connecticut
London

**Library of Congress Cataloging-in-Publication Data**

Arbatov, Alekseĭ Georgievich.
    Lethal frontiers.

    Translation of: Voenno-strategicheskiĭ paritet i
politika SShA.
    Bibliography: p.
    Includes index.
    1. United States—Military policy.  2. Nuclear
warfare.  3. United States—Foreign relations—
1981–   .  4. Nuclear arms control.  5. Soviet
Union—Military policy.    I. Title.
UA23.A68813        1988         355'.0335'73         88–15538
ISBN 0–275–93017–3 (alk. paper)

Library of Congress Catalog Card Number: 88–15538
ISBN: 0–275–93017–3

First published in 1988

Praeger Publishers, One Madison Avenue, New York, NY 10010
A division of Greenwood Press, Inc.

Printed in the United States of America

The paper used in this book complies with the
Permanent Paper Standard issued by the National
Information Standards Organization (Z39.48–1984).

10   9   8   7   6   5   4   3   2   1

# Contents

# Abbreviations

| | |
|---|---|
| ABRES | Advanced Ballistic Reentry System |
| ABM | Anti-Ballistic Missile |
| ACDA | Arms Control and Disarmament Agency |
| ALCM | Air-Launched Cruise Missile |
| ASAT | Anti-Satellite |
| ASBM | Air-to-Surface Ballistic Missile |
| ASW | Anti-Submarine Warfare |
| ATBM | Anti-Tactical Ballistic Missile |
| BMD | Ballistic Missile Defense |
| $C^3$ | Command, Control, and Communications |
| $C^3I$ | Command, Control, Communications, and Intelligence |
| CIA | Central Intelligence Agency |
| CMC | Cruise Missile Carrier |
| CONUS | Continental United States |
| CPSU | Communist Party of the Soviet Union |
| CSB | Closely Spaced Basing |
| DARPA | Defense Advanced Research Projects Agency |
| DDR&E | Director, Defense Research and Engineering |
| DEW | Directed Energy Weapon |

| | |
|---|---|
| DoD | Department of Defense |
| DSARC | Defense Systems Acquisition Review Council |
| ELF | Extremely Low Frequency |
| FY | Fiscal Year |
| GLCM | Ground-Launched Cruise Missile |
| ICBM | Intercontinental Ballistic Missile |
| INF | Intermediate Nuclear Forces |
| IRBM | Intermediate-Range Ballistic Missile |
| JCS | Joint Chiefs of Staff |
| JSTPS | Joint Strategic Target Planning Staff |
| KEW | Kinetic Energy Weapon |
| LoADS | Low-Altitude Defense System |
| MAD | Mutual Assured Destruction |
| MAPS | Multiple Aim Point System |
| MARV | Maneuverable Reentry Vehicle |
| MIRV | Multiple Independently-Targetable Reentry Vehicle |
| MIT | Massachusetts Institute of Technology |
| MPS | Multiple Protective Shelters |
| MX | Missile, Experimental |
| NASA | National Aeronautics and Space Agency |
| NATO | North Atlantic Treaty Alliance |
| NAVSTAR | Navigation Satellite Timing and Ranging |
| NESC | Net Evalutation Subcommittee |
| NSC | National Security Council |
| NSDM | National Security Decision Memorandum |
| NSSM | National Security Study Memorandum |
| PD | Presidential Directive |
| PRM | Presidential Review Memorandum |
| SAC | Strategic Air Command |
| SALT | Strategic Arms Limitations Talks |
| SATKA | Surveillance, Acquisition, Tracking, and Kill Assessment |
| SDI | Strategic Defense Initiative |
| SIOP | Single Integrated Operational Plan |
| SLBM | Submarine-Launched Ballistic Missile |
| SLCM | Sea-Launched Cruise Missile |

| | |
|---|---|
| SOI | Strategicheskaia oboronnaia initsiativa [Strategic Defense Initiative] |
| SSBN | Ballistic Missile Submarine, Nuclear-powered |
| SSN | Submarine, Nuclear-powered |
| START | Strategic Arms Reductions |
| TACAMO | Take Charge and Move Out (Airborne Strategic Communications System) |
| TEL | Transporter-Erector-Launcher |
| TVD | Teatr voennykh deistvii [Theater of Military Operations] |
| UN | United Nations |
| USSR | Union of Soviet Socialist Republics |
| VSTOL | Vertical/Short Take-off and Landing |
| WTO | Warsaw Treaty Organization |

## Western and Soviet Designations of Soviet Missiles

| | |
|---|---|
| SS-4 | R-12 |
| SS-5 | R-14 |
| SS-11 | Soviet designation still classified |
| SS-12 | OTR-22 |
| SS-13 | RS-12 |
| SS-17 | RS-16 |
| SS-18 | RS-20 |
| SS-19 | RS-18 |
| SS-20 | RSD-10 Pioneer |
| SS-23 | OTR-23 |
| SS-24 | RS-22 |
| SS-25 | RS-12M |
| SS-N-6 | Soviet designation still classified |
| SS-N-18 | RSM-50 |
| SS-N-20 | Typhoon |
| SS-N-23 | Soviet designation still classified |
| SS-CX-4 | RK-55 |
| | |
| R | Raketa [Missile] |

RS          Raket strategicheskaia [Strategic Missile]

RSD         Raketa srednei dal'nosti [Intermediate-Range Missile]

OTR         Operativno-takticheskaia raketa [Operational-Tactical
            Missile]

RSM         Raketa Strategicheskaia Morskaia [Strategic Naval Missile]

RK          Raketa krylataia [Cruise Missile]

# Foreword

For over fifty years the United States has had formal diplomatic relations with the Soviet Union. For most of this period, with a few brief interludes, the relationship has been deeply troubled, often hostile, and confrontational. Contacts were usually confined to official representatives. There were occasional cultural exchanges and other meetings, but on the whole there was an amazing lack of communication between two countries and two peoples whose destinies were so deeply intertwined.

Perhaps in recognition of this dearth of contact and communication there grew up over the last twenty years an informal network of exchanges, contacts, discussions, and debates. On the Soviet side there was a group of scholars belonging to institutes (such as the Institute for the Study of the USA and Canada and the Institute for the Study of the International Economy) who had dedicated themselves to the study of the United States and its relations with the Soviet Union, especially in the matter of arms control. This coterie of intelligent and unusually well-informed Soviet scholars gradually became better known in the United States not only to their counterparts in U.S. institutions and universities, but eventually recognized by the U.S. media. One could even observe on U.S. television some of these Soviet experts debating openly with Americans.

Americans also found that on the Soviet side there were often interesting new ideas, novel analyses of old problems, and innovative solutions to difficult issues. Gradually it became apparent that this group of Soviet scholars had a latitude to explore even sensitive issues. Moreover, they were even free to question, albeit carefully, the policies of their own government.

In sum, there was a dialogue developing between the United States and the Soviet Union taking place on an informal but well-informed level. One participant was the author of this book, Alexei Arbatov.

Yet, strangely, there was not a great deal of written material. Soviet publications remained largely for Soviet audiences and American publications were designed for audiences in the United States. To be sure, there were exchanges of informal papers between groups and between scholars but little was published in the United States or in the Soviet Union by authors from the other side.

For example, in the American quarterly, *Foreign Affairs*, there was only one contemporary Soviet author—Nikita Khrushchev—who wrote on "peaceful coexistence" in 1958. This invisible barrier began to break down as Soviet articles began to circulate more freely, but the other half of this process did not proceed as well. In other words, few U.S. articles or books on sensitive political and strategic matters were published in the Soviet Union.

One hopes that the appearance of Mikhail Gorbachev's book, *Perestroika*, will be a breakthrough and will lead in fact to the publication of more books and articles on politics in both countries.

In this light, this volume by Alexei Arbatov is to be welcomed by U.S. readers. Mr. Arbatov is one of the young generation of Soviet scholars who have made a major effort to understand the arcane subjects of strategy, arms control, and strategic forces, as well as to understand the thought processes on these issues in the United States and in his own homeland. In the pages that follow, Mr. Arbatov succeeds in illuminating from a Soviet perspective the last two decades of interaction between the United States and the Soviet Union on strategic affairs. One will find some surprising conclusions—things do indeed look different from the other side. One will also find, however, penetrating insights into the arms control process as well as viewpoints on both sides.

For those of us who participated in many of the events described in this book, Mr. Arbatov brings some fresh interpretations that are indeed thought-provoking. But one does not have to be a participant or even an expert to appreciate the value of this book. It is the beginning, we can only hope, of a new level of exchange in which books are written in order to be published inside the Soviet Union or the United States, and written by scholars who have broken free of most of the ideological constraints that have so badly marred the relationship between the two countries in the past.

William G. Hyland

# Translator's Note

An earlier version of this book was originally published in the Soviet Union in 1984 under the title *Voenno-strategicheskii paritet i politika SShA* [Military-Strategic Parity and U.S. Policy]. A number of changes besides the title, however, distinguish the present volume from the original. Various insertions have been added by the author to Chapters 1 through 6, usually in order to juxtapose a point with some aspect of Soviet strategic forces, doctrine, or policy. The result is to create a more balanced treatment. Chapter 7 has undergone substantial revision, particularly concerning its original description of events preceding the Soviet walkout from the negotiations in late 1983. Most significant is the addition of a completely new Chapter 8 and Conclusion, reflecting events through January 1988. Throughout the book, minor changes of a semantic nature (for example, softening inflammatory text of no substantive import that was solely inserted for domestic consumption) have been made.

This translation was undertaken for three main reasons. First, the book is arguably one of the most sophisticated and intellectually honest interpretations of U.S. strategic policy and U.S. -Soviet relations to come out of the Soviet Union in the postwar era. By that virtue alone it commends itself to a wider, especially American, readership. One measure of the book's significance in Soviet eyes was its publication by the CPSU Central Committee's prestigious press *Political Literature Publishers* in a run of 100,000 copies, far above the circulation that might normally be expected for a book of this nature. Second, this translation is offered with the hope that its publication will inspire others to help fill the

...ous gap in good Soviet scholarship available to those in the West ...ersed in Russian. In the social sciences the vast majority of translated ...iet monographs have been made available either through the U.S. ...epartment of Defense and related agencies (and only then on strictly ...nilitary topics of dubious utility for all but the narrowest of specialists), or through publishing houses in the Soviet Union, whose self-selection of those works to be translated render them unacceptable to a broad Western audience for obvious reasons. Finally, the translation of this book has been accompanied throughout by the hope that, as Robert Legvold suggested, it may serve as the basis for an intellectual and constructive dialogue between U.S. observers and their Soviet counterparts.

A number of individuals have contributed directly or indirectly to the fact of this book's translation. Greatest thanks of all goes to Edward Beliaev, without whose native expertise and willingness to give me academic credit for my work I would never have been allowed to complete this translation while still in graduate school. Professor Marshall Shulman's praise of Alexei Arbatov as perhaps the most outstanding and objective of the new generation of specialists in the Soviet Union on U.S.-Soviet relations and arms control spawned the very idea of translating this book. Also deserving of special thanks for his encouragement is Professor Robert Legvold, Director of the W. Averell Harriman Institute for Advanced Study of the Soviet Union. Vladimir Pechatnov and Vitaly Zhurkin generously helped transport a nearly 500-page manuscript between New York and Moscow. Bryan May of the Columbia University libraries was instrumental in helping me track down obscure government documents. Dan Eades of Praeger deserves much credit for his willingness to take a chance with this book's publication. Finally, I am greatly indebted to Melanie Allen, without whose initial collaboration this translation would never have gotten underway.

Comments on the quality of the translation are of course welcome. Needless to say, any inaccuracies are solely my responsibility.

# Preface

The elimination of U.S. nuclear superiority and the emergence of strategic parity in the late 1960s and early 1970s, and its consolidation in the course of the last decade, is a historic achievement of the Soviet people. Parity plays a most important role in the global correlation of forces between socialism and capitalism, and provides an opportunity for agreements to curb the arms race and to avert thermonuclear war.

For the United States, this objectively established strategic equilibrium, or parity, has put it in an essentially new situation. Washington's policy has made armed force an invariable attribute of U.S. foreign policy, which constantly strives for military superiority over all potential enemies. The U.S. doctrine of nuclear superiority occupies a special place in this regard. Having been the first to create and use the atomic bomb, the United States made the atomic monopoly the foundation of its relations with the surrounding world after World War II. After Washington lost its atomic monopoly in the 1950s, and after it lost its invulnerability to weapons of mass destruction in the first half of the 1960s, U.S. foreign policy was built upon the doctrine of nuclear superiority. This doctrine was the foundation of the U.S. policy of confrontation with the Soviet Union, and became the most important instrument of its "crisis diplomacy." Superiority over the USSR has been made a pledge of U.S. nuclear guarantees to allies and a central pillar of the leading U.S. position in the bilateral and multilateral military-political blocs of imperialism that have secured the unprecedented economic, political, and military expansion of the United States abroad.

Finally, this doctrine has been the means for strengthening the domestic political influence of the conservative wing of the U.S. ruling class, and has become undisputed dogma and a guide to action for the powerful military-industrial complex.

It is obvious that the formation of the Soviet-U.S. strategic balance has given rise to extremely complex and highly contradictory processes in all these aspects of U.S. foreign and domestic policy. As events of the 1970s and 1980s have shown, the results of these processes are hardly consistent. On one hand, they have been expressed at a certain level in the United States' attempts to adjust itself to parity. Its participation in arms control agreements and in certain steps directed toward relaxing tensions was connected with the strengthening of realistically thinking circles in the general public and in the U.S. ruling class itself. On the other hand, Washington has not abandoned efforts to tip parity in its favor, to impose upon the USSR unequal agreements in the nuclear arms area. These efforts continued throughout the 1970s, and at the beginning of the current decade U.S. military programs were accelerated. Washington's policy of global confrontation with socialism and the national liberation movements was invigorated, and the influence of hardliners inside the United States grew. The further development of these contradictory tendencies will directly affect the intensity and scale of the arms race, the prospects for a dialogue on limiting and reducing the growing arsenals of destruction, the future of relaxing international tension, and the possibility of decreasing the threat of thermonuclear war.

The situation of strategic parity was new not only for the United States but also for the Soviet Union. In the course of the 1970s and 1980s in Soviet policy as well took place a process of adaptation to the new realities, a process that at times was highly complex. Until the attainment of parity by the early 1970s the USSR's maximum efforts in constructing its strategic forces automatically strengthened its security, since they reduced U.S. nuclear superiority. In subsequent years, in the conditions of strategic parity, it was realized that the efforts of one side to strengthen defense facilitate security only up to certain limits, at which point they begin to pose a larger threat to the other side's security. In such an event this gives rise to countermeasures by the opponent and the growth of tension, and ultimately damages its own security. The realization of this natural law became one of the main principles of new political thinking and the "philosophy of mutual security" in Moscow in the second half of the 1980s. Also in the period of U.S. nuclear superiority in the 1950s and 1960s, as a certain compensation, asymmetries were accumulated in intermediate-range nuclear forces and conventional armed forces in Europe. The equalized correlation of forces at a higher level has put on the agenda the elimination of disproportions at lower levels of the military balance.

The importance of a comprehensive study of these subjects is borne out, on the one hand, by the significance of the problem of restraining the arms race and averting war in contemporary conditions, and on the other, by the most serious negative changes that have occurred in the 1980s in the sphere of U.S. strategic arms policy. When speaking of the military-strategic balance, or parity, one must first of all clarify the meaning of this most important political concept. It is true that the military correlation of forces can be calculated by various measures, since it has a great number of different parameters in a process of constant and multiphased change, and quite often leaders in the West associated with the campaign on "Soviet superiority" profit by this. The quantity of nuclear launchers (both cruise and ballistic missiles, and heavy bombers able to deliver nuclear weapons a corresponding distance) as well as the number of nuclear warheads and their total yield all relate to the objective criteria of parity on global and regional (European) levels. Thus parity, of course, cannot signify an absolute, mirrored balance of the two sides' strategic forces, which differ substantially from each other in structure, geostrategic position, military doctrines, and operational concepts.

At the same time it is obvious that the notions of "equality," "equilibrium," and "parity" have a broader meaning than simply a characteristic of the balance of strategic forces in respect to launchers, warheads, total yield and other quantitative indices. It is obvious because the strategic arms race is now increasingly moving into a qualitative area. And here the main hopes are connected with replacing present strategic weapons systems with new, much more effective ones, and also with securing improved means of their control, which in principle can be accomplished even without a noticeable change in the number of nuclear launchers and warheads, total weapons yield, and so forth. Consequently, in approaching the strategic balance as the most important condition for strengthening security and averting nuclear war, a study of the entire complex of qualitative and other factors in the nuclear balance, along with a quantitative comparison of military potentials, will acquire increasingly greater significance.

Negotiations and agreements on limiting strategic arms create an opportunity for a fundamentally new approach to the entire complex of the contemporary problems of war and politics. Security cannot be based on a "balance of terror" in which a constant buildup of nuclear arsenals raises the threat of universal destruction to higher and higher lethal frontiers. Arms control negotiations can actively influence the strategic balance in the direction of reducing its levels, limiting and prohibiting new kinds and types of destructive technology, and decreasing the possibility and probability of a nuclear Armageddon with the goal of strengthening the stability of the strategic situation.

# LETHAL
# FRONTIERS

# 1

## The Emergence of Strategic Nuclear Parity

In the late 1960s and early 1970s the change in the overall correlation of forces in the world arena became so apparent that Western leaders were forced to undertake a reevaluation of their foreign policies, which from the late 1940s had been based on U.S. global hegemony. The most important of the new realities was the formation of approximate parity in the quantitative balance of U.S. and Soviet strategic forces, which undermined the foundation of postwar U.S. policy—the doctrine of "nuclear superiority." Attempts by leading U.S. circles to adapt to the fundamentally new strategic situation in the late 1960s and first half of the 1970s had a highly contradictory character. On the one hand, the attempts included measures directed toward changing the nuclear balance, toward attaining unilateral military advantages. At the same time, the significance of the changes that had taken place in the U.S. approach to strategic nuclear arms and the balance of forces made possible a number of significant steps in the area of arms control and the general easing of military and political tensions in East-West relations.

President Richard Nixon's administration came to power at one of the most difficult and dramatic moments in U.S. history. Serious defeats in the international arena, economic and social shocks, a deep internal political split, and an unprecedented wave of disillusionment with traditional U.S. ideals and institutions had led to a national crisis in the United States. The most acute and pressing problem was connected with the failure of U.S. aggression in Southeast Asia. For all its importance, however, the difficulties that confronted the United States were still deeper. For the defeat in Indochina was not an isolated episode, but only the most eloquent manifestation of the failure of the whole "cold war" policy, of global politics "from a position of strength," pursued by Washington after World War II. Having come to power in 1969, the Republican administration encountered essentially two kinds of circumstances in the world arena. On the one hand, it had to deal with the further development of tendencies and realities that had become unmistakably apparent the decade before. On the other hand, it inherited the failures and problems brought on by the Democratic administrations' policies in the 1960s, which themselves had been conceived as the answer to the realities of the surrounding world.

In this background can be found the sources of the revision of U.S. foreign policy, in all its contradiction, which was outlined at the beginning of the 1970s. U.S. policy in the strategic arms area, formulated within the overall framework of the emerging reappraisal of U.S. foreign policy as a whole, was especially tightly rooted in the events of the previous decade. It was precisely in that period—the 1960s—that the ideas and concepts of U.S. nuclear strategy were formulated and became the "coordinate axes" or main point of departure for U.S. strategic thought in a fundamentally new situation for the United States—the condition of the vulnerability of U.S. territory to the other side's nuclear weapons. At that very time—because strategic arms require many years of development and production—the majority of the strategic weapons systems that the United States has or is now putting into service was deployed or began to be developed. At the same time, the 1960s have exceptional significance in the history of U.S. foreign policy in another area. Precisely then, after an unprecedentedly large, expensive and futile buildup of strategic nuclear potential, the idea of Soviet-U.S. negotiations on limiting strategic arms received sufficiently broad recognition in the United States.

Elected president in 1968, Richard Nixon, despite his conservative reputation, turned out to be sufficiently flexible politically to understand the importance of the changes in the surrounding world, within the country, and in the attitudes of the U.S. ruling circles, who had allowed him to take the helm of the state machine. Indeed, the new realities were becoming so apparent and urgent that it was impossible not to reckon with them. The changed mood of the ruling circles, stunned and split by the U.S. defeat in Vietnam, and the broad antiwar movement of the American public demanded the reduction of the burden of the U.S. expansionist global policy, the curtailment of excessive U.S. intervention abroad, and the bringing into line of the instruments of U.S. policy with its capabilities and resources. At the same time, with the exception of a small domestic alignment of "neoisolationists," U.S. finance capital and the military-political elite did not wish to allow the downfall of U.S.

economic and political hegemony in the nonsocialist world, something which Harvard professor Stanley Hoffman has called "the American system" abroad. The complex and contradictory process of U.S. accommodation to the changed objective situation at the beginning of the 1970s was substantially reflected in its foreign and overall military policy, strategic concepts and plans, decisions on strategic nuclear programs, and in the Nixon administration's approaches and tactics in the sphere of the SALT negotiations.

## Toward the First Nuclear Frontier: The Kennedy and Johnson Administrations' Bid for Superiority in the 1960s

In the views of the "establishment"—that powerful force of U.S. state-monopoly capital that determines Washington's foreign policy—the notion of national security is by no means limited to the security of the population, territory, and state of the United States. It is equivalent to supporting a certain world order in which the United States must maintain a dominant position. This order was established in its basic features in the late 1940s and in the course of the 1950s. It was based upon the dominance of the United States in the West's economic relations, in trade and financial institutions. It was consolidated in a system of multilateral and bilateral treaties by which Washington spread its political influence to more than 40 countries of the world. And most important of all, it was supported by the enormous U.S. military potential, by hundreds of thousands of American soldiers on different continents, dozens of the U.S. navy's carrier battle groups on the oceans, and many hundreds of bases and installations abroad.[1] The Eisenhower-Dulles strategy of "massive retaliation" was the heart of the U.S. global military-political policy, which exerted constant pressure on the socialist countries with the threat of massive nuclear strikes from an airborne armada consisting of 1,850 long- and medium-range bombers able to deliver in a single sortie more than 4,700 nuclear bombs, each of which was tens and even hundreds of times more destructive than the bombs dropped on Hiroshima and Nagasaki, and also hundreds of nuclear-capable fighter-bombers at forward bases and on a aircraft carriers.[2] U.S. expansionism and militarism, undertaken in the twentieth century on an unprecedented scale, were the clearest illustrations to V. I. Lenin's conclusion that " 'world supremacy' is, to put it briefly, the substance of imperialist policy, of which imperialist war is the continuation."[3] In the event of such a war, as the U.S. military-political leadership calculated, the colossal power of its nuclear potential multiplied by the inaccessibility of its territory to weapons of mass destruction automatically guaranteed the U.S. victory over the socialist countries.

But despite the monstrous arsenal of destruction built by the United

States and its allies, the downfall of the U.S. atomic monopoly, namely the development by the Soviet Union of long-range bombers and, in the late 1950s, intercontinental ballistic missiles, entailed qualitative changes in the strategic correlation of forces on which the U.S. "deterrence" and "cold war" policies had earlier been based. After the United States lost its inaccessibility in the event of a global war, the nuclear threat became for it a less attractive instrument of politics toward the socialist countries "from a position of strength," or of "brinksmanship" in crisis situations, for in a military conflict it could entail catastrophic damage for the United States itself, in spite of its enormous predominance in the number of strategic launchers, nuclear charges, and their total destructive power.

The continuation of the previous policy in the changed situation put the Republican administration under a barrage of criticism inside and outside the United States. However, the majority of the opposition to the Eisenhower government called not for a revision of foreign policy, for a rejection of the "cold war" and confrontation that had now created a direct threat to the United States itself, but for reforms of U.S. military policy, so that in the new conditions U.S. policy rested to a lesser degree on the unconvincing and potentially suicidal nuclear bluff, and more on truly usable military force. This meant in the first place the buildup and modernization of conventional forces. In the area of strategic arms the overwhelming share of U.S. ruling circles reacted as Pavlovian dogs to the creation of ballistic missiles in the USSR. It supported a comprehensive nuclear arms buildup, proceeding from an unconditional adherence to the idea of U.S. nuclear superiority, which was regarded as the basis of national power in the United States, an integral condition and central pillar of the policy of "containing communism." On the basis of such sentiments the "missile gap" controversy developed in the United States in 1958 to 1960. An important motivating force was the U.S. military-industrial complex, which had grown to enormous dimensions in the soil of militarism and anticommunism. These circles used the changing of the situation in the world arena and the difficulties of U.S. foreign policy for urging forward the arms race, for obtaining multibillion dollar profits, for increasing their influence in Washington's foreign policy, and for the even greater consolidation of their position inside the country.

Despite the arguments of many Western apologists for the arms buildup, the creation of U.S. ballistic missiles was by no means a "reaction" to the Soviet Union's missile program, but rather had been prepared long before the "missile gap" campaign. From 1954 to 1957 a number of missile programs were begun in the United States: the Atlas, Titan, and Minuteman intercontinental ballistic missiles (ICBMs); the Polaris submarine-launched ballistic missile (SLBM); and the Jupiter and

Thor intermediate-range ballistic missiles (IRBMs). Simultaneously, in the "think tanks" and scientific centers of the so-called strategic community new military doctrines were being developed that called for finding a way out of the "balance of terror" dead-end for the United States on the basis of missile technology.

In the late 1950s the National Security Council's Net Evaluation Subcommittee (NESC) under General Charles Hickey carried out a study by Eisenhower's order, NESC-2009, which developed the National Strategic Targeting Attack Policy and advanced the concept of an "optimum mix" of nuclear strikes on the strategic forces, conventional forces, and cities of the USSR, China, and other socialist countries. As a result, the Joint Strategic Target Planning Staff (JSTPS) was formed in August 1960 in Omaha, Nebraska under the headquarters of the Strategic Air Command (SAC). By December 1960 JSTPS had developed the first Single Integrated Operational Plan, SIOP-62, constructed according to the principle of a massive nuclear strike of "optimum mix." It called for employing totally and immediately all alert strategic forces on all listed targets, including the cities of socialist countries.[4]

The Democratic administration that came to power in 1961 considered it necessary to rebuild the U.S. arsenal and reformulate the prevailing strategic concepts in order to support the planned activation of U.S. political and economic expansion abroad not only by nuclear threat but also by truly usable military force. Thus, in order to make U.S. military policy "rational and consistent" in the new conditions, the president announced in his address to Congress of March 28, 1961 that what is needed "are entirely new types of non-nuclear weapons and equipment—with increased firepower, mobility and communications, and more suited to the kind of tasks our limited war forces will most likely be required to perform."[5] In place of the strategy of "massive retaliation" came the strategy of "flexible response." Besides expanding and modernizing conventional forces the Democratic administration considered the buildup of nuclear superiority necessary as well. The U.S. leaders considered that the United States should have a genuine capability to conduct and win a thermonuclear war, to limit damage to the United States in the course of it, and to recover after the cessation of hostilities. Since U.S. territory was henceforth vulnerable to nuclear weapons, the task was placed before U.S. strategic forces not only to have the capability to deliver a massive nuclear strike on the socialist countries but also to be in a position under any conditions of the outbreak of war to survive in the course of an international exchange and destroy the armed forces and administrative-industrial centers of the other side, while having maximally reduced U.S. losses. Thus did the Kennedy administration see the way to increase the effectiveness of the nuclear threat as a means of

Washington's foreign policy. This demanded not simply a further buildup of the thermonuclear arsenal but also a qualitative reconstruction of its technical components and plans of practical applicability.

The period from early 1961 until late 1962 was characterized by an extreme aggravation of international tension. Peoples of the world felt with growing fear that the time had come for a decisive test of strengths between the United States and the USSR in the entire arena of international relations. Shortly after his inauguration Kennedy sanctioned the implementation of the plan to invade Cuba, later followed by the events in Laos, the diplomatic confrontation at the Vienna summit, and a near-military confrontation in Berlin. After the Berlin crisis, atmospheric thermonuclear tests were resumed by the USSR and the United States on an unprecedented scale after a two-year moratorium. In 1962 tensions continued to build in West Berlin, Southeast Asia, and Central Africa. A largely uncontrolled chain of events in October 1962 led to the Caribbean crisis, which nearly spilled over into an open military conflict between the great nuclear powers.

But the U.S. government's approach to building up its military power was influenced not only by the antagonism between the two systems. Changes in the Soviet-U.S. strategic balance on the threshold of the 1960s shook the strength of U.S. guarantees to NATO to employ nuclear weapons in the event of war on the European continent. Along with the economic recovery of the European allies the changes in the military-political situation strengthened the centrifugal tendencies in the North Atlantic alliance. Pressure on the part of the United States to build up conventional forces met resistance from the European members of the alliance, who did not wish to overburden their economies with military expenditures. (NATO's strategy was officially reformed only in 1967.) Therefore U.S. nuclear superiority, according to the Democratic administration's scheme, should have convinced the European allies of Washington's resolution to use nuclear weapons first in accordance with its obligations.

The revision of the Republican government's military programs, begun immediately by the new leadership, was crowned with a large increase of the military budget, including appropriations for strategic nuclear forces. In the course of the first year of their tenure in power the Democrats increased total military appropriations by 20 percent (from $40 billion to $48 billion). The first measures were reflected in the presidential addresses of January 30 and March 28, 1961. They resulted in the significant acceleration of construction of the Polaris ballistic missile-carrying submarine program and an expansion of the Minuteman-I ICBM deployment program—in sum by 20 percent in the number of ballistic missiles.

In late March of 1961 work was begun in Secretary of Defense Robert

McNamara's staff on revising the Eisenhower document "Basic National Security Policy." The working group was headed by Paul Nitze, and the main members were Henry Rowen, William Kaufmann, and Daniel Ellsberg—all former RAND Corporation alumni. Their project included the necessity of different nuclear war attack scenarios and were reflected in the secretary of defense's official document on nuclear weapons employment policy. McNamara also published a series of directives, in accordance with which the higest Pentagon agencies began to revise the Joint Chiefs of Staff's SIOP. The targets of the other side's armed forces were separated from its cities on the target list; a strategic reserve was to be kept in the United States in the course of the war; the command was to be able to ensure "controlled attacks" with nuclear weapons; China and other socialist countries were separated from the USSR in planning nuclear operations; and the Soviet system of command and control was not to be subjected to strikes at the initial stage of a war. The new operational plan, SIOP-63, included five basic strike options: (1) on Soviet strategic forces (missile sites, bomber bases, and submarine pens); (2) on Soviet air defenses covering U.S. bomber routes and on conventional forces (the result of which should have left the Soviet Union with at most seven divisions and the other Warsaw Pact countries with ten divisions); (3) on Soviet air defenses near cities; (4) on Soviet command and control centers and systems; (5) the massive destruction of population and industrial centers. The overall strategic target list was expanded to 6,000 targets. The Joint Chiefs of Staff approved SIOP-63 in December 1961, and JSTPS in Omaha adopted and entered it into its computers in June 1962.[6]

Addressing Congress in January 1962, the secretary of defense for the first time announced the adoption of a new concept in U.S. nuclear strategy—the concept of "counterforce." On June 16, McNamara delivered his famous speech at the University of Michigan-Ann Arbor. He stated:

The U.S. has come to the conclusion that, to the extent feasible, basic military strategy in a possible general nuclear war should be approached in much the same way that more conventional military operations have been regarded in the past. That is to say, principal military objectives in the event of an atomic war ...should be the destruction of the enemy's military forces, not of his civilian population....In other words, we are giving a possible opponent the strongest imaginable incentive to refrain from striking our own cities.[7]

However, despite McNamara's public proclamations of a "retaliatory counterforce strike," the Pentagon's real plans, which underlay the official concept, envisaged mainly a disarming nuclear first strike. Now, when a total nuclear strike on all targets would have brought destructive retaliation on the United States; it was considered especially necessary to destroy the overwhelming portion of the Soviet capability to deliver nuclear weapons, to deprive the other side of the capability of a retaliatory strike. This was precisely how the U.S. leadership saw "meaningful" U.S. nuclear superiority. The unofficial statements of a number of Pentagon officials that year and their memoirs in our time confirm this fact. For example, Jack Ruina, the former director of the Defense Advanced Research Projects Agency (DARPA), wrote: "Broadly stated, the original aim was a war-fighting force that included the possibility of obliterating the emerging Soviet [intercontinental] nuclear force." Other authoritative specialists on military affairs, former Defense Department officials Morton Halperin, George Rathjens, Herbert Scoville, and Herbert York, remarked, "If we were not going to strike first, it was asked, would we not be aiming at only empty holes? DoD said the Soviets might have a 'reload capacity.' In fact, DoD was assuming, as usual, that war would begin in Europe with a Soviet aggressive act and that the United States might well strike first on the nuclear level."[8] After many years had passed McNamara himself acknowledged that on November 21, 1962 he sent a top-secret memorandum to President Kennedy, in which was set forth the plan for developing the U.S. potential for a disarming strategic first strike on the USSR, advocated most of all by the air force command and SAC.[9] By 1964, according to the Pentagon's calculations, the ratio of strategic launchers and warheads between the United States and the USSR should have been so favorable to the United States that it would have achieved the capability to destroy on the ground the majority of Soviet nuclear forces, and in the event of a nuclear exchange, to inflict four times as many losses on the other side as the United States itself would suffer. Of course, even in this event, the damage to the United States (according to estimates, approximately 30 million casualties) would be unprecedented in history, but as an instrument of political pressure the threat to conclude the war with such an unequal loss ratio was considered in Washington as evidence for an unconditional U.S. nuclear superiority and, in some sense, of the ability to "secure victory" in a global conflict.[10]

Parallel with the development of the new nuclear strategy ran the restructuring of the corresponding missile programs. In the strategic arms sphere the recommendations of the air force and the navy called for the development of more than 3,900 ballistic missiles by 1967. The secretary of defense considered a lesser number of missiles sufficient, taking into account considerations of strategic cost-effectiveness and the real capabilities of the defense budget, which was overburdened with appropriations to expand and modernize conventional forces. On average in the first half of the 1960s expenditures on U.S. strategic forces were already making up around 27 percent of the military budget ($12–

$13 billion per year). Meanwhile, the logic of the "counterforce" concept of a disarming strike on the USSR urged on a further, still greater buildup of strategic nuclear arms. In order to formulate clearer strategic criteria upon which to base decisions on the levels of missile forces, the secretary in the summer of 1962 appointed a working group under the leadership of General Glenn Kent.

The inceasing lack of confidence of the secretary of defense and his closest advisors in the justifiability of the "counterforce" concept in and of itself began to play an important role in their strategic views. The Soviet Union's successes in science and technology and the increases in its defense capability were making the U.S. leadership's calculations for implementing a nuclear attack with impunity increasingly problematic. This concerned first of all the beginning, according to Pentagon information, of the deployment of more sophisticated Soviet ICBMs in hardened silos and the creation of ballistic missile-carrying submarines.[11] As a result of a series of studies, the Kent group in July 1963 presented a preliminary report, the main contribution of which was the formulation of the new strategic concept of "damage limitation."[12]

But implementing the new strategy, that is, the ability for the United States to reduce significantly its losses with a nuclear first strike, was becoming more doubtful in connection with the further growth of the invulnerability of Soviet strategic forces. At the same time the strategy of "damage limitation" aroused fewer apprehensions on the part of the NATO allies, who worried that the United States in a crisis situation would risk beginning a nuclear war in the hope of reducing its damage (but not the damage of Western Europe). Moreover, the new doctrine created fewer disagreements inside the United States and looked, in McNamara's opinion, not so provocative toward the USSR. This doctrine gave the civilian leadership of the Defense Department the opportunity to retreat officially from the strategy of a "disarming strike" as the primary "counterforce" option, which the air force bureaucracy had used for justifying its excessive missile programs. On November 5, 1964, a decision to limit the deployment of Minuteman missiles to a ceiling of 1,000 was officially announced by the secretary of defense. The cancellation of the deployment of 200 additional ballistic missiles provoked the unanimous opposition of the Pentagon bureaucracy and its allies in industry and Congress. But the secretary stated that the military requirements of the "damage limitation" doctrine would be better satisfied by replacing the Minuteman-I portion of the missile forces with the much more effective Minuteman-II missile, not by a further buildup of the number of ICBMs.

In 1966–67 McNamara paid increasingly less attention to the "damage limitation" strategy, an indirect acknowledgment of its military-political untenability. Officially the main emphasis was now being put on another strategy—"assured destruction." In the fiscal year 1968 military budget report, the secretary emphasized:

As long as deterrence of a deliberate Soviet (or Red Chinese) nuclear attack upon the United States or its allies is the overriding objective of our strategic forces, the capability for "Assured Destruction" must receive the first call on all of our resources and must be provided regardless of the cost and the difficulties involved. Damage Limiting programs, no matter how much we spend on them, can never substitute for an Assured Destruction capability in the deterrent role.[13]

In 1967 McNamara defined "assured destruction" as the capability of surviving U.S. nuclear forces to destroy in the course of a "retaliatory strike" up to 25 percent of the population of the "enemy" and around 70 percent of its industry. For this, it was conditionally considered sufficient to detonate 400 megatons of nuclear charges over a corresponding number of the enemy's largest cities. The fiscal year 1967 and 1968 budgets did not call for a quantitative buildup of the Minuteman and Polaris forces above the planned level, although appropriations for substituting Minuteman-II for Minuteman-I ICBMs were continued until 1970.

Meanwhile, Pentagon estimates showed that as little as one-fifth of the strategic forces already built in the United States exceeded these appalling criteria of destruction. "With the forces we are proposing to maintain, we will have even a surplus of nuclear power above our requirements," announced the Secretary of Defense. Publicly the Pentagon leadership advanced two main explanations for the unjustifiably enormous extent of amassed potential. In the first place was emphasized the "conservative" character of military planning, which is carried out at least five years in advance in calculating the "worst case scenario." The principle of "redundancy" was another justification, in accordance with which each component of the strategic "triad" (ICBMs, SLBMs, and bombers) should have the capability for "assured destruction" in the event of the surprise malfunction of one of the U.S. military systems or of the enemy's technological "breakthrough" in some area.[14] The gradual revision of U.S. nuclear strategy in 1961–67 should have been, both according to the logic of things and to McNamara's official statements, to entail the narrowing of tasks and the reduction of the initially planned number of U.S. strategic "retaliatory" forces. But in spite of this, the final plans of missile construction remained almost unchanged in this period.

The actual plans for using U.S. nuclear forces also changed very little. A new SIOP, affirmed in February 1967, and the subsequent one as well, included the very same five basic versions of nuclear attacks as in SIOP-63. The target list was expanded to 10,000, and to it were added the newly constructed Soviet ICBM silos, submarine pens, command centers, intermediate range nuclear forces, conventional forces, and centers of the growing Soviet industry and infrastructure.[15] The number of operational tasks had grown, which the missile forces took upon themselves an increasingly greater role in fulfilling, relegating the bombers to a secondary level and allowing greater possibilities for planning various strike combinations. At the same time, in view of the objective growth of the number, readiness, and hardness of the USSR's strategic forces (which in 1967 already numbered about 600 strategic launchers),[16] the emphasis on purely "counterforce" strikes was by necessity notably decreased in the SIOP, and the set criteria for the destruction of hard targets significantly lowered.

Despite the future arguments of a multitude of apologists for U.S. strategic policy, U.S. missile programs, their technical characteristics and quantitative levels, as well as the SIOP and basic target list were by no means based on the concept of "assured destruction." All these parameters of military policy were adopted in 1961–62 and linked most tightly with the "counterforce" concept. The consolidation of the Soviet potential for a retaliatory strike more quickly than was expected in the United States, as well as economic, foreign, and domestic policy considerations, impelled the Democratic administration to move away from its "counterforce" doctrine through "damage limitation" to "assured destruction." The latter became the official formulation of Washington's policy in the area of the strategic balance. But the criteria of "assured destruction" were inferred in a purely formalistic, statistical way and used to justify the existing number of U.S. strategic nuclear forces. The enormous "surplus of nuclear strength," the significant U.S. military-strategic predominance over the USSR preserved until the late 1960s, allowed the Pentagon, contrary to official doctrine, to plan several missile strike options on a wide range of military targets, and not only on the USSR's cities.

The actual arms buildup in 1961–67 attained rates and scales unprecedented for peacetime. Having come to power in January 1961, the Kennedy government inherited from its predecessors 12 unwieldly first-generation Atlas intercontinental ballistic missiles. Two atomic submarines—the *George Washington* and the *Patrick Henry*—had been commissioned, each carrying 16 Polaris A-1 missiles. By late 1967 U.S. missile forces had grown 40-fold in number of launchers; the United States had at its disposal 1,000 Minuteman-I and Minuteman-II ICBMs, 54 Titan-II heavy ICBMs, and 41 nuclear-powered submarines with 656 Polaris A-3 and Polaris A-2 SLBMs. The actual scale of the arms race in the 1960s was still greater than what follows from these finite quantitative levels, if one considers the more than 500 Atlas, Titan-I, Polaris A-1, and Minuteman-I ballistic missiles added to the arsenal but quickly re-

1967, when the Soviet Union, the United States, and other countries signed the Treaty on Principles Governing the Activities of States in the Exploration and Use of Outer Space, Including the Moon and Other Celestial Bodies, which obligated them not to place weapons of mass destruction in space or on celestial bodies. This success strengthened the hope for the possibility of cooperation between the great powers in curbing military rivalry.

The new views of McNamara and his supporters on nuclear weapons were most systematically put forth in a speech to representatives of United Press International in San Francisco on September 18, 1967. The secretary stated that deterrence of a "deliberate nuclear attack upon the United States, or its allies," is ensured by maintaining a highly reliable ability "to inflict an unacceptable degree of damage upon any single aggressor or combination of aggressors, at any time during the course of a strategic nuclear exchange, even after absorbing a surprise first strike." McNamara also acknowledged that "the blunt, inescapable fact remains that the Soviet Union could still—with its present forces—effectively destroy the United States, even after absorbing the full weight of an American first strike." The logical conclusion drawn from these arguments is the senselessness of a further arms buildup in order to attain nuclear superiority. Nevertheless, the arms race, in McNamara's words, had acquired an intrinsic dynamic of development, its own "mad inertia": "Whatever be their intentions, whatever be our intentions, actions—or even realistically possible actions—on either side relating to the buildup of nuclear forces, be they either offensive or defensive forces, necessarily trigger reactions on the other side. It is precisely this action-reaction phemomenon that fuels the arms race." To escape from this sinister closed circle, the secretary advanced the idea of negotiations between the great powers: "We do not want a nuclear arms race with the Soviet Union—primarily because the action-reaction phenomenon makes it foolish and futile... Both of our nations would benefit from a properly safeguarded agreement first to limit, and later to reduce, both our offensive and defensive strategic nuclear forces... We believe such an agreement is fully feasible, since it is clearly in both our nations' interests."[21]

However, by this time the United States was already deeply immersed in the Vietnam war, and the quantitative and qualitative strategic nuclear arms race of the 1960s continued. Furthermore, the contemplated new approach to the question of nuclear weapons and security had failed to go beyond the bounds of a narrow alignment in U.S. ruling circles, a fact that became obvious during the discussion concerning the new generation of U.S. strategic arms.

From about the middle of the 1960s, two new military programs were found in the center of the U.S. leadership's attention in the strategic arms sphere. These were the antiballistic missile defense (ABM) system, and the multiple independently targetable reentry vehicles (MIRV) systems for strategic offensive ballistic missiles. It is obvious that the programs for developing ABM and MIRVed offensive missiles had already in the early 1960s aroused the enthusiasm of the "strategic community," which began to link certain new strategic ideas with prospective military technologies. Specialists from RAND, the Institute for Defense Analysis, the Hudson Institute, and the Air Force Science Advisory Council began to see in the MIRV system the ability to put at risk a growing number of military targets, not by resorting to a futile and financially exhaustive buildup of ballistic missiles but by replacing single-warhead missiles with missiles equipped with several individually targetable warheads. In their opinion, in the condition of the increased accuracy and yield of these warheads, "the continued policy of targeting a nuclear strike on Soviet land-based strategic forces will become feasible and economical." However, for reviving the strategy of a disarming strike, a "thick" ABM system was necessary along with MIRV systems. It should have been possible, according to this scheme, to ensure protection of the United States from a retaliatory strike in theory significantly weakened by a salvo of U.S. MIRVed missiles. A study of the interaction of MIRV and ABM systems in a first strike strategy, important for its consequences, was conducted under the name "Strat-X" in 1966 with the concerted efforts of the Pentagon, RAND, the Massachusetts Institute of Technology, and aerospace industry research centers.[22]

In the eyes of McNamara and a number of his assistants the ABM system became a symbol of a futile arms race, which in the interests of the long-term national security of the United States he considered necessary to put under definite control. The secretary thought that scrapping the construction of the "Nike-X" ABM system would provide an opportunity to conclude an agreement with the Soviet Union on limiting strategic arms. The deployment of ABM systems, on the other hand, could, in his opinion, destabilize the military balance without having provided the United States with any real defense.

In 1966 the supporters of Nike-X and other strategic programs began an intense effort to spread information about the initial deployment of a supposedly "thick" antiballistic missile defense in the USSR. In this situation a preliminary decision to equip a new generation of ballistic missiles with MIRV systems slipped by without attracting great attention and without the noticeable objection, much less the organized opposition, of any party. Opposing the Nike-X ABM program, the secretary of defense contended that MIRV systems could overwhelm any antiballistic missile defense, and that therefore "the correct response" to the construction of the Soviet ABM should be to begin equipping U.S. missiles with multiple independently targetable warheads, not to create the

United States' own ABM system, which the USSR would also be able to neutralize by way of perfecting its offensive forces. President Johnson and the secretary of defense were also attracted by the fact that equipping missiles with MIRVs would render a manifold increase in the aggregate number of warheads and would, therefore, eliminate the necessity of a further buildup of missile forces by number of launchers. In addition, MIRV systems allowed an increase in the flexibility of using strategic potential, that is, the flexibility to plan various nuclear strike combinations and carry out so-called cross-targeting (in which each given target is covered by several nuclear warheads of different missiles).

In November 1965 took place a decisive meeting of high Pentagon officials on the navy's MIRV program. A decision was made to equip the Poseidon C-3 SLBM with 10-14 Mk-3 MIRVs. In early 1966 it was decided to begin the accelerated engineering development of the improved Minuteman-III ICBM with three Mk-12 independently targetable warheads. This decision, which at that time was known to a narrow circle of U.S. military and political officials and seemed to them, apparently, a purely technical move, subsequently turned out to be a turning point in the evolution of the strategic balance. It entailed long-term destabilizing consequences and negatively affected arms control negotiations and Soviet-U.S. relations as a whole. Many of the problems for which civilian and military specialists in the USSR and the United States are now, in the late 1980s, desperately searching for solutions have their roots in these rather routine and undramatic meetings of Pentagon bureaucrats in late 1965 and early 1966.

On December 6, 1966 the U.S. military-political leadership made a decision to allocate resources for long-term contracts for individual battle components of the Nike-X ABM system. But at the same time the spending of these appropriations and the decision on the specific type of ABM system were set aside until the State Department could confirm the possibility of an agreement with the Soviet Union on limiting antiballistic missile systems. On June 23 and 25, 1967 in Glassboro, New Jersey, meetings took place between Chairman of the USSR Council of Ministers Alexei N. Kosygin and U.S. President Lyndon B. Johnson. On the very first day the secretary of defense stated that the creation of a Soviet ABM would "force" the United States to strengthen its offensive nuclear forces, and he proposed to conclude an agreement limiting antiballistic missile systems. But the Soviet Union at that time did not agree to this proposition. McNamara's logic of stability seemed artificial. Moreover, suspiciously enough, it was applied to the only area in which the USSR was somewhat ahead, leaving aside the still overwhelming U.S. offensive nuclear advantage. This was precisely what was counted on by some officials in Washington who were trying to reconcile the idea of negotiations with the Soviet Union and the principle, still widely held in leading U.S. circles, of maintaining U.S. nuclear superiority.

The Glassboro talks did not give tangible results. In his speech in San Francisco, McNamara announced the beginning of the deployment of a "thin" antiballistic missile defense of U.S. territory for defense from individual missile launches and the "nuclear threat" that China could create for the United States in the 1970s. In the summer of 1968 the army began to prepare sites for the construction of the first complexes and produce the battle components of the Sentinel ABM system (as the Nike-X system was renamed in November 1967). On August 16, 1968, Minuteman-III and Poseidon missiles with multiple independently targetable reentry vehicles were flight-tested for the first time.

But 1968 does not only mark the U.S. transition to direct preparation for a new cycle of the strategic arms race. On July 1 the USSR, United States, Great Britain, and subsequently another 55 states signed one of the most important documents of international law of our time—the Treaty on the Non-Proliferation of Nuclear Weapons. The question of negotiations between the Soviet Union and the United States on another question of cardinal importance was also firmly resolved in the same year. In May 1968 USSR Deputy Minister of Foreign Affairs V. V. Kuznetsov in his speech to the U.N. expressed the readiness of the Soviet government to enter into negotiations on the limitation of strategic arms.[23] In June of the same year Soviet Minister of Foreign Affairs Andrei A. Gromyko proposed to the U.S. government a discussion on the mutual limitation and reduction of offensive and defensive strategic arms.[24] President Johnson responded to the Soviet Union's initiative. On June 1, 1968 he announced the agreement of the United States to begin negotiations on strategic arms issues.

However, on August 21, under the pressure of Western reaction to the events in Czechoslovakia, President Johnson renounced the beginning of the Soviet-U.S. negotiations. Nevertheless, in a significant portion of the U.S. ruling circles and public the idea of strategic arms limitations had already won significant support. On December 15, 1968, McNamara's successor to the post of secretary of defense, Clark Clifford, publicly supported the urgent beginning of the SALT negotiations. President Johnson's final attempts to begin the negotiations and bind by obligations the Republican administration of Richard Nixon, who had triumphed in the November 1968 presidential elections, did not achieve their goals. Nixon, who in the course of the preelection campaign had called for U.S. "nuclear superiority," did not plan to be bound by the maneuvers of the outgoing administration. Subsequently, however, laws of a higher order than the tactics of the preelection struggle bound the new leadership with the idea of limiting the arms race. The objective realities of the nuclear age were compelling Washington to adjust itself to changes

in the world correlation of forces, in the first place in the sphere of the
strategic balance, where a situation of parity between the United States and
the Soviet Union was steadily taking shape.

### The Nixon Administration's Foreign Policy: "Redeployment" of U.S. Power

For the sake of preserving the principal interests of the establishment
and the foundations of U.S. influence in the world arena, a considerable
part of the U.S. ruling circles was forced under the pressure of objective
circumstances to begin a revision of foreign policy, to make certain compromises and concessions and, as was expressed by Henry Kissinger, the
president's national security adviser, to begin the "redeployment" of U.S.
power to new international positions. In this connection the American
scholar Robert Tucker noted that "The leitmotif of the [Nixon] administration has been to change while conserving or to change in order to
conserve."[25] The continuation of the same policies of the past in fundamentally new conditions carried increasingly greater costs and ultimately threatened to damage the principal interests of the U.S. ruling
class. The new U.S. leadership first of all considered changes in the
military-strategic area. Later, commenting on the "Nixon Doctrine," the
president's adviser emphasized the necessity of taking into account the
radical changes in the military correlation of forces: "We are coming
into a new period. No words can explain away the fact that when NATO
was created we had an atomic monopoly, and today the Soviets have
over a thousand land-based missiles. No presidential declaration can take
away that change."[26] Severe limitations on the usability of the nuclear
threat as an instrument of foreign policy pressure are, he considered at
the time, the direct result of such a situation. "The paradox of contemporary military strength is that a gargantuan increase in power has
eroded its relationship to policy," wrote Kissinger in 1969, echoing
McNamara's statements in this regard. "The major nuclear powers are
capable of devastating each other. But they have great difficulty translating this capability into policy except to prevent direct challenges to
their own survival."[27]

The changed situation in the military balance and the international
distribution of forces had placed substantial limitations on U.S. options,
but in the opinion of the new U.S. leaders it could concede advantages
as well, provided that U.S. foreign policy goals and methods were properly adapted to the new conditions: "To act consistently abroad we must
be able to generate coalitions of shared interests. Regional groupings
supported by the U.S. will have to take over major responsibility for
their immediate areas, with the U.S. being concerned more with the
overall framework of order than with the management of every regional

enterprise."[28] The primary interest of U.S. foreign policy, in the judgment of Nixon and Kissinger, was to maintain a global and, in vital areas, a regional "balance of power," but not to resolve every international problem with the forces of the United States itself. The main problem was how to induce other states to act in U.S. interests in the face of the noticeable relative decline of U.S. economic and military influence in the world arena.

Whereas Vietnam was the most acute and urgent problem for the Republican administration, Soviet-U.S. relations from the very beginning occupied the central place in its long-term foreign policy. The new leadership realized that the revision of U.S. policy was impossible without rebuilding relations with the USSR. As the president acknowledged in his 1971 address to Congress, by no means did good will play the main role in Washington's recognition of this truth, long advocated by the Soviet Union. "In earlier periods our strategic superiority gave us a margin of safety," said the head of the U.S. government. "Now, however, the enormous increase in Soviet capabilities has added a new and critical dimension to our relationship."[29] The problems of preventing war, halting the arms race, and easing tension were pushed to the center in Soviet-U.S. relations. In November 1969 negotiations on limiting strategic offensive and defensive weapons were begun. In addition to this most important area of the correlation of the two powers' interests, the USSR's significantly expanded international influence affected a whole number of other spheres of world politics where U.S. interests demanded a search for some level of understanding with the USSR, for example on settling conflicts and contradictions in such crisis-prone regions as Central Europe, the Middle East, and Southeast Asia.

In 1970 the Federal Republic of Germany signed landmark treaties with the Soviet Union, Poland, and a short while later with the German Democratic Republic. The conclusion of a four-party agreement on the status of West Berlin took place in 1971, which defused a long-standing European military confrontation there. The further deepening and broadening of détente was manifested in 1971–72 in the Soviet-U.S. Agreement on Measures to Reduce the Risk of Outbreak of Nuclear War, the Agreement on the Prevention of Incidents at Sea and in the Air, and the Agreement on Cooperation in the Research and Use of Outer Space in Peaceful Goals. Preparation was begun for the Conference on Security and Cooperation in Europe, and also for the Mutual and Balanced Force Reduction negotiations on NATO and Warsaw Pact armed forces and arms. The major positive changes in the international environment and in Soviet-U.S. relations culminated in the May 1972 Moscow summit meeting, at which were signed documents marking a new stage of the two great powers' relations.

As for the Nixon government's policies, they were frequently incon-

sistent and full of the contradictions peculiar to the U.S. ruling circles'
interests in the new conditions. Having advanced the idea of negotiations
with the Soviet Union as one of the central elements of the Nixon Doctrine, Washington at the same time tried to maneuver around the settlement of vital issues of Soviet-U.S. relations. In particular, on the basis
of the first so-called National Security Decision Memorandum, the White
House concluded that the Soviet Union was supposedly more interested
than was the United States in strategic arms limitation agreements, in
solving the problems of Europe, and in trade and scientific-technical
cooperation. According to the designs of Nixon and Kissinger, as a
"price" for U.S. willingness to negotiate these questions the Soviet Union
had to yield to the United States in the resolution of problems in the
Middle East and Southeast Asia. Such an approach, called "linkage," in
an unnatural way perverted the correct idea of the indivisibility of détente and the interdependence of contemporary international relations.
The principle of linkage, which had become a most important element
of U.S. policy in the early 1970s, proceeded from the assumption that
the resolution of separate issues depends not so much on the specific
circumstances as on the overall global "balance of power" and on the
advantageousness of the U.S. positions in it. Accordingly, Washington
considered that since a direct threat approach had proven futile toward
the USSR, unilateral advantages must be attained by way of indirect
pressure, or more precisely, by manipulating the interdependence of
interests in those areas where the United States presumably enjoyed
stronger positions in order to attain Soviet concessions on issues in which
U.S. interests were vulnerable.

These considerations explain in large part the postponement by almost
an entire year of the beginning of the strategic arms negotiations. Washington's desire to "strengthen" its positions in this area through the
accelerated development and deployment of new strategic weapons systems was one reason. The escalation of the Vietnam war up through
late 1972, the continuation of the previous futile policy in the Middle
East in anticipation of "concessions" from the Soviet side, the absence
of good will in European security issues, and a hard line toward reducing
the military confontation in Central Europe were conditioned by the
same motives. Ultimately the U.S. government seriously entered into
negotiations in a number of areas, which in time led to mutually acceptable agreements. But much precious time had been lost. In Vietnam
this meant new victims and devastation, and even heavier U.S. defeats.
In the strategic arms area, as we shall see later, the loss of time in 1969
turned out to have long-term negative consequences for the problem of
curbing military rivalry and reducing the threat of nuclear war.

With the inconsistent and contradictory changes in foreign policy were
associated as well certain changes in the U.S. leadership's perceptions of

the role of U.S. military power and the events in which the threat of force or its direct application was justified. In March 1971 Defense Secretary Melvin Laird detailed these views: "In deterring theater conventional warfare—for example a major war in Europe—U.S. and allied forces share the responsibility. In deterring sub-theater or localized warfare, the country or ally which is threatened bears the primary burden, particularly for providing manpower." But when U.S. interests or commitments are at stake, added Laird, the United States would render military and economic assistance, which would consist essentially of backup logistical support and sea and air combat support. In some special cases, in his words, U.S. assistance could include ground combat support as well.[30]

Military planning now envisioned narrower combat tasks for U.S. armed forces, which entailed changing the criteria for determining force levels and their regional distribution. The principle of "two-and-a-half wars" was replaced by the principle of "one-and-a-half wars." The latter meant that U.S. armed forces must be prepared for simultaneously conducting large-scale combat operations in Europe or Asia (but not on the two continents at the same time, as the previous concept assumed) and a small-scale military operation in some other region. A partial withdrawal of U.S. military bases and garrisons abroad began in 1969. The greatest share of the reductions, in accordance with the policy of "Vietnamization," fell upon Southeast Asia (520,000 troops) and on Northeast Asia (43,000) as well. Less significant contingents were withdrawn from Europe, Latin America, northern Africa, and other regions. By the end of the Republican administration's tenure, the U.S. foreign military presence numbered 460,000 men—40 percent less than in 1964, and 65 percent less than in 1968 (760,000 and 1,300,000 troops, respectively). In fiscal year 1968 the U.S. military budget was $76 billion, and in fiscal year 1976, $98 billion. However, considering the enormous inflation (that is, in constant dollars) in the years 1968–76 U.S. military expenditures decreased by 35 percent, and in comparison with the last "pre-Vietnam" year, fiscal year 1964, by 13 percent. Mass obsolescence and the wearing-out of arms and equipment introduced in the early 1960s at an accelerated rate were not offset by the deployment of a corresponding number of new models, which resulted in the reduction of U.S. armed forces in certain quantitative parameters.[31]

However, these tendencies, although they fed the beginning of a propaganda campaign in the West over the United States' "lag" behind the Soviet Union in various measures of military power, did not appear so striking upon closer examination. In the first place, this reduction took place largely at the expense of forces in the Asian-Pacific region that were not intended for direct use against the USSR. (In 1966 a total of around 380,000 U.S. servicemen were stationed on 480 bases in this area.)[32] Second, one must not forget that a comparison with 1964 is a comparison with a period of an unprecedented and unwarranted burst in the arms race undertaken during the Kennedy and Johnson administrations. One must not disregard the fact that the Pentagon strove to compensate the quantitative reduction of military power in qualitative ways, that is, by means of reorganizing the military machine, introducing improved weapons and equipment, and increasing firepower and mobility. In the Nixon administration's strategy, called "realistic containment," a special place was reserved for the so-called blue-water navy concept, which stipulated the growth of the navy's role in exchange for the partial dismantling of the army's presence. The navy's carrier battle groups, as floating forward airbases, were to replace the airbases on land, and Marines units on amphibious assault vessels, the army garrisons. Along with the closure of many U.S. army units and air force bases abroad, naval bases and installations were expanded in Guam, the Philippines, Okinawa, Bahrain, and Australia. Major new bases were built on the islands of Diego Garcia and Tinian. The shipbuilding program envisioned construction of 36 ships and submarines annually, which according to the navy's plan would have increased the fleet's combat structure from 500 to 630 units by 1995. Nuclear-powered and various missile-launching ships were to be introduced as well.

Finally, in line with compensating for the reduction of conventional forces and troops in U.S. strategy, emphasis on plans to use tactical nuclear weapons at an earlier stage of a conflict was strengthened. In 1971 a decision was made in NATO to lower the "nuclear threshold."[33] There was also a proposal to offset the decreased U.S. force levels to the extent possible by way of enlarging the armies and financial contributions of U.S. allies and clients. As the Soviet scholar Andrei A. Kokoshin wrote, the United States set off on a course "of acknowledging the greater political independence of American allies, while conveniently saying that according to the designs of the American political leadership, a much greater 'responsibility' in questions of 'joint defense' was demanded of them."[34] Simultaneously, great emphasis in U.S. military planning was put on the necessity for the Soviet Union to redistribute its military forces to its eastern border in view of the crisis in Soviet-Chinese relations at that time.

At the same time, détente and East-West negotiations, the antimilitary mood in the United States, and especially the liberal opposition in Congress all doubtlessly played a highly significant role in the reconstruction of U.S. strategy. For example, in the first half of the 1970s Congress cut the budget requests of the Pentagon and the government by a total of $50 billion.[35] In the opinion of Soviet reasearcher Vitaly V. Zhurkin, "the reduction, as well as the withdrawal of a portion of U.S. armed forces from certain regions of the world, were real evidence of the definite limitation of the previous interventionist course and of politics 'from a position of strength'."[36]

## The Revision of U.S. Nuclear Strategy in the Early 1970s

Even before his inauguration, on December 28, 1968 President Nixon directed Kissinger to begin a number of studies on the current state of affairs and prospects in the correlation of Soviet and U.S. strategic forces. Estimates of the possible correlation of damage showed that in the event of a nuclear exchange U.S. losses would now be no less than the other side's. To reduce expected U.S. casualties even to 30 million (as in 1964) would have required fantastic expenditures on forces for a disarming strike, as well as for ABM, antiaircraft, antisubmarine, and civil defenses. The main conclusion was perfectly obvious: no imaginable strategic programs could give the United States the kind of superiority it had had in the first half of the 1960s. The president's adviser recommended renouncing the idea of "unconditional superiority" and, so that the retreat would not appear too striking, to settle on a formula of "sufficiency." In one of his first press conferences, on January 27, 1969, President Nixon noted that "Our objective is to be sure that the United States has sufficient military power to defend our interests and to maintain the commitments which this administration determines are in the interest of the United States around the world. . . . I think 'sufficiency' is a better term, actually, than either 'superiority' or 'parity'."[37]

The new strategic concept of "sufficiency" was deliberately vaguely formulated. Nevertheless, there is no doubt that the public recognition of an approximate military balance between the USSR and the United States was, on the threshold of the 1970s, one of the most important political changes in the formation of Washington's policy in the strategic arms area. Thus in February 1970 in his first message to Congress on foreign policy Nixon stated that "an inescapable reality of the 1970s is the Soviet Union's possession of powerful and sophisticated strategic forces approaching, and in some categories, exceeding ours in numbers and capability."[38] A year later, in his second such message to Congress, the president emphasized:

The doctrine of sufficiency represents, rather, an explicit recognition of the changed circumstances we face with regard to strategic forces. The United States and the Soviet Union have now reached a point where small numerical advantages in strategic forces have little military relevance. The attempt to obtain large advantages would spark an arms race which would, in the end, prove pointless. For both sides would almost surely commit the necessary resources to maintain a balance.[39]

The Republican government's official repudiation of the U.S. doctrine of "nuclear superiority," which for many years had been the foundation of foundations of U.S. "national security" policy, had great significance, whatever new strategic concepts were subsequently interpreted, whatever arms programs were undertaken, and however widely separated were Washington's words and deeds. In this connection the American scholar Jerome Kahan wrote:

By proclaiming the doctrine of sufficiency in 1969, President Nixon officially accepted nuclear parity between the United States and the USSR as a fact of life of the 1970s . . . and informed our adversaries, our allies, and the American people that the years of U.S. superiority had ended. For these reasons, the strategy of sufficiency had real political and military significance for the Nixon administration, and the decision to adopt this doctrine marked a turning point in America's strategic policies.[40]

At the same time, despite the strengthening of sentiments in support of the immediate beginning of the Strategic Arms Limitation Talks with the Soviet Union in Congress, wide circles of the public, and the administration itself, Nixon and Kissinger refused to adopt the initiatives of their predecessors and put them at the foundation of their own policy. They not only planned to use linkage to bind Soviet-U.S. negotiations tightly with the broader plans of reconstructing U.S. foreign and military policy but wished also to examine anew the problems of arms control and determine the influence of different versions of possible agreements on the further evolution of the nuclear balance and on the political position of the United States. In early 1969 under Kissinger's direction was begun a comprehensive interdepartmental study of the global military situation, authorized by the president in accordance with National Security Study Memorandum No. 3 (NSSM-3), in order to determine U.S. military requirements, on whose basis in turn would be determined the U.S. position regarding SALT and would be formulated acceptable arms control measures.

The guiding principles of U.S. nuclear strategy, developed as a result of NSSM-3 by early 1970 and published in Defense Secretary Laird's fiscal year 1972 budget report, appeared as follows:

—Maintaining an adequate second-strike capability to deter an all-out surprise attack on our strategic forces.

—Providing no incentive for the Soviet Union to strike the United States first in a crisis.

—Preventing the Soviet Union from gaining the ability to cause considerably greater urban/industrial destruction than the United States could inflict on the Soviet in a nuclear war.

—Defending against damage from small attacks or accidental launches.[41]

Upon close examination of the doctrine of "sufficiency," it is striking that the first of the above principles is hardly at all distinguishable from the idea of "assured destruction" advanced by McNamara in the second half of the 1960s. The second principle of "sufficiency," from a logical point of view, did not contain any additional meaning. And the third and fourth principles obviously were used to justify the construction of an ABM system.

The main issue in U.S. nuclear policy in the first year of the Republican administration's tenure concerned the fate of the Sentinel ABM program. The president and his adviser considered the program's continuation necessary to guarantee the United States a "strong position" in the SALT negotiations, to exert psychological pressure on the other side in goals of securing unilateral U.S. advantages. The ABM program was considered, therefore, an effective although quite expensive instrument for manipulating Soviet-U.S. relations by strength, despite the fact that the administration realized the destabilizing consequences of this system for the military balance. President Nixon had already made an official statement on the subject of ABM on March 14, 1969, the very same day that the order was given in the form of NSSM-28 to begin preparations for the Soviet-U.S. negotiations. The name of the Sentinel system was changed to "Safeguard" and, rather than deploy an area defense, it was planned to construct a system in the program's first phase for defending a portion of the U.S. land-based ICBM force, now on account of a mythical threat of a Soviet nuclear strike on U.S. ICBMs. With this step the Republican administration hoped to reconcile all sides within the United States. ABM opponents were to have been content with the fact that Safeguard was intended not for defending population centers from the other side's retaliatory strike, a mission that could destabilize the nuclear balance, but for decreasing the vulnerability of the Minuteman force, that is, supposedly for strengthening the U.S. "assured destruction" potential. The Pentagon and its allies could be satisfied with the prospect of the further expansion of the program to a "thick" defense of the entire United States.

But in reality the Safeguard decision—the administration's first step in the strategic arms area—did not turn out to be as clever as the White House had calculated. In 1969 a sharp domestic policy struggle developed around the Safeguard system. The growth of antimilitary sentiments in the United States as a result of the defeats in Vietnam, the beginning outlines of détente and the prospect of the SALT agreements, the discontent with greater arms expenditures in the face of widespread poverty, the widespread mistrust of the Pentagon's competency in guaranteeing U.S. security—all impelled Congress toward an unprecedentedly active intervention in the formulation of the administration's military policy. The protracted debates on the Safeguard program culminated on August 6, 1969, when the Cooper-Hart amendment to the fiscal year 1970 budget, which proposed to delete the appropriations for the construction of the first ABM complexes, came before a Senate vote. The results of the vote produced a domestic political sensation, damaged the reputation of the Republican government, and demonstrated the limited extent of its abilities to force its military policy upon Congress. For the first time in U.S. history a major strategic program, upon which the administration and the president had staked their prestige, did not receive a majority of votes. The senators were divided evenly: 50 for and 50 against. The legislative deadlock was broken by a single vote, cast in favor of the program by Vice President Spiro Agnew, who had the right under U.S. law to vote in such situations. Although the Cooper-Hart amendment was not adopted, it had become clear that the ABM program would meet strong resistance in Congress in the future as well, resistance that could grow with the increase of the program's cost. Under the influence of sentiments within the country the Republican leadership's interest in Soviet-U.S. agreements grew substantially.

Besides the ABM, the Nixon administration inherited from its predecessors the MIRV programs. The military-industrial complex had a great stake in the new offensive strategic nuclear arms programs. In March 1968 the Lockheed Corporation and Autonetics received contracts to build the Poseidon missile. On June 10 of the same year General Electric obtained a contract to develop the warheads for the Minuteman-III ICBM. The following year the manufacture of the new technology had already moved to the production lines, and work continued at full speed in assembly departments.

Meanwhile, in Congress, in some scientific circles, and in the liberal press, anxiety about the MIRV program increased. However, in 1969 the liberal opposition was unable to force the administration to halt the testing of MIRVs before ruling out the possibility of prohibiting these systems through negotiations. The congressional opposition refrained from turning the MIRV program into the central issue of their campaign, since its leaders, such as Senators William Fulbright, Albert Gore, and Stuart Symington, considered the main task to be the defeat of the Safeguard program, and they concentrated their activity on this. Opposing them, the strong and organized pressure of the military-industrial complex favored the continued testing and subsequent adoption of MIRV. Most important of all, it accomplished its plans with the consent and approval of the political leadership, which put all its prestige and administrative authority on the side of these circles.

On the threshold of the SALT negotiations the Nixon administration refused to suspend testing of MIRV systems, contending that the question of MIRV limitations should be resolved only on a mutual basis in the course of the negotiations. But when these negotiations began, Washington combined its proposal to prohibit MIRV testing with conditions unacceptable to the Soviet Union. In the course of the two previous years the U.S. MIRV systems had already been almost fully tested, and such an agreement would have hardly affected the U.S. capability to bring them into the arsenal. In addition, Washington advanced a draft treaty prohibiting the deployment of new weapons systems, which stipulated on-site inspections. Such an agreement would have opened the way to obtaining information about the most delicate technological aspects of the other side's strategic weapons systems—the design of the missile's upper stage. The time was certainly not ripe for that kind of on-site inspection. As even many Western experts consider, such methods of verification were just as unacceptable for the United States as for the USSR.[42] The U.S. proposal had been simply a diplomatic ruse and had deliberately counted on the other side's refusal. With its help the administration secured the deployment of MIRVed missiles, while citing within the country the "impossibility" of reaching agreement on their limitation in the SALT negotiations.

In reality, the Republican administration's choice in favor of adopting MIRV was explained by considerations of quite a different order. The U.S. leadership concluded that it was necessary to maintain the superiority of U.S. nuclear potential in the future in a number of parameters. In the face of an approximate quantitative balance between the USSR and the United States in launchers, a buildup of MIRV-type warheads in U.S. strategic forces was chosen as the main way to maintain such a lead. Throughout 1969 in the NSC and the Pentagon a series of studies was conducted to revise strategic planning in light of the anticipated introduction of many thousands of MIRV-type nuclear warheads to U.S. strategic forces. In the words of the American scholar Ronald Tammen, "the result was a dramatic expansion of the targeting list to include even relatively insignificant and tertiary targets and the overlaying of more important targets with multiple strikes." By 1971 the target list had grown to approximately 16,000 targets and was subdivided into four basic categories: Soviet strategic forces, command and control points, Warsaw Pact conventional forces, and industry. These categories corresponded to the priority of missile strikes in the SIOP.[43]

The main idea behind these amendments was to increase the capability for the flexible or selective use of U.S. strategic forces. In the conditions of Soviet-U.S. parity in launchers and the anticipated limitation of ABM systems, a U.S. advantage in warhead numbers could not ensure a "damage limitation" or disarming strike capability (although MIRV programs increased the U.S. potential to strike the other side's military targets). The concept of "flexibility" became Washington's new route to attain unilateral advantages. On June 18, 1970 the first flight of ten MIRVed

Minuteman-III ICBMs was declared operational at Minot Air Force base in North Dakota and transferred to SAC. Test firings of Poseidon missiles from a submarine off the Florida coast began on August 3. On March 31, 1971 the SSBN *James Madison*, carrying 16 Poseidon missiles with MIRVed warheads, left its Charleston, South Carolina base on a course for the North Atlantic. The United States had begun a new round of the strategic nuclear arms race. This newly opened channel of the strategic competition created great difficulties for subsequent stages of the negotiations to limit nuclear rivalry, decreased the stability of the military balance, and revived dangerous strategic ideas.

In June 1975 the deployment of the third wing of Minuteman-III ICBMs was completed: the last of the 550 multiple warhead ICBMs were brought to combat readiness in their silos at the Grand Forks Air Force base and transferred to SAC. The *Daniel Webster*, the 31st and final *Lafayette*-class SSBN, left dry dock in the spring of 1978. In all, as a result of deploying MIRV systems from 1970–78, U.S. missile forces without changing the total number of ballistic missiles brought an additional 5,000 or so thermonuclear warheads into the arsenal, increasing the total number of strategic warheads to almost 10,000. In comparison with 1970 this represented a growth of approximately 100 percent.[44]

By 1972 the substantial reconstruction that had taken place in the U.S. nuclear arsenal under the influence of the rapid deployment of MIRVed missiles began to be reflected in Washington's official strategic concepts. The administration decided to promulgate the idea of the U.S. nuclear strategy's "increased flexibility." In his message to Congress on February 9, 1972, President Nixon stated:

Our forces must also be capable of flexible application. A simple "assured destruction" doctrine does not meet our present requirements for a flexible range of strategic options. No president should be left with only one strategic course of action, particularly that of ordering the mass destruction of enemy civilians and facilities. Given the range of possible political-military situations which could conceivably confront us, our strategic policy should not be based solely on a capability of inflicting urban and industrial damage presumed to be beyond the level an adversary would accept. We must be able to respond at levels appropriate to the situation.[45]

While insisting on a capability for the "flexible" use of U.S. nuclear forces, the U.S. leadership hoped to obtain additional "bargaining chips" in negotiations with the Soviet Union and new means of psychological pressure in the event of a confrontation in one region of the world or another. In essence, Washington was saying that the use of nuclear weapons had become less unthinkable, because inflicting total destruction was not obligatory. As for U.S. allies, the administration's contentions about its capability to use nuclear weapons "flexibly" were to have strengthened the trust in U.S. military-political guarantees abroad. The U.S. leadership thus saw the need to strengthen this trust in the period of "redeploying" U.S. international influence, revising its global obligations, and reducing its military presence in a number of world regions.

## Moscow, May 1972—The First Steps in Strategic Arms Control

After six months of delaying the negotiations, President Nixon, responding to the Soviet Union's constructive proposals, announced on June 19, 1969 the readiness of the administration to begin a dialogue with the Soviet leadership on strategic arms issues. In a joint statement of the two powers on October 17, it was announced that the negotiations would begin on November 17 in Helsinki.

At the basis of the U.S. approach to the negotiations lay the conviction that the potential advantages of the Safeguard ABM system and its inherent capability to become a "thick" territorial defense gave the United States an opportunity not only to secure the mutual limitation of Soviet and U.S. ABM systems but also to reach an agreement on limits for the growth of the number of Soviet offensive strategic missiles. The Soviet Union considered it necessary in the first place to limit maximally both sides' ABM systems. As to limitations on offensive weapons, the Soviet side considered it necessary to examine this question with consideration of U.S. forward-based nuclear forces, which in practice were a supplement to its intercontinental nuclear potential.[46] In the course of a year-and-a-half no compromise could be found on these questions. A way out of the impasse was outlined in May 1971, when the parties agreed to concentrate efforts primarily on limiting the deployment of ABM systems. In addition to this an agreement was proposed on certain measures to limit strategic offensive arms.[47]

In the spring of 1972 at the Moscow summit a series of important Soviet-U.S. accords outlined the sphere of the two superpowers' general interests at this new stage of their relations. The fundamental principles of Soviet-U.S. relations were defined in the document "Basic Principles of U.S.-Soviet Relations," signed May 29, 1972. One of them was the mutual recognition of peaceful coexistence as the only acceptable basis for the two great powers' relations in the nuclear age.[48] The principles included the direct obligation of both parties "to make special efforts to limit strategic arms." The agreements between the Soviet Union and the United States that crowned the first stage of the SALT negotiations were a major step on this path. The fact that the two great powers could find a compromise on the most complex and delicate military-technical issues that formed the core of their national security demonstrated a practical ability to put limits on the strategic arms buildup, to decelerate this most dangerous process.

The unlimited-duration Treaty on the Limitation of Anti-Ballistic Missile Systems, signed in Moscow on May 26, 1972, stipulated the Soviet and U.S. renunciation to deploy ABM systems for covering the territory of their country or separate regions of it, except for two complexes specifically mentioned in the agreement. Furthermore, the treaty prohibited certain directions in the qualitative improvement of ABM systems. Observation by national technical means of verification was provided to ensure treaty compliance. The terms of this agreement directly blocked the way to the far-reaching plans of certain groups of the U.S. military-industrial complex. In particular, strict limitations on the location and quantitative parameters of ABM complexes ruled out their turning into a "thick" defense of U.S. territory. The prohibition on creating new ABM varieties restricted the ways and prospects of developing a number of long-range technical projects. But no one could have imagined at that time that in 15 years these futuristic limitations, in particular those concerning the development, testing, and deployment of space-based components (Article V), would become the center of the vortex of strategic policy, programs, negotiations, and national and transnational debates. In a broader respect the conclusion of the treaty signified a U.S. repudiation of any substantial capabilities for "damage limitation," as well as of the idea of "meaningful nuclear superiority." Therefore, the treaty of May 26, 1972 exerted then and still exerts a most important stabilizing influence on the Soviet-U.S. military balance, despite the arms race that continues in other directions.

Another achievement was the Interim Agreement on Certain Measures with Respect to the Limitation of Strategic Offensive Arms, signed on the very same day. In accordance with it the USSR and the United States were obliged not to construct additional fixed land-based ICBM launchers as of June 1, 1972. The period the agreement was to be in force was limited to five years upon the exchange of instructions of the ABM Treaty's ratification and of written notices of the Interim Agreement's acceptance. In the same period the increase of the number of SLBM launch tubes and the construction of new missile submarines above those already operational and under construction at the date of the signing of the agreement were prohibited. Furthermore, certain channels for the qualitative improvement of strategic forces were blocked. Verification of the agreement with the help of national technical means was provided for as well.[49]

The Interim Agreement limited U.S. military plans less directly than the ABM Treaty, but it did place a real ceiling on Soviet ICBM and SLBM programs. The U.S. did everything possible to prevent the agreement in the offensive arms sphere from affecting its Minuteman-III and

Poseidon programs. But the treaty had significance as well, legally strengthening the principle of both parties' equal security in the area of offensive strategic arms. It did not legitimize a disproportion in favor of the U.S. but counterbalanced the differences in the nuclear arsenals on a mutually acceptable basis. Furthermore, the clear definition of the levels of strategic nuclear potential in the future, as well as both sides' commitment to continue the negotiations with the goal of reaching a long-term and comprehensive agreement, was in and of itself a stabilizing factor in the further evolution of the military balance.

Appraising the results of the Soviet-U.S. summit, Leonid I. Brezhnev emphasized: "The agreement on the Basic Principles of Relations between the USSR and the U.S., the Treaty on the Limitation of Anti-Ballistic Missile Systems, the Interim Agreement on Certain Measures with Respect to the Limitation of Strategic Offensive Arms, and other agreements—all of these are very important and concrete steps in the direction toward a more lasting peace, which is in the interest of all peoples."[50] This evaluation reflected the opinion of the Soviet government, Party leadership, and public opinion.

In the United States itself, a sharp struggle flared up between the supporters of the agreements and their opponents. The Senate Foreign Relations Committee and Armed Services Committee hearings devoted to the SALT agreements, held in June and July of 1972, were the main arena for these arguments. The decisive vote on the ABM Treaty took place on August 3, 1972. The treaty was ratified by an overwhelming majority of votes: 82 versus 2 (Senators Buckley and Allen voted against). On September 14 of the same year the Senate affirmed the Interim Agreement as well. It is true that in the latter case Senator Henry Jackson's amendment was adopted, an amendment that advised the government to achieve "equal levels" in limiting the basic components of U.S. and Soviet strategic forces in subsequent agreements. Congress simultaneously adopted an amendment to the fiscal year 1973 military budget in connection with the agreements concluded in Moscow. In accordance with the conditions of the ABM Treaty, the Safeguard program was sharply reduced, its appropriations cut by $650 million. Total savings in the course of the next five years were estimated at $5 billion. At the same time Congress also approved the accelerated development of a number of military-technical projects.[51]

In the course of discussing the Moscow agreements and amendments to the fiscal year 1973 military budget on Capitol Hill, administration and Defense Department spokesmen urgently recommended the continuation and even acceleration of several basic strategic programs. The defenders of the new programs maintained that their development was necessary for the United States as a "bargaining chip" in future negotiations with the Soviet Union. In addition, U.S. leaders considered the approval of new military programs a necessary concession to the Pentagon for its consent to the 1972 Moscow accords. In the final stage of the first round of the negotiations (in spring of 1972), when the parameters of the future agreements were defined in principle, the Joint Chiefs of Staff laid out the conditions with which it linked its approval of SALT to the U.S. political leadership. Among them were "accelerated programs of research and development." Thus, in accordance with the fiscal year 1974 budget, the deployment of the Poseidon and Minuteman-III missiles was continued, and a fiscal base was laid for new types of strategic weapons as well: the Trident SLBM, the B-1 supersonic long-range bomber, and the highly accurate air- and sea-launched cruise missiles.

The development of new strategic arms as "bargaining chips" in the SALT negotiations was one of the most important elements of the Republican administration's approach to problems of the strategic nuclear balance, a concept that remained at the center of the discussion throughout the 1970s and was transformed into an integral and extremely contradictory aspect of U.S. policy in the conditions of parity. The SALT negotiations indeed opened the possibility for limiting the strategic potential of one side in quantitative and qualitative parameters in exchange for corresponding limitations on the other side. However, practice in most cases demonstrated the counterproductiveness of the idea of manipulating military programs to achieve additional concessions from a negotiating partner. The United States frequently aspired to "trade off" its new military projects not for the USSR's analogous future weapons systems, but for certain components of its existing strategic nuclear forces, which were an integral part of the already-established military balance. That is, they tried to change the latter unilaterally in their favor. Often Washington tried to link the limitation of Soviet and U.S. weapons systems comparable neither in their characteristics nor their strategic significance. And this was at a time when even the mutual limitation of analogous arms was no simple matter, on account of the differences in their role in the two powers' asymmetrical military potentials and of the failure of their strategic programs to coincide in development phases.

At the same time it is impossible to agree with the opinion of certain Western specialists, including those of the liberal school, that the SALT process itself urged forward the creation of new arms as "bargaining chips." In reality, the argument for the necessity of "bargaining chips" was used for approving a number of military programs in the face of parity and the SALT dialogue, when the many previous arguments of the arms race adherents became much less persuasive. However, it should not be forgotten that when parity was not yet attained and the SALT negotiations were not yet underway, for example in the 1960s, a still more intensive buildup of the U.S. nuclear arsenal continued with an open orientation toward superiority. And in conditions of the strategic balance and Soviet-U.S. negotiations, the implementation of programs under the pretext of "bargaining chips" ran into tangible internal and external limitations, especially in the rate and scale of weapons development and deployment. Thus the aggregate of internal and external factors in 1969–72 forced the Nixon administration to the radical limitation of ABM systems. In the early 1970s the debates concerning MIRV programs and the course of the negotiations were reflected in the scale of the deployment of the Minuteman-III system. In 1971–73 the liberal opposition managed to slow down the Trident program and in subsequent years to hamper seriously the development of the B-1 system. From year to year in Congress appropriations for increasing the accuracy and effectiveness of ballistic missiles were cut, and certain projects were eliminated altogether.[52] Parity, détente, and the SALT dialogue, together with other factors, undoubtedly played a great role in this.

Soviet military programs were also limited, though in the context of a quite different decision-making mechanism. This relates to the ABM system, in favor of which in the 1960s there remained some technical and institutional enthusiasm. It pertains as well to ICBM missile and silo construction, SLBM production lines, and SSBN shipbuilding programs. Unlike in the United States, the "bargaining chip" arguments were never put forward or seriously considered in the Soviet political-military establishment. Weapons were not developed and deployed to be bargained away at arms control talks. But since negotiations by definition had to do away with some arms and limit the development and deployment of others, certain complications emerged in the process of the USSR's mutual adjustment of military programs and negotiating positions. This was reflected during the 1970s, for example, in the fact that the USSR had to dismantle considerably more strategic delivery vehicles than the United States to comply with the limits of the arms control agreements.

\* \* \*

In analyzing U.S. foreign policy of the early 1970s it is easy to give way to the temptation to attribute its positive results to the rejection of "cold war" era views, and to ascribe the negative results to the manifestation of vestiges of the past. Certainly, the latter were often perceptibly felt in this period. However, the U.S. leadership of those years disposed of their own concepts as well, which in a number of aspects diverged significantly from the views and perceptions of the rules of détente and competition inherent to the Soviet Union's policies. From the very beginning in Washington détente was considered less a fundamentally new stage in East-West relations that was called upon to promote the strengthening of peace than one of the tools of foreign policy for ensuring the "redeployment of American power." The U.S. leadership considered other means that supposedly supplemented détente: shifting the military-political burden to the NATO and Japanese allies; strengthening key pro-Western regimes in the Third World in order to defend by their hands the privileges of capitalism there; and steps in U.S. relations with China. On account of this approach, Washington's interest in détente diminished from year to year. As a measure of the decline of Washington's interest in détente in various aspects of international politics, as a measure of the reorientation of U.S. policy to goals that contradicted détente, the SALT dialogue—by force of the objective state of affairs in this area—remained in practice the only U.S. sphere of interest in negotiations with the USSR. The reluctance of these circles to recognize the much broader link of true U.S. national interests with détente subsequently bore bad fruit: the aggravation of international tension and acceleration of the arms race, which hampered most seriously the very process of arms control itself.

The Republican administration's theory and practice in the use of military force also testifies that not always did it surmount the past's dangerous heritage but sometimes even augmented it, finding new justifications for it. The Republicans combined a great emphasis on diplomacy in solving international contradictions with an increased readiness to conduct demonstrations of force in buttressing their political line in the crisis situations of 1969–74 in Southeast Asia, Korea, the Middle East, and the Indian subcontinent. The reduction of U.S. military presence abroad was combined with intensified pressure on the allies to expand their military contributions, with enormous supplies of arms and technology to U.S. clients, especially the Shah of Iran, and with the increased role of nuclear weapons in U.S. strategy. The dialogue with socialist countries on disarmament issues was slandered by conditions unrelated to the matter through the principle of linkage and connected with new military programs as "bargaining chips" for the negotiations. And it is precisely in the strategic weapons area, more than in any other, that both the positive results and the negative sides of the Republicans' activities entailed broad and long-term consequences.

The Soviet Union, while hoping for improved political relations with the West, expanded economic cooperation and progress in nuclear and conventional arms control, did not consider itself obliged to stop supporting the national-liberation movement or progressive and anti-Western regimes in Asia, Africa, and Latin America. As the political, economic, and arms control relations with the United States encountered the growing resistance of anti-Soviet and hard-line U.S. political echelons—at the beginning unrelated to events in the Third World—the Soviet policy of supporting prosocialist forces in the developing countries intensified. It was caused also by the Nixon-Kissinger efforts to "elbow out" the USSR from important areas of the Third World. At the same time a strong momentum in Soviet military programs (in fields unrestricted by arms control agreements), undertaken since the mid-1960s in response to the U.S. crash defense buildup of the first half of the 1960s, carried over into the 1970s and continued out of phase with U.S. policy, while the United States was engaged in reducing its overextension and "redeploying" its military presence in the world. This was portrayed in the West as the "Soviet quest for military superiority."

Détente and the first SALT accords clearly demonstrated in the early 1970s that the military-industrial circles were not omnipotent and that the arms race could be curbed. However, the resistance of the U.S. military-industrial complex and conservative circles to positive changes became increasingly more stubborn. As one of the main instruments of their struggle, these forces chose to undertake a mass campaign on the "Soviet military threat." New strategic concepts were put forward to justify the deployment of the next generation of arms and give it a purposefulness in the conditions of quantitative strategic parity. The new strategic concepts, themselves born of the arms race, thus paved the way for its subsequent acceleration.

## Notes

1. See Yurii M. Mel'nikov, *Ot Potsdama k Guamu: Ocherki amerikanskoi diplomatii* (Moscow: Nauka, 1974); Aleksandr N. Yakovlev, *Ideologiia amerikanskoi "imperii": Problemy voiny, mira i mezhdunarodnykh otnoshenii v poslevoennoi amerikanskoi burzhuaznoi politicheskoi literature* (Moscow: Mysl', 1967).

2. *Otkuda iskhodit ugroza miru*, 2d ed. (Moscow: Voenizdat, 1982), 34; John M. Collins, *U.S.-Soviet Military Balance: 1960–1980, Conflicts and Capabilities* (New York: McGraw-Hill, 1980), 37.

3. V. I. Lenin, *Polnoe sobranie sochenenii* (Moscow: Politizdat, 1966) 30:85.

4. Fred Kaplan, *The Wizards of Armageddon* (New York: Simon and Schuster, 1983), 269.

5. "Special Message to the Congress on the Defense Budget," March 28, 1961, *Public Papers of the Presidents of the United States, John F. Kennedy, 1961* (Washington, D.C.: U.S. Government Printing Office, 1962), 236.

6. Kaplan, *The Wizards of Armageddon*, 279; Milton Leitenberg, "Presidential Directive 59," *Journal of Peace Research* 18:4 (1981): 312; *Fiscal Year 1968 Defense Budget* (Washington, D.C.: U.S. Government Printing Office, 1967), 38–39.

7. *Department of State Bulletin* 47, no. 1202 (July 9, 1962): 67.

8. Kosta Tsipis et al., eds., *The Future of the Sea-Based Deterrent* (Cambridge: MIT Press, 1973), 14; Federation of American Scientists, *FAS Public Interest Report* 27:2 (February 1974), 3.

9. Robert Scheer, *With Enough Shovels: Reagan, Bush and Nuclear War* (New York: Random House, 1982), 216.

10. Zbigniew Brzezinski, "How the Cold War Was Played," *Foreign Affairs* 51:1 (Fall 1972): 192.

11. Vladimir F. Tolubko, *Raketnye voiska* (Moscow: Voenizdat, 1977), 24; Sergei G. Gorshkov, *Morskaia moshch' gosudarstva* (Moscow: Voenizdat, 1976), 293.

12. "Department of Defense Appropriations for FY 1965, Part 1," *Hearings*, Committee on Appropriations, U.S. Senate (Washington, D.C.: U.S. Government Printing Office, 1964), 31.

13. *Fiscal Year 1968 Defense Budget*, 38–39.

14. "Military Posture," *Hearings*, Committee on Armed Services, U.S. House of Representatives (Washington, D.C.: U.S. Government Printing Office, 1962), 3185.

15. Leitenberg, "Presidential Directive 59," 312–13.

16. *Radi mira na zemle: sovetskaia programma mira dlia 80-kh godov v deistvii, materialy i dokumenty* (Moscow: Politizdat, 1983), 195.

17. Desmond Ball, "The Strategic Missile Programme of the Kennedy Administration," Ph.D. diss. (Canberra: University of Australia, 1972), apps. 1–3.

18. In accordance with this concept of the strategy of "flexible response," the United States planned to have the capability of conducting simultaneously two large conventional wars (in Europe and Asia) and also of carrying out a minor operation in another region.

19. Lawrence Korb, *The FY 1981–1985 Defense Program: Issues and Trends* (Washington, D.C.: American Enterprise Institute, 1980), 45.

20. Henry L. Trewhitt, *McNamara* (New York: Harper and Row, 1971), 115–16.

21. Robert McNamara, *The Essence of Security: Reflections in Office* (New York: Harper and Row, 1968), 51–67.

22. Ted Greenwood, "Qualitative Improvements in Offensive Strategic Arms: The Case of MIRV," Ph.D. diss. (Cambridge, Mass.: The Massachusetts Institute of Technology, 1973), 57, 174.

23. *Pravda*, May 22, 1968.

24. *Pravda*, June 28, 1968.

25. Robert W. Tucker and William Watts, eds., *Beyond Containment: U.S. Foreign Policy in Transition* (Washington, D.C.: Potomac Associates, 1973), xxxii.

26. Henry Brandon, *The Retreat of American Power* (New York: Doubleday, 1973), 82.

27. Henry A. Kissinger, *American Foreign Policy: Three Essays* (New York: Norton, 1969), 59–60.

28. Brandon, *Retreat of American Power*, 40.

29. "Second Annual Report to the Congress on United States Foreign Policy," February 25, 1971, *Public Papers of the Presidents of the United States, Richard M. Nixon, 1971* (Washington, D.C.: U.S. Government Printing Office, 1972), 305.

30. *Department of Defense Budget, Fiscal Year 1972* (Washington, D.C.: U.S. Government Printing Office, 1971), 22.

31. If one compares these parameters in 1974, when President Nixon resigned, with 1964, the time of increasingly greater U.S. intervention in the affairs of Indochina, then the number of U.S. armed forces personnel decreased by 26 percent; the number of tactical air wings, by 46 percent; the number of naval forces, by 47 percent; and the number of divisions, by 16 percent. But if one draws a comparison with 1968, the peak year of U.S. aggression in Vietnam, then in naval forces and divisions the decrease is 50 percent and 30 percent, respectively. See Korb, *The FY 1981–1985 Defense Program*, 30–32.

32. *The Washington Post*, February 27, 1966.

33. B. M. Khalosha, *Voenno-politicheskie soiuzy imperializma* (Moscow, 1982), 32–36. See also N. Petrov, N. Sokolov, I. Vladimirov, and P. Katin, *SShA i NATO: istochniki voennoi ugrozy* (Moscow, 1979); and Rair G. Simonian, *Voennye bloki imperializma* (Moscow: Voenizdat, 1976).

34. Andrei A. Kokoshin, *Prognozirovanye i politika* (Moscow: Mezhdunarodnye Otnoshenii, 1975), 166.

35. Korb, *The FY 1981–1985 Defense Program*, 32.

36. Vitaly V. Zhurkin, *SShA i mezhdunarodno-politicheskie krizisy* (Moscow: Nauka, 1975), 274.

37. *Public Papers of the Presidents of the United States, Richard M. Nixon, 1969* (Washington, D.C.: U.S. Government Printing Office, 1971), 19; Chalmers M. Roberts, *The Nuclear Years: The Arms Race and Arms Control, 1945–70* (New York: Praeger, 1970), 97–98.

38. "First Annual Report to the Congress on United States Foreign Policy for the 1970's," February 18, 1970, *Public Papers of the Presidents of the United States, Richard M. Nixon, 1970* (Washington, D.C: U.S. Government Printing Office, 1970), 172.

39. "Second Annual Report to the Congress on United States Foreign Policy," *Public Papers of the Presidents of the United States, Richard M. Nixon, 1971*, 311.

40. Jerome Kahan, *Security in the Nuclear Age* (Washington, D.C.: Brookings Institution, 1975), 144.

41. *Department of Defense Budget, Fiscal Year 1972*, 62.

42. John Newhouse, *Cold Dawn: The Story of SALT* (New York: Holt, Rinehart and Winston, 1973), 180.

43. Ronald L. Tammen, *MIRV and the Arms Race* (New York: Praeger, 1973), 114.

44. *Otkuda iskhodit ugroza miru*, 33.

45. "Third Annual Report to the Congress on United States Foreign Policy," February 9, 1972, *Public Papers of the Presidents of the United States, Richard M. Nixon, 1972* (Washington, D.C.: U.S. Government Printing Office, 1974), 307.

46. These forces—the several hundred fighter-bombers at airbases and on U.S. aircraft carriers in the European theater—were capable of reaching Soviet territory with nuclear weapons on board.

47. Alexei G. Arbatov, *Bezopasnost' v iadernyi vek i politika Vashingtona* (Moscow: Politizdat, 1980), 139.

48. *Pravda*, May 30, 1972.

49. *Pravda*, May 28, 1972.

50. *Pravda*, June 6, 1972.

51. "Fiscal Year 1973 Amended Military Authorization Request Related to SALT Agreements," *Hearings*, Committee on Armed Services, U.S. Senate (Washington, D.C.: U.S. Government Printing Office, 1972), 4196.

52. These include, for example, a system intended to improve the accuracy of the Poseidon SLBM, and the *Sanguine* and *Seafarer* submarine communications systems.

# 2

## The Consolidation of Parity: Logic and Contradictions

In 1974–75, the most substantial change in U.S. nuclear strategy since the mid-1960s took place. On the one hand, the dynamics of the military balance and the evolution of U.S. strategic policy over the course of previous years had paved the way for the alteration of U.S. strategic concepts in the mid-1970s. On the other hand, both the overall international situation and conditions inside the United States played a great role. Negative changes were manifested in Washington's overall military policy and nuclear strategy, and in U.S. foreign policy as a whole, which came into increasingly greater contradiction with the interests of détente and arms control.

### The Schlesinger Doctrine: The Strategy of "Limited" Nuclear War

In the face of the growing Watergate scandal the appointment of a new secretary of defense was in and of itself an insignificant event and should not be considered the primary reason for the subsequent changes in U.S. nuclear strategy. But it was an additional factor, a final jolt, that to some extent determined the specific nature of the changes. James Schlesinger was one of the few U.S. secretaries of defense who had come to the leading post of the Pentagon already possessing professional experience in the military field. His strategic views had been formed in the RAND Corporation, where he had risen to become head of the strategic studies division. Schlesinger belonged to the conservative wing of the Republican party and, upon becoming a state official, began increasingly to express his adherence to a "hard-line" policy. This policy was not noted for being particularly sophisticated. In a series of press conferences in late 1973 and early 1974, he declared that the United States required increased military power and greater defense spending. In January 1974, Schlesinger announced the most significant changes in U.S. nuclear strategy in the past ten years. "City-bashing," in his words, was no longer a sufficient deterrent. "It should not be the only option and perhaps not the principal option" available. U.S. nuclear strategy, he asserted, had "to develop a wider variety of options ... in crisis situations." Accordingly, Schlesinger introduced a new strategic concept— the "retargeting" of a portion of U.S. intercontinental missiles from administrative-industrial centers to other targets to give them a capability to implement "certain counterforce options" for nuclear strikes."[1]

Just as the secretary of defense had promised, the military budget for fiscal year 1975 (published in February 1974) represented a noticeable growth in appropriations (from \$87.1 billion in 1974 to \$92.6 billion in fiscal year 1975). Its significance in the history of U.S. military policy was that this budget marked a turning point in the 1970s, when the reduction of U.S. military spending in real terms, which had taken place after the peak of the Vietnam war in 1968, was ended, and a new annual growth of defense appropriations was begun. A large share of these resources were earmarked for expanding and increasing the readiness of U.S. conventional forces. But the principal innovations took place in the strategic arms area, including targeting and war-fighting concepts and modernization programs.

The secretary of defense noted in his budget report that a fundamentally new situation had been established in the strategic balance by the mid-1970s. On the one hand, he emphasized that U.S. superiority had disappeared in almost all categories, but on the other, that the Soviet Union had acquired the indisputable capability for a devastating retaliatory strike, as the overwhelming portion of its nuclear potential had become invulnerable to a hypothetical U.S. first strike. In this situation Schlesinger called for a revision of U.S. nuclear strategy, which since the mid-1960s had been based on McNamara's doctrine of assured destruction:

Today, such a massive retaliation against cities in response to anything less than an all-out attack on the U.S. and its cities appears less and less credible ... .[T]o be credible, and hence effective over the range of possible contingencies, deterrence must rest on many options and on a spectrum of capabilities (within the contraints of SALT) to support these options.

Regarding U.S. strategic nuclear programs Schlesinger asserted that to enhance deterrence, we may also want a more efficient hard-target-kill capability than we now possess....In the meantime, I would be remiss if I did not recommend further research and development on both better accuracy and improved yield-to-weight ratios in our warheads. Both are essential . . . for *a more efficient hard-target-kill capability.*[2] (emphasis added)

Thus for the first time since 1969 a U.S. official had openly declared the policy to increase the "counterforce" potential of nuclear forces, despite the leadership's official assertions to the contrary over the course of the previous several years. To justify these plans Schlesinger cited information that the Soviet Union had begun testing a MIRVed ICBM, and that this had taken place much sooner than the United States had expected.

Upon close examination it is easy to see that Schlesinger's strategic innovations consisted of two main and carefully differentiated elements. First, there was an acceleration of military programs to maintain in the future a so-called "essential equivalence" with the USSR in hard-target-kill capability. Second, the principle of "selective" nuclear strikes for conducting "limited nuclear war" not only at the theater level but even at the intercontinental level was advanced, supposedly to strengthen "deterrence" in the conditions of the new correlation of strategic forces.

In fact the USSR, in response to the U.S. MIRVing of ICBM and SLBM programs already in a high deployment state, began testing its own MIRVed ICBM systems: the RS-20 (SS-18) type heavy missile and the RS-16 (SS-17) and RS-18 (SS-19) type light missiles. The three types of new ICBMs did not represent the "unprecedented scale of the Soviet program," as the secretary of defense put it, but rather the technical and organizational features of the USSR's strategic modernization policy—not surprisingly, quite different from that of the United States. Of course, the eventual deployment of MIRVed missile systems in the USSR gave it a largely expanded capability to cover U.S. military and civilian targets. But this expansion was not conceived of in the USSR as a desirable operational or strategic goal, and rather was the consequence of the Soviet response to the U.S. MIRV programs of the 1960s and 1970s. New Soviet forces were fit into the same strategy and basic operational plan of massive retaliation in response to the contingency of a U.S. strategic first strike, with broader target coverage and more redundancy.

It was not the "threat" of new Soviet ICBMs that obliged the U.S. secretary of defense to demand the development of U.S. "counterforce" weapons and options. To the contrary, the legitimate and necessary steps of the Soviet Union to restore the military balance, undertaken in response to the U.S. MIRV program, were used in the United States to justify a new round in building up its nuclear potential. The equalization of the correlation of strategic nuclear forces presented the United States with the prospect of losing its principal advantage, which it had expected to preserve for itself, in total number of nuclear warheads. From late 1973 to early 1974 the secretary began to intimidate the U.S. Congress and public with the alleged threat of a "counterforce gap" with the USSR in order to secure the acceleration of modernization programs of U.S. strategic offensive forces.

According to Schlesinger and those of similar mind in the upper echelons of the military-industrial complex, in conditions of the future overall equilibrium of the Soviet-U.S. strategic balance both in launchers and in the long run in warheads as well, the United States had to obtain advantages by way of a qualitative arms race. They made their stake on the threat of "selective" nuclear strikes on the land-based component of the Soviet Union's strategic arsenal and on the broad spectrum of its military and industrial targets. At first glance these ideas recalled McNamara's strategic concepts of the early 1960s. But at the same time there were also radical differences between these two stages of Washington's nuclear policy. McNamara's counterforce concept in 1961–63 envisaged, essentially, the creation of a capability for a disarming strike on Soviet strategic forces. In the 1970s, owing to the growth of the Soviet Union's retaliatory capability, its creation of a powerful hardened land-based missile force and ballistic missile-carrying submarine fleet, the potential for a disarming nuclear strike became in reality unattainable for the United States. The 1972 ABM Treaty and its 1974 Protocol all the more deprived the United States of grounds for hoping that they would be able to implement nuclear aggression with impunity.

Schlesinger's main idea, which he evidently fostered while still at RAND, was to advance such a strategy in which the objective capability of both sides to inflict unacceptable damage on each other would essentially be removed "beyond the brackets" of the nuclear balance. Thus, taking the factor that deters the use of nuclear weapons, Schlesinger decided to make it a condition enabling the creation of a credible threat to use missile forces. For this, he argued, the United States needed the potential of delivering highly accurate "selective" nuclear strikes on the other side's land-based strategic forces and other military and economic targets. If such attacks would not entail great collateral casualties among its civilian population, then a retaliatory strike on U.S. population centers would be deterred by the powerful U.S. reserve potential able to destroy the enemy's cities. In this event it would remain for the latter either to do nothing or to retaliate with "limited" strikes, in the conduct of which the United States should have had an advantage due to the accuracy and flexibility of its own strategic forces. The threat of "limited nuclear war," from Schlesinger's point of view, could become a new form of a U.S. unilateral strategic advantage and an instrument of foreign policy even in the situation of an overall military balance. But for this it was necessary to create the corresponding arms as well as convince the political leadership of the United States and other countries of the feasibility of such actions. In early February 1975 in the fiscal year 1976 budget report Schlesinger cast off the camouflaged wording and declared quite bluntly that

since both we and the Soviet Union are investing so much of our capability for flexible and controlled responses in our ICBM forces, these forces could become tempting targets, assuming that one or both sides acquire *much more substantial hard-target kill capabilities* than they currently possess. If one side *could remove the other's capability for flexible and controlled responses*, he might find ways of exercising coercion and extracting concessions without triggering the final holocaust.[3] (emphasis added)

On the basis of a number of additional studies carried out upon Schlesinger's arrival at the Defense Department, an important document—National Security Decision Memorandum (NSDM) 242—was drafted, which Nixon signed in January 1974. Three new points were contained in the memorandum. First, in comparison with the period from the late 1960s to the early 1970s, the accent on hard-target-kill capability and, at the same time, on expanding the set of programmed strike options on a wide range of other military and economic targets was strengthened. Options were broken down in much more detail, right down to the use of several warheads. Second, the concept of "escalation control" was detailed, which concept required raising the survivability, reliability, and flexibility of the U.S. leadership's command and control over strategic forces. Thus the condition was set that at each level of escalation the United States would be able to secure advantages and at the same time retain additional options for moving to a higher stage without resorting to the total destruction of administrative-industrial centers. Third, the other side's administrative-industrial centers, as such, ceased to be considered as targets of nuclear strikes. Instead, industry was subdivided into "industry supporting military activities" (military factories, petroleum refineries, transportation centers) and "industry of postwar recovery" (coal and steel industry, power stations, and so on) as special target sets. Political leadership centers were not supposed to be destroyed at the initial stage of the "exchange" but kept targeted by reserve strategic forces.[4]

In accordance with these points a new version of the Nuclear Weapons Employment Plan was developed in the Pentagon, which Schlesinger signed in April 1974. In it were specifically defined the prerequisites for planning, attack options, targeting tasks, and required levels of inflicted damage (for example, the capability for destroying under all conditions up to 70 percent of "industry of postwar recovery"). A new SIOP was drawn up on this basis. It included four basic categories of operations: "major attack options" (on industry); "selected attack options" (on military targets); "limited attack options" (on single targets); and "regional attack options" (on separate areas). Of paramount importance—especially concerning strikes on the USSR's hardened missile forces—was missile accuracy and cross-targeting.[5] The new SIOP was approved in December 1975 and entered into JSTPS computers in January 1976. Its corresponding target list was expanded to 25,000 targets on the territory of the socialist countries.[6]

One of the first acts of the Pentagon's new leadership was to sanction the intensification of technological efforts to improve the accuracy of strategic missiles. This decision was made without the knowledge or approval of Congress, which in fact the year before had refused to approve the administration's budget request for improving missile accuracy. In January 1974 the secretary of defense announced in the budget report a program to increase the counterforce potential of existing Minuteman-III missiles. An improvement of their inertial guidance systems allowed accuracy to be doubled. Schlesinger planned to begin installing the missiles' new guidance systems in 1977. In addition, the miniaturization of thermonuclear warheads at Lawrence Livermore Laboratory provided an opportunity to approximately double the yield of the warheads without changing their weight or size. In February 1974 the secretary recommended that development begin on a new warhead model, the Mk-12A, in order to begin retrofitting Minuteman-III missiles with it by 1979.

But the main plans of the military-industrial circles that Schlesinger represented were connected with the long-term program of the MX ICBM. Initial studies on the next-generation ICBM system to replace Minuteman had been in progress since the late 1960s. The MX program was begun in 1972, and in 1974 Schlesinger put it at the center of his "selective counterforce strike" concept. According to the plans of the Air Force Space and Missile Systems Organization, the MX was to be a much larger three-stage ICBM than Minuteman, have almost three times the launch weight (80–90 tons), and quadruple the throw-weight (to four tons). Officially, the secretary of defense justified the MX program with arguments of the necessity to reduce the vulnerability of U.S. land-based missile forces by moving to a mobile launch mode. Furthermore, the MX system's increased hard-target-kill capability, by his assertions, would supposedly have assured the U.S. "counterforce parity" with the Soviet Union in the 1980s. This dual substantiation was used to justify the new strategic program's enormous cost in the eyes of the U.S. public and Congress.

In early 1974 the Pentagon leadership was forced to lower the projected deployment rate of the gigantic *Ohio*-class (Trident) submarine from three to two per year, and in 1975 this output schedule was lowered to three every two years. The first ten *Ohio* SSBNs were to have become operational from 1979 to 1985. The Defense Department's decisions were the result of serious technical difficulties encountered in the course of the system's development and of economic problems connected with the earlier accelerated production schedule. Thus, considering sentiments in Congress in favor of limiting military spending and arguments in the Senate against accelerating the Trident program, Schlesinger linked his "targeting options" strategy primarily with the development of air force programs and preferred the redistribution of military appropriations precisely in their favor.

A different issue was connected with air- and sea-launched cruise missiles. The Pentagon's civilian leadership had already in its first months decided to resume development of the air-launched cruise missile, which the air force staff had cancelled in mid-1973 (in order to facilitate as an alternative the development of the B-1 bomber, a supersonic, low altitude penetrating bomber), and also to accelerate sharply the development of the strategic version of the sea-launched cruise missile. In the opinion of Schlesinger and his supporters, the strategic cruise missile systems could not have fitted the strategy of "selective nuclear strikes" better. On the one hand, the secretary was attracted by their comparatively low cost and ability to be launched from various platforms. This allowed cruise missiles to be deployed in quantities of many thousands and dispersed in all possible secret and mobile launch platforms. The Pentagon planned to use accurate cruise missiles, which would be difficult to intercept at low altitudes, as a means of destroying various economic and military targets under the scenario of a level-by-level nuclear strike escalation. Moreover, according to Defense Department plans, cruise missiles were to have freed MIRVed ballistic missiles for striking time-urgent targets (for example, ICBM silos, command centers, bomber bases and so on).

Along with the intensification of work on various cruise missiles was accelerated the development of new nuclear weapons systems for theater military operations. This concerns mainly the development of the highly accurate Pershing-II IRBM, for which a new guidance system and nuclear warhead were created. It is important to note that these measures had already been laid out several years before the beginning of the propaganda campaign on the "threat" of the new Soviet RSD-10 (SS-20) IRBM, and that these military programs were mainly connected with strategies for the "flexible" or "selective" use of U.S. nuclear forces, including for striking Soviet strategic forces.

Nor did programs for increasing the survivablity and reliability of command, control, and communication ($C^3$) systems escape the attention of the secretary of defense. The creation of the E-4 improved airborne command post is an example. A so-called command data buffer system, based on new computer technology, permitted the rapid retargeting of ICBMs to different targets. Such a capability had great significance in plans for "controlled counterforce strikes," since it permitted surviving missiles to assume the tasks of destroyed ICBMs and offered the possibility of retargeting missiles from the enemy's used silos to his unused ones. Finally, the so-called Program 647 of geosynchronous-orbit satellites promised to guarantee the observation of relevant regions and of possible missile launches "in real time" (that is, simultaneously transferring information to receiving stations). The NAVSTAR navigational satellites would have also used infrared sensors to pinpoint the location of nuclear explosions, determine their yield, and estimate inflicted damage.[7]

The shift in U.S. strategic policy that had begun by the mid-1970s had great significance and long-term consequences. At the beginning of that decade an approximate numerical parity was established between Soviet and U.S. strategic forces. It is no less important that the Soviet strategic nuclear potential had become invulnerable to U.S. first strike, that the majority of Soviet strategic forces could now survive under any circumstances the unleashing of nuclear war and inflict catastrophic losses on the United States with a retaliatory strike. This situation was symmetrical for both sides, despite disproportions in the structure and technical features of their nuclear potentials. In a certain sense McNamara's prediction had come true: the mutual capability of both powers to inflict unacceptable damage on each other with even a retaliatory strike made a first strike unthinkable and the strategic balance stable. However, in practice parity turned out to be a much less attractive situation for Washington than certain U.S. politicians and strategists had assumed in the mid-1960s, when the United States still retained a significant strategic predominance. The entire military policy, the "grand strategy" of the United States, its arms programs and overall foreign policy were oriented toward the preservation of, if not nuclear superiority, then in any event substantial U.S. strategic advantages. Giving them up would have demanded much more substantive changes in U.S. "grand strategy" and foreign policy than those upon which U.S. ruling circles were ready to embark. Instead, Washington began to search for ways to secure strategic advantages in the conditions of overall strategic nuclear parity as well. At first these efforts took the form of MIRV programs and concepts of the "flexible" use of nuclear power. Later, when it became clear that the Soviet Union would soon eliminate U.S. advantages even in MIRVs, concepts of "limited nuclear war" or "selective counterforce strikes" were advanced, and programs for improving the nuclear arsenal qualitatively were accelerated.[8]

The long-term military-technical policy to build up and modernize

U.S. strategic arms was directed at reorienting U.S. global strategic policy, which since the second half of the 1960s had envisaged primarily the maintenance of the threat of the assured destruction of urban-industrial centers. From the mid-1970s Schlesinger began to openly "reorient" nuclear strategy toward the tasks of "selective" strikes, including on hard targets. Thus he planned in addition the creation of a threat to destroy the most important components of the other side's strategic forces along with the preservation of a nuclear reserve to deter its retaliatory strike by threat of the massive destruction of industrial complexes and their population.

The immediate goal of the Pentagon's strategic reforms was to create the ways and means for the political use of qualitatively new strategic arms in the face of quantitative strategic parity. The goal was to use military-technical progress, the development of new arms, and the growing strategic power in order to escape from the recurrent nuclear deadlock that paralyzed the use or threat of force at the nuclear level. This was the essence of the "targeting options" or "limited nuclear war" concept. Appeals to increase U.S. "counterforce" potential and corresponding military programs were intended to render diplomatic pressure on the Soviet Union. The concept of "essential equivalence" required the next SALT agreement to "even out" the disproportions in those places where they were not in the United States' favor (that is, in the number, megatonnage, and throw-weight of ICBMs), but without considering those aspects of the strategic balance that favored the United States itself (such as total warheads, the payload, number and weapons of heavy bombers, and the warhead number and patrol rate of the SLBM force). Obviously, such an approach to the question was calculated to improve unilateral advantages.

The ideas of "selective nuclear strikes" were also calculated with U.S. allies in mind. In the situation of a nuclear balance, under which a global war would be suicidal for the United States, Schlesinger was worried, as he said, "by Europe's growing skepticism that U.S. strategic forces are tightly coupled with European security, despite our repeated commitments over the course of many years." Alliance relations in NATO were aggravated by the U.S. domestic opposition's strong pressure to reduce unilaterally the U.S. military presence on the European continent in the early 1970s. According to the Pentagon's plan, U.S. declarations of its readiness to engage in the "limited" use of its strategic forces in the event of a military conflict in Europe, despite the Soviet-U.S. strategic balance, should have strengthened the U.S. nuclear guarantee to end military-political influence in NATO.

To a great degree the new strategic concepts also pursued domestic policy goals. In the early 1970s in the conditions of détente and the SALT negotiations, the antimilitary movement in U.S. society and the influential opposition in Congress impeded the development of new strategic nuclear weapons systems by the military-industrial complex. Schlesinger and his supporters began a massive campaign to intimidate Congress and the public with the "threat" of Soviet MIRVed missiles. Under the pretext of preventing Soviet "counterforce superiority," the Defense Department vociferously began to demand Congress's approval of new U.S. military programs, supposedly to insure "essential equivalence" in this sphere. The military-industrial complex and its allies needed to reverse sentiments within the United States that favored the SALT negotiations and a reduction of the arms burden.

## Vladivostok, November 1974: The Codification of Parity

The reorientation of Washington's strategic policy and the accelerated development of new nuclear arms in the mid-1970s provoked the criticism of realistically thinking liberal and moderately conservative U.S. scientists and politicians, and strong debates regarding this raged in Congress. But the Schlesinger doctrine and arms programs connected with it forced their way into Washington's state policy. Moreover, after a "state of siege" of several years, the military-industrial complex and conservative political circles began to close ranks under the leadership of Secretary of Defense Schlesinger and Senator Henry Jackson, preparing for a counteroffensive along a wide front. The main thrust of their activities was to undertake a massive campaign to intimidate the public with the mythical Soviet "military threat." On Capitol Hill Senator Jackson criticized the 1972 Interim Agreement for the fact that it supposedly ceded "major advantages" to the USSR. A special emphasis was placed on the issue of ballistic missile throw-weight.[9] The arguments of Schlesinger and Jackson held that Soviet missiles' "manifold advantage" in throw-weight would supposedly lead to Soviet "superiority" in the number and yield of nuclear warheads after the deployment of MIRVs. Some supporters of increased U.S. military power, such as Senator Sam Nunn, emphasized the alleged expansion and buildup of the socialist countries' conventional armed forces in Europe. Others, like retired admiral Elmo Zumwaldt, even made assertions about the growth of the "threat" of the Soviet navy, despite obvious U.S. and NATO naval superiority, especially in aircraft carrier strike groups.

Other pretexts as well were used to exacerbate anti-Soviet feelings in the West. The new Arab-Israeli war, which broke out in the Middle East in October 1973, and the subsequent oil embargo that plunged capitalism into an energy crisis (which aggravated further still the general economic recession), were placed in full measure at the service of the anti-Soviet campaign. Here, too, U.S. Zionist circles united in a single front with the conservatives and the military-industrial complex. The U.S. campaign on "human rights violations" in the Soviet Union and other socialist countries seriously damaged détente, without, of course, any improvement in the U.S.-Soviet dialogue on this important problem. By the efforts of Senator Jackson and his supporters, both houses of Congress passed trade legislation in December 1974 that linked the conferral of trade credits and most-favored nation status to the Soviet Union with the state of the level of yearly emigration from the USSR. On account of such unprecedented interference in the Soviet Union's internal affairs, the 1972 agreement on the development of trade and economic cooperation did not enter into force. Economic cooperation—in itself a useful stabilizing factor of political relations—suffered greatly. Without seriously damaging the Soviet economy, this action deprived détente of a significant element of mutual vested interests that could have moderated political rivalry between the principal states.

Events inside the United States also affected the process of détente. The Watergate affair reached its culmination in the summer of 1974. On August 9 President Richard Nixon resigned from office. A serious collateral effect of Watergate was the great damage to détente. From late 1973 to mid-1974 the administration's leadership was practically paralyzed in the foreign policy sphere. Losing as he was the vestiges of authority and influence inside the country, it was increasingly more difficult for President Nixon to bring about practical steps in the area of détente and arms control. The Watergate scandal absorbed increasingly greater attention in U.S. liberal circles as well, diverting them from the problems of foreign policy and the arms race. Opponents of détente in the United States, to be sure, did not fail to take advantage of the existing foreign policy situation in order to cast a shadow on the successes of Soviet-U.S. relations. They began to suggest persistently to the public that the Republican leadership had allegedly allowed the Soviet Union to obtain unilateral political and military advantages for the sake of its own popularity, which had been connected with the expansion of détente.

Having become president of the United States in August 1974, Gerald R. Ford decided to declare his candidacy in the 1976 presidential elections. For this he needed to win authority and popularity in the United States during his remaining two years. The best means for doing this, naturally, would be the quick achievement of a new agreement on offensive arms limitations, which had been deadlocked during the last two years of the Nixon presidency. Despite the active efforts of the military-industrial complex, the Zionists, and the reactionaries, broad sentiments within the United States remained in favor of détente and limiting the arms race. For example, public opinion surveys showed that only 9 percent of those questioned opposed détente, while 35 percent unequivocally supported it, and 34 percent demanded a reduction in the U.S.

military budget. According to a Gallup poll, 44 percent unconditionally favored reducing military spending, while 12 percent of those questioned favored increasing it.[10]

In November 1972 the SALT negotiations resumed in Geneva. The U.S. side raised the question of establishing equal overall ceilings in Soviet and U.S. strategic launchers, including bombers. It also proposed establishing equal limits on the aggregate throw-weight of both powers' strategic forces. In this way the U.S. representatives sought to limit the deployment of MIRVed ICBMs in the USSR and secure a reduction of Soviet heavy missiles. In turn, the Soviet Union raised the issue of counting U.S. forward-based nuclear forces in the equal numerical ceilings. It acted in accordance with its official declaration in the conclusion of the agreement in 1972 of the necessity to return to this question in preparing a long-term treaty. At the June 1973 Soviet-U.S. summit in Washington it was decided that a permanent agreement would be signed in 1974 and include both quantitative and qualitative strategic offensive arms limitations on the basis of the principle of both parties' equal security and of the inadmissability of either obtaining unilateral advantages. At the Moscow summit in June 1974 it was agreed that the new treaty should "embrace the period to 1985 and address both quantitative and qualitative limitations."[11]

Wishing to facilitate the progress of the Soviet-U.S. negotiations, the leadership of the USSR took an important step to meet the U.S. side's position. As Andrei A. Gromyko, former USSR Minister of Foreign Affairs, recollected later, in the course of the negotiations in the fall of 1974, "in the interests of reaching an agreement we did not propose as an obligatory condition the inclusion in the agreement of a provision to eliminate American forward-based nuclear forces."[12] This Soviet decision was directed at easing the next round of negotiations, while putting aside the issue of U.S. forward-based forces until the future. The United States backed off its demand to limit throw-weight. This permitted the reaching of a new Soviet-U.S. understanding on limiting strategic offensive weapons systems. On November 23–24, a meeting between Leonid I. Brezhnev and Gerald Ford took place in the Vladivostok region. The leaders of both powers resolutely affirmed that they would henceforth develop their relations in the direction that had been determined in the preceding years by the treaties and agreements concluded between them.

As to goals set for furthering progress in this direction, an understanding was reached at the Vladivostok summit that new strategic arms control agreements must include "the corresponding provisions of the May 26, 1972 Interim Agreement" and "cover the period from October 1977 until December 31, 1985." Based on the principle of parity and equal security, a new agreement should have included a number of substantial limitations. In particular, both sides would have the right to set the total number of land- and sea-based ballistic missile launchers, and also strategic bombers, at 2,400 units. In addition, both sides were to have in their force structure not more than 1,320 MIRVed land- and sea-based ballistic missiles. It was proposed to work out the legal details and exact wording and conclude a new agreement by the end of 1975. Both sides planned to continue negotiations not later than 1980–81 on the further limitation and reduction of strategic arms in the period after 1985.[13] The Vladivostok Accord was a most important step on the way to limiting the arms race. It set detailed and equal long-term limits for the number of the USSR and U.S. strategic launchers, for the first time including even long-range bombers. Also for the first time limits were put on the deployment of MIRVed missiles, a first step on the way to limiting the qualitative arms race. The positive role of the Vladivostok Accord was noted in the Report of the Central Committee of the CPSU to the 25th Congress of the CPSU: "An agreement on this question would have very great significance for the further development of Soviet-American relations, for the strengthening of mutual trust, as well as for the strengthening of universal peace."[14]

The Vladivostok Accord was met with approval by a significant part of the U.S. public and ruling circles. In January 1975 the Senate passed S.R. 20, which Senators Kennedy, Mathias, and Mondale had introduced in support of the Soviet-U.S. accord at Vladivostok. In February of that year the House of Representatives passed the almost identical H.R. 160.

But the opponents of the new U.S.-Soviet accord did not retreat from their positions either. On the contrary, they led a broad attack on the Vladivostok Accord, striving to prevent the conclusion of a long-term agreement and to open the way for a continued arms buildup. Several of them (Donald Brennan, Paul Nitze, and Melvin Laird, for example) led a frontal assault on the principles of Vladivostok, contending that the accord supposedly gave the Soviet Union unilateral advantages in heavy missiles, throw-weight, and the likely future number of powerful MIRV warheads. Others chose a more sophisticated maneuver. For example, Senator Jackson, using as a cover the slogan of reducing the Vladivostok ceilings, urged lowering the limit on strategic launchers from 2,400 to 1,760. In this framework according to his scheme both sides would be permitted to have not more than 800 ICBMs, 560 SLBMs, and 400 aircraft. In reality, owing to the unequal structures of the two states' strategic forces, these measures would have affected the Soviet Union much more than the United States.[15] This was a new tactic of SALT opponents that later was used with increasing frequency. Hesitating to oppose openly arms limitations as such, they deliberately began to advance "radical" proposals unacceptable to the Soviet Union in order to wreck the dialogue, put the blame for this on the other side, and justify the continuation of the arms race.

### The Conservative Counteroffensive and the Ford Administration

In 1975–76 the internal political struggle in the United States between the supporters and opponents of détente and arms control entered a critical phase, comparable to that of the debates of 1969–70. But in the past the antimilitary opposition was on the offense and engaged the military-industrial complex on all fronts. Now just the reverse was observed: using the changed foreign and domestic political situation and certain objective complications in the path of détente, hardliners fiercely tried to regain lost positions. The activities of the SALT opponents took two basic directions. First, the Pentagon's official representatives and their allies in Congress, the academic world, the arms industry, and the press began an intensified campaign in favor of new strategic weapons systems: air-, sea-, and ground-launched cruise missiles. Since 1975 pressure from the military-industrial complex had been building up against the limitation of cruise missiles in a future Soviet-U.S. agreement. Meanwhile, considering the character of these weapons, the Soviet Union could not agree to their unlimited and uncontrolled deployment. "At Vladivostok the question was posed differently," Andrei Gromyko pointed out later. "No green light was given there to cruise missiles."[16] However, the Pentagon and its advocates demanded the deployment of these systems without any limitations, not in the least disturbed by the obvious negative consequences for strategic stability and the SALT negotiations.

The second aspect of the campaign of the SALT agreement's opponents was the propagandistic sensation regarding the new Soviet Tu-22M bomber, called the Backfire in the West. The Soviet representatives in the Geneva negotiations gave the U.S. side an unambiguous explanation of the fact that the Backfire was not an intercontinental bomber but a medium-range aircraft. In other words, not being a strategic weapons system, it was not subject to limitations. However, in spite of this, from 1975 assertions were persistently advanced in the United States of the "capability" of this aircraft to reach U.S. territory with the help of in-flight refueling and to complete a round trip by landing in Cuba. Under pressure, the U.S. side at the SALT negotiations began to link quite arbitrarilly the limitation of cruise missiles with limitations on the deployment of the Backfire bomber. In late 1975 the differences between the secretary of defense, who took an extremely hard line on the future

SALT Treaty, and the secretary of state, who was trying to find a compromise solution, became so acute that they practically paralyzed the ability of the administration to carry out a purposeful course. On November 1–3, 1975, President Ford shook up the key posts of the administration. He removed Schlesinger from his post and appointed in his place the White House chief of staff and former U.S. representative to NATO Donald Rumsfeld. Kissinger forfeited the post of national security adviser and became secretary of state. Kissinger's deputy, retired general Brent Scowcroft, was appointed to the position of national security adviser.

Came 1976, the final year of the Republican administration's tenure in power. It began with the appearance of a breakthrough in the SALT negotiations in the course of Kissinger's visit to the Soviet Union in January. The essence of the compromise discussed in Moscow was that bombers with cruise missiles on board were equal to MIRVed ballistic missiles and thus would be included in the ceilings on missiles equipped with MIRV systems (1,320). Simultaneously, the deployment of ground- and sea-launched cruise missiles with a range of greater than 600 kilometers would be prohibited. Upon returning to Washington, the secretary of state announced to reporters that the disputed questions of the new SALT treaty were "90 percent settled."

But a final decision had not been made. The Republican administration's position was perceptibly and quickly turned against the new strategic arms limitation agreement. Secretary of Defense Donald Rumsfeld with the unanimous approval of the Joint Chiefs of Staff opposed the compromise outlined in January 1976. The director of the Arms Control and Disarmament Agency (ACDA), Fred Iklé, fully supported the head of the Pentagon. Ikle obstructed the activities of his agency, which had earlier displayed in accordance with its purpose an interest in negotiations and agreements in this sphere. The military-industrial complex rejected the proposed compromise in the SALT negotiations, not wishing to have their hands bound in the deployment of long-range cruise missiles on the widest scale. The dissatisfaction of military organizations was also explained by the fact that the inclusion of aircraft with cruise missiles in any significant quantity in the MIRVed missile sublimits would have required the reduction of a corresponding number of existing MIRVed ICBMs for every Trident submarine put into service. The generals' sentiments became a problem of the highest importance for the president in the domestic political environment of 1976. In spring the preelection campaign came into its own right. In the struggle for reelection President Ford was faced first of all with securing the Republican party nomination, in which his main rival was California governor Ronald Reagan, the long-time and consistent advocate of "unconditional U.S. nuclear superiority." Reagan, as could be expected, launched his election-year attacks on Ford from the right, criticizing him for neglecting national security and for insufficient efforts in building up military power.

A special fury was aroused in the United States by events in Africa, where in 1975 the disintegration of the bastions of colonialism was at hand. The assistance of Cuban, Soviet, and other socialist countries offered to the MPLA forces of Angola in response to South Africa's direct military aggression was met in the West with a hysterical anti-Soviet campaign. In these circumstances even Kissinger decided to heed the overwhelming anti-Soviet sentiments in the United States to prove his hardline attitude toward the Soviet Union on this occasion. In his speech in San Francisco on February 3, 1976 before the members of the California Council on World Affairs, he stated, shamelessly distorting the true meaning of the USSR's assistance to the national liberation movement, that "when one of the great powers tips the balance of forces decisively in a local conflict through its military intervention—and meets no resistance—an ominous precedent is set, of grave consequence even if the intervention occurs in a seemingly remote area."[17] The secretary of state with righteous anger put the blame for the "loss" of Angola on Congress, which in late 1975 had passed a resolution prohibiting the increase of U.S. military assistance to the separatist counterrevolutionary forces there in order to avoid a new "Vietnam" in Africa. Thus, in the spring and summer, the united pressure from right-wing Republicans, conservatives in the Capitol, and the military-industrial complex forced the administration's leadership to "freeze" the SALT negotiations with the Soviet Union. Ford feared that in the existing circumstances the conclusion of a SALT treaty lessened his chances of remaining in the White House another four years. The U.S. president advanced a proposal unacceptable to the Soviet Union: to sign an agreement on the basis of Vladivostok, but to leave out of its framework the issue of cruise missiles "in exchange" for U.S. consent not to include the limitation of the irrelevant Backfire aircraft. And so again were the negotiations led to a dead end.

The facts show that in 1976 there was a real possibility for fundamental progress on the way to concluding a treaty. It was conditioned by the objective situation of the strategic balance between the USSR and the United States and the long-term genuine interests of both powers' security. But the president had made up his mind not to sign a new SALT agreement and under the pressure of the right began increasingly to show his concern for guaranteeing U.S. defense capability, to do all he could to demonstrate his "toughness" in relations with the Soviet Union. Ultimately Ford even stated that henceforth he would refrain from using the word "détente," and would instead say "peace through strength." Such Washington rhetoric at the presi-

dential level, of course, did not promote Soviet-U.S. mutual understanding. Worse still, these statements were confirmed by real political
and military measures that conflicted with the spirit of détente, negotiations, and cooperation. Thus was a stake made on changes in the
political mood inside the United States, which had originated under
the influence of the growing campaign on the "Soviet threat" and the
aggravation of international tension. In the budgets of fiscal years
1976–78, the Ford government laid out a program of a broad arms
buildup. In accordance with the Republican program it was planned
to build an average of 32 ships and submarines per year in order to
attain a 600-ship navy, and to turn out 500 fighters and 2,000 tanks
and armored personnel carriers. A departure from the strategy of
"one-and-one-half wars," as it had been interpreted under Nixon, was
evidently contemplated. The Pentagon set the goal (until then secret)
to build in addition the potential for conducting large-scale transoceanic combat operations supported by the navy, the Marines, and divisions of mobilized U.S. reserves in new crisis areas of the world.

In the sphere of strategic forces it was planned (in FY 1978) to advance
the schedule of equipping the Minuteman-III missile with the Mk-12A
MIRV, to begin deploying the MX ICBM in 1983, to build three *Ohio*-
class submarines every two years (their construction plan was enlarged
from 14 to 16 boats), and to deploy 244 B-1 bombers in the early 1980s.
The retrofitting of the *Ohio* SSBN with the Trident-II SLBM was planned
for the second half of the 1980s, and in the first half thousands of both
tactical and strategic ALCMs and SLCMs were to have been deployed
as well.[18]

In the Republican administration's final budget report (fiscal year
1978), presented by Secretary of Defense Donald Rumsfeld in January 1977, the strategy of "limited nuclear war" received further elaboration. In comparison with Schlesinger's declarations, several points in
Rumsfeld's report drew attention to themselves. First of all, it was categorically stated that the Soviet Union had supposedly always striven
for a capability "to triumph in a thermonuclear war" and "to recover
after it" and restore its economic and military power at the earliest
date. In addition, the capability "to hold at risk a significant number
of military and industrial targets" and thus "substantially undermine
the USSR's capability to recover after a nuclear exchange" was
adopted as the basis of U.S. nuclear strategy. Amendments introduced earlier by Schlesinger in the SIOP and target list now took
shape in the official strategic concept of "counterrecovery," which determined plans for developing and using strategic nuclear arms. Implementing this concept required in particular, stated the secretary, a
greater number of optimal yield nuclear warheads to be targeted accurately and selectively on the USSR's dispersed and hardened indus-

trial and military targets. Rumsfeld was unambiguously committed to the understanding that the United States intended to construct a full "counterforce potential" against all fixed hard targets of Soviet strategic forces (not just some portion of them, as Schlesinger had publicly announced earlier). For this undertaking the United States required, Rumsfeld explained, a sufficient number of nuclear warheads of increased yield and accuracy, an adequate system of command and control, and a special tactic of avoiding the so-called fratricide effect[19] of warheads in an attack on hard targets. Finally, a new criterion for evaluating the strategic correlation of forces, "the post-strike exchange ratio," was formulated in greater detail. It meant that the side that possessed the greater means for a controlled attacked against "industrial recovery," conventional military forces, and political leadership targets after a maximally effective Soviet-U.S. nuclear exchange on each other's strategic forces could deny the other side "victory."[20]

On the whole, Rumsfeld's strategy, while developing and supplementing Schlesinger's position, was yet another step in reorienting the doctrine of "deterrence" toward creating the capability of gaining a "rational" advantage in strategic nuclear war-fighting. The concepts of "post-strike exchange ratio" and "counterrecovery" raised fundamentally new tasks in the strategic nuclear rivalry and opened the broadest scope for military programs.

In goals of revising U.S. "military requirements" and the approach to the SALT negotiations, the White House in August sanctioned the organization of an independent committee—the so-called Group B—for a high-level study of military issues. It was given access to secret information and the right to dispute the position of the state intelligence organs. "The main quality required for membership in the group," wrote *The New Yorker*, "was a pessimistic view of Soviet intentions."[21] The group was headed by figures whose reputations in this regard were beyond doubt: Richard Pipes, the well-known Sovietophobe from Harvard; Lt. General Daniel Graham, the former director of the Defense Intelligence Agency; and the well-known Paul Nitze. As could be expected, the conclusions of their study drew frightening pictures of Soviet "military superiority" at all levels of arms and in nearly every strategic region of the world. A leak about Group B's study served yet another purpose for the anti-Soviet hysteria raised by Jackson and his supporters in Congress, as well as by the press and right-wing political circles. In the end the Republican administration's actions and statements, undertaken under the pressure of militarist groups inside the country, did not bring President Ford victory in the November 1976 elections. But the turnabout in the administration's political course at the same time interfered with making a most important step in restraining the arms race in the face of dangerous tendencies in the evolution of strategic doctrine and strategic nuclear programs.

* * *

The mid-1970s were marked by the growth of the difficulties in accomodating Washington's policy to the new realities and by the aggravation of tendencies in U.S. foreign policy that ran counter to détente. On the one hand, the fruits of détente had largely not turned out to be what the West's ruling circles had expected, and on the other, détente seriously hampered the achievement of "parallel" foreign policy goals set by Washington in the early 1970s that were incompatible with it. Toward the middle of the decade the strategic correlation of forces became even more equal and stable. The United States found itself facing the prospect of losing several unilateral advantages that it had sought to preserve for itself even in the situation of overall military-strategic parity. So, having made a number of steps in revising its policy in certain aspects at the beginning of the decade, the U.S. leadership instead demonstrated an unwillingness and inability to reconstruct deeply and comprehensively enough the entire U.S. foreign and military policy, which over the course of the preceding quarter century had been entirely oriented toward U.S. nuclear superiority. In the face of the growing contradiction between objective conditions and U.S. policies since the mid-1970s, the United States activated attempts to change strategic parity in its favor, first and foremost by qualitative changes in the nuclear balance.

Détente entered a period of serious challenges, progress in Soviet-U.S. relations slowed down significantly, and the new strategic arms limitation agreement on the basis of the Vladivostok accord was in limbo. The development of the next generation of strategic weapons was accelerating. Nevertheless, it would be incorrect to show only the negative aspects of the situation of the mid-1970s. In the strategic arms area, although the postponement of a long-term agreement had taken place, the basis of its achievement was preserved. Inside the United States, although the hardliners stubbornly tried to regain lost positions, the situation remained far from their ideal. The doctrine of "nuclear superiority" lost its attractiveness in the eyes of the general public, and the principle of strategic equality, or parity, with the Soviet Union was acknowledged. The SALT agreements became in the minds of the majority of Americans a legitimate and preferable way of ensuring national security.

The coming to power of a new administration in the United States with the Democratic party's victory in the 1976 elections gave rise to the hopes of many supporters of détente for positive changes in the dialogue to curb the arms race. In Soviet-U.S. relations and in world politics as a whole, an exceptionally crucial, and in many ways decisive, period was coming, on which depended the future of détente and arms control for many years ahead.

## Notes

1. *New York Times*, January 11, 1974, 6; *Newsweek*, February 4, 1974, 23.

2. *Department of Defense Annual Report, FY 1975* (Washington, D.C.: U.S. Government Printing Office, 1974), 38, 40–41.

3. *Department of Defense Annual Report, FY 1976 and 1977* (Washington, D.C.: U.S. Government Printing Office, 1975), II–4.

4. Milton Leitenberg, "Presidential Directive 59," *Journal of Peace Research* 18, no. 4 (1981), 314–15.

5. In cross-targeting, MIRVed warheads of different missiles are targeted on the same point to increase the reliability of its destruction.

6. "U.S.-USSR Strategic Policies," *Hearings*, Committee on Foreign Relations, U.S. Senate (Washington, D.C.: U.S. Government Printing Office, 1974), 38.

7. Desmond Ball, *Deja-Vu: The Return to Counterforce in the Nixon Administration* (Los Angeles, 1974).

8. See Rair Simonian, "Kontseptsiia 'vybora tselei'," *Krasnaia zvezda*, September 28, 1976.

9. Throw-weight characterizes the payload that the missile is able to deliver, or more precisely, the weight of the nuclear warheads (or warhead), their guidance systems (in MIRVed missiles), and penetration aids.

10. *Washington Post*, September 16, 1975.

11. *Pravda*, June 4, 1974.

12. *Pravda*, April 1, 1977.

13. *Pravda*, November 25, 1974.

14. *Materialy XXV s'iezda KPSS* (Moscow: Politizdat, 1977), 23.

15. Since ballistic missiles, especially land-based ICBMs, comprise a much greater portion of the USSR's strategic forces, these ceilings would have demanded much greater reductions of Soviet ICBMs and SLBMs than the ICBMs, SLBMs, and bombers of the United States. Specifically, in order to meet the limits proposed by Jackson, the Soviet Union would have had to remove from its arsenal 990 land- and sea-based ballistic missiles, while the United States would have only had to dismantle 350 missiles and around 200 bombers.

16. *Pravda*, April 1, 1977.

17. *Department of State Bulletin*, February 23, 1976, 209.

18. *Department of Defense Annual Report. Fiscal Year 1978 Defense Budget* (Washington, D.C.: U.S. Government Printing Office, 1977), 121–144.

19. In the early 1970s some theoretical research showed that when targeting several nuclear warheads at once on the very same hard target—such as a missile silo or a command bunker—the consequences of the first warhead's explosion (neutron radiation, thermal radiation, shock wave, and the debris cloud) could destroy, disable, or deflect the course of subsequent warheads for a certain time after the explosion and at a certain distance from its detonation point. If the

yield, accuracy, and reliability of the first warhead does not guarantee a sufficient probability of destroying a target of a given hardness, then for increasing such probability the employment of additional warheads demands, in order to avoid the fratricide effect, split-second timing in the coordination of a strike. See "U.S. Strategic Doctrine," *Hearings*, Committee on Foreign Relations, U.S. Senate, 97th Congress, second session, December 14, 1982 (Washington, D.C.: U.S. Government Printing Office, 1983), 37–92.

20. "U.S. Strategic Doctrine," 59, 68, 70–78, 124–25.

21. *The New Yorker*, April 4, 1977, 104.

# 3

## The Carter Presidency: Inconsistency of U.S. Policy

As the strategic balance increasingly enveloped the interaction of Soviet and U.S. strategic nuclear forces in the second half of the 1970s, Washington's unwillingness to resign itself to the objective situation was ever more distinctly manifested in U.S. policy. While acknowledging in words, even at the beginning of the decade, their adherence to the principles of approximate equality and parity, the U.S. ruling elite did not want to accept all of the inevitable consequences of a strategic equilibrium: the significant differences and disproportions in individual elements of the military balance, the legitimacy of Soviet advantages in some aspects in connection with U.S. advantages in other parameters, the increasing complexity of traditional force planning on the basis of greater-than-expected threat scenarios, the maintenance of the principle of "redundancy" among the elements of the triad, and the growing doubtfulness of planning selective nuclear strikes, including options against the USSR's increasingly invulnerable strategic forces. In the political scheme parity even more strictly limited U.S. opportunities to use the nuclear threat in the international arena, lowered the credibility of its obligations to use nuclear weapons first (which underlay the foundation of NATO's strategy of flexible response), and impeded the direct or indirect use of conventional forces generally in various crisis regions of the world.

The U.S. government's temptation to change the military-strategic balance in its favor and reinvigorate power politics on a global scale was in many respects intensified by the powerful upsurge of the national liberation movement which enveloped Africa, Asia, and Latin America in the second half of the 1970s, and by the direct and/or indirect military support rendered to the movement by the USSR and other socialist states. In the developing countries one antipopular regime after another supported by the West tumbled down, bringing with it a weakening of the economic and political positions of neocolonialism. The answer of the right-conservative circles in the United States and other capitalist countries to these events was to toughen their policy of East-West confrontation, exacerbate international tension, and increase the pressure for the buildup of military force and the conduct of a more hard-line foreign policy.

Upon coming to power, the Carter administration shifted somewhat the accent in U.S. strategic programs and attempted to achieve its strategic goals to a relatively greater degree by way of imposing inequitable SALT agreements upon the Soviet Union. After this attempt failed, the center of gravity of U.S. strategic policy more perceptibly shifted to changing the military correlation of forces in its favor by means of new strategic nuclear (and also conventional) programs. In the end this course strongly collided with the development of the arms control dialogue. This was a major political requisite for the failure of the SALT-II Treaty to be ratified and the further aggravation of international tension on the threshold of the 1980s.

## The Democratic Administration in the World Arena

"The lessons we have learned can be a basis for dramatic improvements in the prospects for world peace and the solutions for international problems."[1] This reasonable judgment was offered in May 1975 in Tokyo by a guest from the United States, governor of the state of Georgia, Jimmy Carter. Hardly anyone could have foreseen at the time that less than two years later, having secured the White House's Oval Office, he would have the opportunity to demonstrate in practice his understanding of history and contribute to the development of international relations.

The speeches Jimmy Carter delivered in the course of his presidential campaign contained many statements on questions of a military détente. He set an ultimate goal "for the reduction of nuclear weapons in all nations to zero," and in the meantime, for achieving a radical reduction of strategic arms in the SALT negotiations, for halting nuclear testing completely, and for suppressing effectively the proliferation of nuclear weapons. The Democratic party candidate pledged also to strive to reduce the level of conventional arms and armed forces, limit the weapons trade and arms transfers, remove U.S. troops from South Korea, and conclude a treaty to contain the militarization of the Indian Ocean. He also stated his intention to reduce annual U.S. military expenditures by approximately 5 billion dollars. However, U.S. policies in practice in the period of Carter's tenure in the White House not only abandoned the majority of the president's preelection commitments in this area but, even worse, in many cases created major additional difficulties for détente and arms control, including the SALT negotiations. The reasons for this are largely to be found in the Democratic administration's unrealistic initial assumptions and contradictory goals in the international area.

The so-called trilateralism theory, which had become popular in the mid-1970s, exerted great influence on the political world outlook of the Democratic government. It arose and gathered force under the banner of reversing the doctrines of the Republican administrations. The organizational nucleus of this political current was formed in 1973. The Trilateral Commission was a nongovernmental international forum, which united in its ranks distinguished politicians, businessmen, and scholars from the United States, Western Europe, and Japan. The views of future president Jimmy Carter were formed in this commission, and collaboration with certain officials of his future administration began there as well, including Zbigniew Brzezinski (the chairman of the commission), Walter Mondale, Cyrus Vance, Harold Brown, and Michael Blumenthal. By the time the Democrats came to power, a broad political alignment that opposed the Ford government and appeared as a third force apart from the liberal Democrats (led by Edward Kennedy), and the right-wing Republicans (led by Ronald Reagan) had united around the Trilateral Commission.

The main idea of trilateralism was that the consolidation of the course of the three imperialist power centers—North America (the United States and Canada), Western Europe, and Japan—in economic, social-ideological, and military-political relations should be the central direction of the policy of the United States (and, hopefully, its principal capitalist partners as well). This unity was considered necessary both in and of itself and for the restructuring on conditions favorable to the West of its relations with the socialist bloc and the developing countries—from positions of the united economic, military, and political power of capitalism. Washington's foreign policy priorities as well were supposed to be revised accordingly: U.S. relations with the major capitalist powers were put on the first level; on the second, relations of the capitalist camp with the developing countries, particularly those exporting raw materials; and only in last place were found Western relations with the USSR and other socialist countries.[2] Brzezinski justified this hierarchy of goals by arguing that "from an American standpoint, the more important and promising changes in the years to come will have to involve Western Europe and Japan. The ability of these areas to continue to grow economically and to maintain relatively democratic political forms will more crucially affect the gradual evolution of a new international system than will likely changes in American-Soviet relations".[3]

At the same time, Carter and his closest aides did not reject the idea of détente per se. It is noteworthy, however, that in contrast to the Republican leadership's views in the early 1970s, they did not at all perceive the positive side of Soviet-U.S. relations as a broad system of negotiations, political accords, cooperation in the area of economics, science and culture, and dialogue on curbing the arms race. Rather, they saw relations much more narrowly, reducing them to practically only arms control negotiations, and to a great degree at the USSR's expense.

The idea to limit the role of military force in contemporary international relations was by all appearances not just propagandistic, but a real element of the political philosophy of the Democratic administration. It was conditioned by the lessons of the U.S. defeat in Vietnam and by the realization of the narrow objective limits on the direct or indirect use of military power by the United States in the conditions of the changed global balance of forces. At the same time the Democrats also linked considerations of a different order with the process of military détente. The notion that arms control should promote a reduction of the USSR's role and influence in the world arena ran through the administration's approach to this problem. This concept, advanced especially by Zbigniew Brzezinski, and taken up by other U.S. officials, was based on the thesis that the Soviet Union's international status supposedly rested only upon its military power. The U.S. desire to weaken at any cost the Soviet Union's international positions, even to the extent of using to this end negotiations on a military détente, also stipulated the U.S. unwillingness to conduct an equitable dialogue on these issues with the other side. In place of a patient search for mutually acceptable agreements, Washington intended to develop a common model of a "stable military balance" for both sides and through agreements eliminate all arms that did not fall into it. In reality such a "universal" model corresponded much more to the specific nature of the geostrategic position and technological development of U.S. strategic nuclear forces and far more severely infringed upon Soviet strategic potential.

The majority of executive posts connected with foreign policy under Carter went to representatives of three social-political alignments in U.S. ruling circles. A number of cabinet posts and advisory positions went to figures of the moderate liberal school (Harold Brown, Cyrus Vance, Paul Warnke, and Marshall Shulman) which, because of its participation in formulating the Johnson administration's Vietnam policy, labored under the "Vietnam syndrome". Another alignment, intransigently anti-Soviet, attributed the "Vietman syndrome" to the failures of U.S. policy in the 1970s and was represented by such figures as the president's national security adviser Zbigniew Brzezinski, Secretary of Energy James Schlesinger, and Samuel Huntington on the NSC staff. Finally, to the policy-implementing posts of the federal bureacracies came appointees who mainly represented the intellectual community of Harvard University, the Massachusetts Institute of Technology (MIT), Columbia University, and the Brookings Institution, the world outlooks of whom had taken shape under the influence of the powerful protest movement against the war in Vietnam in the late 1960s and early 1970s. Among these appointees were Roger Molander and James Fallows in the NSC and on the White House staff; Andrew Young, Leslie Gelb, and Anthony Lake in the State Department; Jerome Kahan, Barry Blechman, and John Newhouse in the Arms Control and Disarmament Agency; and Walter Slocombe, Robert Murray, Lynn Davis, and others in the Pentagon.[4]

A discussion of the Carter administration's entire foreign policy is not the task of the present book, since it has already received comprehensive analysis in the works of other Soviet specialists. Therefore, several general remarks will suffice. Despite trilateralism's scheme, relations between the USSR and the United States, the socialist and capilalist camps, continued to exert if not the only, then in any event the dominant influence in world politics. Similarly, despite the importance of other issues, the problems of the continuing arms race and the threat of global war remained at the center of international relations. The pivotal and, as subsequent events showed, fatal flaw of Carter's foreign policy was the reluctance to recognize these realities, a reluctance that in practice led to inconsistency and in large part the failure of its efforts in the world arena. In practice, in contrast to the speculative concepts, it was impossible simultaneously to minimize the significance of Soviet-U.S. relations, sacrifice them to the politics of consolidating NATO and to maneuvers in the Third World in order to weaken Soviet influence there, and count on Soviet passivity in guaranteeing the interests of its own security and in rendering support to allies and friends. And, to be sure, it was completely unrealistic on Washington's part to trample down the first sprouts of Soviet-U.S. trust and cooperation and to conduct abusive attacks on the socialist countries on human rights issues, while at the same time striving for more radical and broad arms control agreements. Finally, the depth of economic and political contradictions among the leading Western states was obviously underestimated, and NATO's cooperative military programs did not smooth them out. In a number of cases the latter only strengthened these differences. The same concerns the divergence of interests of the capitalist West and the developing countries, which Washington could not surmount, either by way of a widely advertised "North-South dialogue," by large arms transfers to reactionary pro-Western regimes, or by the threat of direct U.S. military intervention.

Along with the foreign policy reasons for the Carter administration's failures, domestic factors played a growing role in the late 1970s. In this respect a most serious influence was exerted by the constantly growing pressure of the conservative opposition in Congress, the press, and right-wing organizations (such as the Committee on the Present Danger), which significantly strengthened the positions of the opponents of dé-tente and SALT. It was also supplemented by factors having little to do with foreign policy. This concerns, for example, the discrediting of lib-eral neo-Keynesian methods of state regulation of the economy, which had produced quite negative side effects in the form of rampant inflation (up to 13 percent a year) and a growing budget deficit (up to $60 billion), but did not prevent a protracted economic recession and increase of unemployment. The strengthening of the conservatives' influence on account of U.S. economic difficulties was amplified by a number of social-economic and demographic processes that had eroded the traditional bases of liberalism (for example, the "northeastern establishment" was squeezed out of the economy by the conservative West and the South, large cities fell into decay, unions lost influence, and the relative pro-portion of youth declined in the general make-up of the population).[5] The powerful offensive of Congress, the press, and various pressure groups on the prerogatives of executive power after Watergate could be put in the same category.

While delivering U.S. public opinion from the "shock of Vietnam" that had taken place in the early 1970s, the strengthening of conservative sentiments in the United States allowed right-wing and conservative cir-cles to increase significantly their influence inside the country. The cam-paign to intimidate the public with the "military buildup" in the USSR was simultaneously stepped up. The systematic manipulation of U.S. public opinion in the face of worsening world tensions was gradually bearing its bad fruit. Already in 1978 56 percent of the participants in Gallup and Harris surveys said that the United States lagged behind the USSR militarily, and 70 percent supported increasing the U.S. military budget (as opposed to 13 percent in 1974).[6]

The Carter administration itself played up the "Soviet military threat" in search of support for its foreign and military policies and also in trying to appease the right opposition. Upon coming to power, the Dem-ocratic leadership encouraged the hopes of the broad public for a quick and easy process in disarmament affairs. When the dialogue on these issues began to run into difficulties, U.S. leaders began to blame the other side, themselves undermining support for the negotiations inside the United States. Hasty decisions and their quick rejection, oscillations from one extreme to the other, and sudden zigzags of policy strongly undermined the government's authority and became a distinctive feature of White House policy in the late 1970s. The absence of a coherent and realistic foreign policy and Carter's personal weakness as a leader deeply split the administration. This concerns not only the disagreements of National Security Adviser Brzezinski and Secretary of State Vance but also the conflict of both of them with U.N. Ambassador Andrew Young, the constant contradictions between the president's domestic and foreign policy advisors, between the State Department's regional and functional bureaus, and between ACDA and the Pentagon. Such conflict had always existed to some degree or another. But in the years of the Democratic administration's tenure the president arbitrarily changed the state policy, being led first by one adviser and then another. Moreover, each group had an opportunity to launch its own initiatives in U.S. foreign policy, and rivals tried to neutralize them with their own countermeasures.

In all fairness, it is necessary to point out that the deepening stagnation in all areas of the Soviet economy, as well as in social and political conditions, could not help but influence the USSR's foreign policy. Bureaucratic inertia, narrow-mindedness, and the absence of an innovative outlook and new ideas in the matters of international relations and security caused great damage in all spheres of Soviet life. Such was the result of the obvious lack of new thinking at a time when it was tremendously needed because of the growing and threatening problems and also because of certain opportunities for arms control and cooperation that were not taken advantage of. All of these factors, of course, played into the hands of the right opposition in the United States, helped them close their ranks, and ultimately, as Stanley Hoffmann wrote, "gain control of the agenda and of the minds of the American people."[7]

These foreign and domestic circumstances of the Democratic administration's activities were most directly reflected in the development of its military policy. Upon coming to power, the new U.S. administration inherited from its predecessors intelligence estimates prepared by the official intelligence organs with the participation of the above-mentioned Group B. This study pointed out the "threatening" U.S. lag in most measures of the military balance and the Soviet Union's approach to strategic superiority and capability to "win" a nuclear war.[8] On February 20, 1977, soon after the president's inauguration, an interdepartmental group was created under the aegis of the National Security Council, which was charged with preparing a comprehensive analysis of Soviet-U.S. relations and the global military balance. This fundamental study, designated Presidential Review Memorandum-10 or PRM-10, expressed the general philosophy of Carter, Brown, Vance, and their closest aides in the military-political sphere. It concluded that the military balance has an important but gradually diminishing significance in international relations; that the state of the military balance is not "threatening" for the United States and, moreover, is characterized by significant stability;

that the importance of conventional forces in U.S. strategy will relatively increase and should therefore receive priority in resource allocation; that the fundamental emphasis in developing conventional forces must be on ground forces oriented toward the European theater, and also on maintaining their air and naval support, with some additional forces set aside for use in the event of a conflict in the Middle East, the Persian Gulf zone, or the Korean peninsula. Another important recommendation of PRM-10 was for a real increase of the military budget of the United States and its allies by 3 percent annually.[9]

After discussing the positions of PRM-10 in the NSC, President Carter issued Presidential Directive No. 18 (PD-18). It determined the basic tendencies and actions of U.S. military policy in subsequent years. At the same time the strategic concepts of PD-18, as in all documents of similar origin, were highly generalized and left significant freedom for specific interpretation in terms of programs and appropriations. The president and the Pentagon's civilian leadership decided privately to especially concentrate resources on raising the combat capability of U.S. troops and conventional forces both deployed in Western Europe and intended for transport there from U.S. territory. Forces for "flexible" use in Asia, the Persian Gulf zone, and even for combat operations on NATO's flanks were, in the first years of the Democrats' rule, pushed into the background.[10]

In 1977 the decision of the previous administration to increase the number of active U.S. divisions from 13 to 16 was carried out in practice (to a great degree by way of reorganizing the army and strengthening combat units at the expense of rear support). U.S. troops in Europe swelled by 20,000, the first such increase since the early 1960s. Simultaneously, great pressure was put on the NATO allies. In contrast to the Republicans, who in the early 1970s attempted to stimulate greater defense efforts from the allies by the threat of reducing U.S. contributions to NATO, the Democrats tried to encourage them by force of the U.S. example. At the North Atlantic alliance's May 1978 session a long-term military program was adopted that included the members' commitment to increase yearly military appropriations in real terms by a minimum of 3 percent, and detailed some 100 programs and projects for the 1980s and 1990s at an overall cost of about $90 billion dollars.[11] From a fiscal point of view U.S. military policy under Carter represented a steady increase of defense spending in current prices and in real terms. However, this buildup was smoother than the growth of the military budget that had been outlined by the Democrats' predecessors and, needless to say, was less significant than that demanded by the right-wing opposition in the late 1970s. Inflation, which reached unprecedented rates in these years, to a growing degree depreciated the increasing outlays of the federal budget, and greater state spending, especially for military purposes, brought on new rounds of inflation—and so on without end. The Democratic government was compelled, primarily for economic reasons, to reduce the shipbuilding program outlined by its predecessors by almost half, and aircraft and tank production by approximately 20 percent, although it tried to compensate for these steps in other aspects of the arms race.[12] The administration's overall military policy, like its foreign policy, was characterized by inconsistency. The greater attention to Western Europe in developing armed forces and preparing U.S. military plans had given way in late 1979 and early 1980 to a sharp shift in emphasis on the Persian Gulf zone and the Indian Ocean basin, which entailed the hasty restructuring of military programs and operational plans and was accompanied by an abrupt increase in the Pentagon's budget, to be addressed at greater length below.

## Cruise Missiles and the Democrats' Strategic Innovations

Perhaps no other U.S. secretary of defense could have compared with Harold Brown in his deep knowledge of technical and military-political issues upon coming to power. In 1977, as far as can be judged, Brown's strategic views coincided with the ideas of the McNamara Pentagon. On the whole he adhered to the doctrine of "assured destruction" in combination with certain "selective nuclear strike" options, including the other side's military targets. In a March 1975 lecture, Brown argued that as long as no one becomes deluded that the presence of the means, options, and plans for a strategic counterforce exchange created the capability for survival of the United States or the Soviet Union in a nuclear war, the presence of such plans and the development of such means is acceptable.[13] The above-mentioned PRM-10 study formed the basis of the initial phase of the Carter administration's strategic policy. One of this study's sections predicted the further evolution of the nuclear balance. Considering the probable Soviet and U.S. military programs, the authors concluded that the strategic correlation of forces remained acceptable for the United States, since whichever side launched a limited nuclear strike on the ICBMs of the other side would be in a much worse position by virtue of the ratio of the remaining missiles and missile warheads on both sides.[14] This opinion was highly significant, since this issue subsequently became one of the main aspects of Washington's strategic policy.

Until the completion of a more detailed revision of strategic concepts, PD-18 acknowledged NSDM-242, which had been developed by Schlesinger, as the basis of U.S. nuclear operational planning. At the same time the prioritization of several goals that had been included in the SIOP was changed. As one White House official noted, in the past the emphasis had been on "the efficient destruction of targets."[15] Since hard targets (ICBM silos and command bunkers) are the most difficult of all to destroy, a significant number of the most effective warheads were chosen for strikes on these points. Such planning was stipulated by the doctrines of Schlesinger and Rumsfeld and, since the total U.S. capability of destroying Soviet hard targets in the 1970s was considered quite limited, it was linked with the acceleration of new strategic nuclear programs. Now a greater emphasis was put on spreading warheads over a broader set of targets. Therefore it was considered especially important to put at risk a greater number of targets of the socialist countries' conventional forces, both in Central Europe and in the Far East. The target list for enterprises and installations of an economic character was also expanded.[16]

In his first budget report (FY 1979), Harold Brown stated that it is not "at all clear that an initial use of nuclear weapons—however selectively they might be targeted—could be kept from escalating to a full-scale thermonuclear exchange, especially if command and control centers were brought under attack. The odds are high, whether the weapons were used against tactical or strategic targets, that control would be lost on both sides and the exchange would become unconstrained." At the same time the Pentagon chief said that U.S. strategic planning must proceed from two assumptions: first, that "deterrence might fail," and second, that U.S. strategic forces must have the capability not only for a total strike but also for "limited" strikes, so that the United States would be able "to frustrate any ambition" that an enemy may have in any imaginable nuclear scenario. As one of the measures of this flexibility, noted Brown, the United States should have the capability of delivering controlled strikes against a wide range of targets, "including theater nuclear and conventional forces, lines of communication, war-supporting industry, and targets of increasing hardness: from aircraft runways and nuclear storage sites to command bunkers and ICBM silos."[17] The duplicitous nature of the Democratic administration's nuclear strategy from the very beginning planted seeds of contradictions and problems in its policy, including those that would subsequently be used against the Carter government itself by the right-wing militarist opposition.

Analyzing alternative arms programs, Brown and his colleagues concluded that a still greater emphasis on sea-based missile forces did not conform to the strategic tasks set by the leadership. Owing to the enormous cost and long construction period of missile-carrying submarines, it would be impossible to increase substantially this component of the nuclear triad until the late 1980s. Furthermore, in the absence of a buildup of its two other elements, by 1986 five-sixths of the survivable and penetrable strategic warheads would already be on SLBMs. Brown and his assistants considered this a violation of the principle of a redundant and balanced triad, and especially undesirable in view of possible technological breakthroughs in the spheres of ASW and BMD. As for the buildup of land-based missile forces, the leading Pentagon officials thought this to be inexpedient in view of the contemplated growth of the vulnerability of U.S. ICBM silos in the early 1980s. The deployment of more survivable missiles on mobile launchers—again because of the cost and periods of implementation—could not provide results earlier than the second half of the 1980s. In addition, they considered that a new, more powerful ICBM offered no guarantee in the event of an BMD breakthrough. In this connection the choice of Brown and his closest aides implicitly fell to the air element of the triad, and precisely to the air-launched cruise missile. They were attracted by this system's comparatively low cost and by the capability to rapidly produce and deploy thousands of units of this new type of strategic weapon on various types of aircraft.

Still, on one hand cruise missiles represented to Brown and his like-minded supporters an expedient and even unique strategic weapon system. The distinctive feature of cruise missiles, in the opinion of a number of U.S. experts, is their significant capability to destroy hard targets owing to the combination of their number, supposed capability to penetrate defenses, high accuracy, and sufficient warhead yield. And at the same time, because of the long (many hours) flight time of the aircraft-launcher to a point within range of launching the cruise missiles and the subsonic speed of the flight of the missiles themselves to their assigned targets, this weapon system, from their point of view, was not suitable for a surprise attack on ICBM silos. The secretary of defense, for example, argued that the deployment of MX mobile missiles, because of their short flight time and high accuracy, could increase Soviet anxiety in the late 1980s more than U.S. strides in the air leg of the triad, since the latter, in his opinion, were not first-strike weapons. A corollary thereof was that there would be less pressure for an immediate buildup of U.S. ICBM and SLBM forces, since some of their tasks could be assumed by air-launched cruise missiles. While recognizing that the deployment of cruise missiles substantially changed the strategic balance in a number of aspects in the U.S. favor, Brown also asserted that cruise missiles could in no way create the threat of a first strike. Such categorical judgments suggest that Brown and his closest aides had become captivated by their far-fetched and highly controversial nuclear exchange scenarios. However, it was precisely this approach that significantly determined the Democratic administration's decisions on military programs and its line in the SALT negotiations in this period.[18]

The Carter administration's innovations in the area of strategic doctrine were first of all reflected in the amendments to the Republicans' military budget for FY 1978, which were inserted in the spring and summer of 1977. There were cuts in appropriations for the five main "counterforce" programs (the Mk-12A warhead, the MX, ABRES,[19] the Trident-II SLBM, and programs for increasing missile accuracy).[20] At the same time $450 million was added to accelerate the development of cruise missiles and their aircraft launch platforms.[21]

The Trident program turned out to be the least contradictory of all the fundamental strategic programs that Brown had found upon coming to the Department of Defense. By this time Congress had authorized the purchase of seven of the gigantic submarines, and the navy's long-term plan envisaged the deployment of a battle fleet of 14 *Ohio*-class submarines before 1989, with a construction rate of three boats every two years. Implementing the planned program fit the new administration's nuclear strategy quite well. The naval command for its part pinned special hopes on the future Trident-II SLBM system, which was specifically designed for its *Ohio* SSBNs. At the same time the Pentagon's civilian leadership was against the excessive emphasis on sea-based missiles, but not only because of possible breakthroughs in ASW in the 1990s. The secretary of defense noted in this connection: "I have considerable doubt that SLBM command, communications and control ($C^3$), responsiveness and accuracy can ever be made as reliable as a CONUS-based ICBM force, especially while maintaining the requirement for enduring survivability of the SLBMs."[22] The political leadership's doubts were strengthened by the economic and technical difficulties with which the program collided in the construction stage. The slowdown of the construction timetable of the nuclear-powered *Ohio* submarine, like the slowdown of the development of the Trident-II SLBM, was evidence of the intention of Brown and several of his assistants to downplay somewhat the role of sea-based strategic means in U.S. nuclear forces. Thus there was a relative reduction of this component's role, or more precisely, a slowdown of its growth as measured by the increase of the total number of strategic nuclear warheads, since in this category sea-based forces would no matter what still retain their dominant positions in the triad in the 1980s.

By the time the Democrats came to power, the procurement and deployment of the new B-1 bomber, it seemed, was guaranteed. In late 1976 flight and equipment testing was completed. At the direction of the secretary of the air force a commission of experts on military-economic issues, including Edward David, Michael May, and Paul Nitze, recommended in favor of developing the B-1. In December 1976 the Defense Department's Defense Systems Aquisition Review Council (DSARC) in its third session on the B-1 decided to put the system into serial production. In the spring of 1977 President Carter became deeply involved in the technical, strategic, and economic details of the issue. Gradually he came to the conclusion that the enormous cost of the new supersonic bomber was not justified by its advantages over the existing

B-52 aircraft, particularly if both systems were considered as launch platforms for cruise missiles. Carter held a final meeting with the secretary of defense. Brown was most of all upset with the growth of the program's cost, which according to early 1977 estimates was already $23 billion. The secretary was increasingly attracted by cruise missiles, in the face of which a highly sophisticated bomber system, specially developed for deeply penetrating into the other side's airspace, appeared superfluous. The B-1 embodied exactly that approach to military policy that Brown rejected: an impressive, prestigious, extremely expensive weapon system, little-justified from a pragmatic-strategic point of view and able to divert resources from more cost-effective, in his opinion, programs. The final decision to cancel the B-1 program was announced on June 30, 1977. It was like a bolt from the blue. Air force and SAC officials were indignant. Some officers joked bitterly that the air force had suffered "its highest attrition rate ever on a single day." The military's partners in business were no less disappointed.[23]

The administration and its representatives in the Pentagon assured themselves freedom of hand in developing those military programs that they considered more effective in light of the formulated strategic concepts. Appropriations were increased for the air-launched cruise missile (ALCM) and the Tomahawk sea-launched cruise missile (SLCM). In addition, on the basis of this latter system the development of yet another kind of cruise missile was begun—the ground-launched cruise missile (GLCM). In all, they proposed turning out 3,400 ALCMs.[24] The first squadron of B-52G bombers was to be equipped with cruise missiles in December 1982, and by the late 1980s there were to be around 3,000 ALCMs on the 150 aircraft of this modification. Research was begun on a new wide-body cruise missile carrier able to carry up to 70 ALCMs and projected for the second half of the 1980s. A fleet of 60 missile-carrying aircraft could carry up to 4,200 ALCMs, each of which was theoretically able to destroy not only a major population center but also to strike with great accuracy a hardened military target.[25]

The Carter administration's decisions on the B-1 bomber and programs to develop long-range cruise missiles gave rise to serious domestic policy contradictions and noticeably affected the SALT negotiations, in which limiting cruise missiles was one of the key issues. However, although from start to finish an integral part of the Democratic leadership's concepts of 1977–80, they were not connected with any major nuclear strategy dilemmas that confronted Washington. From this point of view the MX program was as if at a crossroads of diverse strategic concepts that largely determined the U.S. approach to problems of the nuclear balance and arms control. The decisions on this weapon system most vividly reflected the evolution of U.S. nuclear strategy in the period of the Carter administration. By early 1977 the air force's Space and Missile

Systems Organization had practically completed research and development of the MX missile in the so-called "Hybrid-Trench" basing system.[26]
In March 1976 DSARC decided to proceed to the full-scale technical
development of the MX missile and prepare for its production. Deployment of the new ICBM was proposed to begin in late 1983 or early
1984. By the mid-1980s the United States was to have 100 such missiles
and, if necessary, around 300 by the end of the decade at an overall cost
of approximately $35 billion. The new U.S. leadership, however, decided
to set aside the move to full-scale technical development, and the Air
Force was ordered to continue research and development until there
was complete technical clarity regarding the basing system and cost of
the entire program.

The state leadership's approach to the MX program in early 1977 was
determined by several considerations. The new officials in the Office of
the Secretary of Defense and the Department of the Air Force discovered
major technical and economic flaws in the Hybrid-Trench basing system.[27] But strategic considerations also played a role. In the initial period
of the Democrats' tenure in power, less significance was given to the
question of the theoretical vulnerability of U.S. land-based missile forces
in Harold Brown's official statements than in those of Schlesinger and
Rumsfeld. The latter, as will be recalled, turned this essentially contrived
problem into a key aspect of the nuclear balance and U.S. strategy and
arms programs, and especially into the main justification for developing
the MX system. Under the Democratic administration the opinion originally prevailed that the problem of hypothetical ICBM vulnerability
should not be separated from the combined destructive capabilities of
the strategic triad and from the overall context of the Soviet-U.S. strategic balance. Therefore, in view of the decreased theoretical survivability of U.S. silo-based ICBMs expected in the early 1980s, it was decided
to build up the potential of the two other components of the triad:
bombers with ALCMs and the Trident missile submarine system.

As for the disproportions in the strategic equilibrium in land-based
missiles, the Carter government here counted on changing the nuclear
balance primarily through imposing SALT provisions upon the Soviet
Union. Such intentions were reflected in the draft of the so-called Comprehensive Proposal advanced during Secretary of State Cyrus Vance's
visit to Moscow in March 1977, to be examined further below.

## The "Countervailing Doctrine" and the MX Missile

From late 1977 changes took place in U.S. strategic arms policy in
strategic concepts, military programs, and negotiating positions. The
revision of official strategic concepts was most noticeably revealed in the
secretary of defense's FY 1980 budget report, presented to Congress on

January 15, 1979. In it was proclaimed the "countervailing strategy," which simultaneously concerned both U.S. armed forces as a whole, and its strategic nuclear forces in particular. As for the latter the Pentagon's chief revealed its meaning in the following way:

As a reasonable minimum (but this may also be the best we can do), we can make sure that, whatever the nature of the attacks we foresee, we have the capability to respond in such a way that the enemy could have no expectation of achieving any rational objectives, no illusion of making any gain without offsetting losses.[28]

It was clear from the secretary's report that the Pentagon's strategic emphasis had shifted to a scenario of nuclear strikes on missile silos, underground command centers, and other targets that in the specialized lexicon of the United States are called "primary (time-urgent) hardened targets." In Brown's previous budget report, targets of this type were mentioned in a number of "broad spectrum" military objectives, and strikes on them as "one aspect" of strategic "flexibility." Now the U.S. necessity to acquire hard-target-kill capability was especially highlighted, not only in view of inflicting any selective strikes but also in view of a coordinated salvo on the entire set of such targets. The secretary of defense saw the U.S. guarantee of such a potential as lying

first, in being able to cover hard targets with at least one reliable warhead with substantial capability to destroy this target and, second, in having the retargeting capability necessary to permit reallocation of these warheads either to a smaller number of crucial hard targets, or to other targets on the list. Even with slow-reacting capabilities such as cruise missiles, this would ensure that an enemy's silos are not a kind of sanctuary from which he can shoot with impunity.[29]

Even if this had concerned only cruise missiles, the Pentagon leadership's assertions that the other side should not fear a preemptive strike on its missile forces were unconvincing. Why should the Soviet Union have had in mind only a single U.S. scenario that had been publicly announced—a first strike with ICBMs and a retaliatory strike via SLBMs and bombers with cruise missiles? In fact, according to other scenarios (which incidentally, come closer to reality), the conflict could begin with conventional combat operations in a particular region, providing enough time for bombers to come within range of launching their cruise missiles. Moreover, in an armed conflict situation the United States in any event intends to shift its strategic aviation to airborne alert. Furthermore, it is obvious that in the context of the changed strategic concepts cruise missiles do not any longer play a main role. For it was apparent from Brown's explanations in another section of the report that ALCMs do not answer a number of the primary requirements of the "countervailing doctrine." In particular, it was emphasized that in contrast to SLBMs and ICBMs, cruise missiles do not have an assured capability to penetrate the enemy's defense; in comparison with SLBMs they cannot preserve their survivability for a long time, and together with their aircraft-launchers are vulnerable at airbases without the timely warning of a nuclear strike. In comparison with ICBMs in fixed underground silos, bombers in flight have an insufficiently reliable link with the command, do not possess the capability of flexible retargeting, and cannot deliver a rapid strike on "time-urgent" targets.[30]

In accordance with the new strategic criteria, land-based ballistic missiles came more distinctly into the foreground in the administration's nuclear strategy. Hence the heightened attention to the question of the vulnerability of U.S. ICBMs. In contrast to what had been said a year earlier, in the Pentagon's January 1979 report this issue was advanced to the forefront of Washington's strategic policy:

There are, nonetheless, several reasons why it would be unacceptable not to take measures to correct our impending vulnerabilities [of land-based missiles]. Although the total number of warheads in the U.S. force will be increasing with the deployment of Trident and ALCM, the destruction of the ICBM force could result in a net loss of second-strike target coverage with our forces on day-to-day alert, decrease our ability to attack time-urgent targets, and reduce the flexibility with which we could manage our surviving forces.[31]

Although Brown, just as before, emphasized that this pertained to a U.S. retaliatory strike, from the other side's point of view the strategic nuclear potential that the United States planned to create could just as well be used for delivering a surprise attack.

At that moment preparation for the NATO decision to deploy in Western Europe 572 U.S. intermediate-range ballistic and cruise missiles had already been completed. Simultaneously, there was a proposal to link forces in the European theater of military operations (TVD)—with the goal of creating so-called escalation dominance—with the U.S. central strategic arsenal by way of expanding plans to use the latter in the TVD. As is known, the operational plans of U.S. strategic forces have always included various combinations of strikes on Soviet intermediate-range nuclear forces. Now, as followed from the Pentagon's explanation of the "countervailing doctrine," such peripheral tasks were multiplied significantly and plans for striking targets of the Warsaw Treaty Organization's conventional forces were substantially expanded. It is obvious that this targeting of nuclear forces and the planning of operations assumed the first use of tactical nuclear weapons by NATO in the TVD—which has never been publicly denied—and the subsequent escalation of nuclear strikes. In accordance with the principles of "escalation dominance" the

NATO leadership planned each time that the enemy would retaliate in an analogous fashion to step up or escalate nuclear attacks to a higher level (that is, using longer-range and more destructive forces on targets of the other side farther removed from the forward edge of the battle area and more important for conducting the war).

At a certain "rung" of the "escalation ladder" the question of using U.S. strategic forces would arise. The Defense Department's budget report in January 1980 offered an important revelation in regard to first-strike plans at this level:

We would not want the Soviet to make the mistaken judgement, based on their understanding of our targeting practices, that they would be spared retaliatory attacks on their territory as long as they did not employ strategic weapons or attack U.S. territory.[32]

Intended to be used for such attack were not only the missiles of Poseidon submarines assigned to NATO but also the more accurate and rapidly retargetable land-based ICBMs. But it was precisely their use against targets in the TVD that the Pentagon considered undesirable in the event that the enemy possessed the capability to destroy this component of U.S. strategic forces in a retaliatory strike on U.S. territory. Hence the Pentagon's emphasis on the necessity of eliminating the hypothetical vulnerability of the silo-based missile force. Moreover, "escalation dominance"—an important element of the "countervailing strategy"—required an increase of the threat of a preemptive coordinated strike on the Soviet Union's ICBMs. Not to dwell on the criticism of the unrealistic concept of "escalation dominance," one must also note that together with the doctrine of "limited nuclear war" in the European theater it was invoked primarily to provide the political requirements for the U.S. nuclear guarantee in the North Atlantic pact. It was therefore exceptionally important that the problem of ICBM vulnerability, despite U.S. leaders' public declarations, increasingly hindered not a "retaliatory" strike (because for this the United States had not only significant land-based forces but also air- and sea-based) but in fact a "selective" first strike of U.S. strategic forces in the European TVD at a high stage of the conflict's escalation.

The real reason for the changes in U.S. nuclear strategy, as usually happens in such events, was a whole array of various kinds of factors. Representatives of the administration tried to explain the matter by citing the Soviet Union's "military buildup." Information was leaked to the press about a significant increase in the accuracy of Soviet MIRVed ICBMs, not only of the RS-20 (SS-18) type heavy missiles but also of RS-18 (SS-19) type light missiles which, according to statements by U.S. intelligence organs, continued to be deployed at launching sites at a high

rate. However, if changes in Washington's military policy were conditioned by Soviet measures to strengthen its strategic capability, then this
was only to the extent that the overall equalization of the strategic balance
did not suit the Carter administration in light of its goals at home and
abroad. Such interests demanded the attainment of unilateral U.S. strategic advantages. And in the final analysis it was precisely the political
factors that played a determining role in the revising of official U.S.
strategic views. This fact reflected the dominant functions of military
doctrine and concepts as instruments of U.S. foreign policy, which at
that time itself was at the center of a sharp domestic policy debate.

In 1977–79 the international situation deteriorated significantly. After
a brief warming of Soviet-U.S. relations in the fall of 1977, marked by
the resumption of the search for a compromise in the SALT dialogue,
the commitment of both powers not to violate the Interim Agreement
(which was to expire on October 3), and their joint declaration to settle
problems in the Middle East, the situation again sharply deteriorated.
One after another international problems arose and began to snowball.
In the winter of 1977–78 the anti-Soviet campaign intensified in connection with the conflict on the Horn of Africa, and later followed events
in Lebanon in March 1978, in Afghanistan in April, in Zaire's Shaba
province in May, in South Yemen in June, in Iran in November, and in
Indochina in December of that same year. The aggravation of international tension manifestly intensified the U.S. leadership's general desire to build up its military potential, including strategic nuclear, and to
elaborate strategic concepts for exerting political pressure on the Soviet
Union. A hard-line policy toward the Soviet Union implied a greater
readiness to use force in this or that crisis situation, which in turn required greater resolve—or the creation of an appearance of resolve—
to rise up the "escalation ladder" to the uppermost, the strategic nuclear,
"rung."

In the sphere of the strategic balance, the failure of the U.S. attempts
of March 1977 to change the balance of forces in its favor through
imposing revised Vladivostok provisions on the Soviet side provoked a
reorientation in Washington to attain these goals militarily. In the highly
complex strategic balance the Soviet advantage in land-based intercontinental missiles (on which were deployed about 70 percent of Soviet
nuclear warheads) was a fully legitimate factor. It was conditioned by
the objective disproportions between the nuclear forces of both powers
and was compensated for in the overall military balance by the U.S.
advantages in the number of bombers, and in the number of warheads
on strategic bombers and SLBMs (on which were concentrated around
70 percent of all U.S. nuclear warheads).[33] The key idea, which from
the early 1970s was periodically advanced in the U.S. strategic community and in 1978 was again taken to arms, was to use the greater

proportion of land-based missile forces in the Soviet strategic arsenal, which by itself also conditioned Soviet advantages in this component in U.S. interests. The supporters of this idea pointed out that, having put the land-based element of Soviet nuclear forces at risk by a comparatively small portion of the U.S. arsenal, it was possible to change substantially the strategic balance in favor of the West.

Another consideration connected with these arms and their corresponding concepts was the creation of the much-maligned "bargaining chips" for the SALT negotiations. The administration's position in this respect had notably changed in comparison with early 1977. Having failed to impose inequitable SALT provisions on the Soviet Union in March 1977, the Democratic leadership concluded that it was necessary to develop and deploy the MX system, particularly to pressure the other side in the negotiating process. Such a phrasing of the issue was encountered increasingly more often in official U.S. sources in 1978–79. In one, for example, it was pointed out that "the development of this system . . . may help to persuade Soviet leaders of the futility inherent in the present competition, of the capacity of U.S. technology to outpace Soviet advances, and of the United States' will to utilize that capacity as necessary."[34]

Relations with NATO were still the single most important political factor in the changes in U.S. nuclear strategy. In the face of recurrent complications in the North Atlantic bloc's alliance relations, in the center of attention, as always, were issues that went to NATO's core–the U.S. nuclear guarantees and related strategic doctrines and weapons systems. The aggravation of economic, trade, and financial problems was amplified by political cleavages regarding events in the Persian Gulf zone. The latter were aggravated by disagreements on the bloc's military policy. The neutron bomb issue in 1978 served as the main pretext for these disagreements, giving rise to sharp recriminations among the allies and corrupting the picture of NATO unity presented at the Washington session in May. Along with the plans to build up NATO's conventional and nuclear forces on the European continent, an important instrument for Washington in its attempts to mitigate alliance differences were the steps examined above in strategy and weapons programs at the strategic nuclear level. Expressing the point of view of those who demanded such steps in right-wing circles that opposed Carter and, undoubtedly, of those who took an increasingly similar attitude in the administration itself, Henry Kissinger observed that "the equality in destructive power and even the capability of 'assured destruction' of both sides was a revolution in the strategic balance . . . . Therefore I believe that it is urgently necessary . . . that U.S. counterforce capability in strategic forces be rapidly built . . . just as I believe it is necessary that we develop a military purpose for our strategic forces and move away from the senseless and demoralizing strategy of massive civilian extermination."[35] Such considerations, as is known, have traditionally served to cover attempts to make strategic nuclear power a more effective and active instrument of U.S. foreign policy.

Along with the foreign policy aspects, a growing influence on the administration's strategic policy was exerted by the U.S. domestic political situation. The upsurge of the national-liberation movement in a number of world regions and some direct forms of military assistance to it on the part of the socialist countries, the aggravation of resource problems and difficulties in the state of the U.S. economy, the inconsistency of the administration's policy, and the disagreements with allies—all of this strengthed the displeasure of the broad U.S. public and the mass media and thus created a favorable political climate for an offensive by the right. The Committee on the Present Danger, the Institute for Contemporary Research, the Georgetown University Center for Strategic and International Studies, the University of Southern California, the University of Chicago, the Fletcher School, conservative members of Congress, and such journalists as Richard Burt, Rowland Evans, and Robert Novak noticeably strengthened their criticism of the Carter administration. The latter's policy began to be characterized as the "philosophy of weakness." A number of administration decisions on military policy, beginning with the cancellation of the B-1 bomber and ending with the postponement of developing the neutron bomb aroused the indignation of military circles. An increasingly pointed discussion raged around the opposition's arguments of the supposed present "inadequacy" of U.S. strength and the growing U.S. "military lag" behind the USSR. The right-wing offensive was also facilitated by the fact that from the winter of 1978 the president himself and his associates began increasingly to play up the "Soviet threat" campaign.

In debates on strategic issues in 1978, the problem of ICBM vulnerability and the Soviet-U.S. correlation of forces in this component was finally pushed to the foreground. In the manner of past campaigns on the "bomber and missile gaps," the "ABM gap," and others, a massive campaign was begun in the United States on the so-called "window of vulnerability." Both the administration's military programs and its line in the SALT negotiations came to be discussed primarily in connection with this question. The resumption of a search for compromises in the SALT negotiations in Geneva and the U.S. government's retreat from the March 1977 proposal provoked bitter attacks from the right. A report released by Paul Nitze asserted that SALT II would supposedly allow the USSR such an "overwhelming advantage" in throw-weight that 90 percent of the Minuteman force would become vulnerable well before the mid-1980s.[36] Senator Jackson attacked the White House on the same pretext, which was in practice a divulgence of secret information provided in a closed session of his subcommittee. The differences regarding the future SALT agreement were becoming increasingly acute, and continuous leaks of information on the course of the negotiations to the press immediately became a cause for the campaign of the opponents of arms control. An important watershed in the history of SALT II came in late 1977 and early 1978, since precisely at this time the more or less coherent and organized opposition to the treaty in the Senate was formed. For its part the administration abandoned attempts to draw opponents of SALT II to its side through imposing unilateral limitations on the Soviet Union and, for better or worse, went on the defensive against the opposition. But in order to buy off the military circles and weaken the onslaught of criticism, the administration increasingly began to yield to the pressure of the right in favor of stepping up the strategic nuclear arms race.

By December 1978, in accordance with the conditions of the "countervailing doctrine," work was concluded on a new SIOP. The target list was expanded from 25,000 to 40,000, and attack programs were fed into JSTPS computers in Omaha, command centers, and missile launch control points.[37] The new SIOP added numerous economic and defense targets of the socialist countries. In connection with the changed operational tasks and plans the criteria for the sufficiency of U.S. strategic forces were also subjected to revision. The "post-strike exchange ratio" was used more and more often as a method of evaluating the military balance. The main evidence for this is the increasingly important place given to this criterion in each successive budget report of the secretary of defense and final report of the JCS representative for the 1979–82 fiscal years. Having assumed from the outset the possibility of a "limited" nuclear exchange, the Pentagon's civilian leadership had to develop corresponding points of reference for comparing the two powers' strategic forces and estimating the sufficiency of U.S. potential. The established criteria, naturally, began to determine as well the orientation for the development of U.S. strategic nuclear forces. To remain in the obscure zone between concepts of "selective strikes" (including those on military targets) and a full-scale counterforce strategy turned out to be extremely difficult. From "limited options" the Pentagon's strategic planning was inexorably pushed—in accordance with "post-strike exchange ratio" criteria—toward the concept of "changing the balance of forces" by means of a preemptive strike on Soviet land-based strategic targets. But behind it already loomed the strategy of "damage limitation" with its assumptions of the possibility of "victory" in a thermonuclear war. Technical progress, the development of military programs, the growing pressure of the echelons of the military-industrial complex, the right-wing opposition in the foreign policy establishment and scientific-strategic community all pushed Washington's strategic policy in the same direction.

The question of silo-based ICBM vulnerability was transformed in the late 1970s into a central feature of the U.S. approach to evaluating the strategic balance and Soviet military capabilities and intentions. It became a major factor in the development of U.S. nuclear strategy and arms programs. Finally, the "window of vulnerability" campaign served for hardliners as a fundamental lever to undermine the SALT II Treaty and the arms control dialogue as a whole. However, the thesis of ICBM vulnerability as well as the concepts of "selective strikes on hard targets," "post-strike exchange ratio," and the entire U.S. theory of "strategic stability" that were built around this problem, quite obviously have extremely vulnerable points. First of all, many authoritative experts are of the opinion that mathematical calculations of the vulnerability of reinforced concrete silos (scaled from test simulations of questionable accuracy) underestimate the true survivability of these targets against a nuclear explosion and overestimate (probably deliberately) the effectiveness of ICBMs in destroying such hard targets that one could expect not in theory but in practice.[38] Furthermore, from the point of view of military-political reality, a nuclear strike on several or several tens of missile silos would be a monstrous adventure, no less mad an act than a suicidal total strike on cities. Such a step would leave the other side without any doubt that nuclear war had begun on a global level, and at the same time would relinquish to it the strategic initiative for using its enormous remaining thermonuclear potential at its discretion. When one speaks of a coordinated missile salvo against the entire land-based component of strategic forces, one has in mind a holocaust on the territory of the other country with at a minimum 2,000–3,000 nuclear warheads with a yield from hundreds of kilotons to several megatons apiece. Such a strike (which could not help but affect submarine and air bases as well) would certainly entail many tens of millions of victims among the world's population and the devastation of enormous areas. In contrast to the scenarios of U.S. strategic scholastics, in real life such an attack could be in no way distinguished from a massive strike on the territory of the other power and would therefore inevitably provoke a full-scale retaliatory strike on the aggressor, including on its administrative-industrial centers.[39]

Thus the aforementioned "Nitze scenario" that lay at the center of U.S. strategic policy in the late 1970s—a strike on ICBM silos and the threat of the subsequent destruction of cities in the event that the victimized side retaliated on the aggressor's administrative-industrial centers with its sea- and air-based forces—was a purely academic nation, absolutely detached from reality. It was based only on the fact that under equal conditions land-based missiles would have, possibly, a greater chance than other types of strategic forces of destroying the other side's silos. As for the "post-strike exchange ratio," even this approach is based only on the fact that as a consequence of the deployment of MIRVed missiles and the increase of their effectiveness, the capability may appear in theory for a lesser number of one's own missiles to destroy more of the enemy's missiles. But in reality the massive use of strategic forces in these goals would give rise to such horrible consequences for both sides that such calculations would be devoid of any meaning, even if anyone were to remain to make them.

Thus the strategic meaning of the theoretical vulnerability of ICBM silos in reality comes down mainly to a question of the degree of the vulnerability of strategic forces as a whole, of their ability to deliver a retaliatory strike. As the means for such a strike, land-based missiles are not inferior to sea-based forces or aviation and cannot be considered more "destabilizing." A much more reliable two-way communication is maintained with land-based missile forces than with bombers in flight or with submarines at sea. ICBMs also are constantly found in a higher state of readiness and are better adapted for launch on warning (as a final factor of deterrence if not of operational planning), but are less dangerous from the point of view of unauthorized use. Finally, silo-based missiles are relatively less expensive to produce and maintain than bombers or nuclear submarines.[40]

If the issue of ICBM survivability is examined as only one of the aspects of the problem of the vulnerability of strategic forces as a whole, then no Soviet "superiority" existed here. Even if the dubious calculations of Nitze and his supporters are taken on trust, the destruction of 90 percent of U.S. missiles in their silos, considering the role of the latter in U.S. strategic forces, would mean the loss of about 20 percent of all strategic warheads. On the other hand, were the United States to obtain the capability of putting at risk a similar or even a lesser portion of the USSR's land-based missiles, then this could mean a significantly greater threat to the Soviet retaliatory strike potential, since around 70 percent of Soviet nuclear warheads were deployed on land-based ICBMs. Without the deployment in the United States of the MX system or other new forces for more effective destruction of hard targets, an approximate strategic balance would be preserved between the two powers not only in the quantitative measure of the strategic arsenals but also in their overall ability to survive in the event of a hypothetical attack and to deliver a retaliatory strike. The introduction of the MX system into the force structure might upset this balance and give the United States certain unilateral advantages. Those in the West who exaggerated the ICBM vulnerability issue and demanded the deployment of the MX system had, in fact, made a stake on precisely this calculation.

After the cancellation of the Hybrid-Trench basing system in November 1977, an examination was begun anew in the Pentagon for numerous options of both the basing modes and the MX missile itself. Having examined a multitude of alternative MX basing systems, a working group of the Defense Science Board under the direction of Michael May recommended a project of multiple protective shelters (MAPS, but subsequently MPS), among which the missiles would periodically be transported on the surface in launching containers by transporter-launchers. A coalition of generals and scientists, held together by the alliance of Paul Nitze and Air Force Chief of Staff Lew Allen, wished to deploy 200 MX missiles of maximum weight and size in 4,500 vertical shelters.[41]

On December 5, 1978 Deputy Secretary of Defense William J. Perry chaired a DSARC meeting devoted to this program. However, the Defense Department's civilian leadership did not accept the military's recommendation. From their (and the White House's) point of view the MX/MPS project had a number of serious deficiencies, despite the enthusiasm of the air force command and its supporters. Placing the new missiles in vertical shelters threatened to undermine the entire SALT process. Although adherents of the MPS project strongly contended that the missile container, not the shelter, was the launcher, from the point of view of verification satellites such shelters would be indistinguishable from an ICBM launching silo, and moreover a missile could be launched from it. In addition, the construction of several thousand such targets would be a direct violation of the SALT I Interim Agreement (Article I). The construction of numerous such shelters would open the possibility for secretly producing and stockpiling a large number of containers and missiles and, when the opportunity arose, quickly deploying them in the prepared silos. In making a decision on whether to move its land-based missile forces to MPS launchers, Washington thought over beforehand the possible consequences of the other side's analogous measures and could not help but consider the probability that in the future the United States itself would be faced with the impossibility of distinguishing an empty missile silo from an occupied one and with the uncertainty of the number of the other side's ICBMs. The White House and its representatives in the Pentagon were also displeased by the military deficiencies of the air force's choice.[42]

On June 8, 1979 it was officially announced that preference was ultimately given to the largest and most powerful version of the MX missile.[43] The fact that this statement was made ten days before the signing of the SALT II Treaty in Vienna can hardly be considered an accidental coincidence. Besides everything else, this decision was a concession on the part of the administration to the military-industrial complex. Shortly afterward the decision to equip the new missile system initially (the first 100 ICBMs) with Mk-12A warheads and improved guidance systems, and in subsequent modifications to use an even more effective type of warhead, also became public knowledge.[44]

Meanwhile, the decision on a basing system had repeatedly been set aside, first from March until June 1979, then from June to September. The top OSD officials leaned in favor of the multiple protective shelters systems (although not of a vertical, but rather of a horizontal configuration) in which a missile would be hauled around by a transporter-erector-launcher.[45] The construction of 4,600 shelters and deployment of 200 missiles among them was chosen as the optimal project, calculating on a minimum 50 percent survivability of the force—100 ICBMs with 1,000 warheads.[46] On September 7, 1979 the government announced its final choice. This so-called Racetrack project envisaged the construction of horizontal shelters in the deserts of the states of Utah and Nevada.[47] According to official data, the cost of the entire program was projected at $33 billion. But the Office of Management and Budget issued an estimated cost of $37.7 billion, and a figure of $55 billion was leaked from circles close to the air force.

The enormous probable cost of this weapon system immediately provoked critical commentary in Congress and the press. Representatives of the administration pointed out in reply that as a result of implementating the MX program, the number of nuclear warheads in U.S. strategic forces would have grown by 20 percent in comparison with 1979 and the prompt hard-target-kill capability, by 300 percent.[48] However, these arguments met with far from unanimous agreement even inside the United States. The most serious opposition to the MX program was launched from an unexpected direction. It came from environmentalists who were concerned that the construction of the launch complexes in Nevada and Utah would cause irreparable damage to the economic and social balance of these regions.[49] In the subsequent period the movement to protect the environment increasingly gathered strength and became a major factor in the fate of this program.

But for all the importance of the ecological debates in the United States, the main significance of the MX program was nevertheless determined by its potential influence on the strategic balance and by its interaction with the SALT negotiations. These questions remained in the focus of the Carter administration's policy. They were at the epicenter of the U.S. domestic policy debate on a wide circle of national security problems, the unprecedented aggravation of which attended the preparation of SALT II and later the debate on the ratification of the Vienna agreements.

\* \* \*

In 1978–79 the orientation toward a capability for quick, effective strikes on the land-based components of Soviet strategic forces was significantly strengthened in the strategic doctrine, operational plans, and

military programs of the United States. The campaign on the "vulner-
ablity" of U.S. land-based missile forces, called upon to justify U.S. plans
and programs, reached its apogee. Among strategic programs, foremost
was the development of the MX system, with whose help the U.S. leadership calculated to put at risk the Soviet Union's ICBM silos and thus
eliminate Soviet advantages in land-based missiles, without which the
other disproportions favorable to the United States could upset the strategic balance. Closely connected with these calculations, the emphasis
on the "limited nuclear war" concept was strengthened in U.S. strategy
as a whole, with all the ensuing consequences for the probability of a
preemptive strategic nuclear strike and the stability of the strategic balance.

This tendency obviously contradicted the overall evolution of the strategic correlation of forces, which had been leading to a steadier and
broader balance of the two powers' forces. It invariably increased the
obstacles that confronted U.S. attempts to obtain unilateral political and
military advantages. Nevertheless, the attempts of the United States to
upset parity were again substantially invigorated in the late 1970s with
the development of the next generation of strategic nuclear weapons.
This inevitably put U.S. policy on a collision course with the progressive
development of the SALT process, for which an objective strategic equilibrium as measured by the entire sum of its parameters could serve as
the only possible basis.

## Notes

1. From Carter's address to the American Chamber of Commerce, Tokyo,
Japan, May 28, 1975. See *The Presidential Campaign 1976, Volume 1, Part 1; Jimmy
Carter* (Washington, D.C.: U.S. Government Printing Office, 1978), 66.

2. G. A. Vorontsov, *SShA i Zapadnaia Evropa: novyi etap otnoshenii* (Moscow:
Mezhdunarodnye Otnoshenii, 1979), 298–307.

3. Zbigniew Brzezinski, *Between Two Ages: America's Role in the Technetronic
Era* (New York: Viking Press, 1978), 293–94.

4. Coral Bell, *President Carter and Foreign Policy: The Costs of Virtue?* (Canberra,
1980), 11–13.

5. Anthony King, ed., *The New American Political System* (Washington, D.C.:
American Enterprise Institute, 1978).

6. Harris survey, September 9, 1978; Associated Press/NBC Poll, October
1978; Gallup Poll, November 1977.

7. Stanley Hoffman, "Requiem," *Foreign Policy* 42 (Spring 1981): 10.

8. Lawrence Freedman, *U.S. Intelligence and Soviet Strategic Threat* (London:
1977), 196–197.

9. *The Washington Post*, July 7, 1977; *International Herald Tribune*, January 7,
1977.

10. Lawrence Korb, *National Security Organization and Process in the Carter Administration* (Washington, D.C.: American Enterprise Institute, 1978), 8–10.

11. "U.S. Ground Forces: Inappropriate Objectives, Unacceptable Costs," *The Defense Monitor* 7: 9 (1978).

12. Lawrence Korb, *The FY 1981–1985 Defense Program: Issues and Trends* (Washington, D.C.: American Enterprise Institute, 1980), 4–5, 32–34.

13. Harold Brown, "Statement in the USA Institute," Unpublished report from the Institute for the Study of the USA and Canada, of the USSR Academy of Sciences, Moscow, March 1975, 3.

14. *The New York Times*, July 8, 1977, A1, A4.

15. *The New York Times*, December 16, 1977, A5.

16. Desmond Ball, "Developments in the U.S. Strategic Nuclear Policy under the Carter Administration," ACIS Working Paper no. 21 (Los Angeles: University of California, 1980), 10–11.

17. *Department of Defense Annual Report, Fiscal Year 1979* (Washington, D.C.: U.S. Government Printing Office, 1978), 53–55.

18. "Military Posture, Part 1," *Hearings*, Committee on Armed Services, U.S. House of Representatives, 95th Congress, first session, March 2–3, 1977 (Washington, D.C.: U.S. Government Printing Office, 1977).

19. ABRES (Advanced Ballistic Reentry Systems) are improved guidance, penetration, and evasion systems for ballistic warheads.

20. William H. Kincade and Jeffery D. Porro, eds., *Negotiating Security: An Arms Control Reader* (Washington, D.C.: Carnegie Foundation for International Peace, 1978), 64.

21. By this time General Electric had already begun to produce Mk-12A warheads for Minuteman-III missiles. The latter's effectiveness in combination with the new guidance system against targets of a certain hardness, according to calculations, was to have increased by 20 to 80 percent. In other words, if before ten ICBMs of this type with Mk-12 RVs (three warheads) could theoretically destroy six silos, now ten Minuteman-III ICBMs with Mk-12A RVs (also three warheads) could destroy more than 20 hard targets. In May, Carter and Brown decided to accelerate the installation of new guidance packages (NS-20), beginning not in 1978, as had been intended earlier, but in October 1977, and to equip all 550 ICBMs with it. It was also decided to begin refitting 300 of these missiles with Mk-12A warheads in 1980. See Committees on Foreign Relations and Foreign Affairs of the U.S. Senate and House of Representatives, *Fiscal Year 1981 Arms Control Impact Statements* (Washington, D.C.: U.S. Government Printing Office, 1980), 2.

22. *Department of Defense Annual Report, Fiscal Year 1980* (Washington, D.C.: U.S. Government Printing Office, 1979), 118.

23. *Time*, July 11, 1977, 9.

24. Each B-52 bomber was initially to be equipped to carry 12 missiles on underwing pylons, and later another eight missiles were to be stowed in the internal rotary launcher.

25. Committees on Foreign Relations and Foreign Affairs of the U.S. Senate and House of Representatives, *Fiscal Year 1980 Arms Control Impact Statements* (Washington, D.C.: U.S. Government Printing Office, 1979), 30–31.

26. This basing system was a network of concrete tunnels with an overall

length of hundreds of kilometers along which would move transporter-erector-launchers (TELs) carrying MX missiles. The missiles were to be launched directly from the tunnel through openings broken out at certain roof sections by the TEL.

27. For example, the cost of this basing mode was calculated quite arbitrarily, and a great number of technical questions remained unclear. In addition, the "Hybrid-Trench" system would have required much space and large-scale construction, which would have created serious problems for the environment and social-economic conditions in the states of Utah, Nevada, Arizona, and New Mexico. Certain tests, which simulated the influence of the shock wave and overpressures arising from nuclear explosions at the Have-Host testing ground in Arizona in the summer of 1977, compelled the Pentagon to decide against such a basing mode. It became clear that if the trench were destroyed even in one place, the shock wave would travel throughout it, sweeping away all the plugging mechanisms and the mobile transporter-erector-launchers hidden behind them. As a result, in November 1977 the "Hybrid-Trench" basing system was finally cancelled. See "Defense Authorization for Appropriations, FY 1980, Part 6," *Hearings*, Committee on Armed Services, U.S. Senate, 96th Congress, First Session (Washington, D.C.: U.S. Government Printing Office, 1979), 3478–80.

28. *Department of Defense Annual Report. Fiscal Year 1980*, 77.

29. *Department of Defense Annual Report, Fiscal Year 1980*, 78.

30. *Department of Defense Annual Report, Fiscal Year 1980*, 118.

31. *Department of Defense Annual Report, Fiscal Year 1980*, 80–81.

32. *Department of Defense Annual Report, Fiscal Year 1981* (Washington, D.C.: U.S. Government Printing Office, 1980), 92.

33. *Otkuda iskhodit ugroza miru*, 2d ed. (Moscow: Voenizdat, 1982), 8.

34. Joint Committees on Foreign Relations and Foreign Affairs of the U.S. Senate and House of Representatives, *Fiscal Year 1979 Arms Control Impact Statements* (Washington, D.C.: U.S. Government Printing Office, 1978), 18.

35. Keith A. Myers, ed., *NATO: The Next Thirty Years* (Boulder, Col.: Westview, 1980), 9.

36. Strobe Talbott, *Endgame: The Inside Story of SALT II* (New York: Harper and Row, 1979), 99–100, 136–38.

37. Ball, "Developments in U.S. Strategic Nuclear Policy under the Carter Administration," 10.

38. Congressional Budget Office, *Counterforce Issues for U.S. Strategic Nuclear Forces* (Washington, D.C.: U.S. Government Printing Office, 1978), 9–12.

39. See N. A. Lomov, ed., *Nauchno-tekhnicheskii progress i revoliutsiia v voennom dele* (Moscow: Voenizdat, 1973); Vasilii E. Savkin, *Osnovnye printsipy operativnogo iskusstva i taktiki* (Moscow: Voenizdat, 1972); I. Zav'ialov, "Novoe oruzhie i voennoe iskusstvo," *Krasnaia zvezda*, October 30, 1970.

40. E. Klimovich and S. Bukharov, "Strategicheskie rakety," *Voennye znaniia*, January 1980.

41. "Defense Appropriations, FY 1980, Part 3," *Hearings*, Committee on Appropriations, U.S. House of Representatives, 96th Congress, first session (Washington, D.C.: U.S. Government Printing Office, 1979), 320.

42. In particular, it was pointed out that if the enemy should nevertheless

find a method to detect in which shelters were the missile launchers, then it
would be impossible to transfer them to other silos upon warning of attack. With
the vertical configuration of the shelters, the raising, transport, and reinsertion
of an ICBM were laborious and slow affairs. The so-called capability for a final
"dash" was absent, whereby missile crews would quickly move the missile to
another shelter in the event that its true location were discovered. And the
possibility existed that the program, colossal in the cost, complexity, scale, and
time required to implement it, would turn out to be completely in vain on account
of a single intelligence discovery or any unforeseen factor. See especially
Congressional Budget Office, *The MX Missile and Multiple Protective Structure
Basing: Long-term Budgetary Implications* (Washington, D.C.: U.S. Government
Printing Office, 1979), 97–119.

43. Besides this version of the 90-ton MX missile, in 1978–79 the Pentagon
examined the possibility of placing a Minuteman-III ICBM on a mobile launcher
in a system of multiple protective shelters, and also a project of a fully common
air force and navy missile that would be somewhat smaller in size and power
than the MX, and that could be deployed both in an MPS system on land and
in the *Ohio* submarine's launching tubes as the Trident-II SLBM. Ibid., pp. 71–
96.

44. *Final Environmental Impact Statement: MX, Milestone II* (Washington, D.C.:
Department of the Air Force, 1981), Pt. 1, I–11, I–15.

45. From their point of view, such a basing system had, in the first place, the
advantage that shelters equipped with a viewing hatch would be easier to verify
from satellites for the presence or absence of ICBMs in them. Second, after a
missile attack signal from warning systems, the TEL, controlled remotely, as it
was planned, would be able to get a "dash" of several minutes to move the missile
from one shelter to another in the event it became known to the enemy in which
of them the ICBMs had been previously emplaced. See *Aviation Week and Space
Technology*, November 12, 1979, 19.

46. *Survival*, March/April 1980, 60.

47. Besides the Racetrack scheme, in 1978–79, as in 1975–76, the option of
basing the MX missile on transport aircraft was considered anew. However, this
option was rejected as too cumbersome and expensive.

48. Korb, *The FY 1981–1985 Defense Program* 45–46.

49. As an illustration of the problems that could arise, Congressman James
Santini pointed out that the implementation of the project would attract to his
region (with a total population of 7,000) a contingent of 20–30,000 construction
workers. In these dry zones an enormous amount of water (up to 7 million tons)
would be required for the production of concrete. The construction works as a
whole would cover up to 380,000 square kilometers of desert land and would
require building around 9,900 kilometers of roads, of which 2,400 kilometers
would be asphalt roads seven meters wide. See Office of Technology Assessment,
*MX Missile Basing* (Washington, D.C.: U.S. Government Printing Office, 1981),
64–81; *U.S. Defense Policy: Weapons, Strategy and Commitments*, 2d ed. (Washington,
D.C.: Congressional Quarterly, Inc., 1980), 33–34.

# 4

## The SALT II Treaty and the Deterioration of Détente

The Carter administration's policy in the strategic arms control area was begun with an attempt to revise the 1974 Vladivostok accord and compromises on a number of issues that had been discussed on its basis. The U.S. proposals, advanced in March 1977, pursued the goal of significantly changing the strategic correlation of forces in the U.S. favor, of imposing strict unilateral limitations on the Soviet Union. This attempt damaged the SALT dialogue and impeded the preparation of a new treaty.

Since this attempt failed, a review of U.S. policy in the strategic arms area was begun anew in Washington. Having set far-reaching goals for its own military programs and strategic concepts, Washington began to approach the SALT negotiations more flexibly with respect to limitations on Soviet forces. As a result of negotiations at the foreign minister level, a so-called three-tiered scheme for SALT II was developed. The first tier, a treaty that would run until the end of 1985, contained the basic provisions of the Vladivostok accord. The second tier, the protocol to the treaty, would have regulated the problem of limiting cruise missiles and mobile ICBMs. And in the third it was proposed to talk about more radical SALT measures in the next stage after 1985. The mutual understanding in principle achieved between the two sides concerning the general framework and parameters of a future treaty was a most important political prerequisite for moving toward the resolution of SALT's numerous concrete issues in Moscow, Washington, and Geneva. Andrei

A. Gromyko later offered an eloquent commentary on the true seriousness of the problem:

It seems well and easy to say: "The principle of equality and equal security." Who would ever be against this principle? But it is another matter when negotiations are being conducted, especially on an exceptionally important question—difficulties arise, indeed even great difficulties. To one side it seems that it is adhering to the principle of equality and equal security; to the other it seems that precisely it is acting so, but not the first side. But there is only one truth.[1]

The long and difficult search for this sole truth was ultimately crowned by the set of SALT II agreements signed by the two powers at the Vienna summit in June 1979. The Vienna treaty clearly fixed the Soviet-U.S. strategic balance and stipulated reducing the levels of destructive potential and limiting the number of new military programs. It represented a precisely regulated balance of Soviet and U.S. interests and embodied the principles of the equality and equal security of both sides. The ratification of the treaty would exert a stabilizing influence on the strategic situation and on the whole international political situation.

But U.S. strategic nuclear policy and U.S. foreign policy as a whole on the threshold of the 1980s increasingly diverged from the interests of maintaining the strategic equilibrium and stability, restraining the arms race, and deepening détente. Washington's policy ultimately came into direct conflict with these interests, a conflict that was especially manifested during the debates over the ratification of SALT II in the United States.

The events of late 1979 and early 1980 served as the final jolt to the shift in U.S. policy that had been evolving for a long time. President Carter announced this turning point with the introduction of Soviet military forces into Afghanistan, but at the foundation of these changes undoubtedly also lay reasons of a different order. The inconsistency, which characterized the implementation of the Democrats' unrealistic political views in practice, the attempts to combine the incompatible, presented a clear picture. The United States moved to a policy of confrontation and severed all remaining threads of political and military détente. In the strategic arms sphere destabilizing tendencies were manifested still more boldly under the influence of the overall situation, in particular in certain military concepts peculiar to the new stage of U.S. strategic policy.

## March 1977: U.S. Deviation from the Vladivostok Accord

In his inaugural address Carter proclaimed the intention of the new U.S. leadership to review without delay its approach to strategic arms control, to put before it more ambitious tasks. "We will move this year a step toward our ultimate goal—the elimination of all nuclear weapons from this earth," he announced.[2] The elaboration of a new approach had already begun in the winter of 1976–77. Disparaging the international political significance of the SALT negotiations, the new Washington leaders criticized the Vladivostok accord for the fact that it "hardly" limited the arms race and only "codified" the attained levels of arms and programs intended for the future. President Carter was troubled by the growing criticism within the U.S. concerning the Vladivostok decision. Senator Henry Jackson, with whom the administration flirted while seeking to improve cooperation with Congress, held great influence with the president. Upon replacing the Ford administration, Carter's group immediately shifted attention in the sphere of the unresolved issues of Vladivostok from the question of cruise missiles and the Backfire bomber to the problem of the vulnerability of U.S. land-based ballistic missiles.

On March 12, 1977 Carter led a meeting of the administration's highest echelon. The president received a detailed briefing of the ideas developed in the preceding three months by the Special Coordination Committee and readily approved them. After this, Brzezinski directed former Kissinger assistant William Hyland to compose a specific draft of an agreement for Vance's trip to Moscow, planned for late March 1977. Hyland and his NSC colleague David Aaron produced a draft of the so-called Comprehensive Proposal presented by Vance in Moscow. Sensing how much the U.S. proposals were directed at unilaterally constraining the Soviet Union, Hyland and Vance proposed including in the U.S. position an alternative "deferral" option, which proposed concluding a treaty on the Vladivostok basis and setting aside negotiations on the Backfire and cruise missiles until the future.[3]

On March 28 the U.S. delegation arrived in Moscow. In the course of the negotiations both U.S. drafts were rejected by the Soviet side. Appearing before a press conference immediately after the conclusion of Vance's trip, Brzezinski stated in his own peculiar way that the Soviet leadership's reaction was explained by the fact that it was supposedly caught by surprise and was unable to understand the essence of the U.S. proposals. But the fact of the matter, to the contrary, was that Moscow understood perfectly well the U.S. scheme. The reduction of the total number of strategic launchers to a level of 1,800–2,000 would have required the USSR to remove 500–700 launchers, and the U.S., only 300–500. Much more important, the limitation on heavy ICBMs affected the United States in no way whatsoever but would have cut in half the pivotal element of Soviet missile forces. The limitation on MIRVed ICBMs at a level of 550 launchers coincided exactly with the number of such missiles possessed by the United States. And the Soviet Union would have been forced to rely much more heavily upon sea-based ballistic missiles in deploying MIRVed launchers up to the prescribed limit. In other words, it would be forced to restructure its nuclear forces.

This same tendency was evident in the qualitative limitations proposed by Washington. True, the prohibition to develop, test, and deploy new land-based ICBM systems would have halted the MX program. However, the provision prohibiting the modification or modernization of existing ICBMs would much more heavily impinge upon Soviet strategic forces. It would prevent the United States from even further replacing Minuteman-II missiles with Minuteman-III, which the Carter administration would have rejected in any event, but it did not hinder the placing of Mk-12A warheads on the Minuteman-III.

The provision to ban the deployment of the Backfire bomber in the Soviet Union's northern regions seemed to have been deliberately intended to provoke a negative reaction from the USSR. The proposal of "strict limitations" on cruise missiles in reality meant that cruise missiles of all types with a range of up to 2,500 kilometers would not be subject to any limitations; at the same time it permitted nonpenetrating bombers, submarines in the eastern Mediterranean and Norwegian seas, and land-based launchers in Western Europe to prepare to hit their targets in the greater part of the European territory of the Soviet Union. The promise not to equip tactical aviation with long-range cruise missiles had no great significance, since it did not hinder in any degree their deployment in the thousands on bombers, heavy transport aircraft, submarines, ships, and land-based launchers.

Appearing in a press conference after the Moscow meeting, USSR Minister of Foreign Affairs Andrei A. Gromyko pointed out that "it is easy, after an objective study of these proposals, to draw the conclusion that they pursue the aim of getting unilateral advantages for the USA to the detriment of the Soviet Union, its security and the security of its friends and allies. The Soviet Union will never be able to agree to this."[4] The glaring imbalance of the U.S. plan as a whole could not have been missed even by one of its authors. Brzezinski's advisor David Aaron noted that in the event of the realization of the Comprehensive Proposal, "we would be giving up future draft choices in exchange for cuts in their starting line-up."[5] One detached Western observer drew the following, quite widely held conclusion: "This radically altered proposal would have deeply cut into the strategic 'muscle' of both sides, but it would have taken a greater bite out of the Soviet arsenal than the American."[6] As for the "deferral" proposal, it was also unacceptable to the USSR, since for its right to deploy medium-range aircraft (not the subject of these negotiations) outside the SALT framework, the United States sought to reserve for itself the right to build up strategic cruise missiles without limits.

The question naturally arose: What was the U.S. leadership counting on in proposing such inequitable terms to the Soviet Union as the Comprehensive Proposal? It was especially strange that its fundamental ideas came mainly from liberal politicians and academics who favored limiting the arms race. Apparently these officials were so spellbound by their concepts of "strategic stability" that they lost the ability to look objectively at the state of affairs. They had become captive to the scheme that held that silo-based ballistic missiles are first-strike weapons and therefore exert a "destabilizing" influence, but that the sea-based missile forces and bombers with cruise missiles are "stabilizing" retaliatory strike weapons. These officials did not wish to see that this theory is objectively driven by the geostrategic, technical, and doctrinal peculiarities of the development of U.S. nuclear forces. They tried to impose this scheme on the other side as well, in spite of the fact that it is far from acceptable to the Soviet Union, and in practice would mean the unilateral infringement of Soviet interests. Certain adherents of U.S. nuclear superiority, tempted with the possibility of getting unilateral advantages, joined with the administration's liberal representatives, and in the event that the USSR rejected the offer, they planned to put the blame on the Soviets for the breakdown of the SALT dialogue and to justify an acceleration of the arms race.

Moreover, even the general climate of Soviet-U.S. relations was not conducive to the spirit of mutual understanding and good will necessary in such delicate negotiations. It had already been overshadowed by Carter's campaign on human rights violations in the USSR. The day before Vance's flight to Moscow the president hailed the U.S. initiatives in a speech on U.S. television and criticized all previous SALT agreements. This was done in order to impede the Soviet Union's rejection of Washington's inequitable terms. These rash and shortsighted actions, so typical for the Carter administration, caused significant damage. They subsequently created the opportunity for attacks on the negotiations on the part of SALT opponents, who would raise an uproar over the repudiation of any of the unacceptable U.S. proposals made in March 1977. Any compromise would be branded as "capitulation to the Russians" or a unilateral U.S. "concession."

With all this in mind, it is necessary to point out that there were certain positive elements in the U.S. March 1977 Comprehensive Proposal, especially the notion to reduce and limit strategic arms more radically, in particular certain especially destablizing weapons. In a more benign overall political situation these would have deserved more careful and serious consideration. They could have served as the basis for a more radical arms control agreement, provided that limitations affected both sides more equally.

Despite the sharp conflict of positions at the Moscow meeting, the parties agreed to continue the SALT dialogue. It was also resolved to begin a discussion of certain other questions: limiting weapons trade and arms transfers, limiting military activity in the Indian Ocean, limiting antisatellite weapons, and completely prohibiting nuclear tests. In the main sphere—strategic arms control—more than two years of the most complicated negotiations in Geneva were required, as well as eight meetings at the foreign minister level for resolving the multitude of difficult problems remaining after Vance's March visit. As in no other sphere, as in no other historical period, no provision for limiting strategic nuclear arms has value in and of itself, in isolation from concrete military-political realities. It has meaning only in a strictly defined political situation, in a strictly defined strategic context. For the dynamics of the military balance and the volatility of the international situation are capable of rendering useless the most detailed and thoroughly prepared treaty if too much time is lost in the course of its development. The principle of "all or nothing," more than anywhere else, is inappropriate in this area.

## The SALT II Negotiations: In Search of Equal Security

Numerical ceilings on Soviet and U.S. strategic launchers were a necessary basic limitation without which any other SALT provisions would have been meaningless. The Soviet Union adhered to the Vladivostok levels—2,400 total strategic launchers for each side and 1,320 with MIRVed warheads. The latter ceiling was also to have included heavy bombers with cruise missiles with a range of more than 600 kilometers. In May 1977 in Geneva U.S. Secretary of State Cyrus Vance proposed reducing these levels by 10 percent—to 2,160 and 1,200 launchers respectively.[7] Simultaneously the U.S. government advanced the idea of establishing a 250 launcher limit on heavy MIRVed ICBMs and the same such level for heavy bombers with cruise missiles. For the Soviet Union, reducing the overall numerical SALT ceilings was more painful than for the United States. Proceeding from the existing strategic forces (2,500 and about 2,300, respectively[8]), the Soviet Union would be required to reduce more launchers than the United States, and U.S. forward-based nuclear forces (numbering about 700)—a substantial component of the actual nuclear balance—would not be affected at all by the SALT limits. The 250 launcher ceiling was based on a dubious principle. It would have forced the USSR to reduce a number of its most powerful and already deployed missiles, and "in return" the United States would have been permitted to equip anew 250 bombers with ALCMs. The Soviet Union should not have had to pay any additional concessions for its right to have heavy missiles, since these forces were an integral element of the already-established military balance.

However, in the summer of 1977 Washington revised its claims regarding heavy ICBMs. For the administration it was a major departure from the idea of limiting them, an idea that had been rooted in the U.S. negotiating line since the late 1960s. The administration's interdepartmental SALT working group developed a new proposal that stipulated limiting the overall number of MIRVed ICBMs at a ceiling of 800 launchers. In order to secure the Soviet Union's agreement on this additional subceiling, the U.S. leadership decided to accept a provision to include heavy bombers within the 1,320 launcher sublimit, that is, practically abandoning hopes to worm out ALCMs from under the SALT limits. The White House and NSC staffs advanced as well the idea of introducing yet another sublimit at 1,200 launchers, which would apply to MIRVed intercontinental and submarine-launched ballistic missiles. In the overall 1,320 launcher ceiling it was possible to have more then 120 heavy bombers with cruise missiles, with the condition of removing for every new aircraft one MIRVed ballistic missile (launcher). At the same time, however, it was prohibited to build more than 1,200 MIRVed missiles, independent of the number of ALCM-carrying bombers. A compromise resolution, subsequently embodied in the text of the SALT II Treaty, established an ultimate ceiling of 2,250 total launchers for each side, with a 1,320 launcher subceiling for MIRVed ballistic missiles and heavy bombers with cruise missiles with a range greater than 600 kilometers. Within this subceiling a side could have no more than 1,200 MIRVed ballistic missiles, and no more than 820 of them could be MIRVed ICBMs.[9]

Yet another question connected with quantitative limitations concerned the Soviet Tu-22M intermediate-range bomber, called Backfire in the West. The U.S. Joint Chiefs of Staff demanded the inclusion of these bombers in the overall SALT II ceilings for strategic launchers. Discussion of this question continued right up until the very signing of the SALT II Treaty. In the end, pursuant to the achieved accord, the Soviet Union made a statement to the United States that it did not intend to give this aircraft the capability for operating at an intercontinental range; that it would not increase the radius of operation in such a way as to enable it to destroy targets on U.S. territory; that it would not give it such a capability in any other manner, for example with the help of in-flight refueling; and that it would also not increase the production rate of this aircraft.[10]

Progress in the September 1977 negotiations on the main parameters of the SALT II Treaty offered the hope for a speedier and easier resolution of the remaining problems. As it turned out, more than one and one-half years were required for this, and the most difficult obstacles would still have to be overcome. The negotiating process deepened in the sphere of qualitative limits on the arms race. Limiting the qualitative aspect of strategic nuclear rivalry was long an urgent issue for SALT. Since the late 1960s the main resource expenditures and strategic plans in the United States were connected precisely with the qualitative side of building up its nuclear potential—modernizing existing weapons systems and replacing old arms with newer, more improved ones.

The question of limiting the increase of the number of strategic nuclear warheads and the further improvement of their combat effectiveness arose first of all in the discussion of qualitative limitations. Since early 1978 this problem occupied a key place in the SALT negotiations. At the May 1978 Washington meeting the representatives of the two powers discussed a most important question: the possibility of prohibiting in the context of the treaty the development, testing, and deployment of any new types of ICBMs, without any exceptions.[11] This clear and strict measure, easily amenable to verification and eliminating any loopholes for continuing programs in this direction, could have demonstrated the breadth of the approach to issues of security, the desire to strengthen it by means of agreements, not through creating new arms. But the U.S. military-industrial complex greeted this idea with little enthusiasm. It would have interfered with the continuation of the MX program, which Washington sought to protect from SALT by any means in all its proposals for limiting new types of ICBMs. The MX program, starting in 1978, was already looked upon by the Carter administration as a necessary means of securing advantages in its long-term strategic policy, as an irreplaceable "bargaining chip" in light of the growing criticism from the right, and also as an obligatory condition for the ratification of the future SALT II Treaty in the Senate. Thus the most effective accord on this issue could not be reached. A compromise solution, achieved in the course of further negotiations, prohibited new types of ICBMs, except for one light system for each side, with either multiple or single warheads.[12]

As for prohibiting new types of SLBMs, the U.S. side, considering its strategic position here stronger, generally was not interested in any limitations. A complete ban on new SLBMs turned out to be impossible, since the cancellation of the Trident-I system, intended for deployment in 1979 on *Lafayette*-class submarines and from 1981 on *Ohio*-class SSBNs, was unthinkable for the Pentagon. To the extent the question arose about permission for both sides to create one new type of SLBM each, it was necessary to consider that the Soviet SLBM comparable to the Trident I was the *Typhoon* system (by U.S. designation the SS-N-20, a second-generation MIRVed SLBM). However, the United States tried to prohibit this system, drawing an analogy between it and the U.S. Trident-II SLBM. Such a limitation would have prevented the Soviet Union from creating a counterweight to the Trident-I system and at the same time during the operating period of the treaty would have in no way affected the development of Trident II. As a consequence of the position taken by the United States, a compromise on limiting new SLBM types could not be attained, although they could create a significant threat, even against silo-based strategic forces. Instead, the agreement prohibited both sides from developing new types of SLBMs with more MIRV-type warheads than the greatest number on systems already deployed, that is, 14, as on the Poseidon missiles.[13]

Reaching an agreement on limiting the number of warheads on land-based missiles (that is, "fractionation") was considerably more difficult. Here the United States tried to impose stricter limits on the USSR. As for limiting the number of warheads on the one new type of light ICBM permitted to each side, U.S. representatives once again regarded the inviolability of the MX system as sacrosanct. All the fundamental participants in developing the U.S. negotiating position concurred in the opinion that it was necessary to guarantee the United States the right to place on a new missile up to 10 warheads. Thus the United States simultaneously tried to secure the minimum fractionation for existing models of Soviet missiles and the maximum for U.S. ICBM systems.

The United States perceived the problem of fractionation quite differently when the question of cruise missiles arose. An obvious analogy existed between ballistic missiles with MIRVs and heavy bombers with cruise missiles, which were all included together in the 1,320 launcher ceiling. When the question arose in the negotiations of limiting the number of ALCMs that could be placed on such aircraft, the Pentagon immediately objected. Development had begun in the United States on a wide-body cruise missile carrier (CMC) aircraft capable of carrying up to 70 ALCMs. Therefore, the U.S. side did not agree with the proposal that heavy bombers, including future CMC systems, be limited to carrying on average no more than 20 cruise missiles apiece. The problems of limiting bomber and missile fractionation were interrelated both by the logic of the strategic balance and by the practical logic of the negotiations, and the search for a compromise continued almost until the very signing of SALT II.

Ultimately it was decided that there could be placed on average no more than 28 cruise missiles on bombers. The parties also agreed to state that no more than 20 missiles apiece would be placed on existing bombers (B-52, B-1, Tu-95, and Miasishchev). Soon afterward an accord was reached as well on limiting the fractionation of MIRVed warheads. On each existing missile type it was prohibited to increase the number of warheads beyond the maximum number with which missiles of that type had been tested by that time. No more than 10 warheads were permitted on the one new light type of ICBM.[14] The parties also agreed to quite strict limitations on the modernization or modification of existing types of ICBMs according to the number of launcher stages, length, diameter, launch- and throw-weight of the missile, weight of the warheads, and also the type of propellant in each stage. The significance of these limits was to rule out the possibility of creating more than one new ICBM system under the pretense of modifying missiles already in the force posture.

Insisting on maximally strict qualitative limitations on land-based ballistic missiles (so long as this did not impede the MX program), the U.S. leadership at the same time took a quite liberal approach to the regulation of the varieties of cruise missiles. In this military-technical sphere, Washington, with its unjustified aspirations, undermined even more the SALT measures, which were difficult enough because of the complexity of verification. For example, after the cancellation of the B-1 bomber the Department of Defense began to shun the 2,500-kilometer range limitation for ALCMs, as well as the 600-kilometer limit for SLCMs and GLCMs. U.S. diplomats in Geneva tried to argue that range should be understood not as the maximum distance that a missile could cover until it exhausted its fuel, but as the distance from the launching point to the target with a large (up to 50 percent) allowance for all possible maneuvers in flight. Secretary of State Vance and ACDA Director Paul Warnke opposed such a phrasing of the question, justly assessing it as a mockery of arms control. But the leadership of the Defense Department won the support of the National Security Council, and its demand became the official U.S. position in the negotiations, as a result of which the resolution of the question was long delayed.

On questions concerning the limitation of cruise missiles, the State Department and ACDA as a rule took a more flexible position than the other agencies. While carrying out the official U.S. line at the negotiating table, Vance, Warnke, and Ralph Earle (who replaced Warnke as head of the U.S. delegation in September 1978) often disputed it within the administration, and called for a compromise with the Soviet Union. However, the Pentagon's point of view frequently prevailed, since it had the approval of the White House and NSC, largely through the efforts of presidential adviser Zbigniew Brzezinski. Washington's line did not permit the resolution of questions of qualitative limitations on cruise missiles until late 1978, and in a number of aspects, until March 1979. And since one of the most important tasks of SALT II was the establishment of limits on cruise missiles, the unjustified U.S. demands delayed negotiations on other SALT issues as well. Ultimately the parties agreed generally to remove the range limitation on ALCMs, but the United States conceded to the strict definition of a 600-kilometer range limit for GLCMs and SLCMs.

Among certain arms control supporters in the United States, not to mention the treaty's opponents, there was the opinion that SALT II supposedly insufficiently limited the arms race and was basically a "license" for its continuation in the directions intended by both sides.[15] Such an impression could have arisen largely because of an underestimate of the complexity of the problem, of an unjustified expectation of easy successes in this undertaking unprecedented in the history of humanity. An objective analysis permits the conclusion that both sides in SALT II sacrificed certain not-unimportant elements of their military plans and capabilities for the sake of mutually limiting the nuclear arms race.

The Soviet Union agreed to reduce its strategic forces by approximately 250 launchers, that is, by 10 percent. The USSR also cancelled a number of programs found in various stages of development or deployment. The fractionation limits on MIRVed ICBMs (especially heavy ICBMs), according to many U.S. estimates, significantly reduced the potential number of individually targeted nuclear warheads that could confront the United States in the very near future.[16] And this is far from the complete list of limitations that the Soviet Union took upon itself. It stands to reason that the numerical ceilings and subceilings required upon their being reached—what with the coming into service of new strategic missiles, submarines, and aircraft—the reduction of a corresponding number of existing arms.

In the United States the planned ballistic missile programs would have run against the 1,200 launcher limit by the mid-1980s.[17] However, some barriers were placed before U.S. cruise missiles. Plans to equip 150 B-52 aircraft with ALCMs—in view of the established ceiling of 1,320 MIRVed launchers—would have compelled the United States to remove 30 MIRVed missiles. In connection with the obligation not to place more than 20 ALCMs on existing heavy bombers, the United States could deploy a maximum of around 3,000 air-launched cruise missiles within the framework of SALT II. But as far back as 1977, after the cancellation of the B-1 system the air force planned to equip around 250 B-52 aircraft with this weapon, which would have meant adding to the arsenal up to 5,000 cruise missiles. In the event of such a decision the SALT II limits would have forced the Pentagon to scrap up to 130 MIRVed ballistic missiles in the near future as compensation. Limiting the average number of cruise missiles on each heavy bomber to 28 and stipulating that new launchers could not be reconfigured from existing transport aircraft in turn appreciably contained the buildup of new ALCM launch platforms. The Protocol to the SALT II Treaty had great importance. It prohibited the deployment of ground- and sea-launched cruise missiles (intended for forward deployment near the USSR's borders) with a range of more than 600 kilometers, as well as the testing and deployment of ICBMs on mobile launchers and of MIRVed air-to-surface ballistic missiles (ASBMs). True, these programs were planned for a later stage, after the expiration of the Protocol (December 31, 1981). But at the same time the Protocol created a political premise for continuing future negotiations on these questions in the context of SALT III. This was openly stated in a third document—the Joint Statement. In addition, the strict definition of cruise missiles impeded the Pentagon's search for loopholes for moving these arms out from under the established limitations.

A most important aspect in assessing the influence of SALT II on military policy is that its provisions began to exert pressure on programs well before the signing of the treaty in Vienna. As one article or another was being agreed to in the course of the negotiations, they were becoming important factors in annual decisions on the development and deployment of certain weapon systems. These plans had to be adjusted beforehand under SALT II (although the reverse also took place—the adjustment of the agreements to the programs), in order to avoid major economic and military-technical costs when the treaty's provisions came into effect.

This tendency of the anticipatory restructuring of both sides' programs in expectation of the SALT agreements is exceptionally important. Purely on the surface, from a "publicity" point of view, it seems to dampen the effectiveness of the agreed limitations. But in reality it means precisely that the SALT process actually became an inherent and integral factor of the strategic balance. Although the Vienna treaty ultimately was not ratified, in light of the above-noted circumstances it had already exerted a restraining influence on the arms race. This influence cannot be annulled even by new military programs simply because of the fact that their effect would now be more significant if in the second half of the 1970s the arms race had continued at a faster rate and on a wider scale.

No doubt, SALT II was far from perfect. Both sides could have gone much further in reducing and limiting their strategic offensive forces, especially if the overall political situation had been more favorable to arms control, and if the two great powers had been more determined to exercise new political thinking in this area and emphasize political solutions to the problems of security. Nevertheless, for its time SALT II was a reasonable and important compromise.

Considering the extraordinary complexity of comparing the technical, strategic, and political importance of one limitation or another imposed on both parties, it should be emphasized that a mechanical calculation of concessions made by each power in the course of the negotiations fails to reveal the essence of the achieved agreements. A thorough comparison of the two states' mutual concessions—both with respect to the limitations directly accepted by them on their existing and future strategic forces and with respect to the anticipatory adaptation of military programs to the expected treaty—leads to the conclusion that the set of 1979 Vienna agreements was the embodiment of an equal and delicate balance of interests and compromises between the USSR and the United States.

## U.S. Debates over the Vienna Treaty

On June 18, 1979 President Carter presented the Vienna treaty for examination to a joint session of Congress and formally opened the greatest debate on strategic questions in U.S. history. However, U.S. ruling circles had already split long before that time into camps of opponents and supporters of SALT II. Although the Vienna treaty was the occasion for the domestic political melee that had been building up for a long time, the discussion quickly enveloped the broad field of issues of the strategic balance and of the military and entire foreign policy of the United States, raising major problems for détente, nuclear parity, and arms control. Since 34 votes against could prevent ratification (that is, one-third of the Senate members plus one), and since around 15 senators were unambiguous opponents of the treaty, the struggle between the two camps was immediately associated with winning over around 20 vacillating senators. Essentially, two ruling class alignments engaged in a duel for determining subsequent U.S. policy: on one hand, the moderate-conservatives and liberal echelons of the "establishment" holding power; and on the other, the cohort of conservatives, hardliners, and the "New Right" aspiring to block the state leadership.

An analysis of the arguments of the hard-line opposition suggests that its greatest dissatisfaction was connected not so much with the SALT II provisions themselves as with a number of aspects of the strategic balance, on which were hung the provisions of the treaty like legal tissue on a military-technical skeleton. In other words, the main criticisms of the treaty were that it did not limit the Soviet Union even more strictly and that the significance of its provisions for each side reflected the objectively established disproportions of the strategic correlation of forces.

By the end of the summer, in the course of stormy debates over the SALT II Treaty, a pivotal balance of interests in the political alignments that comprised the prevailing segment of the ruling circles had crystallized. The set of Vienna agreements was considered "peripherally" advantageous to the United States in the context of the established strategic correlation of forces, but this correlation itself and the tendencies in its evolution for the 1980s were considered unfavorable to the United States. The discussion on the ratification of SALT II was used by the significantly strengthened conservative circles and the main elements of the military-industrial complex to ensure in the new decade a much more intensive buildup of U.S. military power, including the strategic arsenal. In addition, the extreme-right alignment of militarists and the "New Right" was convinced that only a dramatic repudiation of the treaty and the entire SALT process, a severance of the remaining threads of détente, could serve as an adequate stimulus for mobilizing U.S. resources for the resurrection of "military superiority." Their "cavalry charge," unable to topple SALT II with one fell swoop, bogged down in the first stage. Their arguments, as Soviet historian Sergei P. Fedorenko notes, displayed obvious inconsistency and bias.[18] However, these circles consolidated their achieved gains, waiting for an opportune moment to resume the offensive. They were able to penetrate much further on another front—in the campaign to increase military spending, where their pressure coincided with the prevailing sentiments of the U.S. ruling circles.

In the course of the Senate Committee on Foreign Relations hearings the Joint Chiefs of Staff, on whose judgment largely depended the treaty's ratification, in fact made their support of the Vienna agreements conditional on an annual real increase of defense appropriations by 5 percent over a five-year period. Otherwise, they warned, the United States would have to change its military strategy, resigning itself to more limited goals.[19] In early August, at the request of the JCS, former President Gerald Ford joined in and stated that he would not approve of SALT II unless Carter would commit himself to an annual real increase of military spending by 5 percent and would add to the fiscal year 1981 budget, at a minimum, ten billion dollars.[20] At his Senate appearance Henry Kissinger in turn called for a substantial increase of appropriations and programs for the arms race, although he refrained from advancing specific numbers. In late July Senator Sam Nunn, recognized on Capitol Hill as an authority on military issues, publicly announced that he would not support the ratification of the treaty if the president would not promise to increase significantly appropriations for defense requirements and drive their yearly growth to 4–5 percent considering inflation.[21] In early August Nunn, in coauthorship with Senators Jackson and Tower, sent the White House a letter which stated that without an annual real increase in the defense budget of 4–5 percent the SALT II Treaty was not worthy of support.

The right-wing and conservative opposition, acting in concert, decided to achieve at any cost a turning point in its favor, to crush the liberal alignment in Congress and put the administration under its control. Against the backdrop of sentiments raised in the course of the Senate hearings, on August 29 a sensation arose in the United States over the so-called Soviet combat brigade which supposedly showed up in Cuba. Bitter attacks on the administration's policy from representatives of right-wing circles in the press and in Congress continued throughout September. Senate Democratic majority leader Robert Byrd favored postponing the ratification of SALT II, and Senators Jackson, Tower, and Baker attacked the Vienna treaty with renewed strength. The administration ultimately capitulated under the pressure of the militarists' campaign. On December 12, speaking to members of the Business Council, President Carter announced that the FY 1981 military budget would surpass the previous one by 5 percent in real terms. In the future, he said, independent of the inflation rate, the rates of defense spending growth in constant dollars would be maintained at a yearly level of 5 percent, and for the five-year period would total over 1 trillion dollars ($1,013 billion, to be exact). This sum was $224 billion (28 percent) greater than that proposed by the administration only four months earlier.[22]

The hardening of Washington's policy was felt along all lines. At the NATO Brussels session on December 12, 1979 under intensified U.S. pressure a resolution was adopted to deploy from 1983 to 1986 108 intermediate-range Pershing II ballistic missiles and 464 ground-launched cruise missiles on the territories of the Federal Republic of Germany, Great Britain, Italy, Belgium, and the Netherlands, capable of delivering nuclear strikes to the heart of the European portion of Soviet territory. The USSR tried unsuccessfully to block this resolution with a proposal made literally on the eve before: to reduce the number of intermediate-range nuclear forces deployed in the European zone of Soviet territory, if the new U.S. intermediate range nuclear missiles were not deployed in Western Europe.[23]

By that time, after numerous interruptions and delays (including such holidays as Thanksgiving, which tend to distract senators from their work), the Senate Foreign Relations Committee hearings on SALT II had been concluded. Failing to have discredited the treaty as a whole, its opponents tried to attach to the Vienna agreements amendments that would have grossly encroached upon the most intricate structure of the SALT articles and required that negotiations begin anew with the Soviet Union. The Senate Committee rejected these amendments by a majority of votes. However, a number of amendments, supplements, and interpretations were adopted that, in the Committee's opinion, did not require the resumption of negotiations. But the matter progressed toward ratification ever more sluggishly. Domestic political conditions in the United States and the situation in the international arena were becoming increasingly less favorable for the treaty. The attention of Congress, the administration, and the public—apart from the traditional turkey and anticipated Christmas holidays—was riveted on the problem of U.S. hostages in Tehran, the crisis flaring up in the Persian Gulf zone, to which a U.S. naval armada consisting of two aircraft carrier battle groups and marine amphibious landing ships had been transferred. On December 15 Senators John Warner and Sam Nunn sent the president a letter signed by 17 of their colleagues which emphasized that their final position concerning the treaty would depend on the further development of the administration's overall foreign and military policy.

A tremendous though in no way unexpected outburst of anti-Soviet sentiment in the West on December 27, in connection with the introduction into Afghanistan of a Soviet military contingent, dealt the final blow to SALT II. On January 3, 1980 President Carter recommended to Senate majority leader Robert Byrd that consideration of the question of ratifying the treaty be set aside indefinitely. At the same time it was announced that the United States would not violate the provisions of SALT II, as long as the USSR followed this example.

Just as far-sighted experts had expected, after the administration's great concession to the right opposition, the attacks of the militarist circles were resumed with still greater strength following the Christmas holidays. Senator Henry Bellmon blamed the White House for the inadequacy of its trillion-dollar program, and the Committee on the Present Danger published a report in which it was argued that a 5 percent annual real increase in military spending could not turn back the tendency toward "Soviet superiority." Former ACDA director Fred Iklé contended in an article that the United States needed military appropriations of a trillion dollars not over five years, but every year.[24] The liberal alignment in Congress was alienated and stifled. In such a gloomy situation the Carter administration entered the final year of its rule. The SALT II Treaty and together with it the entire arms control process seemed to be at a dead end.

In a retrospective view of the U.S. debates over SALT II it becomes obvious that by the end of August 1979, especially after the Joint Chiefs of Staff expressed their support of SALT II, the chances were quite good for ratification. But after the Cuban episode the situation sharply deteriorated. The aggravation of international tension, the reaction in the West to the socialist states' support for the national-liberation movement (in particular to direct military forms of this support), not surprisingly was not conducive to an objective evaluation of SALT II. These factors led to the formation in the country of a much broader political faction that regarded SALT negatively or with reservations than had existed in 1972, 1974, or even 1976. And all this significantly predetermined that SALT II's ratification could succeed only in coordination with the toughening of foreign policy and the acceleration of U.S. military programs.

It is worthwhile to note that the Carter administration committed several errors in 1979 that prolonged and impeded even more the Vienna treaty's passage in the Senate. Certain decisions on strategic programs in 1979 that were intended to appease militarist circles in reality produced the opposite effect. In particular, the decisions on the MX missile system and on its basing mode on June 8 and September 7, respectively, did not placate opponents of SALT II. They were dissatisfied with the basing system, considering it too complex and expensive, and blamed the administration for sacrificing military effectiveness to considerations of SALT verification. The militarists interpreted the MX decision as the final recognition by the leadership of the importance of the problem of silo-based ICBM vulnerability, and, thus, recognition of the erroneousness of its initial approach to this problem as well. On the other hand, the adherents of SALT II also were seriously disappointed, thinking that the costs of implementing this program exceeded the advantages of the limitations contained in the treaty. Finally, many of those on whom the president could count for support of SALT II remained aloof from the debates or criticized the administration for plans of developing still more dangerous strategic nuclear arms.[25]

And nevertheless right up until late December 1979 the administration apparently could still have secured the ratification, if not for one additional circumstance. With the aggravation of tension in the world and the growing revelry of the right forces, it was becoming politically unsafe for members of the Senate to vote in favor of the treaty. However, the administration could have forced a vote, having wholeheartedly put all its remaining political capital behind the treaty. In this case the fluctuating alignment in the Senate most likely would not have decided to oppose the president and SALT II. But instead the Democratic leadership itself waited and maneuvered. Weakness and inconsistency, so typical for the Carter administration, and the absence of a coherent policy played a mortal role in the fate of the SALT II Treaty.

The treaty's significance for strengthening security and limiting the arms race has been significantly minimized and eroded. An agreement achieved with such labor ended up being cast to the mercy of the raging political seas.

It is possible that the White House even breathed a sigh of relief after SALT II was "frozen." As Paul Warnke noted, the administration had begun to regard arms control as a burden and a liability.[26] But such a reaction was obviously unfounded. In fact even without a formal failure of the treaty in the Senate the Democratic leadership with this step had resigned itself to the defeat of its own policy. Having sacrificed the Vienna treaty, it inflicted enormous damage on the matter of curbing the arms race and weakened still further its own political positions.

## Moving to a Higher Frontier: The Carter Doctrine and PD-59

The anti-Soviet campaign in which the White House engaged while trying to divert public attention from its inability to resolve the hostage problem noticeably affected sentiments inside the United States. According to public opinion surveys in the summer of 1980, 68 percent of those questioned (versus 27 percent) now considered that the United States was lagging increasingly further behind the USSR in strength and world influence.[27] In the president's State of the Union message to Congress on January 23, 1980, the so-called Carter Doctrine was proclaimed. The president stated: "An attempt by any outside force to gain control of the Persian Gulf region will be regarded as an assault on the vital interests of the United States, and such and assault will be repelled by any means necessary, including military force."[28] If in fact someone was actually trying to control Persian Gulf oil, it was certainly not the Soviet Union; it was the United States, which had declared at will this region to be within its zone of "vital interests." Washington's actions completely confirmed this suspicion. To the Indian Ocean came an armada of three aircraft carriers and more than 20 other ships from the sixth and seventh Fleets. The Rapid Deployment Force, which had been planned as far back as August 1977 by Presidential Directive 18, was formally organized on March 1, 1980 with an orientation to the Persian Gulf

More than four army and Marine divisions, three aircraft carrier battle groups, four tactical air wings, major elements of transport aircraft, heavy weapons cargo-warehouse ships, and so forth were earmarked to it. Negotiations were begun on the construction of U.S. military bases and support points in Oman (Masirah), Somalia (Berbera), and Kenya (Mombasa). The construction of a complex of bases and military installations on the island of Diego Garcia was undertaken on a still greater scale.

In a broader respect, the acceleration of the arms race, the more than 5 percent annual real increase in military spending, the indefinite postponement of the ratification of the SALT II Treaty, the "freezing" of all other arms control negotiations, and the embargo of a number of exports to the Soviet Union were all connected with the Carter Doctrine. Simultaneously, Washington increased its pressure on the NATO allies and Japan in order to subordinate them to the U.S. anti-Soviet line. Officials who had most consistently supported a Soviet-U.S. dialogue and a policy of realism began to abandon the administration. Behind Paul Warnke followed Cyrus Vance, Marshall Shulman, Leslie Gelb, Barry Blechman, and others in 1980 who did not want to accommodate themselves to the changes that had taken place.

The Pentagon's defense policy as a whole reflected the changes in the foreign policy of the White House. Previously it had been repeatedly noted that U.S. military planning was basically concentrated on the European theater and that the simultaneous participation in conflicts in other regions was not likely. Now Brown unambiguously announced that during the past year, we have reevaluated our needs and concluded we need more military capabilities....Our defense establishment could be faced with an almost unprecedented number of demands. And some of those demands could arise more or less simultaneously.[29]

On August 5, 1980 information was leaked to the U.S. press of the fact that President Carter had signed an important document concerning U.S. nuclear strategy—Presidential Directive 59 (PD-59). This provoked a great stir in the press, which prompted a discussion of Washington's adoption of a "new strategic doctrine" and the "sudden turn" in military policy. In reality, PD-59 brought changes of a more modest scale into strategy. However, since they crowned the Carter administration's revision of strategic policy begun in 1978, the final alterations had some importance. PD-59's main distinction from previous strategic concepts was in focusing greater attention on the problems of command, control, and communications ($C^3$). Soviet $C^3$ installations have always been included as one of the basic SIOP sections in Omaha. However, this list was now expanded, and besides targeting the main command centers and communications nodes of the military-political leadership and armed forces, numerous political and economic leadership concentration points were targeted not just in the center but in the outlying regions as well.[30] Whereas earlier a strike on this target set had been considered part of "assured destruction" in the final total stage of a nuclear war, in accordance with the new directive it was added to the category of limited attacks and divided into subgroups of "limited," "selective," and "regional" options.

Programs for increasing the effectiveness of U.S. strategic arms and their command and control systems in the 1970s and even more so in the 1980s served as a prerequisite for augmenting the emphasis on strikes on the Soviet $C^3$ complex and dividing them into special operational spheres of U.S. strategic planning. At the same time the coordination of this concept with the "countervailing strategy"—both in its declaratory and practical aspects—was a much more complex matter for the U.S. leadership, even apart from the adventuristic political ring to the concept of "counter-control" targeting. First, the majority of targets in this category were inseparable from population centers, which essentially made "counter-control" and "assured destruction" equivalent. Second, the Pentagon did not know whether a selective neutralization of the $C^3$ system would paralyze the strategic forces or whether a massed retaliatory strike on all the other side's surviving forces, including the option of "launch on warning," would take place. Thus a strike on the $C^3$ complex could completely nullify the "limited war," "escalation dominance," and "controlled strike exchange" concepts that Brown continued to insist were the most important elements of the "countervailing strategy."

The Presidential Directive of July 25, 1980 also included a number of other new points. Even greater significance than before was given to the effectiveness of nuclear strikes on Soviet strategic forces. In anticipation of the new strategic weapons due to enter the arsenal in the 1980s, the SIOP criteria set for destroying hard targets (ICBM launch silos, command bunkers, and nuclear warhead depots) were increased. The target list for WTO conventional forces was expanded still further in the new SIOP approved simultaneously with PD-59.

Yet another feature of PD-59 was the recognition of the inadequacy of the U.S. $C^3$ system for the posited strategic tasks. In this connection the directive pointed out the necessity of additional programs and organizational measures in this area (with a total cost of around $15 billion over a five-year period) directed at increasing the survivability and flexibility of the U.S. $C^3$ system. In this respect PD-59 was closely correlated with PD-53 and PD-58. PD-53 dictated the necessity of improving the top national leadership's communications with strategic forces "before and after a nuclear exchange." PD-58 stipulated measures for decreasing the vulnerability and increasing the continuity of the functioning of the U.S. leadership, and ensuring the constitutional transfer of power in conditions of a nuclear war.[31]

In justifying their measures, Pentagon representatives broadly cited the "necessity for countermeasures" to certain Soviet "strategic plans" that supposedly assumed the possibility of "victory" both in a short-term and "protracted" nuclear war. However, the main reasons behind the Carter administration's decisions connected with PD-59 were quite different. In the summer of 1980 the election campaign was in full swing. The administration's weakness in the face of the Iranian hostage crisis and the ignominious failure of Desert One on April 24, 1980 exposed the administration even more to attacks from the reactionary alignments that gathered at the Republican Party convention on June 15, 1980 in Detroit. The Republicans' preelection platform became a kind of anthology of the theses of the militarist circles' long campaign. In it the Carter government was accused of cancelling or delaying all of the Ford administration's strategic nuclear programs and reducing military appropriations planned by Ford by $40 billion. On nuclear strategy, the Republican platform noted that

our objective must be to assure the survivability of U.S. forces possessing an unquestioned, prompt, hard-target counterforce capability *sufficient to disarm* Soviet military targets in a second-strike. We reject the mutual-assured-destruction (MAD) strategy of the Carter administration which limits the President during crises to a Hobsen's choice between mass mutual suicide and surrender.[32] (emphasis added)

It is obvious that the sensation in the press over PD-59 was provoked to counter criticism from the right, to create the impression of the offensive and aggressive character of the administration's nuclear strategy, and to emphasize its "counterforce" and multiple option aspects. However, apart from the election-year considerations, the new presidential directive had a deeper and longer-term military-political significance. Essentially, PD-59 was the next stage in the two-decade-long evolution of U.S. nuclear strategy. With a few deviations and retreats, this evolution progressed from principles of totally destroying the opposing side's population and economy to a concept of inflicting "selective damage" while pursuing specific military-political goals (to be sure, always keeping in reserve a potential for a total strike as well). The fundamental motivating factors of this evolution were, first of all, the dynamics of the Soviet-U.S. strategic balance and the formation of an increasingly broader military equilibrium, which compelled Washington to push into the background one massed nuclear strike option after another and adopt ever more selective options; and second, the development of military technology in the direction of increasing the effectiveness, accuracy, and flexibility of using the growing quantity of nuclear warheads.

At the same time PD-59, as well as the new SIOP itself with its attached target list, was regarded by U.S. leaders not only as the guidance for actual operations in the event of war but was in still greater measure considered an instrument of U.S. foreign policy. In his August 20, 1980 speech in Newport, the secretary of defense openly stated:

It is obvious that the details of our planning remain a carefully guarded secret. Nevertheless, fundamental statements of policy can be publicly disclosed, not putting at risk security. Moreover, the American national interest would be very in hand, if our policy of deterrence . . . were understood by both our allies and opponents.[33]

PD-59 and its strategic innovations were yet another step in U.S. attempts to increase the credibility of its threat to use nuclear weapons, to obtain what the apostle of strategic "theology," Herman Kahn, called "a not-incredible first-strike capability." [34] Such a capability was becoming increasingly doubtful for the United States because of the further evolution of the strategic balance on the threshold of the 1980s in favor of a more comprehensive and even parity. While searching for increasingly newer ways to employ its nuclear threat, the United States decided to give greater consideration to the $C^3$ problem and to use it for its own goals.

The U.S. desire to strengthen the credibility of its nuclear threat as a means of pressuring the USSR grew especially in connection with the aggravation of Soviet-U.S. relations and the deadlock in the SALT process that arose in 1980. To a great degree Washington's new initiative was also explained by the desire to reinforce the U.S. nuclear guarantee to NATO. The resumption of direct U.S. military expansion in resource-rich regions of the world created an additional stimulus for the promulgation of PD-59. Plans to use nuclear weapons in the Persian Gulf zone, whose existence had been leaked to the press, were to some degree the administration's response to criticism from the right-wing opposition alleging the "insufficiency" of U.S. capabilities to conduct conventional combat operations there.

* * *

Having come up against a continuous sequence of failures abroad and the growing onslaught of the right-wing alignments inside the United States, the Carter administration in late 1979 and early 1980 turned onto the well-trodden path of the "cold war," of torpedoing détente, and of a comprehensive buildup of military power. But in conducting its policy of confrontation and in accelerating the arms race the Democrats had a much stronger competitor—the right wing of the Republican party and the most aggressive echelons of the military-industrial complex. This extreme right-wing cohort subordinated and later completely swept away the Carter administration, eventually seizing the commanding heights of U.S. state power.

The strategic arms area was but a microcosm of this general political picture. Having come to power at a time when the formation of some basic parameters of strategic parity was being completed (mostly in the numbers of launchers and warheads, along with a more balanced Soviet strategic triad emerging through SLBM deployment), the Carter administration did bring with it some good ideas for "stabilizing" the military balance. In 1977–81—the years of its rule—along with the continued development of a new generation of nuclear weapons systems the actual deployment of strategic arms took place, for a number of reasons, at a lesser rate and scale than over the previous twenty-odd years. However, the new leadership's ideas about SALT and its notion of "strategic stability" were quite detached from reality, hardly considered legitimate Soviet security interests, and frequently did not even conform with U.S. practice. In the Geneva negotiations—of course, not without the influence of the military-industrial complex—these ideas took the form of attempts to secure the United States great unilateral advantages through arms control agreements.

The United States failed to impose discriminative SALT measures on the Soviet Union. At the same time Washington was unwilling to accept all the practical consequences of parity: the necessity of a mutual and balanced calculation of Soviet and U.S. interests; the narrowing of the political role and military usability of nuclear weapons; the legitimacy of certain Soviet advantages in the face of U.S. advantages in other areas (that is, ICBMs vs. SLBMs and heavy bombers); and the growing difficulty of implementing traditional measures of strategic force planning introduced in the era of great U.S. superiority (that is, redundancy, greater-than-expected threat contingency planning, "escalation dominance," and so on). Then the Carter administration, under the growing pressure of the militarists, changed its strategic doctrine. The positions of the right alignments, who criticized the government for the "inequality" of the Vienna treaty and the "insufficient efforts" at building up strategic power, were in this way significantly strengthened.

The Democrats left as their legacy the SALT II Treaty, achieved with great efforts, the ratification of which was in fact doomed to failure. They also left vast military programs, the deployment of which after a number of delays proceeded at an even greater rate. Thus both in this fundamental aspect of Soviet-U.S. relations and foreign policy as a whole, progress not only ceased but was actually reversed. On the threshold of the 1980s, the highly alarming prospect of an uncontrolled nuclear arms race arose before the great powers and the entire world in fundamentally new conditions—in conditions of strategic parity, with the colossal amassed nuclear arsenals and development of dangerous concepts for conducting and possibly winning thermonuclear war in one form or another.

## Notes

1. *Pravda*, June 26, 1979.
2. Roger P. Labrie, *SALT Handbook: Key Documents and Issues 1972–1979* (Washington, D.C.: American Enterprise Institute, 1979), 381.
3. Strobe Talbott, *Endgame: The Inside Story of SALT II* (New York: Harper and Row, 1979), 54–63.
4. *Pravda*, April 1, 1977.
5. Talbott, *Endgame*, 61.
6. Jane E. Stromseth, *The SALT Process*, (Geneva, 1981), 11.
7. Labrie, *SALT Handbook*, 386–87.
8. *Otkuda iskhodit ugroza miru*, 2d ed. (Moscow: Voenizdat, 1982), 73.
9. *Vneshniaia politika Sovetskogo Soiuza i mezhdunarodnye otnosheniia: 1979, sbornik dokumentov*, (Moscow: Mezhdunarodnye Otnoshenie, 1980), 95–97.
10. "The SALT II Treaty, Part 1," *Hearings*, Committee on Foreign Relations, U.S. Senate, 96th Congress, first session (Washington, D.C.: U.S. Government Printing Office, 1979), 81–82.
11. Talbott, *Endgame*, 159–60.

12. *Vneshniaia politika 1979*, 96.

13. *Vneshniaia politika 1979*.

14. *Vneshniaia politika 1979*.

15. "The SALT II Treaty, Part 2," *Hearings*, 105–16.

16. *Department of Defense Annual Report, Fiscal Year 1980*, 72; "The SALT II Treaty," *Hearings*, pt. 1, 90–105.

17. In 1979 it was proposed to construct seven *Ohio*-class submarines by 1986, the funds for which were already completely allocated by Congress. This would raise the number of MIRVed missiles to 1,214 and would compel the United States to remove 14 Minuteman-III ICBMs or 16 Poseidon SLBMs. If this ceiling were to be preserved after 1985, it would be necessary to dismantle with each subsequent *Ohio* SSBN either 24 Minuteman-III ICBMs or two submarines with 32 Poseidon SLBMs.

18. Sergei P. Fedorenko, "Ideologicheskie aspekty sovremennoi voennoi politiki i strategii SShA," in V. I. Gantman, ed., *Razriadka mezhdunarodnoi napriazhennosti i ideologicheskaia bor'ba*, (Moscow: Nauka, 1981), 140.

19. "The SALT II Treaty, Part 1," *Hearings*, 368, 373, 385–431, 483–95.

20. *The Washington Post*, October, 19, 1979, 3.

21. *The Baltimore Sun*, July 28, 1979.

22. *Department of Defense Annual Report, Fiscal Year 1981* (Washington, D.C.: U.S. Government Printing Office, 1980), 2, 14, 16.

23. *Pravda*, October 7, 1979.

24. *The Christian Science Monitor*, January 24, 1980, 6; *The New York Times*, February 5, 1980, 23.

25. Herbert Scoville, Jr., *MX: Prescription for Disaster*, (Cambridge, Mass.: The MIT Press, 1981), 110–111.

26. "U.S. Defense Policy," *Congressional Quarterly*, 1980, 100.

27. *Newsweek*, October 27, 1980, 50.

28. "Carter: America Will Meet Soviet Challenge," *Congressional Quarterly Weekly Report*, January 26, 1980, 171.

29. *Department of Defense Annual Report, Fiscal Year 1981*, 3, 5.

30. Desmond Ball, "Counterforce Targeting: How New? How Viable?," *Arms Control Today*, 2: 2 (February 1981): 7.

31. Ball, "Counterforce Targeting," 7–8; John D. Steinbruner, "Nuclear Decapitation," *Foreign Policy*, 45 (Winter 1981–82): 25.

32. "1980 Republican Platform Text," *Congressional Quarterly Weekly Report*, July 19, 1980, 2049.

33. Harold Brown, "Speech at Naval War College: Official Text," August 20, 1980 (Washington, D.C.: U.S. Government Printing Office, 1980), 5.

34. "First Strike: An Interview with Daniel Ellsberg," *Inquiry Magazine*, April 13, 1981, 16.

# 5

## The Reagan Administration's Military-Political Platform

During the 1980 election campaign Ronald Reagan was asked in an interview why he wanted to become president of the United States. "Maybe those circumstances," he replied, "the experience that I had, has made me believe that I can do what needs to be done." Implicating the age of the Republican leader and his reactionary preelection slogans, a caustic reporter asked: "Would you turn the clock back to the fifties?" To this Reagan quite seriously answered:

Well, maybe in one sense, but then you would have to go back beyond the fifties....One thing is that I believe the American people have the greatest capacity for great deeds of any people on Earth....I want to help us get back to those fiercely independent Americans, those people that can do those great deeds, and I've seen them robbed of their independence....[1]

Behind these ringing phrases there was hardly any specific program of action for solving problems inside or outside the United States at the beginning of the 1980s. Indeed the future president himself did not pretend to be an expert on the economy, foreign policy, or military strategy. In any event, it would be incorrect to consider Reagan's above response and his numerous other statements in the same spirit as simply noncommittal preelection slogans. For in these words were reflected the starting point of the political outlook of the new president and those surrounding him. Speaking of Americans' "robbed independence," Reagan was referring to (since this concerned the domestic situation) state interference in the economy and social welfare programs, significantly expanded in the postwar years, which had been called upon to ease the social-economic contradictions and crisis phemonena of modern capitalism. As for events abroad, Reagan blamed the realities of international life, increasingly felt by the United States, which had driven further and further into the past the notions of U.S. global hegemony—the *pax americana* of the 1940s and 1950s.

Having confided his dream to return to "the good old days," the 1950s and the even more distant past, the leader of the Republicans in this way expressed his rejection of deep changes within the United States and the surrounding world, his unwillingness to recognize their inevitability, and the necessity to adapt to these changes. Referring to a "revival of independence," he was appealing precisely for independence from current realities, for not having to adapt to these realities, but for adapting and adjusting the realities to the interests and goals of the United States. In this respect Reagan and his closest aides saw as their goal the revitalization of the classical motivating forces of private enterprise to effect rapid U.S. economic growth, on whose basis the lost U.S. military superiority over the Soviet Union would be recovered and U.S. economic and political domination in the nonsocialist world restored.

The fact that attempts by the United States throughout the 1970s to adapt itself to the new realities were deeply contradictory and produced extremely ambiguous results should hardly be surprising. But it is astonishing that in the wake of the previous decade, during which the new realities became even deeper and stronger, the right-wing Republican U.S. ruling class and the public supporting it rejected not only the possibility but even the very necessity of adapting to the changed situation. Nevertheless, such a rejection took place, and the administration loudly declared its intention to surmount the objective realities and achieve U.S. global hegemony. Political doctrines and propagandistic declarations in the style of Acheson, Dulles, and the worst days of the "cold war," which, one would have thought, had been completely discredited by history and scrapped in the late 1960s and the 1970s, became fashionable again in official Washington on the threshold of the 1980s. In reinforcing these doctrines the U.S. government initiated a vast set of economic, political, and military measures. The threat of a new world war was growing again.

## Turning Back the Clock: The Republican Leadership's Approach to International Affairs

Researchers and observers disagree on the reasons for what happened on November 4, 1980, the day of the U.S. national elections. But in any event it is impossible not to recognize that Carter did not simply lose the election but, together with the Democratic party and

a major share of the U.S. ruling elite and their corresponding political ideas, suffered a crushing defeat. The Democrats' awkward campaign tactics, the personality of Jimmy Carter, which set Americans'
teeth on edge, his inconsistency and "wimpiness," the peculiarities of
the two-party political system and the U.S. electoral college—all undoubtedly, played a role in the downfall of the Democrats in November 1980. Domestic social-economic and political factors and the
noticeably more conservative mood of the ruling class and the U.S.
public had had significant effect. It is doubtless that foreign policy
circumstances as well played a great role in the elections, especially
the long and intense "Soviet threat" campaign with which the Carter
administration itself had been associated.

Nevertheless, it is necessary to emphasize that the new leadership's
"mandate" in November 1980, especially in foreign policy, was much
less strong, and the support of Reagan's slogans among the American
people significantly less broad, than can be concluded by the results of
the vote. Only 53 percent of all U.S. voters took part in it, and of them
51 percent voted for Reagan (Carter received 41 percent, and independent candidate John Anderson, 7 percent). Subsequent polls showed
that approximately half of this share of the population supported the
Republican candidate only because it did not wish to reelect Carter and
had no better alternative.[2] Thus at most around 14 percent of the voters
stood directly behind Reagan. As columnist George Will noted, "it was
not a national conversion to a conservative ideology. It was a desire to
see Carter gone."[3]

However, the newly elected leadership regarded the election results
precisely as a broad mandate for its ultraconservative slogans. More
important, these slogans themselves were not simply a flirtation, custom-
ary for U.S. campaigns, of aspirants with the right-wing foreign policy
alignments, but fully reflected the world outlook of the new president
and his closest advisers. Indeed, the pronounced swing to the right and
hardening of U.S. state policy on the threshold of the 1980s was caused
by a number of tendencies within the United States and the surrounding
world that had come to fruition long before the events in Iran and
Afghanistan. And the fact that this change, upon which the Reagan
administration based its policy, took such an abrupt and dangerous turn
was also explained by a whole array of attendant points. The ultraconservative faction of the Republican party came to power on a wave of
jingoistic slogans, of the unprecedented rage of militarism and anti-
Sovietism connected with the U.S.-Iranian crisis and the events in Afghanistan. It took advantage of the worsening U.S. economic situation
and the numerous blunders of the Democratic government and President Carter himself, and intended to carry out its reactionary ideas at
any price.

If any observers entertained the hope that after moving into the White House President Reagan and his advisers would begin to shift from the right to the center of the U.S. political spectrum (by analogy with President Richard Nixon in 1969–72), this hope was quickly dashed. The situation in the world and inside the United States was different, and the people who swept down on Washington in search of state posts were different also. The new administration's first political appointees already indicated better than any official statements what the Republicans' policy would be.

Directly involved in the selection of personnel was Reagan's so-called kitchen cabinet—his group of rich friends from California who first had made him governor of the state and then helped him become president.[4] In the military-political bureaucracy the following figures obtained key positions: George Bush as vice president, Caspar Weinberger as secretary of defense, and Donald Regan as secretary of the treasury—all multimillionaires, very conservative, and even extremely conservative representatives of the "establishment." Especially befitting the latter description was Secretary of State Alexander Haig, who in 1972 as Kissinger's aide had called for widening the "carpet bombing" of Hanoi and in 1979 had testified against the SALT II treaty in the Senate. Richard Allen, one of the leaders of the Committee on the Present Danger, became assistant to the president for national security affairs. William Casey similarly became director of the CIA. People who came into the administration's second echelon, to the policy-implementing posts, had reputations still more unambiguous. Richard Pipes, also a former activist of the Committee on the Present Danger and a director of Group B in 1976, was named NSC adviser on the Soviet Union. In the State Department Richard Burt, who invariably opposed SALT II as a reporter for *The New York Times*, became chief of the Bureau of Politico-Military Affairs. In the Pentagon Fred Iklé, a former member of the Committee on the Present Danger and one of the most zealous supporters of increasing the military budget, received the post of undersecretary of defense for policy. Richard DeLauer, a vice president of TRW, Inc., one of the Pentagon's major contractors, became undersecretary of defense for research and engineering. The post of secretary of the Navy fell to one of the "New Right's" leading representatives, John Lehman, also an activist of the Committee on the Present Danger. Richard Perle, in the past a close adviser and supporter of Senator Henry Jackson, occupied the key post of assistant secretary of defense for international security policy.

Still more significant were the nominations to the Arms Control and Disarmament Agency—the main state organ responsible for negotiations to curb military competition. The directorship was given to "superhawk" Eugene Rostow, one of the main supporters of escalating aggression in

Vietnam in the 1960s and the leader of the Committee on the Present Danger in the 1970s. Later, the negotiations in Geneva, the Strategic Arms Reduction Talks (START), were headed on the U.S. side by General Edward Rowny, who had retired from the armed forces and resigned from the U.S. delegation at the Geneva negotiations in 1979 in order to make an unprecedented demand in the Senate for the repudiation of SALT II. And the main U.S. representative in the Geneva negotiations on Intermediate-range Nuclear Forces (INF) was none other than the oft-mentioned Paul Nitze.[5]

The selection of personnel for the military-political bureaucracy in the Reagan administration is very revealing: with the exception of a few figures who had a reputation as moderates, the overwhelming majority of officials belonged either to strongly conservative or openly reactionary circles. The Committee on the Present Danger and the former members of Group B, who took more than 50 such vacancies in all, were represented especially fully in administrative posts. Even if one had tried very hard, one would hardly have been able to find in the United States people capable of inflicting greater damage on Soviet-U.S. relations, on the matter of curbing the arms race. In the words of the U.S. commentator Arthur Macy Cox, in 1980 "the Committee on the Present Danger [took] control of American national security policy."[6]

On the whole, as Soviet scholars Andrei Kokoshin and Yurii Abramov have noted, the composition of the Reagan administration's top bureaucracy, in comparison with previous administrations, reflected the economic influence, perceptibly strengthened in recent years, of the Californian monopolist alignment that had pushed aside the northeastern banking-monopoly-legal establishment as the main traditional supplier of state personnel. Simultaneously, the representation of the patrician "big business" families and European-oriented transnational corporations was comparatively reduced, whereas the participation of the nouveau riche companies (whose interests were closely connected with the Asian-Pacific and Persian Gulf regions and oriented primarily toward the domestic market) and military-industrial corporations was significantly expanded. In place of specialists from the liberal and moderately conservative academic centers and public organizations (such as the New York Council on Foreign Relations, the Brookings Institution, Harvard, and MIT), to many administrative posts at the policy-implementing level came experts from right-wing conservative organizations such as Georgetown University, the Hoover Institution, the American Enterprise Institute, the Heritage Foundation, and the Committee on the Present Danger.[7]

The foreign policy philosophy of the new administration's ruling body, with the various nuances of its separate representatives, on the whole represented a quite monolithic bloc of ideas and notions about the United

States, the surrounding world, the character of existing problems, and the best ways to resolve them. In this respect the Republican leadership significantly differed from its Democratic predecessors, who in their policies had tried to carry out essentially incompatible approaches, the main spokesmen for which were Brzezinski and Vance. One of the most authoritative U.S. political scientists, Stanley Hoffmann, was able to express in a "decalogue" the main theses of the new leadership's political philosophy, which came down to the following:

—The failures of the Carter administration sprang from its lack of a single political philosophy; therefore a unity of views in the administration must be restored.

—The Carter government criminally neglected U.S. power and conducted policy from a position of weakness; therefore the United States' military strength must be revitalized.

—The Soviet Union had significantly increased its military potential and expanded its international influence; therefore the United States must contain and confront the adversary.

—The "hand of Moscow" is behind all regional and local conflicts—therefore the United States and its allies must suppress the "interventionism" of the Soviet Union and its allies in crisis areas.

—The United States must rally as many countries as possible in a united anti-Soviet front.

—The problems and contradictions of relations of the United States with its main allies under Carter were caused by Washington's lack of will and resolve; therefore these difficulties must be eliminated through reviving a hard-line U.S. leadership.

—The first half of the 1980s will be an especially dangerous period because of the "window of vulnerability"; therefore this window must be closed as soon as possible.

—The United States must move from defense to offense in the world arena, search for and exploit Soviet "weak points," and exert strong pressure on Soviet allies and friends.

—The resolution of the developing countries' problems is primarily through "emphasizing their own strengths" and using domestic and foreign free enterprise as the source of development.

—The American people are tired of failures, weakness, and decline and strongly support a policy of strength and resolve.[8]

The Reagan administration's desire to revive a "cold war" policy with its predominant emphasis on military force, exaggerating the political capabilities of U.S. science and technology, declaring messianic ideas, erecting openly hegemonistic and neocolonialist goals, and attempting to create a bipartisan foundation for its policy in Congress all strikingly recalled a stage of history that had long ago passed. One would have thought that its revival had been tightly sealed off by the events of the 1960s and 1970s: by the catastrophic failure of the years of U.S. aggression in Vietnam; by the radical changes of the global correlation of forces and broad transformation of the entire international situation; and by the tangible success of détente and cooperation of states with different social systems. It was as if all of this did not exist for the new U.S. leadership; it "punched a hole" in the wall of history and escaped from these two decades that were saturated by events, full of drama and cardinally important for history and the fate of humanity. On this basis, analyzing the initial period of the Republican leadership's rule, Soviet scholar Genrikh Trofimenko noted: "Presently the U.S. ruling class, after a certain revision under the influence of objective circumstances in the late 1960s and early 1970s of the fundamental concepts of American messianism and power-politics hegemony in the world arena, is returning to its more traditional great power interpretation."[9]

In this connection an exceptionally significant question arises, the answer to which is important not only and not so much for a correct interpretation of history, as much as for an evaluation of the prospects for international politics, peaceful coexistence, and the prevention of nuclear war. If positive changes in U.S. policy were conditioned by objective circumstances on the threshold of the previous decade, then what happened to these circumstances in the early 1980s and why did the Reagan administration find it possible not to reckon with them and in fact to deny their presence generally? In fact the revision of Washington's policy at the time was in no way an act of charity on its part. We recall with what difficulty the first successes of détente were achieved and with how much effort and even victims the realization of the new realities by the U.S. ruling circles and their initial adaptation to them had cost. Undoubtedly, the U.S. international position in the late 1940s and the 1950s had been simpler and more advantageous for them than the situation that arose after the late 1960s. And it is likewise obvious that any U.S. government would prefer to continue a policy of hegemony in the world arena (that is, the policy to which the Reagan administration aspired), if only the insurmountable circumstances and ever-growing costs of that policy would not make its revision a vital necessity in view of the true national interests of the United States itself. Thus the main question raised by Trofimenko largely comes down to the following: what was transient and accidental, and what is objectively inevitable and long-term in U.S. policy? A movement toward détente and negotiations, which prevailed in the early 1970s, or a return to confrontation and an emphasis on competition, which increasingly characterized Washington's policy from the late 1970s and moved from a quantitative accumulation to a new quality with the coming to power of the Reagan government?

## U.S. Foreign Policy Moves in the Early 1980s: Confrontation along All Azimuths

On the international level, the new administration considered a comprehensive buildup of military power abroad the most important lever for turning the course of history in the favor of the United States. At home, correcting the U.S. economic situation as promised to Americans before the elections was at the center of the attention of the president and his closest aides from the very first days. The views of such pillars of bourgeois economic science as Milton Friedman, George Shultz, and George Gilder were taken as the basis for Reagan's economic program (known pejoratively as "Reaganomics"), which was promulgated on February 18, 1981. They argued that all the troubles of the modern capitalist economy resulted from excessive state regulation, which allegedly constrained the "healthy motivating forces" of the free market, private enterprise, and competition. Representatives of the Friedman school contended that to free these forces it was first of all necessary to reduce taxes and give Americans an incentive to make greater capital investments and purchase more. To prevent the reduction of state revenues from leading to a budget deficit and a growth of inflation, they suggested sharp reductions of federal spending. And in order to liberate business from unnecessary expenses and limitations that interfered with increasing profits and labor productivity, social-economic regulations had to be removed to as great an extent as possible. Then, the supporters of this school promised, business activity would develop with a fury, an intensive and inflation-free economic growth would begin, and state revenues would increase continuously in absolute terms, despite a reduction in taxes.[10]

Through precisely this approach the Republican leadership perceived a way out of the U.S. economic crisis that had begun in 1980 and was accompanied by a more than 8 percent drop in industrial production after only six months together with an unprecedented rate of inflation. This ultraconservative economic policy, it must be said, was an integral part of the Reagan administration's overall political world outlook. The president stated that he would not allow the further expansion of government regulation or the growth of the federal budget, that he would free business from the "fetters" of excessive social regulation, reduce taxes to achieve a balanced federal budget, and carry out a limited monetary policy. To offset the planned sharp increase of military spending, he proposed to reduce budget outlays by cutting expenditures for social programs. Under the guise of "New Federalism," he planned to transfer part of these programs to the authority of state and local government. In following this policy, declared Reagan, the United States would enter into a time of "prosperity and abundance for all."[11]

However, without waiting for the sought-after fruits of its economic program, the administration set about rebuilding U.S. foreign policy. In the spirit of the "Soviet threat" campaign Washington's official rhetoric was sharply inflated, and the new U.S. leaders overstepped all permissible norms in anti-Soviet statements, leaving far behind all that had been said on the subject under Carter. In fact it would seem that the president had decided to outdo the provocative attacks of all his fore-runners, even Acheson and Dulles. For example, in one of his first press conferences President Reagan, replying to a question about the feasibility of détente, said:

So far detente's been a one-way street that the Soviet Union has used to promote its own aims....[They are determined] that their goal must be the promotion of world revolution and a one world socialist or communist state....[T]he only morality they recognize is what will further their cause, meaning they reserve unto themselves the right to commit any crime, to lie, to cheat, in order to attain that....[12]

There are grounds for considering that the most important motive of the new administration's official line was a policy to exhaust the Soviet Union economically. In Washington, the thesis that the Soviet economy was allegedly "dangerously overburdened" and "on the verge of collapse" was taken as indisputable dogma. A new round of an accelerated arms race, both nuclear and conventional, both on land and at sea, in the air and in space, according to the designs of U.S. policy-makers, would undermine, so to say, the "Achilles' heel" of the economy of the USSR and other socialist countries. According to their calculations, this would force the Soviet Union to abandon not only military competition with the United States but almost all foreign policy activities in general and would resign it to the status of a "third-rate power." These same goals were called upon to serve the administration's efforts to sever the United States' and its capitalist partners' trade and economic cooperation with the Soviet Union. The goal to thus impede Soviet economic growth was set quite openly. The Reagan administration also demanded curtailing economic ties under the dubious pretense that the Soviet Union uses trade and scientific-technical cooperation with capitalist countries for its defense needs.

This policy was considered so important in Washington that not only the president, his national security adviser, and the secretary of state but even the secretary of defense, who by definition should have been busy with other issues, gave foreign trade paramount attention. For example, in Weinberger's first budget report, the weakness and superficiality of the statements in the strategic sections are striking, and many pages are devoted to the theme of an economic boycott of the USSR.[13]

Finally, still another fundamental element of Washington's policy was the idea of negotiating "from a position of strength." Such an approach, of course, was not a novelty in U.S. politics. But the Reagan administration's line was notable for the fact that it attached no serious importance whatsoever to negotiations and was in no hurry to resume the dialogue broken off by the United States itself in late 1979. The pervasively recognized goal within the administration's top bureaucracy was first to increase substantially the U.S. strategic potential, to achieve strategic superiority, and only then perhaps to take up a dialogue with the Soviet Union. (For what? To accept a Soviet capitulation?) Stated the secretary of defense:

I don't think that we should enter those negotiations from a position of weakness, and I think that we do have to demonstrate that we are gaining strength and improving our strength when we enter into subsequent negotiations of that kind....I would certainly not want to enter it from the point of view of feeling if we didn't get a treaty it was a failure. Sometimes the failure to get a treaty is a success.[14]

The Republican leadership opposed the ratification of SALT II as "not in the interests of national security," and refused to resume negotiations at once on the limitation of strategic and other arms. The avalanche of anti-Soviet rhetoric, declarations in the spirit of irreconcilability and confrontation, that came down from Washington in 1981 and outlined the basic contours of the Republicans' foreign policy itself became a serious factor in aggravating international tension.[15] In practice the Reagan administration undertook an unprecedented increase in military spending, a sharp expansion and acceleration of almost all military programs both in the nuclear and conventional weapons areas with the obvious goal of obtaining overall military-strategic superiority over the Soviet Union.

Events in Poland led to a furious anti-Communist campaign. In response to the imposition of martial law there in December 1981 the United States imposed economic sanctions against Poland and announced an embargo on the export equipment to the Soviet Union for "the deal of the century"—the construction of an enormous gas pipeline from Siberia to Western Europe. Simultaneously the United States began to exert the strongest pressure on the European allies in order to compel them to follow the U.S. example. However, the participants in the contract (West Germany, France, Italy, and even Great Britain) did not wish to follow the United States blindly to the detriment of their own interests and did not yield either to the persuasions or the threats heard from the other side of the Atlantic. The policy of crude economic blackmail and intense political pressure, conceived of in Washington as a model of the new "hard line" and U.S. leadership in the Western world, was a complete failure. It did not have an effect on either the Soviet Union or Poland and was repudiated by the Western European states.

To its consternation, the conservative administration discovered that criticism had been launched against it even from the right. Former Secretary of State Henry Kissinger, now playing the role of "superhawk," blamed the administration for not taking an even "harder line" with respect to the West European allies, for not declaring Poland financially insolvent, and for not demanding payment of its foreign debt in gold from the USSR.[16] Weinberger and U.S. Ambassador to the U.N. Jeane Kirkpatrick had subscribed to this point of view in the administration. But Alexander Haig and his deputies Walter Stoessel and Lawrence Eagleburger considered that such a policy would be a much too risky test of the "resiliency" of alliance relations. Treasury Secretary Donald Regan and Commerce Secretary Malcolm Baldridge maintained that the proposed steps would deliver a most serious blow to the Western banking and credit system in the face of the worsened economic crisis, with unpredictable consequences for NATO.

The failure of U.S. economic sanctions demonstrated before their eyes that a tough policy is much easier to carry out in words than in practice, where U.S. possibilities face quite perceptible limitations. In reality, as Kissinger's former assistant, William Hyland, noted at the time:

The growing web of economic relationships between East and West raised a serious question for American policy: could the United States afford to stand on the sidelines criticizing and carping while this relationship developed? Or should it modify its own position as the basis for attempting to forge a new Western consensus?[17]

In a broader respect as well the Reagan administration's policy, despite its theoretical assumptions, not only did not eliminate the problems in U.S. relations with its imperialist allies but exaccerbated them to an unprecedented extent. The Republican leadership's militant anti-Sovietism, its "dramatic measures" for accelerating the arms race and unwillingness to enter into negotiations to limit military rivalry, its intensified pressure on the allies to increase their contributions to NATO, and the irresponsible statements of U.S. leaders on the possibility of a "limited nuclear war" in Europe—all of these provoked a mass protest movement among the European public. Laying bare the sources of this movement, retired Admiral Gene Laroque emphasized in his speech at a Netherlands peace conference in the spring of 1981 that "there is a feeling that we are moving inexorably toward a nuclear war in Europe. It seems unfair that nuclear war will be fought over and in the nations which have nothing to say about whether nuclear weapons are to be used."[18] Even NATO Secretary General Joseph Luns, who had by no means become famous during the many years of his tenure for peace-making ideas, was forced to scold the Reagan administration timidly for the fact that it had allowed "the impression, albeit false, to grow that it is reluctant to pursue the subject [of arms control] and is preoccupied with the pursuit of military superiority."[19]

It is obvious that the Reagan administration's attempts to resolve all problems and contradictions within NATO at the expense of returning to the economic and military-political dictates of the United States, to a revival of East-West confrontation on the European continent, produced a directly opposite effect. These policies sharply aggravated relations between the Allies and whipped up anti-U.S. sentiments in Western Europe and anti-European sentiments in the United States, including the administration and Congress. Robert Osgood, one of the "elders" of U.S. political science, noted in this connection, in the early 1980s, that

differences between the United States and several of its allies had created a more deep-seated challenge to the cohesion and security of the Atlantic Alliance than any of the half-dozen previous crises. What made this crisis more serious was that it turned upon fundamentally divergent approaches to East-West relations and that it occurred when the United States had lost the economic and military primacy—and therefore much of the confidence of its allies and its influence with them—that it had enjoyed before the 1970s.[20]

The new administration interpreted all international events exclusively through the prism of Soviet-U.S. competition and confrontation. Secretary of State Alexander Haig blamed the Soviet Union for supposedly being the "main source of international instability" and for having allegedly "funded, supported, equipped, and transported Cuban mercenaries" and terrorist groups around the world.[21] Secretary of Defense Caspar Weinberger did his part in pouring oil on the fire:

It would be dangerously naive to expect the Soviet Union, if it once achieves clear military superiority, not to try to exploit their military capability even more fully than they are now doing....This Soviet activity, unchallenged in recent years by the United States, has led to Soviet gains and the growing perception that the Soviets and their proxies can act with impunity. This trend must be halted and then reversed. But that can happen only if we manifest the capability and the will to follow through.[22]

The Republican leadership similarly perceived United States policy toward the developing countries exclusively from the standpoint of confrontation with the Soviet Union, having pushed far into the background the Carter administration's ideas of expanding the West's economic influence on free states, reducing the relative emphasis on direct military intervention, and cultivating reformist, pro-Western regimes as an alternative to revolutionary national-liberation movements. Even the standard "human rights considerations" as applied to relations with developing countries was thrown out. The Reagan government openly proclaimed that the only criteria for choosing allies in the Third World would be the anticommunism or anti-Sovietism of one regime or another, regardless of its domestic policies. Therefore, for the sake of the client's support, it was announced, the United States would be prepared for direct military intervention in any region of the world and in any circumstances of conflict. The fact that the "Vietnam syndrome" had passed—that the public and Congress were no longer unwilling to be drawn into armed adventures abroad—was one of the main features of the Republican leaders' foreign policy doctrine.

It would be incorrect, of course, to forget that the tendency toward conducting politics "from a position of strength", toward intervention in the affairs of other nations, and toward a cavalier disregard of their legitimate rights has always been present in United States international policy. These impulses were often felt even in the best years of détente. But at the same time it is impossible not to see that in the late 1960s and the 1970s, under the inexorable pressure of the new realities in the international arena and inside the country, the United States ruling circles had made a number of steps in favor of adapting to the fundamentally new established situation, in the direction of limiting the use of force abroad, curbing the arms race, peacefully settling international conflicts, and cooperating in the resolution of global problems facing humanity. Even if these steps have been contradictory and frequently inconsistent, their significance should not be underestimated. For when we speak of the policies of the Reagan administration's first years, we speak of the United States departure from preceisely these attempts to accommodate itself to the objective conditions, of the White House's incredible effort to escape from the rigid bounds of the new realities and conduct all affairs, as in previous times, without considering the interests of other nations or wishing to compromise on anything.

That this policy on the threshold of the 1980s was manifested not only in a rather narrow alignment of reactionaries from the "old guard of the cold war" but received a major reinforcement through the comparatively young cohort of the New Right, and that this policy significantly revived certain ruling circles and strata of United States society is a historical phenomenon conditioned by a complex combination of circumstances. Taking the foreign policy side of the question, it is possible to observe that by the early 1980s problems of essentially three kinds stood before the United States.

On the one hand, there were the objective and inevitable aspects of contemporary international relations: the absence of an invulnerable

United States territory in conditions of the accumulated arsenals of nuclear weapons and means of their delivery; the growing dependence on
imported resources and the world economic situation generally; the limits of political influence on the resolution of various international problems; and the necessity of foregoing particular goals in some areas for
the sake of achieving a compromise on the grounds of general interests.
In fact, the majority of the world's countries had been living in such
conditions for a long time and made no tragedy of this. But for the
United States which in former times had found itself in a special position
and which had emerged directly from its relative prewar isloation to a
period of postwar temporary economic and military-political global domination, these circumstances were an unpleasant discovery. Adapting to
them was becoming increasingly more painful by the late 1970s, giving
rise to a desire to put to the test other, easier, but, alas, unrealistic courses
of action. The journalist and former White House staffer James Fallows
described accurately enough this political-psychological tendency:

It is no accident that John F. Kennedy has been invoked more often than
any Republican to bless the administration's programs, for his was the age of
few obvious limits on American power....Yet in the twenty years since his
inauguration, the U.S. has encountered one limit after another, and has de-
scended from a peak of military and economic domination uprecedented in
this century. This descent may have been inevitable, as Europe and Japan re-
built from war, as the world broke into squabbling, independent nations—
and as the Soviet Union did what we were powerless (short of preemptive attack) to prevent, namely build a force of nuclear weapons. However inevitable it may have been, it is nonetheless disquieting, and the current reaction
has the qualities of denial—of wishing away any reminder of how closely the
limits even to mention the possibility of limits is, in the current climate, to
demonstrate a failure of will.[23]

Problems of another order are the consequences of the policies of the
United States in the 1970s, the fruits of the contradiction and inconsistency of its attempts to adjust itself to the new realities. While engaging
in arms control negotiations with the Soviet Union, the United States at
the same time sought to secure unilateral advantages for itself (for example, MIRV) in a number of aspects, which provoked the other side's
justified countermeasures and complicated the position of the United
States itself. Having temporarily refrained from direct military intervention in Asia, Africa, and Latin America after the Vietnam failure,
Washington, in its policy to "elbow out" Soviet influence in the Third
World, made a stake on pro-Western dictatorial regimes, rendered them
broad economic and political support, and supplied them with enormous
arsenals of weapons in order to suppress internal revolutionary forces
at somebody else's hand. And the United States prepared for itself a

series of major defeats when these regimes began to tumble down one after another (for example, Iran under the Shah).

The many problems and complications that arose before the United States in the late 1970s and early 1980s can hardly be explained by a deficit of "American military power" or "a lack of resolve to use force" in the 1970s, as hard-line circles in the West have attempted to show. For the U.S. difficulties and failures would now surely have been even greater if in the past decade the arms had continued still more intensively and if the United States had been involved in new military adventures abroad. The sources of the problems are found in precisely the opposite—the manifested reluctance and inability of U.S. leading circles in the 1970s to go significantly further down the road of fundamentally restructuring Washington's relations with the surrounding world, of justly settling international conflicts with the participation of all sides involved, of considering the legitimate interests of the USSR and its allies, of negotiating broad and radical arms control agreements, and of seeking a general normalization of the international climate.

Finally, the U.S. and Western reaction in general to Soviet foreign policy actions during the second half of the 1970s greatly aggravated existing perceptions. Direct forms of military support of the USSR and its allies to the national-liberation movement and left-radical forces in Africa and Asia were perceived in the West as a broadening "Communist expansion" that had to be stopped by any means, including military confrontation. The Warsaw Pact's efforts to strengthen its conventional forces in Europe and the programs of the USSR to modernize and improve its strategic and theater nuclear arsenals were looked upon in the United States as a determined policy aimed at achieving military supremacy at all levels of military power. Obviously, this Western perception of the policy of the USSR and its allies, the scale of the negative reaction in the United States, and the magnitude of U.S. counteractions were greatly underestimated in Moscow and in some cases simply misunderstood or indignantly rejected.

In this connection the abrupt shift that took place in U.S. policy at the turn of the decade is not only explainable but to some extent even natural. History, and not just U.S. history, has provided more than a few examples of how a country's inability or reluctance to revise consistently and fundamentally its policy in accordance with the changed realities entails growing difficulties and failures that, in turn, engender a desire to return to the past, brush aside entirely the complexities of the objective situation, and disregard the new realities. At best this tendency leads to the stagnation and deterioration of many aspects of the life of a nation and at worst, to crisis or even catastrophe.

All of the above, however, does not mean that the positive changes in U.S. policy of the early 1970s and détemte were a historical accident caused by a temporary confluence of domestic and foreign circumstances, and that the U.S. shift in favor of confrontation and its bid for military superiority is a return, so to speak, to the "normal" state of affairs. Precisely to the contrary, the positive changes in the early 1970s were objectively inevitable and necessary: they reflected fundamental and irreversible changes in the world arena. Thus Washington's policy in the early 1980s is an attempt to escape from reality, to veer from the path preordained by objective world processes. In the November 1982 Plenum of the CPSU's Central Committee it was emphasized that "the 1970s, which passed under the banner of detente, were not, as certain imperialist figures are contending today, an accidental episode in the difficult history of humanity. No, the policy of detente is in no way a stage which has passed. The future belongs to it."[24]

U.S. policy in the early 1980s, independently of the desire and intentions of its creators, confirmed this truth in its own way. It is indisputable that Washingon saw as its task to sharply aggravate international tension and whip up the arms race, and such a task was fulfilled. However, in and of itself this scarcely can be considered the only goal of foreign policy. Its goals, obviously, must consist in exerting influence in the direction necessary for the United States on U.S. adversaries as well as on allies and supporters in the international arena. It is here that the preliminary results of the Reagan administration's policy in the first half of the 1980s are highly problematical, but to some extent indicative as well. Having badly complicated the entire world situation, the Republican administration could hardly boast of any major sucesses or achievements, not only in comparison with the Nixon and Ford administrations but even with the Carter government, which Reagan and his supporters had most zealously attacked for the inconsistency and fruitlessness of its foreign policy.

It is obvious that the explanation for this should be sought not only and not so much in individual virtues, in the level of intellect and professional training of one leader or another in the administration. Thus the Republican leadership's initial foreign policy philosophy, which proved quite useful as a club for beating the Carter government during the election campaign, turned out to be a poor means for implementing foreign policy in reality, for working out a purposeful policy around which could be united if not the public and Congress, then at least the administration itself. The apparent simplicity and integrity of its philosophy had the pleasing shape of castles in the air that, upon contact with the ground, immediately begin to tumble down

Former U.S. Secretary of State Cyrus Vance described the political views of the administration's leaders in the following way:

Their rhetoric is very strongly anti-Soviet. It implies that the source of most problems that arise around the world is Moscow, and that therefore that problems presents a basic confrontation between East and West. I think that's a vast oversimplication and is incorrect and will lead us into making erroneous decisions. The world is much more complex than that. It is a world of great change. It is a world where problems which have local roots—economic, political and social—have produced local conflicts which can only be resolved by dealing with the grassroots causes, and not by trying to make it into an East-West confrontation. And if we don't realize that and we don't attack those problems in a way that gets at the root causes, we are going to get ourselves into situations where we will make great mistakes and perhaps get hurt.[25]

The past years of the administration's rule have provided a great number of confirmations to Vance's forecast. Despite every kind of intensification of tension and unprecedented buildup in military preparations, Washington did not manage to achieve its main goal—to crush the realities of the contemporary international situation, to fit them on the procrustean bed of its unrealistic and reactionary foreign policy philosophy. The opposite happened earlier: in colliding with objective conditions, U.S. policy in practice disintegrated into uncoordinated measures, not only insufficiently interconnected, but frequently contradicting each other and leading to unpredictable results. With time, analysts and commentators in the United States and Western Europe began to speak increasingly more seriously about this situation. For example, Stanley Hoffmann wrote that the past period of the Republican administration's activities has had two features:

The first is the frequent incoherence that results from the tug-of-war between ideology and reality, between assertion and accommodation. The second is the absence of a genuine foreign policy in a number of important spheres because of the wide gap between Reagan's dogmas and the world.[26]

Robert Osgood, hardly a liberal analyst, observed:

The overriding goal of the Administration's foreign policy was to make American and Western power commensurate to the support of greatly extended global security interests and commitments....In pursuit of this goal the Administration's determination to increase the U.S. defense budget was clearer than its strategy for applying military resources to foreign policy requirements.[27]

Even so conservative a foreign policy expert as Robert Tucker cautioned:

A period of withdrawal and passivity has come to an end. If it is to be succeeded by a period of America everywhere resurgent and activist, we will risk jeopardizing those interests that are critical to the nation's security and well-being.[28]

Analyzing the political actions of the Republican leadership in the first half of the 1980s, one may divide them conditionally into four categories. Into the first go those cases in which the administration's political world view has turned out to be completely inapplicable and policy has had to be worked out in a purely practical way. They include the government's inability to guarantee a deficit-free federal budget while at the same time reducing taxes and sharply increasing military spending; Washington's approach to the issue of China and Taiwan[29]; simultaneous arms transfers to Israel and Saudi Arabia; and the war between Great Britain and Argentina over the Falkland Islands (Malvinas) in the summer of 1982. U.S. zigzags in 1986–87 in the Iran-Iraq conflict could also be included. The second category concerns those areas of international politics in which the U.S. administration's attempts to follow its ideology in practice has had dangerous consequences or produced an effect opposite to that expected in Washington. This pertains, for example, to the U.S. efforts to impose at any cost a policy of economic blockade of the USSR on its Western European allies; to the U.S. policy of encouraging the aggressive actions of Israel in the Near East and South Africa in its region of the African continent; and to Washington's general policy in the sphere of arms sales and nuclear nonproliferation. In the third category are those issues in which by virtue of objective circumstances the government was forced to adapt itself, retreating from its initial position. Finally, the fourth category constitutes a broad range of problems, in which sometimes dogmatism and sometimes pragmatic adaptation alternately win over policy, rendering it inconsistent and ineffective.

Beside the examples enumerated above there are many other cases that fall under one section or another or under several at once. But perhaps no other sphere of the Reagan administration's policy can provide a clearer illustration of all the aforementioned categories, taken together, than its course of action in the arena of military policy, strategy, and arms programs.

## Power Politics: The Gap between the Desirable and the Possible

Since the core of the Republican administration's political designs was to revive the conduct of politics "from a position of strength," emergency measures for building up military power were not to be kept waiting long. The bounding growth of the military budget, the sharp intensification and expansion of arms programs, was the red thread running through the Reagan administration's policy. Moreover, the unprecedented peacetime acceleration of the arms race became, as if an end in itself, almost the main feature of U.S. foreign policy. And this, generally speaking, is quite explainable. To pile up mountains of weapons while

Congress releases the necessary appropriations is much easier than solving the real international problems. Here one need not fear direct confrontation from without or opposition from within for some time. Here it is easier to show "courage" and "resolve." Therefore, as the blunders and failures of the Reagan administration's policies within the United States and abroad became increasingly obvious, the administration's persistence in whipping up the arms race only grew all the more.

Defense Secretary Weinberger's first speech in the Senate on March 4, 1981 contained quite panicky pleas on developing the theme of the USSR's "colossal military buildup" and global "military-political offensive." "It is critical to recognize, however," said the secretary, "that it is the across-the-board suppression of past defense budgets that is the direct cause of the need now for across-the-board increases." Amendments proposed by the Pentagon to the previous administration's defense budgets (in the 1981 and 1982 fiscal years) totaled almost $32 billion. This meant a real increase of outlays (total obligational authority) in comparison with the Carter request for this same period by more than 13 percent.[30] Besides increasing combat readiness, enlarging reserve forces, and upping the salaries of military personnel, this budget supplement was earmarked for expanding the DoD's previous procurement program of arms and combat supplies, in particular for buying an additional 170 aircraft and helicopters, 700 tanks and armored personnel carriers, 200 pieces of artillery, and 6,000 various tactical missiles and guided munitions. The greatest share of the resources requested ($8.2 billion) was allotted, however, to increasing the shipbuilding program for the Navy and Rapid Deployment Force (in total to nine ships and vessels).[31] As for strategic arms, $2.4 billion were earmarked for developing a new heavy bomber to replace the B-52, although the usual air force special investigation was needed to determine the specific type of new system. Additional outlays ($130 million) were also allotted to the development of an ABM system.

The administration advanced a program for a colossal increase of military spending over the long term. In place of Carter's trillion-dollar program came Reagan's more than one-and-one-half-trillion-dollar program. In accordance with the latter the annual real growth of the military budget was already projected not at 5 percent but at more than 7 percent. In current dollars the DoD budget for five years was to increase from $222 billion in FY 1982 to $368 billion in FY 1986. This meant that the share of military spending in the U.S. gross national product would grow for that period from 5.9 percent to 7.2. percent, and in the total federal budget, from 25 percent to approximately 35 percent.[32] Such an unprecedented peacetime increase of military appropriations is even more striking, considering that quite detailed and long-term budget projections had been planned long before even the most general contours of

U.S. military-political strategy in the 1980s had become clear, not waiting for the formation of strategic concepts and decisions on the main arms programs. From this one cannot help but conclude that the abrupt increase in military spending was largely considered in Washington a political action as well. The Center for Defense Information, a liberal research organization in Washington, emphasized that

military budgets have recently been used by politicians as vehicles for sending "messages" and "symbols" of will and intention. As Mr. Weinberger said at the start of the Administration, "a time has come when we should be seen as getting stronger"; ergo, we should spend more money.[33]

The innovations of the Republican administration's military strategy became apparent in the course of 1981 in the speeches and reports of Pentagon officials, in separate decisions on military programs, and in a summarized respect—in Weinberger's first budget report (for FY 1983) on February 8, 1982. Most prominent was the greater, in comparison with the preceding administration, emphasis on the possibility of using nuclear weapons in both the TVD and globally and, in turn, on the growth of the share of strategic nuclear programs in the Pentagon's budget. "This Administration does not regard nuclear strength as a substitute for conventional strength," explained Weinberger in his report.

However, it does place the highest priority on the long overdue modernization of our strategic forces. While this modernization program is not designed to achieve nuclear "superiority" for the United States, by the same token, we will make every necessary effort to prevent the Soviet Union from acquiring such superiority and to insure the margin of safety necessary for our security.[34]

The real meaning of the "margin of safety" concept will be explored in greater detail below, but here it need only be noted that the share of appropriations for strategic programs, on average 10 percent of the DoD budget in the 1970s, grew under the new government to 15 percent.

Even with the relative growth of the share of appropriations to nuclear weapons, the overwhelming absolute share of fiscal resources added by the Reagan administration to Carter's five-year program went to conventional forces. This was connected with the significant expansion of tasks put before them. One of the first and major steps of the Reagan government in military strategy was in officially repudiating the "one-and-a-half war" doctrine, which from the early 1970s determined the sizes and plans of U.S. conventional forces and provided for the capability of simultaneously conducting a conventional "large war" in Europe and a limited military operation (such as the Marines' excursion into

Lebanon in 1958) in another region of the world. The change of basic strategic doctrine in the conventional forces area was conditioned by plans for U.S. military expansion in the Indian Ocean basin, by the spearhead aimed at the Persian Gulf, which was considered as the probable theater for a second "large war" apart from the European continent.

In this connection it is appropriate to recall that plans for military intervention in Southwest Asia appeared much earlier and had been definitively consolidated in the so-called Carter Doctrine in early 1980. The distinction here in the new leadership's approach was that earlier the Pentagon had assumed that the conventional forces already possessed by the United States, apart from their main concentrations oriented toward the European TVD, would be sufficient for use in other regions.

Proceeding from this assumption, the overall size of conventional forces under the Carter administration was determined in accordance with the "one-and-a-half war" doctrine, and emphasis was laid on preparing forces of the strategic reserve for combat operations in various climates and conditions, with the use of different arms and tactics. Ensuring military plans in the Indian Ocean zone under the Carter Doctrine was to be chiefly accomplished not through enlarging the size of the armed forces, but through expanding U.S. air- and sea-lift capabilities, securing for troops the right to use in-place air bases and ports, and also permanently deploying in the Indian Ocean cargo ships with heavy weapons (which are difficult to deliver with transport aircraft). To the Rapid Deployment Forces were added from the existing force structure four divisions, four tactical air wings, and three aircraft carrier battle groups,[35] which were to be specially trained and equipped for combat operations in the burning deserts around the oilfields of the Persian Gulf.[36]

Under the Reagan administration this approach began to be revised. In his March 1981 speech Weinberger, having groundlessly blamed the Soviet Union for encroaching upon the raw material resources of the Persian Gulf, announced: "We cannot deter that effort from 7000 miles away. We have to be there. We have to be there in a credible way."[37] In the February 1982 budget report the secretary expressed himself even more definitely: "Successful defense depends upon early arrival of U.S. forces—indeed upon their being in place in favorable defensive positions before any major Soviet penetration is achieved."[38] Such a phrasing of the question obviated the necessity for Washington to substantiate "the existence of a threat" in one region or another in order to justify U.S. military presence there. Essentially, it was said that even before obtaining the "facts" of "Soviet intervention," U.S. intervention must be implemented, and if such "facts" subsequently turn out to be nonexistent, then it is only because of U.S. operations put into effect ahead of time. Thus the defense against the "Soviet threat" of practically any region of the world could be justified by way of establishing a permanent U.S. military supremacy in that region.

In addition, the administration did not intend to be limited to the Persian Gulf. The U.S. secretary of defense emphasized in this respect: "While security requirements for Southwest Asia and Europe loom particularly large in our budget, our commitments and interests in other regions will not be neglected. We have important obligations toward our allies in Asia and the Pacific region and toward our friends in Africa. We have a vital concern for the peace and stability of Central America and the Caribbean."[39] So what remained outside of the sphere of U.S. "vital interests" and planned military intervention? Only Antarctica, it would seem. Here was in fact not a return to the "two-and-a-half war" doctrine of the 1960s but the creation of the capability to conduct simultaneously two "large wars" and several local military operations in such distant and isolated regions as Europe, Northeast and Southeast Asia, southern and East Africa, or Central America.

The reorientation of U.S. military planning in this direction was linked with another new strategic concept—the so-called notion of horizontal escalation. It held that in the event of a Soviet-U.S. conflict in any crisis point of the planet Washington would not limit itself only to operations in the given region, especially if the situation there were unfavorable to the United States. In this event it was planned to unleash military operations in other regions more advantageous to the United States, for example, against states friendly to the USSR located far from Soviet territory, such as Cuba, Vietnam, Angola, and Ethiopia, or even to inflict strikes on certain points on the Soviet Union's periphery, such as naval bases and other important installations.[40] In practice this was a most dangerous prescription for the rapid transformation of a local crisis into a global conflict with its subsequent unpredictable escalation.

Still another clearly expressed demonstration of the cavalier U.S. treatment of the interests of peace was the concept of "offensive operations" advanced by the Defense Department. According to a statement by Weinberger, it is impossible to transposition

the defensive orientation of our peacetime strategy onto the strategy and tactics that should guide us in the event of war. A wartime strategy that confronts the enemy, were he to attack, with the risk of our counteroffensive against his vulnerable points, strengthens deterrence and serves the defensive peacetime strategy.[41]

The concept of a "protracted conventional war," which envisaged wearing down the enemy in conventional combat operations through "horizontal escalation" and "offensive operations" in directions favorable to the United States before moving to nuclear weapons, was subordinate to this same idea.

Maintaining that U.S. military doctrine has a defensive character, Washington at the same time put before U.S. armed forces the task to prepare for active, long-term, and deep offensive operations "in the event of war." The other side, it appears, was to have staked its security and put its faith in U.S. declarations that troops offensively oriented in arms and equipment, in deployment and operational plans, would be used exclusively for a "counteroffensive," but in no way for a surprise attack. Of course, such a phrasing of the question is unacceptable. In our time, when the military correlation of forces has become the most important factor of politics, the intentions of a state are judged not by words but by deeds, in particular by its measures in developing its armed forces. Their orientation to aggressive operations "in the event of war" is incompatible with a "defensive" character "in peacetime," considering the situation of the nearly continuous confrontation of the two massed groupings of armed forces, oversaturated with modern technology and destructive weapons, including nuclear, maintained in a high state of readiness for combat operations, and trained to resolve in the shortest period the greatest tasks of crushing the enemy. Therefore the preparation of plans and material capabilities for widescale offensive operations, despite the reasonings of Weinberger and his advisers, in no way strengthens "deterrence," but increases the probability of unleashing war, sharply intensifying the stimuli for either a surprise attack or a preemptive strike.

U.S. measures in practice in the area of developing its armed forces, much more persuasively than official declarations, are indicative of the true character of U.S. military doctrine. U.S. naval forces have received the greatest share of the enormous program to purchase arms, whose proportion in comparison with other types of armed forces has become still more overwhelming under the Reagan administration. Secretary of the Navy John Lehman, one of the most outspoken representatives of the New Right, stated plainly: *"Our national goal must never be less than clear maritime superiority* . . . .Simply put, we must be able to put the Soviet fleet on the bottom if they attempt to interdict our free use of the sea"[42] (emphasis in original). The navy's shipbuilding budget for the 1983–87 period doubled and reached $96 billion (in comparison with $45 billion under the Carter administration). The Reagan administration intended to build and modernize 150 ships and submarines with this money, including two gigantic nuclear-powered aircraft carriers (yet another one was planned for later). It proposed to enlarge the size of the active combat fleet from 460 to 600 ships by the early 1990s, and the number of large aircraft carriers, from 13 to 15. It was also decided to renovate and return to active duty an old aircraft carrier and four World War II-vintage battleships and to reconfigure the latter to fire SLCMs.

Under the leadership of John Lehman, the navy took a course to move from a "one-and-a-half ocean" fleet to a "three-ocean" fleet, that is, to a permanent, broad naval presence with the aim of exerting political pressure and demonstrating force in the Atlantic, Pacific, and Indian oceans. This force was concentrated around powerful aircraft carrier battle groups and large Marine contingents. In the event of war, the emphasis of operational planning was to be shifted from the defense of sea lines of communication, along which troop and supply convoys would have sailed to transoceanic TVDs, to the classical methods of U.S. naval strategy—striking the enemy's fleet, hitting the enemy's coast with sea-based air strikes, and landing massed troops. Thus the navy also responded to Weinberger's strategic concepts of "horizontal escalation" and "offensive operations." Lehman's enthusiasm was especially aroused by the scenario in which U.S. nuclear-powered aircraft carriers under the powerful cover of anti-air and antisubmarine escort would sail right up to Soviet shores and conduct a Pearl Harbor on Soviet naval bases.

Lagging behind the navy in appropriations, the other branches of the armed forces and their industrial contractors also attempted to snatch a larger piece of the ensuing budgetary windfall. In view of the significant expansion of strategic tasks, the army requested that the number of active divisions be increased from 16 to 20 (at the height of the Vietnam war there were 19), and substantially widened the plans for purchasing the latest armored tanks (the M-1 tank production program alone grew to 7,000 units), combat helicopters, mobile air defense complexes, and chemical weapons for increasing the offensive power of land forces. The air force recommended deploying in addition to the available active and reserve tactical air wings another five air wings (around 400 aircraft), with an emphasis on the latest fighter-bombers for achieving air superiority and deep strikes in the enemy's rear. The Marines requested new troop transport ships, attack aircraft, and VSTOL fighters. To expand the capabilities for rapidly transferring troops and combat equipment to overseas bridgeheads, it was decided to construct in addition to the 70 existing gigantic C-5A Galaxy military-transport aircraft another 50 such planes. It was also calculated that the planned expansion of the armed forces' structure required the additional recruitment of 200,000 servicemen beyond the 2.1 million men available in the active forces.[43]

The plans for substantially increasing the overall size of the U.S. armed forces, which Reagan publicly approved in his May 1981 speech at West Point, along with their intensified modernization, fully responded to the overall thrust of the Republican leadership's foreign policy. Washington's attempts to revive "containment" and "roll back communism" in the 1980s, as if to return to the pre-Vietnam period, were accompanied by military measures that, at a much higher qualitative level of arms and combat equipment, in a quantitative respect greatly resembled the powerful surge of the military buildup undertaken by the United States two decades earlier.[44]

In this connection, as well as in the analysis of Reagan's entire foreign and military policy, the question arises: What was the Republican leadership counting on, putting before itself the task of "turning back the clock?" How did it propose to overcome or get around the new realities, which from the late 1960s and first half of the 1970s had forced its predecessors to undertake a pronounced reduction of U.S. commitments and military presence abroad, to recognize the emergence of perceptible limitations on the capability for U.S. armed intervention everywhere? Why did the new administration think that it would not have to take into consideration those same factors that had compelled Washington ten tears earlier to carry out a reduction of excessive military spending (which was undermining the economy) in real terms and be reconciled with reducing in a number of quantitative parameters the inflated armed forces, not only in comparison with the peak of the Vietnam war but in comparison with the early 1960s as well?

The basic assumptions upon which these pretentious military concepts and plans rested were first of all that the administration's economic policy would provoke a furious and inflation-free upsurge of industrial activity, which would permit a sharp increase in military appropriations and a wider and more intensive introduction of the achievements of U.S. scientific-technical progress into the arms sphere. Furthermore, it was assumed that the massive and long-term swing to the right of U.S. public opinion, in contrast to that of the early 1970s, would allow a purposeful increase of military power and the conduct of an aggressive policy abroad. In addition, it was pointed out that expanding U.S. interventionist forces to the approximate size of the early 1960s would provide a capability for their use in the Persian Gulf zone and other crisis regions. Finally, Washington seriously hoped that U.S. allies, who had since become significantly stronger economically and militarily, would assume even greater responsibilities for collective defense in Western Europe and the Far East, freeing U.S. hands even further for preparing aggression in other regions.

But as was true for the Reagan administration's entire foreign policy, the main problem of its military-political policy was that this scheme was completely detached from real life. Therefore, the chief difficulties for the administration arose when it tried to move from general arguments to the formulation of a more concrete strategy, in which the practical ways of achieving set goals with a calculation of available resources and obstacles confronting the United States should have been defined.

The new leadership placed its main hopes on the idea that "Reaganomics" would provoke a furious economic advance. However, as warned so authoritative an economist as John Galbraith, in the present conditions of state-monopoly capitalism, the economy did not wish to answer to governmental measures, which were designed for the classical "free market" of the distant past.[45] The enormous increase of military spending not only did not allow for a reduction of the federal budget deficit but entailed its unprecedented growth.[46]

Reagan's economic policy, of course, did not provide the promised "prosperity for all." Its social-economic effect was quite eloquently described by the American specialist Ralph Nader:

The omnibus slogan for the language of mandate was "Getting government off your backs." Behind the semantic curtain something quite serious was going on in the Reagan Administration. Power was being reshuffled in the age old game of politics but this time swiftly away from consumers, small taxpayers, receivers of social programs and workers toward large corporations, especially the multinational corporate type. Not that these popular constituencies ever had that much control under previous administrations. However, the shift to more concentrated power in the hands of the few certainly became more pronounced. The rich are indeed getting richer and more powerful and the middle class and poor are finding their meager economic and political assets slipping, the former less able to buy homes and find jobs, and the latter less able to receive sustenance for the bare necessities of life. . . .

Many Americans must be puzzled by what reducing child immunization and infant nutrition programs or weakening nursing home inspection enforcement standards have to do with getting "government off the backs of the people" or lessening "big government" for that matter. . . .

What is really at work here is the dismantling of government's traditional public role in defending victims abused by established private powers. Reagan's government is getting off the backs of the powerful who coerce the powerless. This translates into a loss of freedom from corporate toxic waste dumps, price-fixers, joblessness, racialism, sexism, and dangerous products or services.[47]

In the face of an unprecedented federal budget deficit and the severe cutback of social programs, the colossal program of increased military spending began to provoke the increasing dissatisfaction of significant strata of the U.S. public. It is indicative that whereas in September 1980 19 percent of the participants in a Harris survey stated that the government's main task is to guarantee U.S. military power, by May 1981 (that is, only eight months later) the proportion of supporters of this point of view fell to 8 percent. In February 1981 54 percent of those surveyed by Harris approved of Reagan's military-political policy, but already in June of the same year the number declined to 48 percent, and 47 percent were opposed.[48] Not surprisingly, the administration's fiscal policy and its program of excessive military appropriations aggravated the ever-present "guns vs. butter" contradiction in state spending. In this connection the Soviet specialist Yurii I. Bobrakov correctly stressed that "the planned unprecedented escalation of military spending is the main factor in the destabilization of the U.S. financial system. At the same time it is radically undermining the administration's very program for 'reviving the economy' and increasingly leading 'Reaganomics' to a dead end."[49] The Reagan administration's measures, openly oriented toward the interests of the most well-to-do of society, the apex of the U.S. exploiting class, provoked the aggravation of class contradictions, and in effect rubbed salt into the social-economic wounds of capitalism.

While striving to enlarge U.S. armed forces across the board for global interventionism, the Pentagon's leadership neglected such factors as the steady rise in real costs of arms and combat supplies. For example, each new M-1 tank cost $2.7 million—three times more than the M-60 tank it replaced; the new Bradley armored personnel carrier was 24 times more expensive than the previous model ($1.9 million versus $80 thousand apiece); a new navy carrier-based F-14 fighter came to $44 million, whereas the F-4 aircraft that was being replaced had a cost of $3 million. Especially striking was the growth of the cost of ships: a new missile cruiser cost 1 billion dollars, a multipurpose nuclear-powered submarine, $900 million, not to mention a nuclear-powered aircraft carrier at $3.5 billion. Norman Augustine, president of Martin Marietta Aerospace division, a major military contractor, calculated in his spare time that from the time of the Wright brothers' plywood aircraft to the modern supersonic fighter, the cost of an individual aircraft has grown, on average, by a factor of four every ten years. If such a trend were to continue, Augustine concluded, "in the year 2054 the entire defense budget will purchase just one tactical aircraft." Of course, new weapon systems and technologies are always more improved than the old, though many specialists have begun to believe that the growth of their cost outstrips by far the increase in their effectiveness.[50]

The arms race program planned by the administration put an enormous burden as well on both the U.S. financial system and U.S. industry. The chairman of the president's Council of Economic Advisers, Murray Weidenbaum, warned in this connection: "I am worried that we might be going faster, on a bigger scale than our economy can sustain."[51] The military monopolies, who received a guaranteed profit of 5–12 percent and more in their contracts, were not at all interested in increasing the economy and efficiency of production. And according to estimates of Congress's Joint Economic Committee, the real cumulative costs of the Pentagon's 1983–87 arms programs were to exceed the official estimate, at a minimum, by $80 billion.[52]

The accelerated arms race promises to intensify significantly the rivalry between the military and civilian branches of industry for scarce equipment, raw materials, and skilled workers. If in the next few years in accordance with the laws of the business cycle any prolonged revival of the economy begins in the United States, then the competition between the military and civilian branches of industry may become a serious problem. First of all, according to the opinion of experts, it will provoke a spillover of inflation from the military to the nonmilitary sectors of the economy, and in the future the acceleration of the arms race, profitable only to the 150 or so largest military firms, threatens to create great obstacles for the development of the United States economy as a whole.

The situation was hardly facilitated by the decision-making system established in the Pentagon. Weinberger came to the post of secretary of defense without having the slightest idea about issues in military policy, strategy, or weapons systems. The actual implementation of U.S. military policy, with the exception of several special cases, was fully transferred to those organizations that manage the development, production, and operation of weapons systems and the drawing up of operational plans for their use, that is, to the branches and agencies of the armed forces and their scientific, design, and industrial contractors. In the words of one of Weinberger's predecessors:

You have to start with foreign policy, and then you make defense strategy, and then you get down to force budgets. . . . Cappy's like a kid going into F.A.O. Schwartz and buying all the toys on the shelf. The services aren't being managed.[53]

The Reagan budgetary windfall that came to the military and its partners in business even entailed the improbable overallocation of resources, inspired by the military-industrial complex. Information about this leaked to Congress and in early 1983 provoked a genuine scandal. Franklin C. Spinney, a Pentagon analyst, appeared before the Senate Armed Services Committee. With facts and figures in hand Spinney proved to the astonished senators that military programs, whose costs had been misjudged by the Pentagon, exceeded by $500 billion the $1.6 trillion military appropriations planned by the administration for a five-year period.[54]

At the same time, the personal qualities of Weinberger or the peculiarities of the decentralized administrative system he introduced were hardly the main sources of the growing uncontrollability of the branches of the armed forces and their industrial contractors. A more important reason for this situation was the Republican leadership's lack of any clear and coherent strategy by which the secretary and his assistants could have recarved the requests of the military services and monopolies in order to reflect the overall military-political interests and capabilities of U.S. ruling circles. To be sure, the overall aggressive thrust of the leadership's arguments and concepts and its desire for military superiority was not to be doubted. But it was impossible to understand by precisely which measures superiority was conceived, in which ways the administration planned to achieve it, and how it was proposed to be used in practice. Still more concretely, exactly which arms and capabilities, supposedly neglected by Carter, did the Republican leadership decide to place at the service of military superiority? In answer to all these questions Weinberger explained with pride that according to the Republicans' five-year program, in comparison with that of the Democrats, it was proposed to purchase 29 percent more tanks and 36 percent more helicopters. Production of tactical aircraft was to be increased by 15 percent, and the navy's combat fleet was to be 15 percent larger by the early 1990s than that which had been planned by the Carter administration.[55]

These plans, although impressive, did not however provide an answer to the main posited questions. Professor Stanley Hoffmann pointed out in this respect: "More of everything is not a policy.... Neither in the conventional nor in the nuclear realm has the Administration offered a strategic doctrine that would provide a rationale for the catalogue of measures it has announced."[56] Robert Osgood in turn recognized:

This ambitious target, however, was arrived at without the benefit of any comprehensive strategic review, and it depended on equally ambitious targets of growth in domestic economic production. The scattershot approach to defense spending, along with Secretary of Defense Caspar Weinberger's decentralization of the management of programs and resources into the hands of the separate armed services, meant that defense expenditures would be undisciplined by strategic guidance until budgetary and other constraints compelled choices among priorities.[57]

Expressing the bewilderment of many Capitol Hill officials, Congressman Les Aspin, an authority on military issues, said:

I don't have any idea what this Administration's defense policy is. And I read the posture statement and I still don't know. And I listen to Fred Ikle and I still don't know. To paraphrase Will Rogers, I think this Administration has never seen a weapons system that it didn't like.[58]

Even so conservative an expert as John Collins, who in the late 1970s had devoted a great personal effort to propagandizing the "Soviet threat" campaign, especially throughout Congress, conceded that "if you don't know what you want to do, you can't plan how to do it." Finally, even Edward Luttwak, perhaps Weinberger's most bellicose consultant, was forced to recognize that "in lieu of strategy at all levels we have only budgeting, programming, and politics."[59]

It is difficult to explain the reasons for the Reagan administration's lack of an intelligible strategy for linking U.S. foreign policy goals with its military resources and capabilities. But the sources for this, no doubt, lie in the fact that having set before the United States the task of securing military superiority over the USSR along the perimeter of its borders and preparing for armed intervention in nearly all crisis regions of the world simultaneously, the Republican leadership failed to take the trouble to harmonize its goals with genuine U.S. capabilities. It did not attempt to understand the profound reasons for which the United States in its time had been forced to depart from an infinitely expansionist policy, just as it refused to recognize that in years past these reasons had not only not disappeared but had become even more profound.

The economic difficulties and costs heaped by military programs upon industry and the U.S. financial system represented, as has already been shown, one of the most important objective limitations on the policies of the administration. In late 1981 the director of the Office of Management and Budget, David Stockman, with the support of White House Chief of Staff James Baker, favored reducing the military budget for the 1983 fiscal year, a proposal that met with violent opposition in the Pentagon. In 1982, in the face of the growing budget deficit, and the fall of the government's popularity, the struggle within the administration intensified significantly. The Department of Defense at this time was forced to concede somewhat, and its budget request was reduced by 4 percent ($11.3 billion) in comparison with the original plan. The first signs of opposition to the administration's military policy appeared in Congress. In 1982 the Pentagon's proposed budget for FY 1983 was cut by approximately $18 billion, and the administration's five-year budget program was reduced by $66 billion. The next year an alignment formed in Congress that favored reducing the military budget by $20 billion, despite Weinberger's warning that this would deprive of funds the planned orders for the production of army helicopters, air force and navy fighters, nuclear-powered multipurpose submarines, the Trident I missile, the MX, and cruise missiles. It is highly significant that among the supporters of such reductions were now such figures as, for example, Senator Sam Nunn, who little more than two years earlier had numbered himself among the main supporters of increased military spending. More than 50 members of Congress, including, besides Nunn, Senators Gary Hart, William Cohen, Warren Rudman, Carl Levin, and Congressmen Newt Gingrich, Les Aspin, and William Whitehurst formed the so-called group of "reformers" who favored more limited strategic goals and the cancellation of outrageously expensive arms.[60]

Having settled on a relative redistribution of the U.S. foreign military presence from Western Europe and the Far East to the Indian Ocean basin, Washington pinned greater hopes on the notorious "strategic division of labor" with its partners. And here the Reagan administration's military policy ran up against another set of great difficulties and problems. In the course of the 1970s Western Europe's share in NATO military expenditures grew from 23 percent to 42 percent under U.S. pressure. The further shifting of this heavy burden to the shoulders of the bloc's Western European members, especially in the face of the economic crisis that had struck capitalism, hardly aroused the enthusiasm of the governments of Western Europe and was met with growing opposition from the peace-loving European public. It became increasingly obvious to everyone that the buildup of NATO's military potential would provoke the Warsaw Pact's corresponding retaliatory measures, would not give the West predominance, but would only increase the economic costs of all sides and aggravate political tension on the continent. The extensive plans to broaden U.S. military intervention in many regions of the developing world represent yet another area of policy fraught with failure for Washington and possibly even greater defeats. Armed intervention against Third World nations has become in modern times an incomparably more difficult and costly enterprise than in the past. The Falklands war in the summer of 1982 serves as an obvious example of this. Having set a significant part of its armed forces in motion, in particular the main formations of its navy, Great Britain won the war, but with losses in manpower and equipment not comparable to those of its earlier colonial wars.

In spite of the opinion of a number of Western commentators, nothing in the events of the early 1980s provides grounds for concluding that "the usability" of military force in politics has grown, although imperialism's inclination toward the direct use of force undoubtedly has. Yes, in Grenada the U.S. invaders succeeded in overthrowing the legitimate government—the world's most powerful imperialist power "dealt with" the tiny island state through the massive use of its military power. But this hardly means that the same maneuver can be carried out in Iran, Nicaragua, Lebanon, El Salvador, or anywhere else. If a different conclusion is being drawn in Washington, then enormous failures in U.S. policy are guaranteed in the future. Such policies will not win support inside the United States and will meet resolute opposition outside. The Republican administration, which in its programs for world military expansion would revive the U.S. dictates of the 1950s, should not forget to what such a policy has already once led. The accelerated buildup of U.S. military power in the early 1960s and its direct use in imperialist goals was ultimately crowned by the crushing defeat of the United States in Vietnam.

The absence of realism, of a sober assessment of the desired with the possible in the Reagan administration's foreign policy designs, eroded the ground upon which could have been built a coherent military strategy. The unrestrained inertia of the arms race prevailed, having snowballed beyond even the greatest budgetary means of the Republican military program. The times are gone forever when the United States could without particular strain on its resources support a massive military presence in two or more transoceanic theaters or without unacceptable financial costs carry out direct armed intervention in developing countries and exert effective pressure with the help of a demonstration of force. This has most convincingly been confirmed by the history of the 1970s and the first half of the 1980s. Neither the United States nor the Soviet Union, if only because of the limits of their economic-military capabilities, excluding political and moral considerations, will henceforth have such capabilities. And the problem is certainly not that the United States has not allocated enough of its resources to defense. Even a still greater buildup of armed forces than that contemplated by the Reagan administration could not have reversed the new realities manifest in the qualitatively changed global correlation of forces, in the fundamentally different economic, political, and moral-psychological situation in the world.

Indicative in this respect is the opinion of Robert Tucker, one of the most influential advocates of building up U.S. strength and spreading its military presence in the 1980s from Western Europe and the Far East to the Persian Gulf zone as well:

A policy of global containment would have to be conducted today in circumstances markedly less favorable than the circumstances of a generation ago. Even if we assume the restoration of a national will and consensus comparable to that of the 1950s and early 1960s, the point would remain that the overall relative advantage we once enjoyed could not be regained without a very considerable effort, and even then it would likely be regained only in part.... That policy must presuppose either the retaining of a position of strategic superiority or, if strategic parity is the best that can be had, the achievement of conventional force capabilities that, which in relation to Soviet forces, are superior to those maintained in the earlier period of containment.[61]

Professor Tucker, far from a supporter of limiting U.S. military power, has increasingly regarded such plans as highly utopian, especially considering the Soviet Union's ability to undertake retaliatory measures, the doubtfulness of sufficiently strong support on the part of U.S. allies, and the immeasurably increased independence and activity of the developing countries and their unwillingness to submit to imperialist dictates.

After only a year in power, the Republican leadership collided with a highly significant indicator of the lack of realism in its military-political policy. Its significance was not connected with any one person in particular, but with the Pentagon's civilian and military environment, that is, with officials who in principle wholly approved of the idea of building up U.S. strength (but with a greater degree of professionalism and a

lesser share of politics), and who actually calculated the "military requirements" of Washington's foreign policy ambitions. Deputy Secretary
of Defense Fred Iklé in early 1982 stated before the Senate Armed
Services Committee that the $1.6 trillion in appropriations would not be
enough to fulfill the tasks set before U.S. armed forces. This opinion
was reaffirmed by Richard DeLauer, Director of Defense Research and
Engineering, who said that the programs planned by the services required increasing the overall budget for the 1984–88 fiscal years ($1770
billion) by another $750 billion (!) at a minimum. As if this was not
enough, Lt. General William Richardson, army deputy chief of staff for
operations and plans, announced that the deployment of four new divisions in addition to the existing 28 (active and reserve) would be insufficient to support the expanded U.S. foreign policy commitments.
Similarly, the director of naval program planning, Vice Admiral Carlisle
A. Trost, stated that 15 aircraft carrier battle groups also were not
enough, and the air force deputy chief of staff for plans and operations,
Lt. General Jerome F. O'Malley, asserted the necessity of expanding air
force tactical aviation by significantly more than five wings.[62]

These revelations shocked members of Congress and the press. Even
Senator Sam Nunn felt that if $1.6 trillion was not enough for the
administration, it should "go back to the drawing board" and formulate
strategy all over again. JCS chairman David Jones offered sobering ad-
vice when, upon retiring, he recommended revising U.S. strategic goals
in order to bring them into line with real capabilities and avoid over-
extending national resources. Senator Ernest Hollings, an influential
figure on the Appropriations Committee, stated that "Weinberger has
really destroyed the consensus that we had going for defense."[63] And
while this consensus, it is true, had not yet been replaced by an organized
opposition, the Reagan administration's ability to carry out its military
policy had undoubtedly begun to experience increasingly more substantial limitations.

The plans to return to the "containment" and "cold war" policies, as
Professor Tucker correctly noted, have created the strongest temptations
to reestablish U.S. nuclear superiority, which had been the most important requisite for U.S. policy in the 1950s and early 1960s. And it is
precisely nuclear weapons that have taken center stage in the Republican
administration's military strategy and foreign policy. In this area the new
realities were, as nowhere else, more tangible and obvious, the desire of
the administration to overcome them, stronger, and the specific plans
for doing so, the most detailedly prepared by Reagan's fellow champions.
It is precisely here that the U.S. administration's measures created the
greatest threat to peace and general security. But at the same time it
was primarily in this very sphere that the inconsistency and futility of

Washington's policy were manifested. It has run against the most serious obstacles, become increasingly more contradictory, and incurred growing costs for the United States itself.

## Notes

1. Robert Scheer, *With Enough Shovels: Reagan, Bush and Nuclear War* (New York: Random House, 1982), 260.

2. *Congressional Quarterly Weekly Report* 38: 45 (November 8, 1980): 1–4.

3. Ronald Brownstein and Nina Easton, *Reagan's Ruling Class* (Washington, D.C.: The Presidential Accountability Group, 1982), xi.

4. Ronald Brownstein and Nina Easton, *Reagan's Ruling Class* (New York: Pantheon, 1983), xvi.

5. Arthur Macy Cox, *Russian Roulette: The Superpower Game* (New York: Times Books, 1982), 90.

6. Cox, *Russian Roulette*, 91.

7. Yurii K. Abramov and Andrei A. Kokoshkin, "Sostav verkhnego eshelona administratsii Reagana," *SShA: ekonomika, politika, ideologiia* (hereafter *SShA*) 11 (November 1982): 117–127.

8. Stanley Hoffmann, "Reagan Abroad," *The New York Review of Books*, February 4, 1982, 16.

9. Genrikh A. Trofimenko, "Osnovye postulaty vneshnei politiki SShA i sud' by razriadki," *SShA* 7 (July 1981): 14.

10. V. M. Shamberg, "Ob ekonomicheskikh kontseptsiiakh respublikanskoi administratsii," *SShA* 5 (May 1982): 36.

11. *International Herald Tribune*, December 31, 1982.

12. "Ronald Reagan's Press Conference Text," *Congressional Quarterly Weekly Report*, January 31, 1981, 238.

13. *Department of Defense Annual Report, Fiscal Year 1983*, (Washington, D.C.: U.S. Government Printing Office, 1981), II–27, II–30.

14. "Nomination of Caspar Weinberger to be Secretary of Defense," *Hearings*, Committee on Armed Services, U.S. Senate, 97th Congress, First Session, January 6, 1981 (Washington, D.C.: U.S. Government Printing Office, 1981), 27.

15. Brownstein and Easton, *Reagan's Ruling Class*, 1983 ed., 562.

16. *The Sunday Times*, January 24, 1982.

17. William G. Hyland, "U.S.-Soviet Relations: The Long Road Back," *Foreign Affairs* 60, no. 3 (1982): 543–544.

18. Brownstein and Easton, *Reagan's Ruling Class*, 1983 ed., 560.

19. Ibid., 561.

20. Robert E. Osgood, "The Revitalization of Containment," *Foreign Affairs* 60: 3 (1982): 478.

21. "Nomination of Alexander M. Haig, Jr.," *Hearings*, Committee on Foreign Relations, U.S. Senate, 97th Congress, first session, January 14, 1981 (Washington, D.C.: U.S. Government Printing Office, 1981), pt. 2, 11.

22. "Department of Defense Authorization for Appropriations for Fiscal Year 1982," *Hearings*, Committee on Armed Services, U.S. Senate, 97th Congress,

first session, pt. 1, Posture Statement, March 4, 1981 (Washington, D.C.: U.S. Government Printing Office, 1981), 545–46.

23. James Fallows, "The Trap of Rearmament," *The New York Review of Books*, December 17, 1981, 31.

24. *Materialy Plenuma Tsentral'nogo Komiteta KPSS, November 22, 1982* (Moscow: Politizdat, 1982), 20.

25. Scheer, *With Enough Shovels*, 229.

26. *The New York Review of Books*, February 4, 1982, 18.

27. Osgood, "Revitalization of Containment," 474.

28. Robert Tucker, *The Purposes of American Power* (New York: Praeger, 1981), 186.

29. Hoffmann, "Reagan Abroad," 17–20.

30. "Department of Defense Authorization for Appropriations for Fiscal Year 1982," 546.

31. *U.S. News and World Report*, March 16, 1981, 25.

32. *U.S. News and World Report*, March 16, 1981, 24–25.

33. *The Defense Monitor* 12: 2 (1983): 2.

34. *Department of Defense Annual Report, Fiscal Year 1983*, I–17.

35. A deployed U.S. division numbers 16–19,000 men; a tactical air wing, 60–80 aircraft; and an aircraft carrier battle group, as a rule, is composed of one aircraft carrier and five to six escort ships and auxiliary vessels.

36. *Setting National Priorities: The 1983 Budget* (Washington, D.C.: The Brookings Institution, 1982), 81–83.

37. "Department of Defense Authorization for Appropriations for Fiscal Year 1982," 546.

38. *Department of Defense Annual Report, Fiscal Year 1983*, 11–20.

39. "Department of Defense Authorization for Appropriations for Fiscal Year 1982," 552.

40. *Department of Defense Annual Report, Fiscal Year 1983*, I-16.

41. *Department of Defense Annual Report, Fiscal Year 1983*.

42. Brownstein and Easton, *Reagan's Ruling Class*, 1983 ed., 490.

43. *Setting National Priorities: The 1983 Budget*, 83–86; *Time*, July 27, 1981, 4–17; *Newsweek*, June 8, 1981, 10–25.

44. In the early 1960s, even before the unleashing of direct aggression in Vietnam, U.S. armed forces were enlarged in number by 270,000 men, the navy's fleet was increased by 60 ships and submarines and reached 880 units, the army received five new divisions, and the air force's tactical aviation, eight additional wings. See Lawrence Korb, *The FY 1981–1985 Defense Program: Issues and Trends* (Washington, D.C.: American Enterprise Institute, 1980), 29.

45. John Kenneth Galbraith, "The Conservative Onslaught," *The New York Review of Books*, January 22, 1981, 30.

46. *Setting National Priorities: The 1983 Budget*, 23–50.

47. Brownstein and Easton, *Reagan's Ruling Class*, 1983 ed., xvii-xxi.

48. P. Odean, *American Security in the 1980s: The Domestic Context* (Williamsberg: IISS, September 10, 1981), 12.

49. Yurii I. Bobrakov, "Ob ekonomicheskoi programme administratsii Reagana," *SShA* 5 (May 1981): 45–51.

50. *Time*, March 7, 1983, 23.

51. *The Defense Monitor* 12: 2 (1983): 4.

52. Joint Economic Committee, U.S. Congress, *Defense Buildup and the Economy* (Washington, D.C.: U.S. Government Printing Office, 1982), 4.

53. Theodore H. White, "Weinberger on the Ramparts," *The New York Times Magazine*, February 6, 1983, 19–20.

54. *Time*, March 7, 1983, 12–30.

55. *Department of Defense Annual Report, Fiscal Year 1983*, I-30.

56. Hoffmann, *Reagan Abroad*, 16–17.

57. Osgood, "Revitalization of Containment," 475.

58. Brownstein and Easton, *Reagan's Ruling Class*, 1983 ed., 451.

59. *Time*, March 7, 1983, 27.

60. *Time*, March 7, 1983, 27.

61. Tucker, *Purposes of Power*, 163–64.

62. *International Herald Tribune*, March 9, 1982, 1–2.

63. *The Washington Post*, January 31, 1983, A4.

# 6

## The Republicans' Nuclear Policy: In Pursuit of Superiority

The achievement of "U.S. nuclear superiority" was not simply a Republican campaign slogan, but an integral element and, moreover, the cornerstone of the entire political philosophy and strategic aspirations of the Reagan administration. Its leading figures perceived the origins of U.S. troubles and failures in the world arena to lie in the U.S. loss of nuclear superiority and strategic advantage in the late 1960s and 1970s. They did not wish to be resigned to strategic parity as an inevitable and objective reality. They attributed everything in the second half of the 1960s to the Vietnam war (which had supposedly "siphoned off" capital investments for strategic programs), in the first half of the 1970s to the pressure of the antimilitary opposition in Congress and the general public, and in the late 1970s to the Carter administration's supposed "neglect" of U.S. strategic power.

Along with this it was firmly maintained that an "unrelenting buildup" of the Soviet arsenal of land- and sea-based ballistic missiles had continued all these years. If in the first instance the Democrats had emphasized Soviet "superiority" in conventional forces, then with Reagan's entrance to the White House "Soviet nuclear superiority" became the central theme of the official "Soviet military threat" campaign. The revival of U.S. strategic superiority was seen by the Republican leadership and its followers as not only entirely possible in the course of the 1980s but absolutely necessary as the main pillar for restoring the global policy of "containing communism." Thus, in the simple logic of the new U.S. leaders, there was no denying that since strategic superiority was in the past inseparably linked with the cold war, an exhumation of the past in turn demanded the revival of U.S. nuclear domination.

## The Nuclear War-fighting Doctrine

Upon coming to power the Reagan administration did not take the majority of "quick fixes" for increasing U.S. strategic power from an extensive list proposed by William Van Cleave and other members of the Republican's Defense Department transition team.[1] Rather, primary attention was to be given to the more important and extensive transformations in the strategic weapons sphere. For this, a broad interdepartmental study was begun in the Pentagon (under the direction of Deputy Secretary of Defense Fred Iklé and Assistant Secretary of Defense Richard Perle), a review of U.S. strategic doctrine and operational plans within the framework of the study "Fiscal Year 1984–1988 Defense Guidance." A consultative commission of experts from the military-scientific community led by University of California physicist Charles Townes was given the task of reforming strategic weapons development and deployment programs. Although the experts operated within their own narrow strategic and technical specialties, Reagan's political views and outlook on the role and utility of nuclear weapons in politics and war underlay their work. These views differed substantially in a number of aspects from the Democratic administration's approach, and still more from notions generally accepted throughout the world community, including the United States for the past two decades or more.

The idea that, despite the enormous potential of mass destruction currently accumulated by both sides, it was nevertheless possible to conduct and win a global thermonuclear war served as the basic premise of the new U.S. leadership's policy. The capability for either side to inflict catastrophic losses on its opponent had not been doubted by anyone for a long time, but U.S. leaders publicly announced that even in a massive nuclear exchange there exists the possibility of limiting damage to "acceptable" levels, allowing for the hope of a postwar recovery of the country's economy and armed forces within an "acceptable" period. And thus Vice-President George Bush explained the idea of survival in a nuclear war:

You have a survivability of command and control, survivability of industrial potential, protection of a percentage of your citizens, and you have a capability that inflicts more damage on the opposition than it can inflict upon you. That's the way you can be a winner.[2]

It is common for calculations of this kind to be justified by the argument that the Soviet Union is supposedly developing analogous plans, and that therefore the United States must do the same if only so as not to be at a disadvantage. But this was merely declaratory rhetoric. At the official level, as U.S. leaders could not help but have known, there were numerous authoritative Soviet declarations that testify that the USSR categorically does not share such views. For example, in the materials of the 25th CPSU congress it was unambiguously pointed out that "to count on victory in a nuclear war is dangerous madness." Soviet leaders have repeatedly emphasized that initiating a nuclear war with the hope of emerging from it as the victor can only be done by those who have decided to commit suicide: "No matter what kind of power the attacker possesses, no matter what kind of capability for unleashing nuclear war is chosen, he will not attain his goals. Retaliation will inevitably follow." All Warsaw Treaty member states unanimously expressed the point of view in the declaration of January 5, 1983 that "In a nuclear war, should it break out, there can be no winner. It will inevitably lead to the destruction of all nations, to colossal devastation and catastrophic consequences for civilization and all life on earth."[3]

The assumption of the possibility of survival in a thermonuclear war, like the rolling stone that starts an avalanche, gave rise to a whole chain of other ideas that shattered the established way of thinking about nuclear weapons. For if it is possible to limit losses in a nuclear war to "acceptable" levels, then it follows that such a war can even be won in the real sense of the word if one can take away the opponent's analogous damage limitation capability. And if a global war can be won, the main tasks of strategic offensive and defensive arms are no longer ones of primarily "deterrence" (the ability to inflict unacceptable damage on the enemy), but ones of conducting intercontinental war-fighting with the goal of destroying the other side's armed forces and economic potential while limiting one's own losses to "acceptable" levels. A disarming first strike (for destroying the maximum number of the other side's nuclear forces on the ground) as well as active and passive territorial defenses[4] against the remaining forces are notions—never before publicly admitted to operate in Washington's official strategic declarations—that are now acquiring legitimacy at the official level.

For example, to a reporter's question of whether the U.S. refusal to rule out categorically the first use of nuclear weapons creates a stimulus for a preemptive strike by the other side, Reagan said:

Don't you open up the possibility of being hit by a surprise nuclear attack far more if you assure the rest of the world that under no circumstances would you ever be the first to fire those bombs? . . . Suppose you're the President, and suppose you have on unassailable authority that as of a certain hour the enemy is going to launch those missiles at your country—you mean to tell me that a President should sit there and let that happen . . . ?[5]

The U.S. government had even earlier adhered to the principle of using nuclear weapons first. But this argument was concerned with, as a rule, the use of tactical nuclear weapons under conditions of widespread conventional hostilities, and is an integral element of NATO's strategy of flexible response. However, in this case Reagan was clearly talking about a strategic preemptive strike that, even if the enemy's attack could be foreseen in practice, had always been carefully avoided and obscured since the early 1960s in official U.S. declaratory policy. Since then the strengthening of the Soviet capability for a destructive retaliatory strike has increasingly put in doubt this aspect of traditional strategic thought.

Actually, in the past, when countries could hope for victory in a war, mobilization and the very act of launching combat operations required a comparatively long period of time for extensive and highly visible maneuvers. The other side was therefore compelled to take early corresponding measures and was simultaneously provided time for additional intelligence concerning the enemy's plans. Finally, there was always the hope of the possibility of stopping escalation in a war or negotiating a cease-fire even after hostilities began. In contrast, today's colossal arsenals of nuclear weapons, a significant number of which are physically invulnerable to surprise attack or are continually ready for launch at literally a moment's notice, and the modern means of observation and early warning available to both sides are changing the situation radically. A preemptive strike is incapable of preventing devastating retaliation. The transition to hostilities may be practically instantaneous. And once begun, the war would become irreversible, quickly and inevitably leading to total destruction.[6]

Therefore, at present, the risk of unleashing war as a result of erroneous information, miscalculation, unauthorized launch, or technical malfunction has become immeasurably greater. In peacetime no one is seriously worried about such an event, although in a crisis situation (such as the Cuban crisis of October 1962) a nuclear holocaust could inadvertently be precipitated. The consequences of a mistake are so enormous that no information of the other side's intentions or preparations, despite Reagan's arguments, can serve as the basis for a preemptive strike. Only signals from various redundant means of early warning that an actual nuclear attack was under way, as well as evidence of the first nuclear explosions, would justify setting into action the potential of devastating retaliation. For ensuring such a possibility, strategic forces and their systems of command, control, communications, and early warning are continually being upgraded and maintained in a high state of readiness. The orientation of strategy and armed forces to a preemptive strike makes the outbreak of nuclear war much more probable, with all its catastrophic consequences, and at the same time does not promise the aggressor any advantages, much less victory, in a global nuclear conflict.

The above considerations were taken into account in the Soviet Union's official decision of June 1982 to make the commitment not to use nuclear weapons first. This step was based on a correct analysis of the strategic situation and on the selection of the only correct way to safeguard security. In this connection, as then-USSR Minister of Defense Dmitrii F. Ustinov stated:

The USSR, renouncing the first use of nuclear weapons, refuses in any instance to harbor plans for a nuclear attack that count on victory in a nuclear war. The state of the military potential and military-technical capabilities of both sides are such that the imperialist forces cannot achieve military superiority, either at a level of preparing for a nuclear war, or at that moment when they would attempt to start this war.[7]

If the other nuclear powers would follow the USSR's example, the common security would become politically more stable. However, the prevailing tendencies of U.S. strategic policy have developed in a completely different direction, most notably after the coming to power of the Reagan administration.

Attempts to revise the views of nuclear weapons in war have also entailed a revision of the notion of their role in politics. If under the Carter administration and its Republican predecessors the presence of an overall Soviet-U.S. strategic parity was fully recognized, the Reagan administration has categorically rejected this opinion and announced that the United States today has supposedly come face-to-face with the "prospect of Soviet strategic superiority."

In our time the understanding of an inevitable total catastrophe in the event of nuclear war has become the foundation of the point of view that with so many nuclear weapons amassed on both sides, the potential for multiple destruction ("overkill") is disproportionate to any rational military requirements. Military superiority in the real sense of the word, as the capability of prevailing in war, has become unattainable, and one partial advantage or another in strategic forces cannot be transformed into means of political pressure. Accordingly, it follows that the overall strategic balance, or parity, formed in the early 1970s was exactly the state of the military balance of forces acceptable to both sides and on the basis of which could be conducted a dialogue on limiting and reducing weapons. Guided by these considerations, the Soviet Union has repeatedly declared at the highest levels that it would not strive for nuclear superiority, that the very notion is devoid of meaning in the presence of the enormous arsenals of already-accumulated nuclear weapons and the means of their delivery, and that approximate equality or parity is sufficient for safeguarding the reliable security of the USSR and its allies.[8] Only on this basis could progress be achieved in the matter of nuclear disarmament. In the 1970s the U.S. government in its public declarations on a whole expressed agreement with these views.

The Reagan administration has handled affairs quite differently. Taking as a premise the possibility that losses may be limited in a thermonuclear war to "acceptable" levels and that victory may be achieved, it has once again dragged out the idea of superiority. The nuclear warfighting doctrine generally excludes such notions as parity or equilibrum. The only remaining possibility is superiority for one side or the other. And Washington, publicly declaring the "unacceptability of Soviet strategic superiority," has chosen the path of achieving U.S. superiority. Certain aspects of the correlation of strategic forces and war-fighting capabilities have acquired decisive meaning for the U.S. leadership (such as the ability to destroy the enemy's strategic forces, the effectiveness of command and control systems, active and passive means of defense from nuclear weapons, and so on). It is not an arms race, fraught with the threat of global war in the event that a crisis situation would get out of control, that seems the main danger to the Reagan government, but rather this or that disproportion in certain parameters of the nuclear balance that are characterized by "Soviet superiority." Now it has been decided to change them in the United States' favor, while simultaneously broadening its superiority in other parameters of the correlation of forces.

Significant in this respect was the statement of former ACDA head Eugene Rostow, who noted frankly in the summer of 1981 that

somewhere in this period there is vulnerability of our ICBMs and of a good deal else, and a terrific asymmetry in the arsenal, and that has to be remedied.... Wars come about not when power is balanced, but when power is unbalanced. ...I do not think that nuclear war is the main threat. It is a possibility. But I don't think it is the main threat to the future. I think the main threat to the future is political coercion based on nuclear blackmail.[9]

In other words, the new U.S. leaders, regarding the objectively established strategic balance as unacceptable, set out to change it at any price, first of all with the help of an accelerated arms race and new strategic doctrines and concepts, regardless of the pernicious consequences of such a course for arms control talks, the increase of tension, and the growing probablity of thermonuclear war. And thus the latter, not surprisingly, was no longer considered the "main threat" in Washington. This mode of political-military thought is fundamental to the elaboration of the Reagan administration's strategic doctrine and nuclear weapons programs.

In Weinberger's first budget report several principles were formulated that by all appearances reflected the process of making nuclear strategy at the highest echelons of the administration's military-political bureaucracy. As for U.S. strategic policy, the secretary said that it was not directed toward achieving U.S. nuclear superiority. At the same time, he said that "We will make every necessary effort to prevent the Soviet Union from acquiring such superiority and to insure the margin of safety necessary for our security."[10] Evidently, taking into consideration the negative reaction of U.S. and world public opinion, the Republican leadership had replaced the term "nuclear superiority," openly used in the 1980 Republican party platform, with the term "a margin of safety necessary for security." However, the meaning remained unchanged, as was confirmed in the Pentagon chief's subsequent pronouncements. Explaining the character of U.S. strategic aims, Weinberger declared that the U.S. goal is "to impose termination of a major war—on terms favorable to the United States and our allies—even if nuclear weapons have been used—and in particular to deter escalation in the level of hostilities."[11] Thus for the first time in more than 20 years in U.S. declaratory policy was heard the idea of victoriously terminating a thermonuclear war without unacceptable damage to the United States.

The revision of U.S. military-political doctrine and strategic concepts was completed by the summer of 1982 and released in a series of official documents, signifying a serious turn in U.S. strategic policy. According to press leaks, in May 1982 President Reagan signed an eight-page document whose contents called for increasing pressure on the Soviet Union across the whole spectrum of U.S. military, economic, and propaganda activities with the goal of undermining the establishment of socialism, destroying the unity of the Soviet people and the socialist alliance. This document reflected the ideas of presidential adviser Richard Pipes, noted for his belief that Soviet leaders had to choose between peaceful change of their system or war. Shortly thereafter the press reported on the completion of the above-mentioned Pentagon *Defense Guidance* study and on the statements of the Defense Secretary. As some commentators noted, the *Defense Guidance* put forward the idea of a "limited and protracted" nuclear war, whereby the United States must be able to prevail and compel the Soviet Union to seek as early as possible a termination of the conflict on conditions favorable to the United States. The *Defense Guidance* also included plans for "decapitating" the USSR with a nuclear strike on the Soviet political-military leadership.[12]

The White House's National Security Decision Document-13 (NSDD-13) sanctioned the Pentagon's development of a plan for necessary military programs and the restructuring of operational planning in accordance with the aim of achieving victory in a "limited and protracted" nuclear war. This plan was presented to the leadership in the summer of 1982 and, according to newspaper reports, stipulated the possibility of conducting nuclear hostilities in the course of up to a six-month period and of limiting U.S. losses to "acceptable" levels of 20 million dead.[13]

Concepts of a "limited and protracted" nuclear war and of strikes on strategic forces, the command and control system, and political leadership, were, of course, not a novelty in U.S. nuclear strategy. In particular, they had been advanced in such important documents as NSDM-242 in 1974 and PD-59 in 1980. At the same time the Republican administration's strategic concepts, to the extent one can judge by the statements of informed persons, went significantly further than all that had been stipulated by U.S. nuclear strategy in the 1970s. In this regard, former Deputy Undersecretary of Defense Walter Slocombe, allegedly one of the authors of PD-59, said in the spring of 1982:

I think the place where there is a discontinuity is that if there are people in the present administration who think that you can fight and win a nuclear war, and that it is reasonable to plan on doing so in the same way the British plan to fight and win a war in the Falklands—if there are people who believe that, then there was nobody at a politically responsible or politically significant level in the Carter administration who thought that.[14]

As for the nuclear war-fighting strategy, an integral part of U.S. strategy that had in part sprung from the supposed existence of Soviet "plans" to survive a nuclear war, even extreme right-wing officials preferred to justify it with the harmonious aim of "deterrence." Weinberger's speeches contained extensive discourses on the "specifics" of the Soviet approach to deterrence and global war, of the supposed efforts undertaken by the Soviet Union to develop the possibility of prevailing in a nuclear war, whether short-term or protracted, by way of striking U.S. armed forces, command, and industry, combined with the vast means and measures of active and passive defense of its own territory.

It must be recognized that a number of works of Soviet military theorists and specialists have contained statements that are widely used in the West to impute to Soviet military doctrine, strategy, and armed forces an orientation toward a first strike, the conduct of a protracted war, and the achievement of victory in it. In part such statements reflected the inertia of traditional thinking, which has to be unequivocally revised in accordance with the radically changed political and military-technological realities. In part it was an ideological approach, a desire to bring up officers and soldiers in a spirit of patriotism, vigilance, and readiness for self-sacrifice in the name of the Motherland (in this respect the doctrine of "deterrence" and the strategy of retaliation create a difficult and unusual state). Finally, in other instances took place narrowly specialist and technical discourses relating to the effective fulfillment of operational and tactical combat tasks (indeed, readiness for such tasks also lies at the foundation of deterrence, as long as these tasks are not based on a strategy oriented toward inflicting a first strike).

As for the overall thrust of the Republican administration's strategic thinking, only informed sources may judge, since such documents as NSDD-13 or the Defense Guidance are highly secret, and Weinberger has spoken quite vaguely in this regard in the defense budget report and in congressional testimony. But some light can be thrown on the problem from the writings and statements of a number of specialists who have occupied administrative and advisory posts under Reagan and were able in one way or another to influence the formulation of U.S. nuclear strategy in the early 1980s. Especially indicative in this respect, for example, are the writings of Colin Gray (an ACDA consultant), which should be examined fully since they were published after the new administration came to power and appear to have served as official guidance. "The important point to recognize," he writes,

is that the United States *may have no practical alternative* to waging a nuclear war. ...The United States requires the capability to strike first with strategic forces and dominate any subsequent process of escalation....Survivable C³I should permit genuine political direction of the war on an hour-by-hour and day-by-day basis. In practice "the fog of battle" may not permit this, but the goal is a sound one....A damage limitation capability comprising counterforce strikes, multilayer ballistic missile defense, air defense, and civil defense—though not perfect or "leakproof"—should make the difference between a United States which could, and a United States which could not, survive a nuclear war.[15] (emphasis in original)

Such arguments cannot but beg the question: does the author actually hold this point of view or does he seek to shock established public opinion for political reasons? Alas, judging by the other works and statements of this specialist, he apparently in fact believes his own ideas and, sadder still, is far from alone in the U.S. "strategic community." Although many top- and second-echelon Republican administration officials to one degree or another share these views, Colin Gray has been the one to deliver them most frankly to the public.

For example, then Deputy Secretary of Defense Frank Carlucci stated to the Senate Armed Services Committee: "I think we need to have a counterforce capability. Over and above that, I think we need to have a war-fighting capability."[16] Another key figure of the administration, Richard Burt, shortly before becoming head of the State Department's Bureau of Politico-Military Affairs, wrote:

"Parity," a political definition of force sufficiency, is not an adequate measure of military effectiveness because it fails to provide any operational requirements for long-range forces. "Flexibility" is likewise a poor measure of effectiveness because limited nuclear options, by themselves, have a suicidal quality, unless they form part of a broader concept for nuclear use and American forces are capable of waging a large-scale, sustained nuclear campaign.... 

For a start, the requirements of military effectiveness necessitate the acquisition of secure and survivable forces capable of threatening a range of military forces, including hardened military targets in the Soviet Union.... [O]n the defensive side of the ledger, there are a number of activities that need to receive more attention, including civil defense, antisubmarine warfare, and air defense. In space, the potential offered by new technologies, primarily lasers, needs to be exercised concurrently with programs to reduce the growing vulnerabilities of American early warning, surveillance, and communication spacecraft.[17]

No less symptomatic were the observations of administration officials on the possibility of defending population and industry from nuclear destruction, which was an additional integral feature of the nuclear war-fighting strategy. The statements in this respect of the deputy under-secretary of defense for strategic and theater nuclear forces, T. K. Jones, caused an uproar. Beginning in 1976, Jones, at the time a chief engineer at the Boeing Corporation, together with retired General George Keegan, led the campaign on the Soviet civil defense "threat" that, by their assertions, could reduce Soviet losses in the event of a thermonuclear war to 5 percent of the population.[18] Moving to the Pentagon in 1981, Jones launched a vigorous effort to intensify U.S. civil defense programs, from enhancing civil defense for industry to plans for evacuating and constructing shelters for the population. His views on survival in a nuclear war left an impression of schizoid nonsense: "Dig a hole, cover it with a couple of doors and then throw three feet of dirt on top. It's the dirt that does it," he said. "If there are enough shovels to go around, everyone's going to make it." Complete recovery after a nuclear war, by his assertions, would take two to four years.[19] These statements on the part of a Defense Department official caused such an outrage in Congress that Assistant Secretary of Defense Richard Perle was instructed to assure congressmen that Jones did not express the Pentagon's official point of view.

The influence of this group of actors occupying key posts in the Reagan administration's military and political bureaucracy was precisely characterized by the respected American scientist Herbert York, a former presidential science adviser and assistant secretary of defense:

What's going on right now is that the crazier analysts have risen to higher positions than is normally the case. They are able to carry their ideas further and higher because the people at the top are simply less well-informed than is normally the case. Neither the current President nor his immediate backers in the White House nor the current Secretary of Defense have any experience with these things, so when the ideologues come in with their fancy stories and with their selected intelligence data, the President and the Secretary of Defense believe the last glib person who talked with them.[20]

At the same time, it is obvious that the higher political leadership had not chosen such officials by chance. The cynical scholastic arguments of adherents to the nuclear war-fighting doctrine, who nevertheless comprised a minority in the U.S. strategic community, attracted Reagan and his entourage especially because their ideas fitted precisely into the overall framework of the Republican leadership's policy. In the 1970s all these experts unanimously opposed détente, strategic party, and arms control agreements, and supported the large-scale buildup of U.S. military power and a policy of pressuring the USSR from a position of nuclear superiority.

But whereas the general thrust of the Reagan administration's strategic thinking left no doubts, specific concepts in its nuclear strategy were much less clear. With all the ambiguity and contradictions of earlier official U.S. concepts (such as "assured destruction," "damage limitation," "counterforce," "counterrecovery," "the countervailing strategy," and others), from 1981 to 1983 neither Reagan nor Weinberger forwarded any analogue to them, even at the same level of abstraction. The secretary of defense's statements in this respect were more unintelligible and contradictory than ever before in the history of U.S. nuclear strategy. So, on one hand, he spoke of the necessity for "a margin of safety in U.S. security," and on the other, maintained that U.S. plans called for "neither military superiority nor one warhead more than the Soviets have." Testifying before the Senate Foreign Relations Committee, the secretary asserted that "we are under no illusions that a nuclear war would be anything less than an absolute catastrophe." Yet literally in the next passage he emphasized that in the event of war the United States plans to prevail "in denying victory to the Soviets and in protecting the sovereignty and continued viability of the United States and of the Western democracies as free societies with fundamental institutions and values intact." Indeed, many characters from *Alice in Wonderland* would probably have envied the following unsurpassed pearl of Weinberger playing the strategic casuist when he stated: "There is no contradiction between our view that there could be no winners in a nuclear war and our planning to prevail, if war is forced upon us."[21] Well, if this is no contradiction, then common sense and logic evidently played no part in the formulation of the administration's strategic concepts.

Strategic arms programs are, undoubtedly, more objective and clearcut criteria of Washington's nuclear policy than its public declarations. For whatever decisions are made in the Pentagon on these programs, whatever considerations play a definitive role at any given moment, the development and deployment of strategic weapons systems have become the material basis and objective reality of the global military correlation of forces.

## The Reagan Administration's Strategic Program

The strategic program announced by the U.S. president on October 2, 1981 was a set of long-term measures for the substantial transformation and buildup of U.S. strategic nuclear strength. As is noted in the Soviet publication *Whence the Threat to Peace*, this program "not only consolidates and expands programs approved earlier, but provides for the creation and deployment of new weapon system as well".[22] In its scale and cost the Reagan-Weinberger program has had no precedent in the twenty-odd years since the decisions of the mid-1950s and early 1960s established the basic levels and structure of the U.S. strategic arsenal up through the early 1980s. The Reagan administration increased appropriations to strategic forces by nearly 150 percent in comparison with the budget estimates of its predecessors; the share of these resources in the annual U.S. defense budget and five-year budget program also grew by one and a half times. Just the direct spending alone on development, production, and deployment of new strategic arms was projected to be $180 billion for the fiscal years 1983–87. And if all related expenses connected with strategic forces are considered (in particular, $C^3I$, nuclear warhead production, rear security and maintenance, personnel costs, and so on), then the strategic force budget reaches on average $50 billion per year and totals $250 billion for the five-year period.[23]

The Reagan program of October 2, 1981 consisted of five parts: measures in each of the three legs of the strategic triad, in the command and control area, and also in the sphere of strategic defense. Without digressing into a detailed description of these programs, which have already been thoroughly examined in the Soviet technical and political literature, it should be noted that these differed significantly from the Carter-Brown programs and plans, in spite of the enormous inertia and continuity inherent in the development of strategic weapons systems. In the offensive strategic arms sphere the new administration's initiatives meant a much greater emphasis on the air and sea elements of the U.S. strategic arsenal with a comparative reduction of the role of ICBMs. Furthermore, the Republicans' measures stipulated a great diversification in strategic forces, that is, expanding the set of the kinds and varieties of weapons systems in the force posture.

One of the main decisions of the Reagan administration was to revive the B-1 bomber program, cancelled in 1977 by the Carter government, in the modified version of the B-1B.[24] One hundred such aircraft were to be deployed from 1985 through 1988 at a total cost of $28 billion or more in 1983 dollars. In addition, ALCM production was expanded from 3,400 to 4,300 units. Not 150, as planned earlier, but all 250 existing later-model B-52 heavy bombers, and in the 1990s also the B-1B bombers, were proposed to be equipped with these missiles, and in the future their follow-on improved supersonic generation as well. Development was also accelerated on the fundamentally new Stealth bomber, widely advertised as an invisible aircraft, of which approximately 130 were planned to be deployed in the early 1990s. The Stealth bomber is to function as a deep-penetrating bomber, whereas the B-52 and B-1B are to be set aside for cruise missile strikes from stand-off positions.

In regard to sea-based strategic forces the Reagan administration's main step was to accelerate the development of the new Trident-II SLBM (D-5 by the navy's classification), which is to significantly surpass the Trident I (C-4) in range, throw-weight, yield, and warhead accuracy. The deployment of Trident II was to begin not in the 1990s, as was earlier planned, but in 1989 on the ninth *Ohio*-class SSBN, after which all subsequent SSBNs were to carry this new missile system. The eight built previously, all carrying the Trident I, were to be retrofitted with Trident II. Simultaneously, the plan to construct the gigantic *Ohio* was expanded from 13 to 16 boats. Later on, top navy officials, with the blessing of the political leadership, planned to increase their total number to 20.[25] Moreover, in addition to the previous administration's plans it was decided to produce and deploy around 700 Tomahawk long-range nuclear-armed SLCMs on the multipurpose *Los Angeles*-class SSNs and on certain surface vessels beginning in 1985.[26]

As for land-based missile forces, the most important decision of the new political leadership was the scrapping of the MPS basing system for the MX. It is interesting to note that this decision was adopted despite the position of the uniformed military, an extremely rare exception to Weinberger's management practice. In 1981 JCS Chairman General David Jones, Air Force Chief of Staff General Lew Allen, his deputy for research and development General Kelly Burke, SAC commander General Richard Ellis, the Air Force Space and Missile Systems Organization, and the Air Force Military Science Council—this entire powerful alignment—continued to support the deployment of 200-plus MX ICBMs in a system of multiple protective shelters. But the secretary of defense and a group of experts from the Townes Commission rejected this basing option, explaining that the MPS system would be so expensive and demand such a long construction period that the other side would have the opportunity to deploy in its missile forces a sufficient number of warheads for reliably destroying all 4,600 hardened shelters.[27]

In place of this strategic program Reagan called for the eventual introduction into the arsenal of 100 MX ICBMs as well as an intensification of the search for a new basing system among a set of several options, including deployment in large transport aircraft permanently stationed on air patrol, in deep underground silos, and with the protection of an ABM system. But in order that the development of a basing system did not delay the movement toward testing and serial production of the powerful new missile, it was decided to begin initial deployment (starting in 1985) of 36 to 40 MX ICBMs in existing Titan-II or Minuteman silos. These silos were to be "superhardened" through the utilization of new technology. The cost of such an initial deployment was estimated at $6–8 billion.[28]

In all probability, the administration's decision was conditioned primarily by political considerations. The nature of Weinberger's arguments against the MPS system and the even more doubtful character of his proposed alternatives force one to think that the president and his advisers from the very beginning had decided for political reasons to scrap the basing scheme advanced by the Carter administration, which had served as a convenient target for attack during the earlier struggle for power. Furthermore, according to some sources, Reagan did not want to complicate relations with the influential senators Paul Laxalt and Jake Garn, who in accordance with the will of their electorate opposed the deployment of the MX system in multiple shelters in their states (Nevada and Utah, respectively).[29] At the same time the Republican leadership, seeking to accelerate the arms race in every possible way and bowing to the interests of the military-industrial complex, wanted to intensify the development and deployment of this very missile, despite the absence of a more survivable basing system (although, as we will recall, it was just such a survivable basing system that from the beginning had served as the integral strategic justification for the entire MX program). The vagueness of alternative basing systems apparently also explained why the Republican leadership did not expand, but in fact narrowed the initial MX deployment phase. Nevertheless, whatever motives in reality dictated the Republican leadership's decision, there is no doubt that the reduction of the number of new ICBMs to be deployed from 200 to 100, the plan to place them initially in existing silos (which, as had been asserted earlier, would lose their ability to survive a nuclear strike by the mid-1980s), and the new delay in selecting a permanent basing mode were all evidence of a certain reduction of the relative importance of land-based missiles in the U.S. strategic triad. It is important as well to consider that the development of new weapons systems (the B-1B, Stealth, Trident-II, and Tomahawk cruise missiles) was intended to accelerate, expand, and diversify the triad's two other components.

However, Congress did not support the Reagan and Weinberger proposals. This was the first sign that, despite the Republican leadership's calculations, the general swing to the right in the political atmosphere on Capitol Hill still did not give the "hawks" a completely free hand in the administration. Congress, echoing its 1976 decision, in March and April of 1982 prohibited the deployment of missiles in both existing Titan-II silos as well as in existing or upgraded Minuteman-III silos. In addition, the Senate refused for the third time, after votes in 1974 and 1978, to finance research on an aircraft basing option for MX. Moreover, before it would allocate resources for the program's further development, Congress required the government to present a final plan for a survivable basing system by December 1, 1982. In the words of then-Deputy Secretary of Defense Frank Carlucci, "Congress didn't just say no. They said, 'Hell, no!' "[30]

In accordance with the legislators' decision a special working group was formed that, jointly with Pentagon agencies, again embarked upon a search for a survivable basing system for the new missile. These findings resulted in the so-called Closely Spaced Basing (CSB) scheme, or Dense Pack.[31] In this basing mode the main stake was made not on a greater number of targets (as with dispersed mulitiple protective shelters) than the number of nuclear warheads presumably targeted on them, but on a completely different principle. This was the so-called fratricide effect, whereby the consequences of the explosion of the first warhead destroys, disables, or deflects from course other incoming warheads at a certain distance from its epicenter. The essence of CSB was to place the MX silos so close to each other and to make them so superhardened that, regardless of the yield of the attacking warheads, each explosion would not so much destroy silos as "shield" them from being destroyed by accompanying warheads. Theoretically, this should have guaranteed the survival of more than 50 percent of the ICBMs in the course of a hypothetical attack.

The total cost of the MX program with such a basing system was estimated at approximately $25 billion. Spokesmen for the Department of Defense also pointed out that CSB, if necessary, could be supplemented in the future by an ABM complex for an additional expenditure on the order of $12 billion. They also reserved the option to construct additional superhardened silos as well within the ICBM deployment region in order to confuse the opponent, that is, to combine the principle of the earlier MPS system with the Closely Spaced Basing scheme.

In December 1982 the secretary of defense presented the new plan for congressional review, having renamed the MX the "Peacekeeper." "[T]he unique capabilities of the Peacekeeper missile, deployed in CSB," said Weinberger, "strengthen deterrence in three ways: by ending the Soviet monopoly in hard target capability; by restoring the effectiveness and survivability of the ICBM force; and by bolstering the resilience of the strategic Triad."[32] But in spite of the administration's intensive lobbying effort, the program came under criticism from various sides. In the first place, a number of experts, including Townes himself, the former head of the president's commission to examine MX basing modes, expressed a lack of confidence in the feasibility of the increase called for in silo hardness. Such experts as Richard Garwin, Barry Carter, and Kosta Tsipis offered the opinion that there were many ways, much quicker and cheaper than the time and money required for the administration's plan, to overcome the fratricide effect.

Serious objections to Weinberger's plan were raised by his predecessor, Harold Brown, one of the most authoritative U.S. military experts:

Incoming reentry vehicles are more vulnerable than hardened silos. Unfortunately, the MX missiles are themselves still more vulnerable during the several minutes of their launch and powered flight and could be forced to remain in their silos, "pinned down" by the incoming Soviet attack . . . .Whether fratricide has a more destructive effect on the attack than pindown has on the residual MX force is a difficult question. . . . My own judgement is that Densepack without an MPS feature is likely to be vulnerable to destruction by a properly executed attack of only a few hundred 1-megaton Soviet warheads, or even fewer larger ones; thus, it is not a good military or technical solution."[33]

Former CIA director Admiral Stansfield Turner stated that, despite the Pentagon's arguments, ensuring the coverage of closely spaced missiles with an ABM system would also be highly difficult: "If there is one thing that you don't want to do with an anti-ballistic system, it is to bunch your targets close together. That makes it easier for the enemy to saturate the system with attacking missiles."[34]

As it turned out, the U.S. military leadership also did not like the idea of deploying one of the main strategic systems while relying on controversial and theoretical calculations unverifiable in practice. JCS chairman Army General John Vessey, who had replaced David Jones, said this about Closely Spaced Basing: "The first time I heard of it, I thought the thing was crazy. For guys like me, who'd been telling troops, spread out, don't bunch up, the idea of everyone bunching up on the bull's eye seemed crazy."[35] True, the president and the secretary of defense ultimately "convinced" Vessey to support the plan, and the air force followed this example. However, the commanders of the army, the navy and the Marines, while approving the deployment of the MX ICBM, opposed the CSB system. A majority of experts from the "strategic community" took the same position. A White House official later acknowledged: "We tried to round up five eminent scientists who would testify to Congress that fratricide would work. We couldn't find one."[36]

There was another side as well in all this, to which U.S. critics of this basing system have devoted insufficient attention. The MX basing schemes advanced by the administration, which pursued the aim of more quickly pushing through the missile system to the testing and production stage at any price, seriously conflicted with the SALT I and SALT II treaties that the administration in May 1982 had pledged not to violate.[37] Washington was officially warned by the Soviet minister of defense on the most serious consequences of such actions.[38] In particular, the construction of superhardened silos according to the CSB plan would have violated one of the central provisions of both agreements, which was the obligation not to create additional fixed ICBM launchers and not to relocate them to other regions (Article IV, Paragraphs 1 and 2 of the SALT II Treaty). The Pentagon's arguments that the missile's "launcher" should supposedly be considered as the mobile launching container, but not the reinforced concrete silo, which was allegedly only a "shelter," were absolutely unconvincing. In reality a missile with a container would be placed in a silo and launched from it. Any attempts to manipulate these provisions casually would deprive of meaning one of the basic SALT limitations—the number of ICBM launching silos—that the United States itself more than anything else sought to attain in the 1970s. Destroying this limitation, should the other side take advantage of it, would put the United States as well in a highly complicated position.

The administration's other option—placing the MX missile in superhardened Minuteman ICBM silos—would have violated yet another provision of SALT II, since it would have required increasing the size of such silos beyond the agreed limit of 32 percent (Article IV, Paragraph 4). Finally, the plans for eventually deploying an ABM system for coverage of the planned MX basing region on Warren Air Force Base in Wyoming would be a direct violation of the ABM Treaty and its Protocol, in accordance with which the United States has the right to move an ABM system from the Grand Forks base region, where its components are presently deployed, only to the region of the U.S. capital.

The above examples serve as a clear illustration of how existing arms control accords, even without being ratified, can impose quite tangible curbs on the arms race. Moreover, this limiting influence appears in such areas that would hardly have been possible to foresee earlier, at the time the agreements were being negotiated. This speaks well for broad, comprehensive, and strict limitations in the strategic nuclear arms area. All these factors, combined with the rise of the nuclear freeze movement, brought about this decision on Capitol Hill, the first serious strike against the prestige and influence of the Reagan administration. Congress refused to allocate resources to the MX program in conjunction with the Dense Pack basing mode. A resolution was adopted to require another review of the entire approach to land-based missile forces and, in particular, a review of the MX missile basing system as a necessary condition for continuing this program.[39] Weinberger threatened to resign, but was not allowed to by the president.

The night after the vote Senators William Cohen and Warren Rudman and White House aide Kenneth Duberstein gathered in the office of Vice President George Bush to find a way to save the MX program and avert a split between the administration and Congress that would paralyze U.S. politics. According to their recommendation President Reagan named a new bipartisan commission under the leadership of retired General Brent Scowcroft, Kissinger's former assistant and his successor in the NSC under President Ford. The commission was composed of a number of well-known experts and politicians,[40] and was to provide (again!) a final decision on the MX issue and to plan for the future more general approaches to policy in the strategic weapons area.

The report of the Scowcroft Commission was presented to President Reagan on April 6, 1983. It was a significant event in the history of U.S. strategic policy, and we will return later to its military-political significance in the broader sense of the word. Here it will only be noted that the Scowcroft Report turned out to be the "saving grace" of the MX program and the administration's prestige. It rejected the idea of combining by technical means two features in a single missile: increased survivability, and enormous destructive power directed primarily at striking a large number of hard targets on Soviet territory. The essence of the commission's recommendation was to divide these two nearly incompatible qualities between two different weapon systems. It was proposed to keep the latter for the MX and deploy 100 of them in the second half of the 1980s in existing Minuteman silos. But the former was to be entrusted to a new small ICBM with a single warhead—the "Midgetman"—which was to be much more survivable, being deployed in significant quantities (around 1,000 missiles) on mobile launchers or in another invulnerable mode in the first half of the 1990s.[41]

As for the future Midgetman system, great technical, strategic, economic, and political uncertainties are connected with it. According to certain competent estimates, the apparent simplicity and low cost of such a system are highly deceptive. For example, guaranteeing adequate survivability for the system, according to one option, would require dispersing 1,000 missiles on mobile hardened transporter-erector-launchers in an area approximately equal to the size of the state of Oklahoma. In this case major complications arise from the problems of ensuring the missiles' protection, combat readiness, retargeting flexibility, maintenance, prevention of unauthorized launch, and so forth. The cost of deploying such a system could reach $46 billion, and total expenses, including operation and maintenance, could amount to $107 billion over the course of 20 years.[42] And all of this would be for the sake of guaranteeing the survival of 600 warheads in a hypothetical nuclear strike—that is, the number of warheads on three *Ohio* submarines.

However, in one respect the "effectiveness" of the Midgetman scheme was indisputable. This small missile of the distant future opened the way politically for the powerful missile of the present—the MX. Having removed the previous problematical task of maintaining the MX's invulnerability, the Scowcroft Commission linked its deployment with a number of other advantages. Among them were the placing of a major "bargaining chip" at Washington's disposal in arms control negotiations with the Soviet Union and the political demonstration of resolve in building up its nuclear might, especially considering the 5 billion dollars already spent on the system. Also relevant was the need to immediately develop a new generation of ICBMs previously planned for the 1990s to replace the aging Titan and Minuteman systems deployed in the 1950s and 1960s, as well as guarantee additional resources for launching satellites into orbit so as not to rely solely on the Space Shuttle. But the main purpose of the MX missile, in the commission's opinion, was that it would provide a means of "controlled limited attack on hardened targets."

True, it was contended that 100 MX ICBMs would have the same total throw-weight and megatonnage as the 54 Titan II missiles retired from the arsenal plus the 100 Minuteman III missiles they replaced. The Scowcroft Commission also tried to demonstrate that its proposed steps did not violate strategic stability, since 100 MX ICBMs would not have "a sufficient number of warheads to be able to attack all hardened Soviet ICBMs, much less all of the many command posts and other hardened military targets in the Soviet Union."[43] A much larger MX deployment, numbering at least several hundred missiles, would be necessary for effectively carrying out the above tasks, the report stated.

President Reagan unconditionally accepted the Scowcroft Commission's recommendations and immediately began to force them through Congress. In particular, he sent two messages to Capitol Hill in which he pledged to organize a bipartisan advisory group in Congress on arms control and in general to more actively draw legislators into decision making on strategic arms. He personally made 20 telephone calls to key members of Congress and the day before the vote gave a banquet for 40 uncommitted congressmen. As a result, both the Senate (59 to 39) and the House of Representatives (239 to 186) approved the commission's and the president's recommendations in votes of late May and early June of 1983 and allocated $625 million for completing development and moving toward the testing and serial production of the new missile.[44] The future of the program at that moment was certain.

In reality the probable consequences of this step, despite the Scowcroft Commission's arguments, will be destabilizing. But to clarify this conclusion it is necessary to examine the MX decision in the context of the Reagan administration's entire strategic program. Its declaratory policy, as observed above, is notable for its significant vagueness and self-contradiction. A complex design of political, strategic, economic, and technical considerations lie at the basis of decisions on military programs. But each strategic weapon system possesses its own unique and exceptionally expensive characteristics, specific advantages and disadvantages, in comparison with other systems in fulfilling a given military task. Therefore, regardless of the political motives that determine decisions at any given moment, arms programs, once launched and having gained momentum, to a certain degree acquire their own laws of development and influence on the military balance, predetermine the shifting of emphasis in strategic doctrine and operational planning, and subsequently influence the options for using nuclear weapons, that is, immediately affect the possible conditions and probability of unleashing global war.

## The "First Strike" Option

Looking at the Reagan program from the above point of view, one's attention is first of all drawn to the fact that in building up the striking power of all three legs of the triad and in replacing old weapons systems with new, emphasis is being made not on increasing the number of strategic launchers (as in the 1950s and the first half of the 1960s), but on increasing the number of nuclear charges deliverable in a single launch or sortie.[45] In the 1980s and first half of the 1990s the total number of launchers will most likely be reduced, since newer, more expensive and complex arms will replace the old at less than a one-to-one ratio.[46] From 1979 through 1983 the number had already dropped from 2,280 to 2,000 launchers. But the total number of individually targetable warheads will substantially grow, from 8,800 in 1983 to 14,000 in 1990, that is, by 60 percent. However, increasing the number of nuclear warheads alone, which permits covering an expanded target set and planning diverse strike options, is not the main direction of the arms race for the United States in the next years. Remember that in the 1970s the number of warheads grew by even more than what is planned in the future, more precisely, by almost 100 percent (from 5,000 to approximately 10,000).[47]

The core of the Reagan strategic program is a buildup of warheads with hard-target-kill capability, that is, possessing the necessary combination of increased yield and accuracy. The number of such warheads with which the MX, Midgetman, and Trident-II missiles, the Tomahawk SLCM, and the B-1B, Stealth, and B-52 bombers (with ALCMs) will be equipped will grow from approximately 2,000 to 6,000 in 1990, and to 9,000 in 1996, that is, by three times in comparison with the present, and by 4.5 times later on. Within these plans the main emphasis will be on an expansion of such counterforce weapons on less vulnerable launchers. Whereas about 1,500 warheads in U.S. strategic forces, according to the calculations of certain experts, now possess such a capability, by 1990 this level will have grown to almost 4,000, and by 1996, to 6,500. Currently almost all such weapons are deployed on heavy bombers,[48] which are considered "slow flying" weapons, since they require several hours to reach their targets. As a result of the Republican administration's program, by 1990 the share of sea-based missile forces will grow slightly to ensure a less vulnerable hard-target-kill potential, and by 1996 approximately 10 percent of such a potential will be concentrated in land-based missiles (mainly on Midgetman), while 45 percent each will be found on the sea and air legs of the triad.[49] Thus the greatest growth in the Reagan program will take place in SLBM forces, the "fast flying" invulnerable forces for destroying hard targets.

By 1990 such U.S. strategic potential is planned to be increased six-fold, and by 1996, almost 20-fold (from 150 warheads to 890, then to 3,470). Sea-based forces, in particular the accurate and powerful war-heads on the Trident-II SLBM, will fulfill the main role here. Thus the Reagan administration's strategic policy implies not simply a buildup of U.S. nuclear might, but a radical restructuring of its strategic arsenal, giving it qualitatively new strategic and operational possibilites.

It must be noted that the Carter administration proposed moving in a similar direction in its military programs, that is, developing forces for promptly destroying hard targets in conditions of either a brief or "protracted" thermonuclear war as stipulated by the countervailing doctrine and PD-59. However, the Republican leadership was committed to moving along this path much further, in a shorter period of time, and along a broader front. For example, appearing before the Senate Armed Services Committee, Weinberger stated that by 1990 according to the Reagan program the United States would have 18 percent more strategic launchers, 11 percent more warheads, and 12 percent more hard-target-kill capability than was planned under the Democrats. Much more important in his opinion was that by 1990 the Republican administration's defense program would allow the U.S. to have 10 percent more warheads and 25 percent more hard-target-kill capability able to survive in the course of a nuclear exchange.[50] In creating less vulnerable hard-target-kill-capable forces the Carter administration proposed to lean mainly on land-based missile forces—200 MX ICBMs in multiple protective shelters. The Democrats' successors made a greater stake on a sea-based missile force of 20 *Ohio* submarines with 480 Trident-II SLBMs, and also significantly increased the reliance on bombers as redundant, although "slow-flying," hard-target-kill-capable weapons.

These differences presuppose certain changes as well in U.S. nuclear strategy. The Democratic administration, at least in its public statements, until the very end denied any intentions to create a hard-target-kill capability for putting at risk the entire set of hard targets of the USSR's

Strategic Rocket Forces, in which are concentrated about 60 percent of its strategic retaliatory forces. The Republican leadership openly adopted a policy to create a full-scale potential for a crushing strike on the entire set of Soviet land-based missile forces and other related strategic targets. The secretary of defense, for example, said in early 1982 that the Trident submarine in combination with the Trident-II missile would enable the United States to strike the entire spectrum of targets from reliable and highly survivable launch platforms.

The significant shift of emphasis in U.S. nuclear strategy to sea-based missile forces as the means for rapidly striking the other side's strategic weapons also presupposes certain changes in the Pentagon's strategic doctrine and operational plans. As first-strike weapons, sea-based missile forces, by ensuring the proper combination of warhead yield and accuracy, can, in the Pentagon's opinion, have a number of substantial advantages. Since the flight time of an SLBM is on average half as much as that of a land-based missile (15 minutes compared to 30), the use of sea-based missile forces can guarantee greater surprise in a strike. Flight time can be reduced still further (to 5–7 minutes) and surpise increased if long-range SLBMs such as the Trident II are launched along a so-called depressed trajectory from a shortened distance. Furthermore, submarines can deliver strikes from different azimuths, that is, from unexpected directions. Thus SSBNs can be considered in the future as effective weapons for surprise nuclear strikes on hard and time-urgent targets. It is much easier to guarantee the command and control system for carrying out a first strike on these targets with the help of SLBMs than a "retaliatory strike."[51] In this respect the writings of Keith Payne, an analyst at the National Institute for Public Policy, seem important, since they have obviously received recognition among the U.S. military-political leadership. Payne holds that the potential for a disarming first strike on Soviet strategic forces, specifically ICBMs, must itself be as invulnerable as possible, as must be its command, control, and communications system. However, the whole idea of counterforce D-5 SLBMs as a potential weapon for retaliatory strikes on "reserve" Soviet ICBMs is highly inconsistent.[52] This cannot but create suspicions that the real employment plan for these missiles will be for a preemptive counterforce attack.

The MX decision in 1983 obviously did not square with the strategic policy noted by Payne, Gray, and other adherents to the nuclear war-fighting doctrine. Missiles with a powerful hard-target-kill potential were to be put in theoretically vulnerable silos, and the development of a survivable ICBM basing system was postponed until the 1990s. The fact that the Pentagon could not find a basing mode for the MX acceptable in technical, strategic, economic, and political respects apparently also explains the decisions from 1981 to 1983 to cut its deployment in half, from 200 to 100. This decision was made despite the fact that in 1979–80 many Reagan supporters insisted on increasing the number to 300-400 or more missiles. But this would have exposed the administration to the charge that it was demonstrably creating first-strike forces which, deployed in vulnerable launch sites, would be a magnet for a nuclear strike.

Weinberger explained the plan to deploy such a number of MX missiles in the following way: "There is no such thing as a first strike weapon—only a first strike force. That is to say, no missile system, however effective, can confer a first strike capability by itself. To have a first strike capability such a system must be deployed in sufficient numbers to enable it to significantly reduce the effectiveness of an opponent's strategic force. At 100 Peacekeeper missiles, the President's deployment plan does not even approach such a capability."[53]

However, in the first place the secretary was obviously being modest: even 100 MX ICBMs is a powerful force, not to mention the possibility of deploying an even greater number of such missiles, by no means ruled out by the administration. Once mass production of the MX gets underway, deploying more than 100 missiles in existing silos will be a problem neither economically nor technically, compared to what the case would be with other proposed basing modes. Second, even 100 MX missiles can exert a seriously destabilizing influence on the strategic balance. In fact, owing to the combination of yield and accuracy of their 1,000 warheads, this ICBM group alone could destroy the greater part of the Soviet Union's hardest targets, such as command centers and MIRVed ICBM silos (820 of them). In addition, the United States would have another 900 or more Mk-12A warheads on Minuteman-III ICBMs, themselves capable of destroying a significant number of such targets.

Moreover, in comparing Soviet and U.S. land-based missile forces, U.S. experts, especially those associated with the current leadership, portray this aspect of the overall strategic balance quite inadequately. They do this in two ways. On the one hand, they omit from their calculations the different relative share of theoretically destroyable strategic forces in the two sides' nuclear arsenals. Land-based missiles now account for around 20 percent of the total warheads in the U.S. strategic triad. In absolute terms even the "reduced survivability" of 90 percent of U.S. ICBMs, repeatedly underscored by leaders of the United States in their "window of vulnerability" campaign, at that time would have meant the vulnerability of only 1,930 warheads (out of 8,800). In comparison, with the same destruction of Soviet forces, that is, 90 percent of its 4,000–5,000 silo-based ICBM warheads, the Soviet Union would have lost the overwhelming share of its retaliatory potential.[54] So is revealed the true nature of the "nonoffensive" plan to deploy the MX system.

On the other hand, when removing the correlation in destructive power of land-based missiles from the overall context, the Pentagon's leadership is also silent on the role the MX missile could play in cooperation with the Trident II in the 1990s. Even without looking at the secret SIOP, one can imagine various operational plans according to which the rapidly retargetable MX would be set aside for "mopping up," for example, surviving targets after a massive SLBM strike, or themselves striking the hardest and most important targets after an SLBM attack against the command and control system. Pershing II missiles, which have exceptional accuracy and an even shorter flight time to their targets than SLBMs, could be used against hardened command centers and missile silos. Both GLCMs and SLCMs, extremely difficult to detect before and after launch, are also capable of striking a wide set of early warning and communications targets.

Another particular danger of the MX program is that placing the missiles in existing silos, whose vulnerability was so often the subject of the writings and speeches of U.S. ruling officials and their advisers in the late 1970s, will create a strong stimulus for the Pentagon to plan to use them in no uncertain terms. The following calculations are cause for serious thought. In the theoretical conditions of a U.S. retaliatory strike the MX would by 1990 contribute less than 3 percent of all survivable warheads able to destroy hard targets in the course of a hypothetical attack on the United States. It is difficult to believe that such a potential justifies the $14 billion planned for the development, production, and deployment of 100 MX missiles. On the other hand, as first-strike weapons these missiles would provide by 1990 16 percent of hard-target-kill-capable warheads. Even more significant, according to U.S. data, is MX's contribution to prompt hard-target-kill capability. The MX will provide 44 percent of this capability in 1990.[55]

The objective military capabilities of the MX provide the grounds for considering this system as precisely a first-strike weapon, regardless of the defense secretary's denials. Weinberger himself, however, inadvertently provided serious confirmation for this point of view. Appearing before the Senate in December 1982 and arguing in favor of the Dense Pack basing system, he stated: "If our purpose in developing and deploying Peacekeeper were to acquire a first strike capability it would not have been necessary to expend so much time and effort to develop a survivable means of deploying it."[56] By reverse logic, then, the decision to deploy these missiles in admittedly vulnerable existing silos must also imply plans for using this weapon system to deliver a first strike.

The concept of a massive first strike to destroy the maximum number of Soviet strategic forces, based on the MX, Trident-II, and Pershing-II programs, is supplemented by the concept of a "limited and protracted" nuclear war on both a regional and global scale. At first glance these two concepts are incompatible. But in the purely academic minds of Washington strategists they would organically complement each other. Indeed, according to U.S. calculations, under any scenario for striking Soviet strategic forces and even after a massive nuclear exchange on each other's military targets, thousands of unspent nuclear weapons would remain in both powers' arsenals that could not be destroyed quickly. In the event that this enormous reserve potential were brought down upon the population and economy of the belligerents in total and final strikes, the horrendous scale of destruction would reduce to nothing all the advantages that the authors of U.S. strategy count on achieving. Therefore, the Pentagon has decided that nuclear forces not spent in the first volleys can still be used selectively over an extended period of time in conditions of a "limited and protracted" nuclear war.

In accordance with previous concepts, nuclear war at the intercontinental level would either begin immediately through a massive exchange on each other's strategic forces, or through a series of selective attacks and counterattacks against military and isolated industrial targets leading up to such an exchange. But after the exchange on strategic forces, military operations would either cease or move to the total destruction of administrative-industrial centers. The "post-strike exchange ratio" was thus transformed into one of the most important criteria of the "sufficiency" of U.S. strategic potential, although no one had devised a way for this ratio to be used to conclude a "truce" or continue the war. Former Secretary of Defense Harold Brown, in particular, recognized that "it would be an equally questionable measure of success to have, after an exchange, a residual capability—whether measured in throw-weight or warheads—that is equal to or larger than the residual capability of the Soviet Union, especially if both nations had been reduced to radioactive rubble in the meantime."[57] But once again the incoming administration devised a way to use the unspent forces of destruction. Continuing to hold the other side's cities as hostages, U.S. strategists now plan for a long (up to several months) period for inflicting limited nuclear strikes on leadership and command posts not yet destroyed by nuclear forces, as well as on various military and economic targets. By that time the United States and its allies would also have undertaken intensive ASW operations against Soviet SSBNs at sea. Along with BMD, air defense, and civil defense, the war would be conducted in space as well. As a result of just such military operations the United States hopes to secure "victory" and reduce its damage to an "acceptable" level.

If Washington's previous strategic concepts were quite removed from reality, then the recent "discoveries" in U.S. strategic theory have severed any past connection with it. In psychiatry this is called schizoid behavior. However, in U.S. nuclear strategy these ideas have received prominent display and have become embodied in certain military programs. For example, *Ohio* submarines with Trident-I and Trident-II missiles could spread among themselves the functions of a massive strike on strategic forces and of a long-standing reserve at sea for use in subsequent stages of the conflict. Multipurpose SSNs with long-range cruise missiles could provide on order "limited" and highly accurate nuclear strikes that, as Weinberger maintains, would guarantee a near-term acquisition of hard-target-kill capability as well as supplement the strategic reserve. These considerations also explain plans to use the B-1B penetrating bombers and future Stealth bombers for repeat attacks against Soviet land-mobile ICBMs, which would be difficult to target in advance with U.S. ballistic and cruise missiles.[58]

Offensive strategic arms programs are not the only ones to demonstrate tangibly and graphically the growth of U.S. nuclear strategy's aggressiveness and war-fighting orientation. The nuclear war-fighting doctrine is also clearly reflected in the Reublican leadership's measures in the $C^3$ sphere. Changes in U.S. strategic doctrine have revealed the inadequacy of the $C^3$ system, which now faces increased demands. The DoD's civilian leadership and experts who had increasingly penetrated the operational side of strategic nuclear policy have come to the conclusion that, despite all the refinements of new weapons and their combat tasks, strategic capabilities are strictly limited by the characteristics of the $C^3$ system.

If one examines the $C^3$ system in U.S. strategic forces, a number of not unimportant conclusions can be drawn. First of all it is obvious that certain concepts in U.S. nuclear strategy and related arms programs directed at changing the nuclear balance in reality are far removed from the capabilities of controlling strategic nuclear operations. The principles of "selective missile attacks," "controlled nuclear exchanges," "escalation dominance," the idea of preserving an extensive "strategic reserve" for conducting a "protracted nuclear war," and calculations of the "poststrike exchange ratio" at each level of military operations correspond very little to the realities of the $C^3$ system. Yet another conclusion is that the generally accepted (in the West) theory of "strategic stability" also in large measure does not correspond with the real situation. The most dangerous weapons from the point of view of crisis stability are obviously not ICBMs, which may theoretically destroy enemy missile silos, but forces that may, with minimal warning of attack, take out early warning systems, communication nodes, command centers, and airborne command posts. Highly effective in this respect are SLBMs with powerful and accurate warheads, such as the Trident-I and Trident-II, which may be launched along depressed trajectories. Such attacks would provide even less warning in the event that submarines launched their missiles just off the other side's coasts. Most destabilizing, in view of the ability to maintain reliable two-way communications and flexible strike coordination, would be highly accurate forward-based intermediate-range ballistic missiles, such as the Pershing-II (whose flight-time is 10–13 minutes), as well as long-range cruise missiles, which are extremely difficult to locate before launch and in flight.

The Reagan administration has devoted primary attention to improving $C^3$, spending nearly $20 billion on it. Plans in this area have been divided into two elements or stages. First, Reagan planned to expand and accelerate the previous administration's programs to deploy more powerful and modernized early warning and long-range detection systems, airborne command posts, and space-, air-, and land-based communications systems for ensuring a capability for rapid and coordinated strategic operations, especially for striking the other side's strategic forces and $C^3$ systems.[59] Second, it is proposed over the long term to create a survivable $C^3$ complex for ensuring extended combat operations in accordance with the "protracted nuclear war" concept.

### Rising to the Space Frontier: The "Star Wars" Vision

Owing to the 1972 ABM Treaty and its 1974 Protocol, an all-out arms race in this area was practically frozen for more than a decade. However, developments in this military-technical sphere not limited by the treaty and not verifiable by the other side's national technical means continued in research laboratories. U.S. annual appropriations for such purposes averaged about $200 million. They were justified by the necessity of "keeping up" with the possible development of such technology in the USSR, of perfecting offensive weapons in a timely manner, and of not allowing the other side to achieve an "unexpected technological breakthrough." But despite these "justifications," it was in the United States itself in the early 1980s that serious discussion was begun of the possibility of reviving ballistic missile defense.

Rapid technological progress in radar and other sensor technologies, high-speed computers, means of interception, expanded possibilities for using space for military purposes, and the development of new operational concepts brought forward a whole series of BMD schemes. This concerns first of all a point defense system developed on the basis of components of the old Safeguard system for defending ICBM sites. The United States could have feasibly deployed such point defenses as early as the mid-1980s. But this system also retained the many technical shortcomings of Safeguard. Considered a much more improved and effective project was the Low-Altitude Defense System (LoADS), which was specially developed for protecting the MX MPS system and could have been constructed in the late 1980s. Still more ambitious plans—the defense of entire regions of U.S. territory—were connected with the scheme for layered defenses, which combined the exoatmospheric nonnuclear interception of enemy warheads with the low-altitude defense of individual targets (for example, with the help of the above LoADS system). Such an ABM option was planned for the 1990s. But with prospects for the twenty-first century, research was conducted with the goal of creating orbiting BMD stations with a fundamentally new means of intercepting ballistic missiles. If accomplished, it would portend a radical shift in the military balance and all strategic doctrines of the nuclear age. The U.S. military-industrial complex and the circles connected with it considered this to be their Rubicon line for moving toward long-term overwhelming strategic superiority.

A most important integral element of these changes was the heavy emphasis on Soviet efforts in active and passive strategic defense as part of the "Soviet threat" campaign. As we will recall, the main argument against ABM in the late 1960s and early 1970s, advanced even by Robert McNamara, was that large programs of this kind would put in doubt the "assured destruction" capability of the retaliatory strike of one or both sides. This development would destabilize the situation of "mutual deterrence," which destabilization would, in turn, sharply push forward the arms race into an offense-defense competition and radically undermine the SALT process. In the early 1980s proponents of BMD began to attract more and more attention and interest in U.S. ruling circles with their assertions that this argument had allegedly proved false in practice.

Expressing such views, Colin Gray, for example, wrote that U.S. experts have concluded that the Soviet Union does not adhere to anything similar to the Western notion of strategic stability, nor does it share the concept of assured destruction. To confirm this thesis, in addition to charges that Soviet ICBM "counterforce" strength had grown, "facts" were marshalled on Soviet developments in the BMD area, on the upgrading of the "massive" Soviet air defenses, on the increased capability of certain radars and air defense missiles to fulfill BMD functions, and also on the extensive Soviet civil defense system. In addition, the champions of this campaign in the United States, citing Soviet MIRV programs in the 1970s, asserted that both powers' repudiation of ABM systems in 1972 and 1974 did not slow the offensive strategic arms race at all. Finally, it was pointed out that despite the ABM limitations the dialogue on containing the offensive arms race had reached a dead end, the SALT II treaty had not been ratified, and the prospects for strategic arms control in the 1980s were not favorable.[60]

None of these arguments stands up to criticism. The "disproportions" in U.S. and Soviet active and passive defense systems cannot be considered apart from the differences in the two powers' geostrategic and political positions. (Nuclear-armed aircraft and ballistic missiles of third powers pose practically no threat to the United States.) An even more substantial factor was Soviet policy in practice. Its consistent line to limit

BMD excluded calculations ascribed to the USSR to "limit" its damage and "win" a global thermonuclear war. The offensive arms race in the 1970s, including the deployment of MIRV systems, was explained by U.S., not Soviet initiatives. All the more reason for there to be no Soviet guilt for the failure of the SALT II Treaty, which was in fact derailed by the United States.

The true motivating forces behind the movement to revive BMD are rooted primarily in the shift of the center of gravity in U.S. deterrence strategy from the concept of "assured destruction" to various options of limited, selective nuclear strikes. As has already been shown, a most important aspect of this strategy—the U.S. creation of a less vulnerable prompt hard-target-kill capability put squarely in the center of attention the idea of defending U.S. ICBMs with LoADS, whose development was sufficiently advanced. And in a broader respect, the nuclear war-fighting doctrine could not help but open the way to reviving ballistic missile defense. Thus even if in the forseeable future BMD offered little prospect for defending U.S. territory from a massive nuclear strike, such a system could play a tangible role in various scenarios of "limited" exchanges, in a protracted war, and in calculating both sides' relative damage and the "post-strike exchange ratio." Moreover, proponents maintained that after a certain point various BMD options in such plans would be more cost-effective than further improvements in offensive weapons systems. The increased attention in official U.S. strategy toward the question of what to do if deterrence should "fail" also strengthened the attractiveness of BMD. "If deterrence fails," wrote one BMD supporter, "the U.S. President will quickly discover that in reality he is very interested in reasonable plans for conducting war and physically defending the United States and less worried about bringing down punishment on Soviet society.[61] The idea, then ascendant in U.S. strategic thinking, that the deterrent effect depends not on overall destructive power, but on the ability to "prevail" in global hostilities against the opponent's military potential, was a major factor in reviving the popularity of BMD in certain circles of the U.S. ruling class. Hopes for economically exhausting the Soviet Union by opening up new channels in the arms race as well played no minor role.

It is also impossible not to note the domestic politics aspect of the U.S. campaign for BMD. As will be recalled, the U.S. liberal opposition to the military-industrial complex and the strategic arms race took shape in the 1967–70 ABM debate. The SALT dialogue began with the limitation of ABM systems, and the 1972 ABM Treaty, apart from its enormous significance, essentially became a symbol of the reality of mutually acceptable agreements for the superpowers on cardinally important questions of their security. Finally, the ABM Treaty remains the only truly radical, unlimited-duration agreement in the sphere of SALT that has been ratified. For all these reasons, the revival of ballistic missile defense with the revision or repudiation of the 1972 treaty became an exceptionally enticing goal for militarist circles. Its achievement would be for them evidence of a complete turnabout within the country, a victory in the struggle for decisive influence over foreign policy. It would carry to its logical end the policy of destroying the fruits of détente of the 1970s and undermine for a long time to come the possibility of continuing the SALT process.

Appropriations for strategic defense programs had already been increased in the latter period of the Democratic administration's rule. But a truly sharp jump in funding took place with the coming to power of the Reagan administration. It involved the intensification of research and development on new BMD projects, including fundamentally new concepts. (About $6 billion was allocated for BMD research and development in the FY 1983–87 program.) It also involved programs for upgrading air defense (which had largely been dismantled and become obsolete in the 1960s and 1970s), including new long-range radar detection systems, AWACS aircraft, and the latest fighter-intercepters. Finally, the Reagan administration proposed reviving broad measures in the area of civil defense, such as constructing shelters and developing evacuation plans for the population, and increasing the hardness of economic installations. Such attempts had twice before (in the early 1960s and the mid-1970s) ended in failure. Civil defense was allocated approximately $2 billion over a five-year period.[62]

U.S. plans for militarizing space were also closely connected with the development of BMD systems. This process had already been going on for a long time; since the early 1960s U.S. forces, especially strategic, had increasingly relied on satellites for early warning of attack, intelligence, communication, and navigation. On the other hand, satellites have begun to play a great role as a national technical means of verifying SALT compliance and in the "Hot-Line" link between Washington and Moscow to prevent miscalculations or misperceptions in a crisis.

The development of various antisatellite (ASAT) weapons systems initiated a truly dangerous phase in the militarization of space. A "Soviet ASAT threat" campaign had already begun in the United States in the 1970s. Yet the precedent belongs to the United States here as well: already in the 1960s it had created a system for destroying the other side's satellites based on Thor missiles on Johnston island in the Pacific Ocean. In the late 1970s ASAT development was seriously accelerated. Soviet-U.S. negotiations to limit ASAT systems, begun in 1978, were frozen in 1979 by the U.S. side.

The Reagan administration from the beginning has made the militarization of space an important link in its military policy. In 1981 appropriations to the Pentagon's military-space programs grew to $6 billion, in 1982 to $9 billion, and by 1988 were planned to reach $14 billion annually.[63] On September 1, 1982 the U.S. Space Command was created at Peterson Air Force Base in Colorado and charged with co-ordinating U.S. military activities in space. The new U.S. ASAT system, initially planned to be operational in 1985, consists of a two-stage missile with a self-guided nonnuclear warhead. It is launched from an F-15 fighter at an altitude of about 20 kilometers and is capable of destroying satellites out to an altitude of 600 kilometers. Still greater hopes are connected with an ASAT system utilizing land- or sea-based lasers.[64] In this realm ASATs are closing ranks with futuristic space-based BMD schemes.

The idea of "Star Wars"—orbiting battle stations and space ships with laser weapons able to destroy enemy satellites at any altitude and ballistic missiles emerging from the dense layers of the atmosphere—has long excited the imagination of U.S. strategists. In the early 1980s schemes of orbiting laser stations were at the center of the attention of Congress and the mass media. According to leaked information, in late 1982 Dr. Edward Teller, the father of the U.S. hydrogen bomb and the indefatigable "pusher" of all new weapon systems, met with President Reagan in the White House and urgently recommended that he authorize the development of a space-based laser system for intercepting ballistic missiles. By all appearances, no great effort was required to captivate the president on this question.

On March 23, 1983 Reagan delivered a speech in which he called for the creation of BMD weapons, including a space-based antiballistic missile system. "Let me share with you a vision of the future which offers hope," said the president. "It is that we embark on a program to counter the awesome Soviet missile threat with measures that are defensive.... What if free people could live secure in the knowledge that their security did not rest upon the threat of instant U.S. retaliation to deter a Soviet attack; that we could intercept and destroy strategic ballistic missiles before they reached our own soil or that of our allies?" Since this will take decades, he stated, it is necessary to begin immediately.[65]

The assertion that new BMD systems promise to save humanity from strategic nuclear weapons is the greatest deception of our time. The danger of these schemes is aggravated by the fact that they appeal to the psychologically natural human desire to find once and for all a defense against the all-destructive power of nuclear weapons. The arguments of a number of "competent" specialists add to this the notion that in accordance with the dialectics of the means of war, the predominance of offense must be replaced by the superiority of defense, as has happened repeatedly in the past. In turn, the type of weapons that have prevailed in the course of several decades, in this case nuclear weapons, must with time cede their place to fundamentally new means of destruction: laser or particle beam weapons.

In reality, the competition between offense and defense historically has taken place with varying success. And one must not forget that parallel to this process the overall tendency to expand the destructive consequences of war, especially for the noncombatants, has developed as well. It is enough to recall World War I as the classic example of the primacy of defense, which stipulated the primarily positional or trench character of the war, but which was accompanied by the massive (for that time) destruction of territory in regions of combat (Marne, Verdun, and so on). Nuclear weapons in this respect occupy a very special place, as weapons specially created and for the first time used for the mass annihilation of civilians and their material surroundings. The prospect of totally annihilating noncombatants and devastating enormous areas has always frustrated the attempts of Western strategists to devise some means for using these weapons to resolve more traditional military tasks, to inflict "limited" or "selective" strikes.

The future offense-defense competition, should the new U.S. schemes be implemented, will by no means eliminate the inevitability of the destructive consequences of a potential war, and even more so will not guarantee a "reliable defense" for the civilian population. Rather, precisely the opposite will prevail: the improvement of offensive forces in order to overcome the defense will entail a still greater absolute growth of losses in the event of war.

Estimates of the probable effectiveness of space-based laser weapons are now clashing with enormous technical uncertainties. There is, however, every reason to assume that even if future scientific-technical breakthroughs nevertheless make possible the interception of a significant share of strategic nuclear forces, the strategic consequences thereof will in no way be stabilizing but rather extremely destabilizing. That is, they will not decrease, but rather increase, the probability of global war. For long before the time when an increase of the effectiveness of space-based BMD systems will permit the solving of the most difficult task of defending oneself against a massive nuclear strike, hopes will appear for its capability to defend against a retaliatory strike (that is, to provide the potential to carry out aggression with impunity).

Furthermore, even if one managed to intercept ballistic missiles as they left the atmosphere, what of cruise missiles flying in its dense layers low to the ground? In fact the United States itself is already planning to deploy many thousands of such missiles in the foreseeable future. If the power of energy sources, the effectiveness of focusing the beam, the accuracy of detecting targets and aiming the lasers at them should someday permit the destruction of cruise missiles (and also low-flying aircraft) as well, then space-based BMD systems will, in fact, develop from systems of defense—in accordance with the dialectics of weapons development—into terrible weapons of attack. In other words, nothing would interfere with using these systems directly in a first strike, that is, for destroying on the ground the other side's armed forces, its command and control complex, economic infrastructure, and population. As Yuri V. Andropov observed in his answers to the West German magazine *Der Spiegel*, "the adventurism and danger of this entire venture is that they are counting on delivering a nuclear first strike with impunity, believing that they can protect themselves against a retaliatory strike. From here it is not far to the temptation to push the button."[66]

Moving the arms race into space, moreover, may significantly aggravate political tension in the world and threatens to undermine arms control efforts. Finally, such an attempt entails colossal expenditures and economic costs. Proponents of increasingly newer weapons should have understood that neither new nuclear weapons systems nor schemes of space-based laser stations can guarantee the security of any state in the event of a general war. Nor will "Star Wars" systems help eliminate nuclear weapons, just as combat aircraft did not lead to the elimination of ground and naval forces, and as nuclear weapons did not help to reduce conventional forces. To the contrary, "Star Wars" will certainly raise the military confrontation to a much higher nuclear-space frontier and may push the world over the last, fatal threshold.

The Reagan administration's plans concerning space have aroused major anxiety in the world community. A large group of scholars from the USSR Academy of Sciences issued an "Appeal to All Scientists of the World," in which it was stated in particular that "Based on the knowledge that we, as scientists, dispose, and proceeding from an understanding of the very nature of nuclear weapons, we declare with all responsibility that in a nuclear war there are no effective means of defense, and their creation is impossible in practice.... The use of antiballistic missile weapons is most of all suitable precisely for the attacking side, which is aspiring to degrade the strength of a retaliatory strike. However, they cannot completely prevent this retaliatory strike."[67] A group of eminent U.S. scientists addressed a telegram to Soviet General Secretary Yuri Andropov in which they emphasized that "the testing and deployment of any weapons in space significantly increases the probability of the outbreak of war on Earth." In response the Soviet leader assured them that the Soviet Union would be even more diligent in exerting all efforts in order that the sinister plans for moving the arms race into space not become a reality. He urged that "space remain forever free from any weapons, that it not become an area of military confrontation, and that the threat not come from space for those living on Earth."[68]

* * *

The Reagan administration's nuclear strategy and military programs were directed at creating a U.S. capability to conduct nuclear warfare and prevail in it by destroying the other side's armed forces, reducing its own damage to an "acceptable" level, and simultaneously depriving the Soviet Union of such capabilities. Illustrating the aggressive nature of U.S. strategy, the Soviet minister of defense emphasized that "Superiority is simply understood as the achievement of the capability to strike the Soviet Union at the place and time of Washington's own choosing, while calculating that a retaliatory strike on the U.S. will be less strong than in other conditions."[69]

The Reagan administration's approach to strategic nuclear weapons, whatever new concepts and military programs have been advanced, vividly demonstrates the return to traditional views of military power in politics and war. The principal, qualitatively new features of nuclear weapons, which caused a revolution in strategy and the approach to war itself, have been rejected. Right-wing representatives of U.S. strategic theory, such as Pentagon consultant Edward Luttwak, are trying to prove that thermonuclear weapons are essentially the same as conventional bombs and warheads, but simply more destructive, in order to use them for achieving fully defined and practical operational-tactical and strategic goals that promise victory at the theater and global level. Other experts of the same school of thought—Colin Gray and Keith Payne, mentioned above—are also fighting for the return to what may be called, by analogy with economics, "neo-classical strategic nuclear theory." Payne, for example, writes:

A force posture consistent with Classical Strategy would entail a counter-political/ military deterrent threat via a heavily counterforce targeting policy, and a survivable hard-target kill capability complemented by both active and passive defenses, i.e., air defense, ballistic missile defense, and civil defense. In the not too distant future, high energy laser or particle beam technology may also be incorporated in an effective system for ballistic missiles defense. . . . There is some indication that the Reagan Administration is moving towards Classical Strategy as the proper approach to deterrence.[70]

Thus the unchanged arguments about "deterrence" by U.S. officials and experts should not deceive anyone. The question is not whether arms are being created to "deter" or "conduct" nuclear war. Any weapons system deployed in the armed forces is counted on for real use in real conditions. What is really of utmost importance is against which targets and for which tasks these weapons and strategic forces as a whole are proposed to be used. Weapons primarily designed, deployed, or effective for a first strike, for depriving the other side of its retaliatory capability, for achieving strategic advantages in any version of "limited nuclear war," undermine deterrence and make thermonuclear conflict more probable. But weapons intended for retaliation, for inflicting a certain level of unacceptable damage on a potential nuclear aggressor under any circumstances of the enemy's unleashing of war, generally strengthen deterrence.

Of course, one cannot reduce everything to an evaluation of the technical characteristics of this or that weapons system, even more so because they rarely predetermine unambiguously the character of the weapon's use. Therefore, the overall thrust of foreign policy and the character of a state's military doctrine and strategy, which set the tone for both war plans and arms programs, have exceptional importance. In fact, in the final analysis even the nuclear war-fighting doctrine and weapons for a disarming first strike, for conducting a "limited and protracted" nuclear war, are primarily means of U.S. foreign policy, instruments of political-psychological influence in political relations with other countries—both opponents, allies, and neutrals.

In this sense, in the early 1980s the Reagan administration's attitude toward the problem of curbing the arms race has created a stark background against which the character of U.S. strategic concepts and nuclear programs stand out even more boldly.

### Notes

1. The "quick fixes" (steps for building up U.S. nuclear strength) that could have taken effect already in the early 1980s included: resuming production of the Minuteman-III ICBM and additionally deploying it in silos or in a mobile mode; equipping more than 300 such missiles with Mk-12A warheads; deploying the Trident-I SLBM on a greater number of Poseidon *LaFayette*-class submarines than on the planned 12 of that class; and speeding up production and broadening deployment of air, sea, and ground-launched cruise missiles. See *From Weakness to Strength*, (San Francisco: 1980), 89–108. William R. Van Cleave, *Strategic Options for the Early 1980s: What Can Be Done?*, (White Plains, MD: Automated Graphic Systems, 1979).

2. Robert Scheer, *With Enough Shovels: Reagan, Bush and Nuclear War*, (New York: Random House, 1982), 261.

3. *Materialy XXVI s'ezda KPSS* (Moscow: Politizdat, 1981), 23. *Pravda*, October 21, 1981. *Radi mira na zemle* (Moscow, 1983), 470.

4. Active defenses are usually understood to be defenses against ballistic missiles, aircraft, and submarines, whereas passive defenses are civil defenses—measures for sheltering, evacuating, and dispersing the population and the economy.

5. Scheer, *With Enough Shovels*, 240–41.

6. See V. D. Sololovskii, ed., *Voennaia strategiia*, (Moscow: Voenizdat, 1968); M. M. Kir'an, *Voenno-tekhnicheskii progress i Vooruzhennye Sily SSSR* (Moscow: Voenizdat, 1982); R. G. Bogdanov, *SShA: voenno-strategicheskie kontsepsii* (Moscow: Navka, 1980); Genrikh A. Trofimenko, *SShA: politika, voina, ideologiia* (Moscow: Mysl'; 1976).

7. *Radi mira na zemle: sovetskaia programma mira dlia 80-kh godov v deistvii, materialy i dokumenty* (Moscow: Politizdat, 1983), 187.

8. *Pravda*, May 4, 1978. Dmitrii F. Ustinov, *Sluzhim rodine, delu kommunizma* (Moscow: Voenizdat, 1982), 50.

9. Scheer, *With Enough Shovels*, 206, 210, 211.

10. *Department of Defense Annual Report, Fiscal Year 1983* (Washington, D.C.: U.S. Government Printing Office, 1981), 1–17.

11. *Department of Defense Annual Report, Fiscal Year 1983*, I–48.

12. *The New York Times*, June 10, 1982, A31.

13. *The New York Times*, May 30, 1982.

14. Scheer, *With Enough Shovels*, 135.

15. Colin S. Gray, "Presidential Directive 59: Flawed, but Useful," *Parameters* 11: 1 (March 1981): 30, 32–34.

16. "Nomination of Frank C. Carlucci to be Deputy Secretary of Defense," *Hearings*, Committee on Armed Services, U.S. Senate, 97th Congress, first session, January 13, 1981 (Washington: U.S. Government Printing Office, 1981), 13.

17. Richard Burt, "The Relevance of Arms Control in the 1980s," *Daedalus* 110: 1 (Winter 1981): 170–71.

18. Samuel P. Huntington, ed., *Strategic Imperative* (Cambridge: Ballinger, 1982), 154–56.

19. Scheer, *With Enough Shovels*, 24–25.

20. Scheer, *With Enough Shovels*, 13.

21. "U.S. Strategic Doctrine," *Hearings*, Committee on Foreign Relations, U.S. Senate, 97th Congress, Second Session, December 14, 1982 (Washington, D.C.: U.S. Government Printing Office, 1982), 7, 13.

22. *Otkuda iskhodit uroza miru*, 2d ed. (Moscow: Voenizdat, 1982), 37.

23. Congressional Budget Office, "Modernizing U.S. Strategic Offensive Forces: The Administration's Program and Alternatives" (Washington, D.C.: U.S. Government Printing Office, 1983), xiv.

24. The B-1B bomber, as designed, differed from its B-1 predecessor in that it had a significantly lower maximum speed but in turn a greater range. Its weight was increased, as was the required take-off and landing distance. The wing-sweep was reduced, and owing to certain design changes and the utilization of new materials the radar cross-section, according to the Rockwell Corporation, was cut by approximately an order of magnitude. The cost of each B-1B aircraft ($200–280 million) is more than double the cost of its predecessor. See *Congressional Policy* (Washington, D. C., 1982), 80–81; *Time*, March 7, 1983, 14.

25. "Strategic Force Modernization Programs," *Hearings*, Committee on Armed Services, U.S. Senate, 97th Congress, First Session, October 1981 (Washington, D.C.: U.S. Government Printing Office, 1982), 175.

26. *Department of Defense Annual Report, Fiscal Year 1983*, iii-59.

27. "Modernization of the U.S. Strategic Deterrent," *Hearings*, Committee on

Armed Services, U.S. Senate, 97th Congress, first session, October 1981 (Washington, D.C.: U.S. Government Printing Office, 1982), 16, 28.

28. "Modernization of the U.S. Strategic Deterrent," 42.

29. Theodore H. White, "Weinberger on the Ramparts," *The New York Times Magazine*, February 6, 1983, 64.

30. White, "Weinberger on the Ramparts," 64.

31. The Closely Spaced Basing plan involved putting 100 MX ICBMs in steel launching containers, to be placed in 100 launching silos or, by U.S. designation, "shelters," which were situated in a column with two to three per row at a distance of 550 meters from each other. See Jeff Romm and Kosta Tsipis, "Analysis of Dense Pack Vulnerabilities," Report no. 8 (Cambridge, Mass.: The MIT Press, 1982), 11–13.

32. "U.S. Strategic Doctrine," *Hearings*, 15.

33. Harold Brown, *Thinking About National Security* (Boulder, Col.: Westview, 1983) 68–69.

34. Scheer, *With Enough Shovels*, 80.

35. White, "Weinberger on the Ramparts," 64.

36. White, "Weinberger on the Ramparts," 64.

37. "U.S. Strategic Doctrine," *Hearings*, 17.

38. *Radi mira na zemle*, 192–99.

39. Congressional Budget Office, "Modernizing U.S. Strategic Offensive Forces: The Administration's Program and Alternatives," 5.

40. Among the members of the Scowcroft Commission and its consultants were the former secretaries of defense Harold Brown, Donald Rumsfeld, James Schlesinger, and Melvin Laird; the former secretaries of state Alexander Haig and Henry Kissinger; the former CIA director Richard Helms; and the following officials who in the past had occupied high positions in the State and Defense departments: William Clements, William Perry, Thomas Reed, Levering Smith, Lloyd Cutler, John McCone, and the eminent MIT physics professor John Deutch.

41. This missile was to have a launch weight of about 15 tons, in comparison with the 100-ton MX.

42. "Modernizing U.S. Strategic Offensive Forces," 58, 72.

43. "Report of the President's Commission on Strategic Forces," April 6, 1983 (Washington, D.C.: U.S. Government Printing Office, 1983), 18.

44. *Time*, June 6, 1983, 21.

45. Estimates of the number of nuclear warheads in existing (and especially in future) strategic forces differ noticeably according to the individual sources. This discrepancy is caused by the fact that aircraft and certain missiles can carry various sets of weapons. For example, the Poseidon SLBM is capable of delivering a maximum of 14 Mk-III warheads, but in practice, according to certain data, it is more often equipped with 10 warheads, and in return has greater range. The same applies to future weapons systems, in particular the Trident-II SLBM, which is capable of delivering 14 Mk-IV warheads (at 100 kilotons each) out to a range of 11,000 kilometers, or eight Mk-21 warheads of a much greater yield (480 kilotons each) a distance of 7,200 kilometers. At a maximum U.S. strategic forces presently are theoretically capable of delivering in a single launch (or sortie) of all delivery vehicles around 13,000 warheads, and by 1990, up to 20,000 warheads, but with a significantly smaller total yield and perhaps lesser range as well than in other configurations.

warheads, but with a significantly smaller total yield and perhaps lesser range as well than in other configurations.

46. V. Bogdanov and A. Podberezkin, "Podlinnyi istochnik ugrozy miru," *Kommunist* 10 (July 1983): 99.

47. *Otkuda iskhodit ugroza miru*, 33.

48. In the United States there are now considered to be around 1,500 such weapons (gravity bombs and ALCMs) on bombers. Minuteman-III missiles with Mk-12A warheads—totaling 900 warheads—also possess hard-target-kill capability, but doubts are expressed as to their survivability. See "Modernizing U.S. Strategic Offensive Forces", 22–24.

49. "Modernizing U.S. Strategic Offensive Forces," 22–24.

50. "Modernization of the U.S. Strategic Deterrent," *Hearings*, 53.

51. In particular, this concerns the creation of the extremely low frequency (ELF) underground system of radio communication with SSBNs, the addition of more TACAMO communications aircraft for maintaining a permanent airborne alert of two such aircraft over the Atlantic and Pacific Oceans, and the development of new satellite communications.

52. Ashton Carter, "Assessing Command System Vulnerability," in Ashton Carter, John Steinbruner, and Charles Zraket, eds., *Managing Nuclear Operations* (Washington, D.C.: The Brookings Institution, 1987), 577.

53. "U.S. Strategic Doctrine," *Hearings*, 15.

54. *Otkuda iskhodit ugroza miru*, 8.

55. "Modernizing U.S. Strategic Offensive Forces," 46–48, 76–87.

56. "U.S. Strategic Doctrine," *Hearings*, 15–16.

57. *Department of Defense Annual Report, Fiscal Year 1980*, 78–79.

58. Scheer, *With Enough Shovels*, 141.

59. V. S. Frolov, "Chto skryvaetsia za modernizatsiei SUS," *SShA* 6 (June 1983): 116.

60. Keith Payne, *The BMD Debate: Ten Years After* (Washington, D.C., 1980).

61. Payne, *BMD Debate*.

62. Congressional Budget Office, "Baseline Budget Projections: Fiscal Years 1983–1987 (CBO Annual Report, Part II)" (Washington, D.C.: U.S. Government Printing Office, 1982), 87.

63. If all NASA appropriations are added to this, part of which also go toward military goals, then the total sum is still more impressive: for example, $11 billion in 1981, $15 billion in 1982, and $20 billion in 1987.

64. SIPRI, *World Armaments and Disarmament: SIPRI Yearbook 1983* (London: Francis and Taylor, 1983), 427–56.

65. "President's Speech on Military Spending and a New Defense," *The New York Times*, March 24, 1983, 8.

66. *Radi mira na zemle*, 38.

67. *Pravda*, April 10, 1983.

68. *Pravda*, April 29, 1983.

69. *Radi mira na zemle*, 184.

70. Philip S. Kronenberg, *Planning U.S. Security: Defense Policy in the Eighties* (New York: Pergamon Press, 1981), 13–31; Keith Payne, *Nuclear Deterrence in U.S.-Soviet Relations* (Boulder; Col.: Westview, 1982), 199, 206.

# 7

## U.S. Policies Clashing with the Realities of the Strategic Balance

The approximate parity of Soviet and U.S. strategic forces that emerged by the early 1970s was the most important and, perhaps, the most tangible factor assuring the reduction of international tension. Parity became the foundation of the first strategic arms control agreements, and in the course of the 1970s the military-strategic balance was inseparably linked with the SALT dialogue and other problems of disarmament. Finally, on the threshold of the 1980s, when détente had been undermined in many areas, the strategic nuclear balance was the chief remaining barrier in the path of global interventionism, direct confrontation, and an uncontrolled strategic arms race.

The preservation of the strategic balance is an indispensable condition for preventing global war and developing the arms control dialogue. But in and of itself an overall military-strategic equality is insufficient for ensuring general security. Indeed, if parity in the course of an unceasing arms race were to be preserved at increasingly higher levels of destructive potentials, the political pressure and economic costs for both sides would continue to grow, as would the threat of thermonuclear catastrophe hanging over the world.

However, in the first half of the 1980s the negotiations on strategic arms limitations reached a dead end. Events of those years showed that the achievement of agreements through negotiations turned out to be an extremely difficult matter in view of the persistent aspirations of U.S. and NATO ruling circles to implement their arms race programs and plans.

## Strategic Stability and the Quest for
## the Nuclear High Ground

Evaluating the true U.S. capabilities to change in its favor the existing military-strategic correlation of forces, one must first of all remember that parity was by no means a U.S. "gift" to the Soviet Union that can be taken back at will. To the contrary, in attempting to escape from the nuclear deadlock and build superiority the United States undertook an accelerated effort in the arms race in the 1960s, and in the 1970s again and again strove to obtain unilateral strategic advantages. Nevertheless, parity was established in the late 1960s owing to the strengthening of the USSR's defense capability, in spite of U.S. efforts. Due to the Soviet Union's measures in response to the U.S. buildup, the strategic equilibrium in the course of the 1970s became more comprehensive. Furthermore, in this period the favorable influence of the strategic arms control dialogue had already begun to take effect, certain channels of the arms race had been closed off by agreements, and strict limits had been established in some parameters of the military balance. It became immeasurably more difficult for the United States to upset significantly the military balance, to obtain strategic superiority in the course of the 1980s, than had been the case at any time earlier.

If one takes the simplest indicators of the strategic correlation of forces, which are politically the most striking, then the irreversibility of the changes that have taken place in the past 20 years becomes quite obvious. A simple calculation on the basis of published data shows that if the United States had decided to revive its quantitative predominance in the total size of strategic forces to a degree comparable to that of the 1966–67 period, then it would have had to deploy around 10,000 launchers and almost 60,000 warheads in place of the approximately 2,000 strategic launchers and 10,000 nuclear warheads existing in the then-current force structure.[1] It is obvious that even military appropriations significantly greater than those planned by the Reagan administration could not guarantee such a buildup of U.S. strategic forces.

At the same time it would be shortsighted to underestimate the danger of U.S. programs and doctrines. In reality, as has been noted above, by force of a number of economic and military-technical reasons the number of nuclear warheads in U.S. strategic forces will grow in subsequent years at a lesser rate than in the previous decade, while the number of strategic launchers will even decrease in connection with the retirement of obsolete missiles, aircraft, and submarines. However, all the above does not mean that the Soviet-U.S. strategic balance will be maintained automatically in the 1980s and beyond. For the essence of such a cardinal factor of contemporary international relations as the strategic balance cannot remain unchanged in the face of the intensive development of science and technology, of the appearance of new kinds and types of weapons, and of the formation of increasingly more dangerous strategic doctrines and concepts.

First of all, at work here is the principle that in addition to the military balance's quantitative parameters, such as the number of nuclear launchers or warheads, with all their importance, factors of another order will exert an increasingly greater influence on the correlation of forces. For the U.S.-Soviet strategic competition is continuing mainly by way of a qualitative arms race, that is, through replacing existing types of strategic weapons (the Minuteman, Poseidon and Polaris missiles, and the B-52 bomber) with new strategic nuclear forces (the MX, Trident-I, and Trident-II missiles, various cruise missiles, and the B-1B and Stealth bombers). The Soviet Union in response is deploying the RS-12M (SS-25) and RS-22 (SS-24) to replace the obsolete RS-12 (SS-13), RS-16 (SS-17) and SS-11 ICBMs, and is also replacing the old SS-N-6 SLBMs and submarines with the SS-N-20 (Typhoon) and SS-N-23 on new submarines (including the *Typhoon*-class). Modern Tu-160 (Blackjack) and modified Tu-95 bombers with cruise missiles will replace the older Miasishchev and Bear types. The new arms will be less numerous, but will in turn be much more effective and will be coupled with an improved $C^3I$ system. In the more distant future destabilizing breakthroughs are possible on the basis of fundamentally new technologies in such spheres as ballistic missile defense, antisubmarine warfare, space-based weapons, and so forth. One must also mention U.S. attempts in the early 1980s to make, so to say, an "end run" around parity by way of deploying intermediate-range ballistic and cruise missiles on approaches near Soviet territory: in Western Europe, in the surrounding seas, in the Far East, and in other regions.

Superiority is now understood as the capability via a first strike to reduce the strength of a retaliatory strike in order to limit the aggressor's damage to some kind of theoretically "acceptable" level. Thus the new U.S. weapons systems, in accordance with the programs and concepts advanced in the Pentagon, are first of all intended for a synchronized surprise strike on the Soviet $C^3I$ and early warning complex, as well as for destroying to the extent possible Soviet nuclear retaliatory forces themselves. Obviously, the "working assumptions" of the purpose of this operation are to drastically alter the Soviet-U.S. force ratio, to deter retaliation or at least disorganize and weaken a retaliatory strike in order to limit U.S. damage and losses. It would not be surprising if the United States were to perceive Soviet weapons programs in the same way, although objective calculations show that it would be harder for the United States to prove this point, considering the composition of its strategic triad and the alert rates of its forces and $C^3I$ system.

In approaching the strategic balance, that is, the correlation of forces, in which the superiority or unilateral advantage of any side is excluded, one must take into consideration not only the quantitative correlation of both powers' strategic forces, but also the overall correlation between the U.S. capability for a first strike and the Soviet capability for a crushing retaliatory strike. Such an approach will acquire growing importance in subsequent years, since it implies calculating the entire set of quantitative and qualitative factors of the contemporary military balance.

In the current decade the strategic balance, both in quantitative parameters and with respect to the impossibility of a decisive first strike on the part of a potential nuclear aggressor, to be sure, will not be maintained automatically without any efforts and expenditures. The futility of schemes to attain strategic nuclear superiority is precisely conditioned as well by the fact that in the existing Soviet-U.S. correlation of strategic forces both sides posses all the capabilities for creating the necessary counterweight to any additional steps of the opponent to build up his military power.

The present administration has on numerous occasions openly declared its hopes for economically exhausting the Soviet Union in the arms race; it has made a stake on the greater U.S. gross national product and defense budget, and on the U.S. lead in certain areas of science and technology. In this respect it is exceptionally important to emphasize that the contemporary strategic nuclear balance is characterized by a significant margin of safety, durability and stability, as a consequence of which it will be substantially more difficult over the long run for one side to violate this stability in its favor than for the other side to interfere with these attempts.

The USSR's strategic nuclear forces, as Marshal of the Soviet Union Nikolai V. Ogarkov has pointed out, "serve as the basic factor deterring aggression and possess the capability, in the event that war with the use of nuclear weapons is unleashed against the Soviet Union and other countries of the socialist alliance, to carry out without delay a crushing retaliatory strike."[2] The different elements of the Soviet strategic forces maintain close interaction and effectively complement each other, not allowing the opponent to count on success by concentrating on any one approach, such as, for example, prompt hard-target-kill capability or means of active or passive defense from nuclear weapons. Approximately 1,400 ICBMs and 6,000 strategic nuclear warheads are the main component of Soviet retaliatory forces.[3] As Chief Marshal of Artillery Vladimir F. Tolubko has pointed out, the most important indicators in the development of missile forces are "improving and modernizing missile technology, reducing preparation time to launch, increasing weapon yield and missile accuracy, improving the operation and maintenance of combat equipment, automating control systems, and increasing the survivability of installations and troops. . . . Strategic missile forces," he emphasized, "are forces of constant combat readiness."[4]

The Soviet ICBM force is supplemented by 160 long-range heavy bombers and a sea-based missile force. The latter's force of 62 submarines and 920 ballistic missiles with 3,000 nuclear warheads,[5] as Navy Fleet Admiral Sergei G. Gorshkov wrote, optimally combines "the latest achievements of science and technology, enormous striking power and mobility, survivability of strategic forces and a high readiness for their immediate use."[6] The fleet's strategic forces can maneuver to launch positions in an area surpassing many times that which is available to land-based missile forces. They maneuver as well by depth, concealing themselves in the water's vastness both for defense and camouflage, thereby increasing their survivability still further. Increasing the range of SLBMs significantly expands the ocean space for their combat patrol and, in addition, facilitates the use of other Soviet naval forces and weapons "for providing submarines combat support and stability and comprehensive protection for the struggle with enemy submarines and antisubmarine forces."[7] The supplementation of Soviet land-based missile forces and long-range aviation by large sea-based strategic forces, which on the whole was implemented in the 1970s in response to the growth of the U.S. nuclear threat, made the Soviet strategic arsenal much more balanced and diverse (while quantitatively unchanged), and the strategic balance more stable.[8] In this respect Soviet military experts wrote that a potential aggressor, "understanding the inevitability of nuclear retaliation from oceanic axes as well, may bow to the necessity to refrain from unleashing nuclear war."[9]

The further improvement of the combat readiness of Soviet strategic forces, their logistical support, and the $C^3I$ system allow the influence of the factor of surprise to be reduced to a minimum. To this one may add that the concentration of U.S. population and industry in comparatively few centers (more than 50 percent of the country's population and industry is concentrated in 150 such centers), as well as the unlikelihood, in the opinion of most experts, of the appearance in the foreseeable future of a sufficiently reliable means of defending broad regions of territory from strategic nuclear weapons, hardly permits even the most scholastic armchair strategists in the United States to realistically count on reducing U.S. damage in a thermonuclear war to any kind of acceptable level.

Yet another phenomenon of the existing correlation of strategic forces is that rapid and comparatively inexpensive measures (such as the additional U.S. deployment of 50 stockpiled Minuteman-III missiles that was discussed in 1981) cannot exert an appreciable influence on the nuclear balance. And major strategic programs require enormous expenditures and long periods of time for their implementation. Of all strategic weapons, cruise missiles and the Trident-I SLBM influenced the military balance in the first half of the 1980s, the MX and B-1B are producing their effect now in the late 1980s, and the Trident-II, Stealth, Midgetman, BMD, and space-based weapons programs might figure in the strategic equation significantly only in the 1990s and beyond. This gives the other side the opportunity to recognize and evaluate the threat ahead of time and undertake the necessary steps. For those in the beginning of the Reagan administration who dreamed of quickly achieving a "position of strength" vis-à-vis the USSR, the collision with these points in real life was quite a painful discovery. Secretary of Defense Weinberger in particular was distressed over the time frame of U.S. strategic programs. "One of the frustrating things, I have to add," he said, "is the length of time all of this takes."[10]

Finally, one must also keep in mind that if indeed the United States for the time being still surpasses the Soviet Union in economic potential, then the United States also puts before itself more pretentious strategic and military-political tasks, calling entire continents and faraway regions of the world spheres of its "vital interests." Washington is seeking to co-opt its allies into building superiority over the USSR in space war systems, strategic arms, and forward-based intermediate-range nuclear forces in Europe, Asia, and the surrounding seas. In addition to the two former TVDs, located on the perimeter of the socialist camp in European Asia and the Far East, the Pentagon has been organizing yet another TVD in the zone of the Persian Gulf and the Indian Ocean, not to mention the one it is organizing in Central America. In this connection, there were "armchair strategists" in the Reagan administration and its immediate environment who dreamed of completing the envelopment by adding both Southeast Asia and South Africa to these "spheres of vital interests." To fulfill these goals the United States has striven to expand its extensive network of foreign military bases, installations, and support points, to deploy additional troop contingents there, to set in place the means for the rapid and massive sea- and airlift of troops to distances many thousands of kilometers away, and to achieve "undisputed" naval superiority in three oceans and air superiority above them.

Meanwhile, the Soviet Union's military doctrine bears a purely defensive character; predatory and interventionist goals are alien to it, and it needs neither foreign military bases nor the natural resources of other countries. As a result the Soviet Union is assured great flexibility in planning its military requirements and the possibility of not squandering its resources in reacting to all of the other side's measures and plans. The Soviet Union should not plan to pursue the United States in each new weapons system, in each military program, but must always concentrate its strengths on the decisive axis for reliably deterring the aggressor's main potential.

In short, despite the differences in U.S. and Soviet economic potentials, the Soviet Union possesses all necessary capabilities for preventing the United States from upsetting the strategic balance both in the conditions of an arms control dialogue and, if worse comes to worst, in the event of a completely unlimited arms race.

Many in the U.S. "strategic community" argue that in view of the existing differences in individual parameters of the military balance, the development of analogous weapons in both countries affects unequally their strategic potentials and the correlation of forces between them. For example, the further improvement of hard-target-kill capability for both sides could allegedly be unilaterally advantageous to the United States, since these types of targets (ICBM silos, command centers, and so forth) play a more important role in the Soviet Union's strategic forces.[11] However, those who would play on the objectively existing disproportions of the nuclear balance in order to change it in the favor of the United States should not forget that, ignoring the difficulty of resolving such a task, other aspects of the military correlation of forces now advantageous to Washington are no "sanctuary" belonging exclusively to the United States. This concerns, for example, U.S. advantages in heavy bombers, cruise missiles, and the number of warheads deployed at sea, plans for using SLCMs for coastal strikes, and also certain factors favorable to U.S. ASW forces.[12]

In a word, in an unlimited arms race the strategic position of the United States would become extremely complicated in comparison with the existing situation, a position that in the future would hardly be more favorable than that of the Soviet Union. Another point is that both powers and other countries as well would face great additional economic costs in such a development, and their security would suffer from the growth of political tension and military threat.

The stability of the existing military-strategic balance also conditions the inconsistency of the U.S. nuclear war-fighting doctrine as a contemporary expression of the idea of nuclear superiority. First of all, Washington's calculations of the possibility that a first strike could decisively weaken the Soviet Union's retaliatory strike force are groundless. Even a sharp increase in U.S. hard-target-kill capability, which is expected from the MX and Trident-II missiles, will not confer on the United States a capability to undertake nuclear aggression with impunity. In this regard Dmitrii F. Ustinov noted quite definitively: "In the face of the modern state of warning systems and the combat readiness of the Soviet Union's strategic nuclear forces, a U.S. disarming strike on the socialist countries will not work. The aggressor will not escape from an

all-destroying retaliatory strike."[13] The USSR will take all necessary measures to ensure that such a situation, which lies at the foundation of the
stability of the military-strategic balance, will be preserved in the future
as well, despite the new U.S. arms programs.

The concept of a "limited and protracted" nuclear war—another major
element of the Reagan administration's strategy—is quite unrealistic in
and of itself and increasingly loses its meaning in light of the U.S. inability
to change sharply the correlation of forces in its favor and weaken substantially the strength of the Soviet retaliatory strike through a massive
first strike on military targets. U.S. plans for unleashing nuclear war at
the regional level, using tactical nuclear weapons and forward-based
forces including intermediate-range ballistic and cruise missiles, while
keeping U.S. territory itself inviolable, are devoid of elementary political
and military-strategic logic. In real life, despite U.S. strategists' abstract
schemes of an "escalation ladder," the horrible consequences of using
nuclear weapons render meaningless the question of where the forces
were launched from. In the event of such a step on the part of the
United States and its allies, a retaliatory strike will inevitably be brought
down not only upon those states from whose territory the launch originated but also upon the territory of the United States itself. In the early
1980s the commander in chief of the Strategic Rocket Forces Vladimir
F. Tolubko wrote in this regard that "A potential opponent must know
that, after launching even a group of his missiles from any basing region
in the direction of our territory, inevitable retaliation will follow without
delay!"[14]

Even more absurd is the concept of "limited nuclear war" following
Soviet and U.S. strike exchanges on each other's strategic forces. Such
an exchange would mean the raining down of, at a minimum, 2,000–
3,000 nuclear warheads on the opponent's territory, each with an explosive power tens and even hundreds of times more powerful than that
of the bombs dropped on Hiroshima and Nagasaki. In this regard, the
Soviet minister of defense has said: "Only completely irresponsible people are capable of maintaining that nuclear war can be conducted by
some kind of rules worked out in advance, in accordance with which
nuclear missiles must be detonated 'in a gentlemanly manner'—only over
certain targets while not destroying the population."[15]

It must be said that the Reagan administration's strategic concepts
have provoked criticism in the United States as well. True, criticism of
the nuclear superiority and war-fighting doctrines and of the "disarming
strike" and "limited and protracted" nuclear war concepts had taken
place in the United States even earlier, when these ideas figured in
debates over military questions. But a distinctive new feature is that
whereas in the past, opposition to such concepts basically originated in
liberal circles, now, when similar ideas have become a part of state policy,

disagreement with the extremist circles of the administration is being expressed by quite conservative officials as well. For example, JCS chairman David Jones, hardly a liberal or a struggler for disarmament, upon retiring in the summer of 1982 stated publicly that preparation for a "protracted nuclear war" with the Soviet Union was for the United States becoming the equivalent of throwing money into a "bottomless pit." "I don't see much of a chance of nuclear war being limited or protracted," said the general. "I see great difficulty" in keeping any kind of nuclear exchange between the United States and the Soviet Union from escalating.[16]

In the opinion of many authoritative U.S. experts, neither new programs in the area of $C^3I$, new space-based or other BMD system schemes, nor civil defense measures allow the United States to count on conducting a "controllable" nuclear war and reducing its damage to an "acceptable" level. Thus former Pentagon chief Harold Brown emphasizes: "As for active defense of populations against missiles or bombers, neither is cost effective. For a given investment, the offense will be able to overwhelm the active defense of urban industrial targets."[17] The eminent U.S. military leader and former JCS chairman General Maxwell Taylor wrote:

One could never hope to foresee where and how to stockpile reserves of food, water, medicines, hospital beds, firefighting equipment and the like needed to deal simultaneously with hundreds of regional disasters. Even if there were warning of attack, how to relocate senior government officials without closing down government itself, how to evacuate urban populations without creating nationwide panic, and how to disperse industry at a time when all communications might be blotted out by nuclear explosions? And after the attack, how to put out fires, restore order, and keep the survivors alive while disposing of millions of dead?[18]

Adherents of the nuclear war-fighting doctrine, such as Edward Luttwak, Colin Gray, Keith Payne, Richard Perle, and Richard Burt, cannot persuasively answer even one of these concrete, practical questions. They can only avoid them with general theoretical pronouncements of the necessity to combine defense and offense for transforming nuclear weapons into forces for "rationally" conducting war with the goal of assuring U.S. survival (we may note in passing that they never remember U.S. allies in this context) and achieving "victory" over the socialist countries in the real sense of the word. Everyone knows Clausewitz's classic dictum that war is the continuation of politics by other means. In view of the fact that neither victory nor any rational political goals in the existing military correlation of forces are attainable for the United States, and that "national suicide" cannot be a political goal, nuclear weapons and U.S. plans to use them can in no way be successfully transformed into effective instruments of foreign policy. Expressing the main aspiration of all those who think like him, Colin Gray contends that with the help of new U.S. nuclear doctrines and arms programs "military power and political purpose would be reunified, and the American president would have gained a useful measure of freedom of foreign policy action."[19]

Many may disagree with Colin Gray, as well as with the majority of "armchair strategists" like him. It is significant that among them are those, such as the late General Taylor, a veteran of many U.S. wars, who are quite far from being sympathetic toward the Soviet Union and its ideals. "[M]ost of my contemporaries concluded," wrote the general, "as I did and do, that there is no conceivable way of hedging adequately against a failure of deterrence. . . . In any major strategic exchange, the reciprocal damage would create conditions that would make victory and defeat virtually indistinguishable."[20]

This naturally raises the issue of the "Soviet SIOP" or "strike plan." In the first half of the 1980s the number of warheads in Soviet strategic forces, in the process of catching up with the United States, increased from 7,000 to 10,000 (by 1987). The concentration of these warheads on the land-based leg of the triad, and especially the 3,000-plus warheads on the heavy RS-20 (SS-18) ICBMs—responsive, accurate, in hardened silos, and of quite high yield—causes Western experts to attribute to the USSR a counterforce, damage limitation, and war-fighting strategy.

The details of Soviet operational planning are of course secret, just as are those of the U.S. SIOP. But in contrast to widespread opinion, quite a bit may be derived from Soviet military writings if a logical analysis of them is combined with an understanding of the Soviet military mentality, tradition, and decision-making mechanisms, including those relating to strategic programs, force deployments, and operational planning in the General Staff of the Soviet Armed Forces.

There is enough reason to believe that Soviet ICBMs are targeted on a comprehensive target list that includes U.S. strategic forces, in particular hardened missile silos. The increase of ICBM warheads in 1975–85 from 1,400 to 6,000 permits a comprehensive target coverage, cross-targeting, and much redundancy in planning major strike operations. From the point of view of Western strategic logic, since certain targets may be destroyed much more rationally in a first rather than a second strike (such as ICBM silos, $C^3I$ points, and airfields), Soviet nuclear targeting presupposes a preemptive, not retaliatory, strategy. And by the same logic thousands of warheads mean a number of limited and flexible options.

Such a view is a vivid illustration of the imposition of one's own logic and mentality on the opponent, which leads to the wrong conclusions. U.S. strategy evolved from 1960–80 to a great extent as a result of civilian specialists' rationalization of nuclear war-fighting, of attempts to introduce logic and discrimination into what is essentially illogical and indiscriminate.

The Soviet strategic forces' "strike plan" is determined by the Politburo and Defense Council guidance not to plan a first or preemptive attack and not to count on limited or selective options (which in any event are considered impossible because of $C^3I$ limitations under conditions of nuclear warfare). On this basis operational plans are worked out, including as comprehensive and redundant target coverage as can be afforded by the number of available warheads, their invulnerability, and levels of the forces' readiness and reliability. Covering U.S. ICBM silos does not mean a first-strike posture in the eyes of Soviet military planners, if only for the reason that alert bombers and submarines at sea cannot be destroyed in any case. In fact such a "first strike" would mean attacking 20 percent of U.S. strategic forces, having great uncertainty of destroying 30 percent (depending on the state of readiness of nonalert aircraft and submarines in port), and leaving at least 50 percent (the alert bombers and submarines at sea) intact. In other words, it would mean inviting at least a 1,000-megaton destructive potential to deliver a strike against the USSR. From the point of view of Soviet military mentality and tradition the advocacy of such a strike would be sheer madness, actually treason, deserving of punishment by court-martial. On the other hand, there is no reason not to target ICBMs in a second-strike operation, together with all other industrial and military targets, if enough warheads are available. In any event, in a second strike there would be no possibility of finding out which U.S. ICBMs were not used and no possibility for the "flexible rapid retargeting" of Soviet ICBMs.

In the highly unlikely contingency of a NATO first strike with intermediate-range and forward-based forces from Western Europe or the Far East against Soviet territory, a comprehensive Soviet retaliation against U.S. targets, including ICBMs, may have more operational logic to it, though it will have nothing to do with a damage-limitation, to say nothing of a war-winning, strategy. With deep warhead reductions, "redundant target coverage" will naturally be reduced, in particular as a growing number of ICBM silos and other targets, whose destruction in a retaliatory strike seems less feasible or logical or both, are dropped from the target list.

It is obvious that the U.S. doctrine of "nuclear deterrence" is currently going through a period of profound crisis. This crisis is explained by the fact that from the very beginning the dialectical seed of its own collapse was built into it, leading to its distintegration in the conditions of strategic equilibrium. First of all, U.S. doctrine stipulates extremely loose criteria for formulating strategic concepts, specific combat tasks, and weapons development and deployment. Essentially it grants the broadest license for an endless continuation of the arms race and the creation of increasingly refined and expensive means of annihilation. Judgment as to what degree these forces and plans strengthen or undermine deterrence is determined by the prevailing notions of Soviet intentions and capabilities and of which factors exert a deterring effect on them. The history of the 1960s and 1970s demonstrates how, under the guise of the campaign against the mythical threat of a "Soviet preemptive strike," the U.S. doctrine of deterrence evolved from the concept of primarily massive strikes on cities, through various options of selective missile attacks, to principles of striking the other side's strategic forces, and ultimately approached the idea of the possibility of "winning" a nuclear war, with its integral features of a first strike, damage limitation with the help of a large-scale BMD system, and so forth. And this idea, needless to say, seriously clashes with the tasks of preventing thermonuclear war, a goal to which all U.S. leaders of the past four decades have publicly given a ritual bow.

Furthermore, it is obvious that even the most reliable means of deterrence, however they may be deduced in theory, in and of themselves still do not offer a guarantee against the unleashing of thermonuclear war. Even in the situation of strategic parity deterrence theoretically can collapse as a result of the escalation of an international conflict, or because of a technical defect or the unauthorized use of nuclear weapons. This possibility is especially dangerous in the face of the activation of U.S. policies of military presence and intervention in crisis regions, the U.S. commitment in certain conditions to use nuclear weapons first, and the ceaseless attempts to expand the applicability of the nuclear threat, often under the pretense that it was for reasons of "deterrence." Hence follows the theological question of U.S. nuclear strategy: what to do if deterrence in spite of everything at some point "fails?" Can one refuse to prepare plans and forces for "limited nuclear war" and limiting damage to an acceptable level in this event? But such measures inevitably produce a feedback effect: they create the illusion of the possibility of limiting the destructive consequences of nuclear war, they make it less unthinkable, and the step toward unleashing it easier. In the course of the 1970s and early 1980s the scale in U.S. strategic policy that measured the probability of the "failure" of deterrence and arguments for preparatory measures for such an event gradually tipped in favor of the latter.

The question of what to do if deterrence "fails" is one of the most important problems of contemporary politics and strategy. Even moderately conservative and liberal U.S. officials and experts fall into the trap of this problem and conclude the necessity of providing for the possibility of "limited" nuclear war. Harold Brown, for example, writes:

It would be highly irresponsible to say that, because we cannot predict how such a war would begin, the United States should make no plans for how it will be fought. Imagine a military planner or political official who had to tell a President who had asked for options in responding to an actual strategic attack that there were no such plans because such a war had been judged inconceivable or unimaginable. Should a nuclear war begin, it is the responsibility of the political and military authorities to try to limit its damaging effects.[21]

From the above statement it is apparent that U.S. strategic theory has become too academic. One must therefore bring clarity to the question. How can deterrence "fail?" The actions of states in the event of the unauthorized use of nuclear weapons are regulated by corresponding international arrangements. In other cases the use of nuclear weapons may be a premeditated military-political act with full consciousness of the grave consequences of such a step. It would mean that the stakes in a conflict were so great that they would think it possible not to consider the risk of escalation and total destruction. This step would be the most heinous crime ever committed against humanity. It is impossible to imagine this act as a misunderstanding that everyone would immediately rush to patch up. Any use of nuclear weapons would be a move across the Rubicon, would put at risk the vital interests of other states, and would immediately entail full-scale crushing retaliation. In arguing about the possibility of nuclear war, we have before us a matter with some kind of overall probability. One does not need to be a military expert to understand that the probability of sanctioning the use of nuclear weapons is immeasurably smaller than the probability of the uncontrolled escalation of strikes to total annihilation. Therefore the only rational goal is to eliminate the first, not reduce the second.

The possibility of preventing the catastrophic consequences of a general war hardly exists in the concepts and weapons systems for "limited nuclear war." It generally lies outside the sphere of improving strategic weapons and developing operational plans for their use. The only real possibility for avoiding total destruction—and the lessons of the past are convincing evidence of this—lies in reducing and ultimately eliminating the probability of nuclear war generally, in the unconditional refusal to use nuclear weapons first, in the limitation and reduction of strategic nuclear arsenals, and in the peaceful settlement and prevention of international conflicts. If such a course is exceptionally difficult, any other is simply impossible, and in many cases could lead to the opposite result.

The durability of the military-strategic balance also explains how the Reagan administration's military policy has run into increasing difficulties. Indeed many of the problems of this policy, at first glance purely economic or technical, have at their roots the objective realities that frustrate U.S. attempts to obtain unilateral advantages or, even more often, superiority, both in terms of required spending as well as technical considerations (for example, the creation of an invulnerable basing system for the MX). During the Reagan administration's rule the unprecedented acceleration of military spending and intensification of the arms race has brought the United States not military superiority or the economic exhaustion of the USSR, but an unprecedented federal budget deficit. It has significantly aggravated the economic situation.

Meanwhile, on the part of Congress, pressure to reduce military spending is growing. It is characteristic that among the supporters of decreased military spending are political figures, military officials, and scientists who as recently as 1980 had been in the vanguard of supporters for increasing the Pentagon's budget. As has already been indicated, Congress's refusal in December 1982 to approve appropriations for the administration's proposed MX basing system and production schedule was a genuine shock. The 1983 Scowcroft decision has been subjected to increasingly sharper criticism, and not only from liberals but from conservative groups as well. Under the pressure of economic and technical circumstances the government was forced against its will to stretch out and cut back certain other strategic and conventional arms programs. SAC commander General Bennie Davis baldly asserted that the government's policy "will weaken the U.S. strategic defense for the next five years." In this connection one of the administration's critics, Senator Carl Levin, charged that "Not only is the strategic program a shambles and a waste, but also funds wasted are draining our real conventional forces' needs and our readiness needs."[22]

All of the above, of course, does not mean that the arms race will gradually wither away, and that the danger of thermonuclear war in the near future will recede in and of itself. On the contrary, U.S. policies in the first half of the 1980s inflicted significant damage worldwide and strategic programs gathered inertia that with each year will become increasingly more difficult to turn off. In even greater measure this situation has affected efforts to limit and reduce nuclear arms.

### Strategic Arms Reductions: The Reagan Administration's False "START"

The original intention of the Republican leadership and its advisers and consultants was to achieve nuclear superiority over the Soviet Union exclusively by way of an accelerated buildup of U.S. strategic nuclear strength and the deployment of U.S. intermediate-range ballistic and cruise missiles in the European theater in an even greater number than was planned in the infamous NATO resolution of December 12, 1979.[23] Even before the negotiations, the new leaders and many of their advisers considered arms control a burden, from which it best be separated in order to prove to the whole world the United States' superiority through an all-out arms race. In his address at West Point in May 1981, President Reagan declared: "The argument, if there is any, will be over which weapons and not whether we should forsake weaponry for treaties and agreements."[24]

In all of his early interviews the president strictly linked the beginning of a dialogue to radical changes in the Soviet Union's entire foreign policy which, obviously, was equivalent to torpedoing whatever negotiations there might have been. "There has to be linkage," he said. "I don't think we can sit there and talk about some agreements on weapons and ignore what they're doing with regard to taking over other countries, intervening in other countries. . . . If we're going to have good relations, then it must be based on conduct different from what they've done in the past."[25] And as noted earlier, Defense Secretary Weinberger considered that "even a failure to reach an agreement is a success." All of the Republican leadership's first steps conformed with such an approach. The SALT II Treaty was said to be as "dead as a doornail" and that therefore the United States did not consider itself bound by its provisions. A dialogue was suspended for a year and a half, in the course of which, as later became known, the question was seriously considered of repudiating the ABM Treaty, the SALT I Interim Agreement, and in general any negotiations in this respect.[26]

But after comparatively little time had passed, it became obvious that events were developing far differently from what the architects of U.S. policy had wanted. The strategic balance turned out to be much more stable in practice than it had seemed to them in theory. Attempts to upset parity in their favor unexpectedly began to collide with growing economic, political, and military-technical difficulties. This development had the most immediate bearing on the state of affairs in the strategic arms control area, for the United States could not free itself unilaterally from the limits and provisions of SALT. And the Soviet Union was not playing into U.S. hands by engaging in an unlimited buildup of its own nuclear arsenal. Thus, according to the calculations of certain competent researchers, in the absence of any SALT constraints the United States could increase its potential to 2,600 launchers and 23,000 nuclear warheads, and the USSR to 2,800 launchers and 22,000 warheads in the course of the 1980s.[27] These numbers, of course, did not reflect real plans and practical considerations, but they quite graphically characterized the opinion of influential circles of the maximum capabilities of the two powers within the most general economic and technical constraints. Thus no matter how much the Republican leadership maligned or wished to withdraw from the SALT II Treaty before coming to power, the inexorable and objective facts testified that in the absence of SALT

I and SALT II the U.S. strategic position would not be more favorable under any conditions.

Apart from the enormous significance of these agreements in the political sphere and in strengthening comprehensive security, they acquired an enormous strategic role as well. In the situation of parity and the colossal levels of destructive capability, of the enormous costs and timeframe of development and deployment of nuclear arms, the SALT process became an integral part of military planning. This, of course, did not mean that arms control was put at the service of the arms race. The arms race and the dialogue to limit and reduce it fundamentally contradict each other. The above has thoroughly examined how military programs and arms control negotiations have continuously clashed with one another. But in the course of such a mutual "grinding," the parameters of and prospects for SALT gradually became a most important element of military policy, without whose consideration the latter would be faced with enormous uncertainty, great miscalculations, and strategic, technical, and economic costs. The breakdown of the SALT II Treaty and the uncertainty of the future prospects of arms control suddenly put this problem into sharp focus.

And it is no accident that precisely the professional military in high offices of the Pentagon as early as 1980 had sounded the alarm in this regard. Such people as JCS Chairman David Jones, Naval Chief of Staff Admiral Thomas Hayward, Army Chief of Staff Edward Meyer, and SAC commander General Richard Ellis were by no means supporters of détente and disarmament. But they, in contrast to such "academics" as, for example, Van Cleave, Luttwak, and Gray, more clearly imagined all the difficulties and costs of an unlimited arms race in the conditions of a strategic equilibrium—a fundamentally new situation for the United States. In addition, the generals did not fear criticism from the right. Thus General Jones stated:

I associate myself with the perspective that SALT II is an agreement of mutual interest between adversaries, not a treaty between friends or a favor we are doing for the Soviets. In fact, I would submit that the deeper our disagreements and the more brittle our relations, the more important become the restrictions on Soviet momentum and capabilities—as well as the predictability of their programs and deployments—afforded by SALT.[28]

In fact, not one of the Vienna Treaty's provisions existed apart from the others. Each was linked to both military-technical realities and to a long chain of other SALT II provisions, both according to the logic of the strategic balance and to the history of diplomatic compromises. For example, conceding the United States the right to heavy missiles, which certain representatives of militarist circles demanded, also meant allowing the Soviet Union to create a new type of heavy ICBM—the very type that the U.S. side had sought with all its might to avoid during the negotiations. Meanwhile the Pentagon was not planning such a system in any event in the foreseeable future since the MX system, being categorized as a light ICBM, satisfied fully its strategic plans. Precisely the same erosion of limitations on certain U.S. programs (ALCMs, for example) would "break" the entire chain of other limitations that the United States had imposed upon the USSR (such as the ceilings on MIRVed missiles and limits on new types of ICBMs and MIRV fractionation). In other words, an analysis of the SALT II provisions once again affirmed that the treaty was carefully balanced and based on objective strategic parity in all of its diverse aspects. Under the existing military balance it would be impossible to change unilaterally the agreement in favor of either power, and a two-way reconsideration or a complete erosion of the limitations could ultimately make the United States the loser. Even the subsequent U.S. declaration in 1986 that it would no longer be bound by SALT I and SALT II, made mostly for political reasons, did not change this reality.

The White House's flagrant propaganda broadsides at the USSR, its irresponsible and cynical statements on the subject of thermonuclear war (such as Reagan's statement on the possibility of limiting a nuclear conflict within the confines of European territory, and Secretary of State Haig's statements about nuclear "warning shots" in Europe[29]) in no way frightened the USSR. But they did provoke a massive protest movement within the West European public and the great anxiety of their governments. An antinuclear movement was born in the United States itself and dissatisfaction surfaced in Congress over concern for the inflated military budget. In turn, the peace-loving policy of the Soviet Union and the fraternal socialist countries and their constructive approach to problems of disarmament made Washington's position still more difficult.

In these conditions the U.S. leadership began to maneuver. In March 1981, and later as well in May 1982, it was announced that the United States would not violate the provisions of SALT II (although a persuasive explanation was never given as to why the Vienna Treaty should therefore not be ratified), and obligations under the ABM Treaty were also affirmed. In November 1981 the Geneva negotiations on limiting nuclear weapons in Europe (the INF talks) were opened, and in June 1982 negotiations resumed in Geneva on limiting and reducing strategic arms (START). However, as quickly became clear, the specific U.S. proposals at the negotiating table pursued identical goals: to change the existing correlation of military forces radically in the West's favor and obtain superiority, although not simply through an unlimited arms race, but also through combining its military programs with inequitable and severe constraints on Soviet defense potential.

According to the so-called START draft treaty advanced by Ronald Reagan on May 9, 1982 in his speech in Eureka, Illinois, it was proposed to reduce the number of Soviet and U.S. sea- and land-based ballistic missiles (about 2,350 and 1,700, respectively) to 850, and the number of warheads on them (approximately 6,500–7,500 each) to 5,000. An additional subceiling of 2,500 was put on ICBM warheads. At first glance the draft START treaty went much further than SALT II, which stipulated reducing the number of launchers by approximately 10 percent. U.S. leaders had apparently in the eleventh hour become fierce proponents of nuclear disarmament. However, such an impression was possible only among the uninformed or extremely partisan.

As is known, by force of the objective asymmetry of the two powers' strategic forces (the USSR had around 70 percent of its warheads on ICBMs, while the United States had about 20 percent), implementing the U.S. draft treaty, in particular establishing a ceiling at 2,500 warheads, would require reducing 50–60 percent of Soviet ICBM warheads and a greater portion of its missiles. Again, because of the fact that sea- and land-based missile forces make up about 94 percent of the Soviet Union's strategic launchers, and 76 percent of those of the United States (bombers account for 6 percent and 24 percent, respectively, of the two powers' strategic launchers), a level of 850 launchers meant that the USSR would have had to reduce its ballistic missiles twice as much as the United States.

Thus under the pretense of equal reductions the U.S. proposals pursued the aim of literally eradicating the central element of Soviet strategic power—land-based ballistic missiles. Submarine-launched ballistic missiles, which by warheads represented a significantly greater share of U.S. capability (more than 50 percent in comparison with less than 30 percent for the USSR), were affected to a much lesser degree in the draft START treaty. And heavy bombers, which were being equipped with thousands of cruise missiles in the United States, a measure that provides the U.S. with its most significant advantages, were outside the limitations altogether. Had Reagan's conditions been implemented, the United States would have obtained, in place of the current overall strategic equality with the USSR, almost one-and-a-half times more of an advantage in launchers and an approximately three-fold superiority in warheads.[30] Such a START for the new administration in the arms control sphere could only be considered a false one in all respects.

The Reagan administration's blatant pressure in the START talks for the discriminatory reduction of the main component of Soviet strategic capability grossly violated the principles of the equality and equal security of both sides. As the foundation of the SALT negotiations in the 1970s, these principles implied that arms control agreements must embrace all Soviet and U.S. strategic forces, not just an arbitrarily chosen few. However, as noted above, Reagan's START proposal cut far more deeply into the land-based component of Soviet strategic forces than into the land- or sea-based elements of U.S. strategic power. And the bomber leg of the triad, in which U.S. advantages remained most significant, was altogether outside the START framework. To justify such inequitable proposals, which would have sharply tipped the entire military balance in favor of the United States, the Reagan administration completely repudiated the principles of equality and equal security and resolved to impose the U.S. concept of "strategic stability" on the Soviet Union as the basis of the negotiations.

The essence of this concept, which has already repeatedly been touched upon above, is the notion that ICBMs are a "destabilizing" element of the military balance, since they are supposedly the best means for delivering a rapid preemptive strike on the other side's strategic forces, especially on hardened missile silos and command centers. The greater the capability of this kind possessed by one or both sides, U.S. representatives maintain, the higher the probability of using strategic weapons in a crisis situation, and in turn, the lesser the stability of the nuclear balance. According to this same theory SLBMs are unambiguously declared retaliatory strike weapons for urban-industrial targets, since thay do not possess a sufficient combination of warhead accuracy and yield, and also allegedly do not have reliable two-way communications with the command for coordinating a first strike. Bombers and cruise missiles are relegated to this same category, since they require long flight times to reach their targets and do not guarantee the necessary surprise of attack. Thus the sea and air components of the triad qualify as "stabilizing" types of strategic arms.

This concept was transformed by the present administration into an instrument for arbitrarily breaking the existing methods for evaluating the military correlation of forces and for subverting previous notions of the presence of an overall Soviet-U.S. strategic parity. The U.S. advantages are represented as "inoffensive," and the Soviet ones as "threatening" and "unacceptable." Thus, for example, Edward Rowny affirmed in the Senate Armed Services Committee: "I think the total warhead number as it now stands is not a very good measure. The advantage which we temporarily enjoy in the total number of warheads is in areas which are not usable in a so-called first strike exchange. Our temporary lead is in the SLBM field and in the bomber field; generally in second strike or follow-on strike capabilities."[31]

In accordance with this theory, the Reagan administration declared its primary goal of START—instead of arms control on the basis of the principles of equality and equal security—to be the "stabilization" of the strategic balance (to be sure, in the U.S. favor). Thus the Reagan START proposals of May 9, 1982 were quite openly tailored to the measures of the Pentagon's strategic program of October 1981, which stipulated, in comparison with the previous administration's policy, still greater emphasis on the sea and air components of the nuclear triad. It is not difficult to see that the draft START treaty was structured in such a way as to reduce maximally the ICBMs and to a much lesser degree affect SLBM forces. It is not without reason that the proposed 5,000 total ballistic missile warheads ceiling prohibited having more than half on ICBMs. Moreover, the subceiling worked in only one direction: many more than 2,500 warheads, even all 5,000 warheads, could be kept on SLBMs, and beyond that, any number on bombers.

The concept of strategic stability, which justifies the emphasis on the sea and air components of strategic forces and quite obviously was adapted to the geostrategic and military-technical peculiarities of the U.S. strategic nuclear arsenal, was in development in the United States long before the Reagan administration. During the 1970s Washington repeatedly tried to apply it to the SALT agreements, in 1973 and 1977, for example. However, the U.S. leadership had never previously tried to impose on the Soviet Union such glaringly inequitable conditions for limiting and reducing arms. Never before had the United States launched in support of its proposals such a massive propaganda campaign and taken such an uncompromising position at the negotiating table based on the gross blackmail of new strategic nuclear programs. The U.S. concept of "stability" has in recent years become a most important instrument, with whose help Washington tries to substantiate the "Soviet threat" thesis, for justifying measures to accelerate the arms race and attempts to recarve according to its taste agreements on limiting strategic arms. But at the same time this concept has a number of extremely vulnerable spots and obviously strained interpretations. Once discredited, the entire façade of apologetics for U.S. strategic policy comes tumbling down like a house of cards.

For example, insofar as a first strike may pursue the goal of preventing or weakening a retaliatory strike, its primary task would theoretically become the destruction or disorganization of the other side's early warning and $C^3$ systems. Best adapted to this task are those nuclear forces that are more difficult to intercept after launch and that can reach their targets in the shortest period of time and from unexpected axes of attack. The most dangerous and destabilizing from this point of view are highly-accurate intermediate-range ballistic missiles (short flight times to targets), GLCMs and SLCMs (difficult to detect), as well as SLBMs (short flight times and unpredictable azimuths of attack).

If one approaches the matter from the standpoint of the capability to limit damage through a first strike, then the most "tempting" targets, besides the command and control systems, appear to be the "soft" submarine pens and bomber bases possessing a large nuclear potential.

SLBM forces are also best suited to this type of attack. For striking hardened ICBM silos, thousands of powerful and accurate nuclear warheads and the close coordination of strategic operations at intercontinental range are in fact required. But this is hardly confirmation of the thesis of the ICBM's "destabilizing" character. Rather, it is evidence of the great importance of this type of weapon as a reliable means of retaliation.

In actual fact, with the development of technology the capability to destroy missile silos and command centers is increasing. But ICBMs have no monopoly on such a capability in this situation. In particular, in terms of range, warhead yield, and accuracy SLBMs are approaching the level of land-based missiles and in the not-too-distant future may even surpass them in hard-target-kill capability. Systems for communicating with submarines are improving, the concentration of missiles on SSBNs is increasing, and in addition, as has been noted, SLBMs have shorter flight times and may come from unexpected directions. Indeed, and to the point, the Pentagon leadership does not in the least conceal that all these qualities are linked with the Trident-I system, and even more so with the Trident-II.[32] Second, one must take into consideration the different share of ICBMs in the two powers' nuclear forces. Consequently even a theoretical future threat to the survivability of this component will appear far from equivalent for the USSR and the United States.

One may also approach the matter from the standpoint of which nuclear weapons are most dangerous in terms of facilitating escalation of a potential conflict or making possible thermonuclear war by mistake or political miscalculation. Then there emerge into the foreground various operational-tactical and intermediate-range nuclear weapons in the TVD, which lower the so-called nuclear threshold, that is, those weapons intended for immediate use in the event of armed conflict. Of strategic arms, especially destabilizing may be bombers, whose mass scrambling in a crisis might be interpreted as the beginning of a nuclear strike. SSBNs for their part may be immediately drawn into conventional combat operations at sea, and they are in fact physically able to launch ballistic missiles even without command authorization, especially if they are the object of pursuit and attack by ASW forces.

There is as well a number of other military-technical spheres that appear outside the framework of offensive strategic weapons but which in theory and in fact already in practice exert a no less destabilizing influence on parity than the capability of land-based ballistic missiles for destroying hard targets. This concerns, for example, the development of ASW forces, which can threaten the survivability of SSBNs; antisatellite systems, whose missions include destroying space-based means of early warning, observation, and communication; and new ballistic missile defense schemes, which are called upon to weaken the force of a retaliatory strike. On all these questions official U.S. propaganda, which fights for "stability," for the most part maintains a cool silence.

Thus under closer examination the U.S. concept of "strategic stability" turns out to be quite vulnerable (much more so than U.S. strategic forces). Washington has no grounds for claiming that it has created the universal and only correct model of "stability" that is mandatory for both sides. Such issues can be resolved only by way of considering the legitimate interests and positions of both powers and persistently searching for mutual understanding and mutually acceptable compromises between them.

Also, one cannot help but notice that the next round of strategic modernization will, as is hoped in Washington, produce a significantly greater strategic and political effect in the lowered numerical ceilings proposed by the United States. In fact the new U.S. military programs keep fully within these limits as long as a certain number of in any case obsolete submarines are retired somewhat prematurely.[33] In this event, Soviet strategic forces not only would have to undergo much deeper reductions and make a significant quantitative concession to the United States, but would also be much more vulnerable to a U.S. first strike.

In 1983 certain changes were undertaken in the U.S. approach to START. They were connected first of all with the intensification of U.S. criticism of the Reagan policy. The one-sided and unrealistic nature of the administration's START proposals was too obvious. Certain U.S. officials had pointed this out from the very beginning. Thus Edmund Muskie, secretary of state under Carter, expressed the opinion that START was "a secret agenda for sidetracking *disarmament* while the United States gets on with *rearmament*"[34] (emphasis in original). Former secretary of defense Brown stated with characteristic caution that "it is too much to expect that any arms control agreements, including SALT— or START—will in the real world live up to our idealized hopes."[35] Roger Molander, who worked on arms control issues as an NSC staff member under the Democrats and with the coming to power of Reagan organized the Ground Zero antinuclear organization, said that "rather than emphasizing the control of different avenues of strategic competition, [the Reagan START proposal] essentially calls for the Soviets to restructure their strategic missile forces along lines much closer to our own."[36]

But this point of view, for the time being, remained a voice in the wilderness. Only the growing dissatisfaction of the broad public and Congress with the U.S. economy, with the unrestrained escalation of military spending, with the contradictions and absurdity of the Republican leadership's statements on nuclear strategy and decisions on arms programs, and with the obvious aggravation of the threat to international (including U.S.) security that U.S. policies had provoked, strengthened the opposition to the administration's unconstructive line in the START dialogue. In this connection the 1982 elections were quite a graphic indicator of the changing sentiments. The Republican party's losses in the Senate and House of Representatives, as well as in the state guber- natorial and legislative assemblies, exceeded those usually anticipated for the ruling party in off-year elections. As Soviet historian Vladimir Pechatnov observes,

the elections clearly showed that the peak influence of the far right forces of the 1980 type had already passed: the long-term shift of mass sentiments to the right, on which the Republicans had counted, in reality turned out to be largely the expression of voters' dissatisfaction with the economic situation. Now, as a measure of the increasingly clear failure of the right-wing conservative exper- iment to solve economic problems, this dissatisfaction is turning against the Republicans themselves.[37]

Simultaneously in U.S. domestic politics the role of the problems of war and peace and of curbing the arms race grew in an unprecedented way. A mass movement to freeze nuclear arsenals was launched, affecting circles that had never previously taken part in the political debate on these issues: small towns, the middle class, part of the upper class, the community of physicians, the Catholic church, and numerous public organizations. Antinuclear demonstrations spread across the country, comparable in scale to those during the Vietnam war. According to various public opinion surveys, in 1982 45 percent of the participants expressed the fear that nuclear war was highly probable in the next ten years; 75 percent stated that it could not be limited, and would inevitably become total; and 83 percent of those polled indicated that too many nuclear weapons were amassed on both sides. Eighty to ninety percent favored freezing Soviet and U.S. nuclear arsenals at equal levels.[38] With his acceptance speech for the Einstein Peace Prize, the noted U.S. public figure George Kennan provoked a widespread discussion. Kennan called for reducing, without delay or "further arguments among experts," the strategic, intermediate-range, and tactical nuclear arsenals of both pow- ers by 50 percent. A vigorous debate was also stimulated as the result of an article by Kennan and three other renowned authors: McGeorge Bundy, Robert McNamara, and Gerard Smith, each of whom at one time or another had played a significant role in the formulation of U.S. policy in the arms and disarmament area. The former statesmen rec- ommended to the U.S. government that it make a pledge not to use nuclear weapons first, after having stipulated as the condition for this a buildup of U.S. and allied conventional forces.[39]

The antinuclear movement spread to Capitol Hill as well, although the Republican party, and especially the bipartisan right-wing militarist alignment, continued to hold the dominating position there. However, even conservative Democratic senators, such as Daniel Moynihan, Henry Jackson, Sam Nunn, John Glenn, and others began increasingly more often to express misgivings regarding the administration's irresponsible approach to the strategic balance and the START negotiations. In 1982 the House of Representatives adopted a nonbinding resolution that urged the White House to consider seriously the idea, supported by millions of Americans, of freezing nuclear arsenals.

On the eve of a deciding vote on the MX program, three influential senators—Nunn, Charles Percy, and William Cohen—sent President Reagan a letter that stated that they would not vote for this system if he did not adopt a new, more flexible position on arms control. Ten members of the House of Representatives sent Reagan an analogous message.

The Scowcroft Commission's report, already mentioned above, greatly influenced U.S. policy in the area of strategic arms. In a practical respect, of course, it played into the hands of the administration, since it was the factor that tipped the scale in favor of MX. However, in the broader political and strategic respect it put at doubt certain key elements of the administration's policy, even if its heartened supporters and frustrated opponents initially paid no attention to this. First of all, beneath the rather strong anti-Soviet rhetoric, the report contained an indirect call for the establishment of a Soviet-U.S. strategic balance and a calmer evaluation, obviously differing from that of the administration, of Soviet strategic forces and military capabilities. Absent in the report were any judgments as to the possibility of guaranteeing U.S. "survival" or "victory" in a thermonuclear war, and strategic tasks were discussed more in the spirit of the earlier countervailing doctrine.[40] Most important, the real significance of the theoretical vulnerability of U.S. ICBM silos was called into question. The commission pointed to the unjustifiable separation of this issue from the overall context and to the necessity of examining it in totality with the capabilities of the other triad components. In other words, the "window of vulnerability," the issue which had become pivotal in U.S. strategy, its defense programs, and its approach to arms control, and around which U.S. militarist circles had conducted their campaign for years, was "closed," not via a military-technical solution but simply as a result of changing theoretical assumptions and conclusions.[41]

Tightly bound with the Scowcroft Commission's conclusions was the idea of the so-called build-down or, more accurately, "reductions through modernization." This idea came directly from Senator William Cohen, who was subsequently supported by Senators Nunn and Percy and Congressmen Les Aspin, Albert Gore, and Norman Dicks. They represented an influential bipartisan group in Congress on defense policy questions. In light of the Reagan administration's accelerated and expanded strategic programs and the deadlock in the START negotiations for which it was to blame, these officials advanced the idea of introducing a certain "price" for modernizing nuclear arsenals by way of agreement. This concept was that for each new nuclear warhead introduced into the strategic arsenal, the parties would be obligated to remove two old ones. Along with the establishment of yearly mandatory reductions of the number of nuclear warheads by a certain percentage, it was thus proposed to achieve lower levels of nuclear potentials in warheads despite the new programs and possibly to slow somewhat these programs themselves.

Initially, this idea was given a hostile reception both in the White House and in ACDA, since it stipulated changing the START proposal and could theoretically reduce the planned buildup of the number of U.S. nuclear warheads from 15,000 to 8,000.[42] But Congress hit the administration with the threat to cancel the MX program, and the government adopted the idea, in October 1983 officially including it in the U.S. START proposal. However, with the efforts of U.S. strategists (in particular, the above-mentioned General Glenn Kent), this approach was modified into the so-called double build-down, according to which arbitrary ratios were established to require the removal of two old ICBM warheads for one new one, while for one new SLBM warhead, only one-and-a-half old warheads. Thus Soviet forces would suffer greater reductions than U.S. forces.[43] And the method advanced by Kent for equating the throw-weight of Soviet ICBMs and U.S. bombers would in practice mean writing off the old B-52 aircraft, which were to be replaced in any event, in exchange for reducing the USSR's most effective silo-based missiles. On the whole, the proposed double build-down yet again was subordinated to the earlier principle of U.S. arms control policy: to impose on the Soviet Union a unilateral, strict reduction of its land-based missiles, epecially its heavy ICBMs, while leaving the United States much greater freedom in developing its own programs, primarily in the triad's sea and air components. In the realm of domestic politics this idea was utilized by the administration to undermine support for the freeze movement in Congress.

In principle the idea of reducing the number of strategic warheads in such a way so as not to increase the vulnerability of strategic forces and not to undermine the stability of the military balance is quite sensible. However, observing the principle of equality and equal security is a necessary precondition. In concrete terms this means that a reduction of warheads and launchers must affect both powers equally and envelop all component of strategic forces, that is, include both bombers and SLBMs, and not be concentrated selectively on ICBMs.

Of no lesser importance is that the double build-down plan failed to offer a guarantee of reducing the probability of a nuclear first strike and of strengthening the general security—the most important goals of the arms control dialogue. In fact, even with significantly fewer nuclear warheads—and many thousands would nonetheless still remain—a first strike could become more probable if within these quantitative limits were to continue the replacement of old weapons systems by more accurate, destructive, and effective ones. This "new approach" was largely an escape from the task of mutually limiting and prohibiting new and much more dangerous kinds of weapons—an urgent task, and extremely complex as well.

To a significant degree the above was expressed in the revisions of the U.S. START position in the summer of 1983 as a result of the Scowcroft Commission's recommendations. While leaving unchanged the ceilings on the total number of ICBM and SLBM warheads, the United States proposed to raise substantially the ceiling on the number of missile launchers themselves, in accordance with the planned deployment in the 1990s of numerous small single-warhead ICBMs. Furthermore, a separate limit of 400 was proposed on bombers as "slow-flying" strategic forces. At first glance the U.S. position had adopted changes in favor of solutions more acceptable to the Soviet Union: fewer ICBM launchers would be cut by the reductions, and limitations were established on bombers, though at a higher level than the United States possessed (about 270). The administration staked its domestic and foreign policy game on precisely such an impression.

But in reality all of Washington's "concessions" had, in effect, a "false bottom." The one-sided selective approach to reducing the main component of Soviet retaliatory forces—MIRVed ICBMs—was retained along with the increased ceiling on missile launchers.

The United States had to accommodate practically nothing of value to the 400 bomber limit on long-range aviation: it had only to eliminate a portion of 230 deeply mothballed B-52 bombers. And, as it turned out, Washington demanded that medium-range bombers of the Tu-22M type (Backfire) be considered in this limit, a question that had already been resolved in the mid-1970s after drawn-out negotiations and that in addition was being discussed in the other negotiations on limiting nuclear arms in Europe.

Finally, although suggesting a maximum number of warheads that could theoretically be deployed on Soviet missiles, the United States refused to establish any limits on long-range ALCMs and SLCMs, whose number in principle could reach 12,000 (up to 8,000 on aircraft and 4,000 at sea).[44] Thus the widely advertised "changes" in Washington's position, far from being a step toward a compromise, were rather intended to be used for deceiving the U.S. and the world public, weakening the growing opposition in Congress, and intensifying political and propaganda attacks against the Soviet Union.

The Soviet START proposal, as is known, called for a first-stage reduction of all strategic forces of both sides (at that time, approximately 12,000) by 25 percent. At the same time, according to the Soviet proposals it would be necessary to focus on strictly prohibiting and limiting the deployment and modernization of new types of strategic weapons, including ballistic missiles, aircraft, and long-range ALCMs and SLCMs. Only after such prohibition and limitation would it be possible to make still deeper reductions.[45] In such an event the reduction of nuclear arsenals would correspond to the goal of stabilizing the strategic balance and decreasing the capability for and probability of a first strike, the task of absolute priority in arms control.

Yet another vital condition for progress on this path was guaranteeing a radical solution to the problem caused by U.S. forward-based nuclear missiles on equal footing with similar Soviet weapons. This matter was especially connected with the problem of limiting nuclear weapons on the European continent, which both politically and in terms of the arms control dialogue became a key issue in the first half of the 1980s.

## Parity and Missiles in Europe

It is generally known that the military-technical differences in Soviet and U.S. strategic arsenals are also supplemented by the geostrategic asymmetries between the two powers. That is, the United States, in contrast to the USSR, is capable of delivering a nuclear strike to the heartland of the other side's territory not only with the help of strategic arms but also by using forward-based and intermediate-range nuclear forces deployed close to Soviet territory.

This geostrategic asymmetry has enormous significance in an objective analysis of both the military balance and the problems of arms control, which Western analysts quite often fail to take into consideration. For thermonuclear war may not only be unleased with a first strike of strategic forces but also through the use of tactical and intermediate range nuclear weapons at the theater level. It is precisely the first use of nuclear weapons in the TVD and the subsequent escalation of nuclear strikes in yield and range that is the cornerstone of NATO's military strategy and is openly proclaimed in the alliance's official documents. It may be that some future arms control treaty will reduce and limit strategic arms to such an extent that a first strike at the intercontinental level would become in practice unthinkable. But if no analogous measures were implemented with respect to nuclear weapons in the European and other theaters, then the threat of thermonuclear war not only would not be reduced but would become greater still, for the factors that deter Washington from using nuclear weapons on transoceanic battlefields, that is, the threat of an intercontinental strategic retaliatory strike on U.S. territory, would be significantly weakened.

It is for this reason that in negotiations to reduce substantially the level of military-strategic parity between the USSR and the United States the problem of limiting nuclear weapons regionally—particularly in the European TVD, where the most powerful destructive potentials in the history of humanity oppose each other—acquires the greatest significance. The plan to deploy the 572 new U.S. intermediate-range missiles (the Pershing II and GLCM) in Western Europe, not to mention the specific destabilizing military-technical characteristics of these weapons systems, added to the significance of the problem. Geostrategic factors and the obvious first-strike nature of these missiles made the negative consequences of their deployment far greater than the purely numerical addition of them to the U.S. strategic arsenal. Such considerations were reflected in the extreme importance attached to the attempts to reach an agreement on this question in the Geneva negotiations.

NATO's "dual track" decision of December 1979, as we recall, was justified by the "necessity" to strengthen U.S. nuclear guarantees with the North Atlantic pact. It was contended that whereas in the 1950s and 1960s the massive U.S. nuclear superiority in strategic weapons and nuclear forces in Europe compensated for the supposed NATO inferiority to the Warsaw Pact in conventional forces, by the 1970s and 1980s the position had changed. Soviet-U.S. parity existed at the level of strategic arms, and the Soviet Union had allegedly obtained superiority in nuclear weapons in the European theater primarily as a result of deploying from 1977 the new RSD-10 Pioneer mobile intermediate-range ballistic missile, called the SS-20 in the West. Accordingly, it was stated that NATO's "only escape" was through "rearming"—building up U.S. nuclear forces on the European continent. This approach was advanced in a speech by former West German Chancellor Helmut Schmidt in London in October 1977. These ideas were subsequently elaborated and even more dramatically expressed in Kissinger's speech in Brussels in September 1979. They formed the basis of a NATO high-level working group's recommendation and ultimately became alliance policy at the December 1979 session of the North Atlantic Council.

But setting aside for the moment the 1979 dual-track decision, it must be noted that in a broader respect the West's entire approach to the so-called problem of U.S. nuclear guarantees is totally bankrupt. There can be no doubt that a large-scale military conflict between the WTO and NATO would inevitably give rise to the use of nuclear weapons and develop into a global thermonuclear war. Such a political reality has existed for the past 40 years and will continue to exist in the future, independent of this or that partial change or disproportion in the military balance. But it is precisely the balance between the USSR and the United States in strategic arms, between the East and the West in nuclear and conventional forces in Europe that makes the unleashing of such a war unlikely. At the same time, the open possibility of radically limiting and reducing the levels of armed opposition, of lessening political tension, goes even further to permit the reduction of this "three-layered" balance, and in the future the complete elimination of the danger of unleashing a third world war in the European theater. As to guarantees of U.S. participation in such a war should it nonetheless break out, they are reinforced by the presence of about 300,000 U.S. servicemen in the European theater, by the deployment of 5,000 nuclear warheads on various U.S. launchers there, and by an enormous number of arms and various combat supplies. Finally, the broad economic, political, and ideological interests in Western Europe have extremely great significance for the United States.

If all of the above was insufficient for the reliability of U.S. commitments to NATO, then 600 new U.S. missiles on the continent could hardly "correct" the situation. If one maintains that the United States would not risk using its strategic forces in the course of the escalation of a possible European conflict, fearing a retaliatory strike on U.S. territory, then what was to be changed by adding the new U.S. missiles in Western Europe? In fact, a nuclear strike with the help of these missiles to the heartland of the territory of the USSR and its allies would be for the victimized side absolutely equivalent to a missile strike from, for example, submarines in the Norwegian or Mediterranean seas or U.S. territory itself. Precisely the same retaliatory strike would be brought down upon the bases of aggression both in Western Europe and on the other side of the Atlantic. If the Europeans, as the late French president De Gaulle said, could not believe that the United States would in the event of war exchange New York for Paris, then why would the NATO allies believe that the United States would exchange New York for the Pershing II?

Another matter is that an overall strategic balance is at root incompatible with the threat of the first use of nuclear weapons as a tool of U.S. and NATO foreign policy. The attempts, in spite of everything, to preserve and strengthen this capability explained Washington's strong desire to deploy the new missiles in Western Europe and in other regions close to the borders of the socialist alliance. Shifting the center of gravity of the nuclear confrontation as much as possible to the European continent was considered a U.S. advantage in Washington, since it would mean creating a first-strike nuclear capability immediately adjacent to vitally important centers of the USSR and other countries of the Warsaw Treaty. Furthermore, such a process would aggravate political tension and the military confrontation in Europe. By these very means Washington expected to block the process of détente, cut off the channels of East-West dialogue, and bind still more tightly the West European allies to Washington's anti-Soviet policy.

Upon coming to power the Reagan administration had in general not planned to begin negotiations to limit nuclear weapons in Europe, in any event not before beginning the deployment of U.S. ballistic and cruise missiles on the continent. As noted above, the U.S. president had stated that nuclear war could be kept confined to Europe, and Secretary of State Haig had said that the United States envisaged the possibility of nuclear warning shots on the European continent. These irresponsible declarations, adventuristic strategic plans, and overall policy of the administration provoked an unprecedented wave of antinuclear and anti-U.S. movements among the broad European public. In October and November 1981, 250,000 demonstrators marched in Bonn, 250,000 took part in demonstrations in London, 400,000 in Amsterdam, and 200,000 in Rome. Many of the major political parties in Western Europe opposed the deployment of the U.S. missiles.[46] On this question as well the Reagan administration was forced to change, if not its policy, then in any event its political tactics.

On November 18, 1981 President Reagan delivered a speech to the U.S. National Press Club with simultaneous radio and television coverage in Europe. He advanced the infamous "zero option" as the solution to the problem of nuclear weapons on the European continent. It specifically proposed that the USSR give up all its intermediate-range land-based ballistic missiles both in the European part of its territory and beyond the Urals.[47] The United States in this event would cancel the deployment of the Pershing II IRBM and the GLCM. The administration had counted on the fact that this proposal would be unacceptable to the USSR. Land-based ballistic missiles made up more than 50 percent of the USSR's intermediate-range nuclear launchers, but no more than 2 percent of NATO's. Moreover, the United States altogether refused to include the nuclear forces of its allies Great Britain and France (27 percent of NATO's potential), which in the 1990s could have numbered more than 1,000 nuclear warheads.[48] Thus the Soviet Union was to demolish more than 50 percent of its existing intermediate-range nuclear forces in exchange for a U.S. promise not to deploy 572 new land-based missiles. NATO's existing nuclear arsenal was in no way affected. As was declared by Moscow, the West as a result would receive a two-fold advantage in launchers and a three-fold advantage in warheads.[49] The United States under this plan reserved for itself the right to build up and modernize its 600-odd nuclear-capable fighter-bombers at airbases and on aircraft carriers in the European theater, and also to deploy hundreds, if not thousands, of SLCMs in all the seas and oceans, as well as to retain complete freedom of hand in regard to forward-based nuclear forces in the Far East.

In fact, at the foundation of the "zero option" lay the exact same logic of the START proposal examined above. Just as START was oriented not toward achieving an understanding in strategic arms control, but toward weakening the growing opposition to the administration's policy in Congress, the "zero option" was directed not at a search for an arms control agreement but at reducing the heat of the antinuclear movement in Europe, "calming" the West European governments, and, by contriving a deadlock in the negotiations, justifying the deployment of the new U.S. missiles. This was recognized by many experts in the West. For example, Arthur Macy Cox observed that "the Reagan speech was clearly a propaganda effort focused on Europe rather than on the Soviet Union."[50] And ACDA chief Eugene Rostow openly declared that the United States' main purpose in the negotiations was not to reduce arms but to unify the North Atlantic alliance.[51]

The Soviet Union, as to be expected, rejected Reagan's "zero option." Moscow stated its readiness to discuss the matter of eliminating all arsenals of nuclear weapons—both operational-tactical as well as intermediate-range—on the European continent, which would be a true zero option. However, since it would be difficult to reach such a goal in the foreseeable period, the USSR proposed reducing on a mutual and equitable basis the intermediate-range forces possessed by the Soviet Union and NATO by more than one-third—to 600 by 1985 and to 300 by 1990.[52] With the aim of facilitating the search for a compromise, the Soviet government unilaterally suspended the further deployment of the RSD-10 (SS-20) IRBM in the European part of the USSR, as well as in those regions beyond the Urals from where they could reach the countries of Western Europe, and continued reducing the overall number of its intermediate-range missiles. Were the United States to have refrained from deploying its new missiles in Europe, the Soviet Union expressed its readiness to reduce its RSD-10 IRBMs to the overall level of British and French intermediate-range missiles, that is, to a level of 162 missiles.

The Soviet government proposed examining other approaches as well: for example, to establish equal Soviet and U.S. limits on both intermediate-range launchers (missiles and aircraft) and their warheads. Under this proposal, in order to ensure equality in warhead number with Great Britain and France (420–430 total), the USSR would have reduced the number of RSD-10 launchers in Europe to approximately 140, that is, to a markedly lower level than the existing British and French missiles. The Soviet side also proposed establishing equal overall numbers of Soviet and NATO medium-range nuclear-capable aircraft at a mutually acceptable level. Finally, having completely dismantled its R-14 (SS-5) missiles, the USSR unilaterally expressed readiness to begin the reduction of more than 200 R-12 (SS-4) missiles and to complete their elimination in the course of 1984–85, should the United States have refrained from deploying its missiles in Europe at the announced time.[53] Carrying out these proposals would have resulted in the removal of about 1,300 intermediate-range nuclear forces from Europe, and in significantly fewer missiles and warheads of this class than existed before 1976 in the European part of the USSR, that is, before the beginning of the deployment of the RSD-10 system.[54]

The United States, on the contrary, sought to upset the then-existing balance of forces at any price. Washington's maneuvers in the Geneva negotiations were subordinated to this goal. In early 1983 the U.S. side, having created a semblance of retreating from the "zero option," advanced a revised proposal by which the Soviet Union "would be allowed" to keep a certain number of its missiles (after having significantly reduced them), with an obligatory equal deployment of U.S. missiles in Europe. Then in the fall of 1983 a new, "more precise option" followed from Washington, which stipulated the establishment of an "equal global maximum level" at 420 apiece on Soviet and U.S. intermediate-range missiles. But this option, too, was not an attempt to find a compromise solution, only another diplomatic trick. The fundamental goal of all these shifts was not to reach an agreement in Geneva, but to pacify the Western European public, ease the anxiety of their governments, and, having pinned the blame on the USSR for the failure of the negotiations, to begin deploying its missiles on the European continent. Vladimir F. Petrovskii, a deputy foreign minister and member of the Soviet negotiating team, justifiably observed in this connection that

all this cannot but lead to the thought that Washington wanted to spoil an agreement in order to deploy its missiles on European soil while citing the failure of the negotiations.... The U.S. in no way wants to refrain from attempts to destroy the approximate equality of forces in the European zone and obtain a decisive advantage for NATO either by way of unilateral Soviet disarmament or, at the opposite extreme, through sharply increasing its already large enough nuclear force in Europe.[55]

In November 1983 the United States began to deploy its cruise missiles and intermediate-range ballistic missiles on the European continent. In the November 24, 1983 statement of General Secretary Andropov was announced the adoption of retaliatory measures by the Soviet Union and the other socialist member states of the Warsaw Treaty.[56] First, since the United States by its actions had destroyed the possibility of reaching a mutually acceptable agreement in the negotiations to limit nuclear arms in Europe, the Soviet Union considered its further participation in these negotiations impossible. Second, the unilateral measures that the Soviet Union had adopted and that were aimed at creating more favorable conditions for reaching an agreement, including a moratorium on the deployment of the RSD-10 (SS-20) in the European part of the USSR, were cancelled. Furthermore, by agreement with the governments of the GDR and Czechoslovakia, it was decided to accelerate the preparatory work for deploying the OTR-22 (SS-12) and OTR-23 (SS-23) extended-range operational-tactical missiles on the territory of these countries. These forces were allegedly aimed at neutralizing the advantage that the United States had wanted to gain on account of the Pershing-II's short flight time, and their range was sufficient to reach the majority of the U.S. missiles' launching areas. Finally, since the deployment of the U.S. missiles increased the nuclear threat for the USSR, corresponding Soviet forces had to be deployed in the ocean regions and seas bordering the territory of the United States itself. By their characteristics these forces, as it was stated, were adequate to counterbalance the threat created by the U.S. missiles, in particular in range, yield, accuracy and, most importantly, in flight time to target.[57] While considering the strategic role of the new U.S. missiles, the Soviet side was also forced to suspend the START negotiations for a comprehensive reappraisal of its position. The magnitude of those retaliatory measures was characterized as strictly corresponding to the threat created by the U.S. diplomats. The response on two levels of the nuclear balance in Europe and one additional level of the strategic balance to deal with U.S. INF systems was quite symptomatic of the approach to the military balance, security, and sufficiency at that time.

In connection with the breakdown of the negotiations in 1983, it is appropriate to raise the question of whether the Soviet Union's decision to proceed with the deployment of the RSD-10 Pioneer missile in 1977 was justified, and whether the Soviet line in the 1981–83 negotiations was correct. It seems that from a purely military-technical point of view the deployment of the RSD-10 was a quite valid step. This system was to replace the technically and physically obsolete R-12 (SS-4) and the R-14 (SS-5) missiles, which had been deployed in the early 1960s. The new system fulfilled the very same tasks, although it was naturally technically more advanced, carried more warheads, and had a land-mobile basing system, which guaranteed higher survivability and hence capability for a retaliatory strike. Intermediate-range missiles have traditionally been the Warsaw Treaty Organization's main nuclear deterrent to NATO's aggregate nuclear potential in Europe and the U.S. nuclear forces in the Far East. Since this element of the WTO was not a subject of negotiation in the 1970s, the question of its necessity and preservation evidently did not arise and a decision was taken to modernize it.

At the same time, the political consequences of this modernization in the conditions of the Soviet-U.S. parity that emerged in the 1970s at the strategic level were, obviously, underestimated. Nevertheless, the main stimulus of NATO's decision to deploy the U.S. missiles was not the RSD-10 system as such, but the new situation of Soviet-U.S. strategic parity, which in the minds of the West's political leadership demanded some major steps in the military area to emphasize the solvency of the U.S. nuclear guarantee, that is, the promise to use nuclear weapons first in the event of a large-scale war on the European continent.

In the course of the negotiations certain political miscalculations were quite detrimental. This relates, in particular, to the fact that the United States was generally not interested in an agreement and considered the negotiations, as well as the "zero option," as simply a means for pacifying the antinuclear movement among the European public. The U.S. goal in the Geneva negotiations was not to reach an agreement but to guarantee a political pretext for implementing the plan to deploy the missiles. At the same time the position (in 1981–83) that security could be guaranteed only on the basis of the arithmetic equality of the intermediate-range nuclear forces of the USSR on the one hand, and the United States, Great Britain, and France on the other, was oversimplified. In this respect the overestimate of the importance of the military factor, and the underestimate of the significance of the political essence of security and the political ways of achieving it were also apparent. In the conditions of the overall military equilibrium, of parity at the global strategic level, disproportions at lower levels of the military balance have to a considerable degree lost their significance. It was possible to be resigned to these disproportions for the sake of strengthening the political basis of security through an agreement to reduce radically Soviet and U.S. intermediate-range missiles to as low a level as possible.

The reformulation of the Soviet approach to the issues after 1985, as the clearest manifestation of new political thinking in the area of security, completely confirms the above assessment. It was applied to the recent successful negotiations on intermediate-range missiles and is being applied now in the negotiations on the deep reductions of strategic arms as well. As recent practice has shown, only bold and radical decisions in these areas can strengthen security and prevent the arms race from outrunning arms control negotiations.

## Notes

1. *Pravda*, December 7, 1982.

2. Nikolai V. Ogarkov, *Vsegda v gotovnosti k zashchite Otechestva* (Moscow: Voenizdat, 1982), 49.

3. *Otkuda iskhodit ugroza miru*, 2d ed. (Moscow: Voenizdat, 1982), 8.

4. Vladimir F. Tolubko, *Raketnye voiska* (Moscow: Voenizdat, 1977), 25–26.

5. *Otkuda iskhodit ugroza miru*, 8.

6. Sergei G. Gorshkov, *Morskaia moshch' gosudarstva* (Moscow: Voenizdat, 1976), 307.

7. Ibid., 319, 454.

8. *Otkuda iskhodit ugrozu mira*, 8.

9. M. M. Kir'an, *Voenno-tekhnicheskii progress i Vooruzhennye Sily SSSR* (Moscow: Voenizdat, 1982), 289.

10. "Modernization of the U.S. Strategic Deterrent," *Hearings*, Committee on Armed Services, U.S. Senate, 97th Congress, first session, October 5, November 5, 1981, (Washington, D.C.: U.S. Government Printing Office, 1982), 17.

11. Harold Brown, *Thinking about National Security* (Boulder, Col.: Westview, 1983), 70.

12. See Gorshkov, *Morskaia moshch' gosudarstva*, 335.

13. *Radi mira na zemle: sovetskaia programma mira dlia 80-kh godov v deistvii* (Moscow: Politzidat, 1983), 186–87.

14. Tolubko, *Raketnye voiska*, 34.

15. *Pravda*, June 25, 1981.

16. *The Washington Post*, June 19, 1982, A3.

17. Brown, *Thinking about National Security*, 77–78.

18. *The Washington Post*, June 30, 1981, A17.

19. Colin S. Gray, "Presidential Directive 59: Flawed, but Useful," *Parameters* 11, no. 1 (March 1981): 34.

20. *The Washington Post*, June 30, 1981, A17.

21. Brown, *Thinking about National Security*, 80.

22. "Modernization of the U.S. Strategic Deterrent," *Hearings*, 47.

23. In particular, it was decided to deploy 400–600 SLCMs, including in the seas surrounding Europe. Plans were considered as well to deploy more than 108 Pershing-II missiles and to equip forward-based aircraft with ALCMs. See SIPRI, *World Armaments and Disarmament: SIPRI Yearbook 1983* (London: Francis and Taylor, 1983), 8.

24. Keith Payne, *Nuclear Deterrence in US-Soviet Relations* (Boulder, Col.: Westview Press, 1982), 207.

25. *U.S. News and World Report*, January 19, 1981.

26. "Arms Control Policy, Planning, and Negotiation," *Hearings*, Committee on Armed Services, U.S. Senate, 97th Congress, first session, July 21, 24, December 1, 1981 (Washington, D.C.: U.S. Government Printing Office, 1982), 86.

27. Congressional Budget Office, "SALT II and the Costs of Modernizing U.S. Strategic Forces" (Washington, D.C.: U.S. Government Printing Office, 1979), 8–21; "The SALT II Treaty, Part 1," *Hearings*, Committee on Foreign Relations, U.S. Senate, 96th Congress, first session (Washington, D.C.: U.S. Government Printing Office, 1979), 107.

28. David C. Jones, "United States Military Posture for FY 1981," in "Department of Defense Appropriations for Fiscal Year 1981, Part 1, Posture Statements," *Hearings*, Committee on Appropriations, U.S. Senate, 96th Congress, second session (Washington, D.C.: U.S. Government Printing Office, 1980), 262.

29. *The New York Times*, November 11, 1981.

30. *Pravda*, June 4, 1982; *Pravda*, January 2, 1983.

31. "Arms Control Policy, Planning, and Negotiation," *Hearings*, 38.

32. *Pravda*, June 4, 1982.

33. For example, under the 850–2,500–5,000 ceilings the United States could have deployed by 1990 100 MX ICBMs in addition to 300 Minuteman-III missiles with Mk-12A warheads, and also eight *Ohio*-class submarines with Trident-I SLBMs in addition to the 12 earlier *Ohios* carrying the Trident I, for a total of

784 missiles and 4,972 warheads (with the retirement of 750 older ICBMs and 304 SLBMs on the 19 *Lafayette* submarines). Within these same limits, considering the planned programs, by 1996 the United States could have 100 MXs, 300 single-warhead ICBMs or 100 Minuteman IIIs, as well as 19 *Ohio*-class submarines with 456 Trident-II SLBMs—in all approximately 650–850 missiles and 4,950 warheads. In addition the United States would have around 330 bombers with approximately 6,000 nuclear warheads not subject to the limitations. See Congressional Budget Office, "SALT II and the Costs of Modernizing U.S. Strategic Forces," 49, 84, 86.

34. Robert Scheer, *With Enough Shovels: Reagan, Bush and Nuclear War* (New York: Random House, 1982), 84.

35. Brown, *Thinking about National Security*, 84–85.

36. Scheer, *With Enough Shovels*, 167.

37. Vladimir O. Pechatnov, "Promezhutochnye vybory: itogi, perspektivy," *SShA* 1 (January 1983): 33.

38. *Public Opinion* 5: 4 (August-September 1982): 33–39.

39. McGeorge Bundy, George F. Kennan, Robert S. McNamara, and Gerard Smith, "Nuclear Weapons and the Atlantic Alliance," *Foreign Affairs* 60, no. 4 (Spring 1982): 753–68.

40. "President's Commission on Strategic Forces," 2, 5, 7–9.

41. "President's Commission on Strategic Forces," 22–25.

42. Alton Frye, "Strategic Build-Down: A Context for Restraint," *Foreign Affairs* 62: 2 (Winter 1983–84): 303.

43. *Time*, October 17, 1983, 16–18.

44. *Pravda*, June 16, 1983.

45. *Pravda*, February 24, 1983.

46. Arthur Macy Cox, *Russian Roulette: The Superpower Game* (New York: Times Books, 1982), 133–44.

47. *The New York Times*, November 18, 1981.

48. *World Armaments and Disarmament: SIPRI Yearbook 1983*, 39.

49. *Pravda*, February 20, 1982; *Pravda*, March 12, 1982.

50. Cox, *Russian Roulette*, 144.

51. Scheer, *With Enough Shovels*, 87.

52. *Pravda*, February 20, 1982.

53. *Pravda*, October 27, 1983.

54. *Pravda*, May 11, 1983; *Pravda*, April 25, 1983.

55. Vladimir F. Petrovskii, "Politicheskii realizm i Evropa," *SShA* 7 (July 1983): 13.

56. *Pravda*, November 25, 1983.

57. *Pravda*, December 6, 1983.

# 8

## A New Era in Soviet-U.S. Relations: Nuclear Arms Reduction and the Prevention of an Arms Race in Space

Opinions differ widely as to whether the suspension of the Soviet Union's participation in the INF and strategic arms negotiations was a necessary and wise act. But there is no doubt that to a great extent this step was conditioned by the uncompromising U.S. line. Washington regarded the negotiations not as an instrument for reaching agreements on limiting and reducing arms but rather as a means of pacifying the U.S. and world public, of weakening the movement against the deployment of U.S. missiles in Western Europe, and of splitting the congressional opposition to the accelerated strategic programs. By late 1983, with the U.S. move to deploy the first missiles on the European continent, it finally became clear that the negotiations had degenerated by their very essence and from a means of curbing the arms race had become a spur for its acceleration.

Came 1984—the first year in the past 15 in which no arms control dialogue at all was being conducted, expected, or planned between the world's two most powerful states. Meanwhile, the arms buildup steadily continued, the world drew inexorably closer to a completely unlimited arms race, and the previous elements of controlling this process were quickly disintegrating. The destabilization of the military-strategic situation was in the closest way interlinked with the aggravation of political conditions. As the American journalist Strobe Talbott perceptively noted: "The crisis in arms control contributed to three others: in the alliance between the United States and Western Europe; in the partnership between the executive and legislative branches of the U.S. government; and in the Soviet-American relationship."[1]

It was necessary to stop the world's slide into a thermonuclear abyss. In November 1984 and January 1985 at the meetings of the Soviet and U.S. foreign ministers in Geneva it was agreed to resume negotiations, the subject of which would be "the set of issues concerning space and nuclear arms, strategic and intermediate-range, all of which will be considered and resolved in their interdependence."[2] In March 1985 the Soviet-U.S. negotiations on nuclear and space weapons began in Geneva. Having come to these negotiations despite the continued deployment of U.S. missiles in Europe, the Soviet Union was guided by several principal considerations.

First of all, the worsening of the global military-political situation and the growth of the military threat provoked a powerful rise of the peace movement in 1984. The questions of war, peace, and disarmament acquired great importance in the course of the U.S. presidential elections. The continued increase in the levels of nuclear confrontation on the European continent became the most important political question for Western Europe. In these conditions the U.S. leadership noticeably changed the tone of its official rhetoric. In January 1984 Reagan stated: "Neither we nor the Soviet Union can wish away the differences between our two societies and our philosophies. But we should always remember that we do have common interests. And the foremost among them is to avoid war and reduce the level of arms." In June the U.S. president declared that "a nuclear war cannot be won and must never be fought. . . . I believe that now it is even more possible to achieve an agreement. . . . I am ready to halt and even reverse the deployment of our intermediate-range missiles in Europe in the event of a verifiable and equitable agreement." In September the U.S. chief said: "We recognize that there is no sane alternative to negotiations on arms control and other issues between our two nations, which have the capacity to destroy civilization as we know it. I believe this is a view shared by virtually every country in the world and by the Soviet Union itself."[3]

These expressions represented a striking contrast to the official statements made by Washington in the early period of the Republican administration's first term. They reflected the major political changes within the United States and abroad, to which the U.S. government was forced to adapt, at least in words. Signs of a struggle appeared as well within the administration between adherents of the earlier hard-line policy and supporters of a more moderate policy, of achieving some level of understanding with the USSR on the most important issues. The absence of negotiations in these conditions had begun to be increasingly costly, if only because it was used by the opponents of arms control for shifting the blame to the other side and for a propaganda campaign on the "nonconstructive line" of the USSR. They hurried to transform this situation into a pretext for accelerating the arms race, imparting to it an irreversible character, and transforming the break in the dialogue into a permanent state of affairs.

Another aspect was the development of the problem of preventing the militarization of space in questions of strategy and international politics and on the disarmament agenda, which became quite acute as the SDI program gathered increasingly greater inertia and exerted a destabilizing technological and political influence. Thus, in order to stem the movement of the arms race into space, it was necessary to begin without delay negotiations on this issue directly. Moreover, this issue was inseparably linked with the problems of offensive nuclear weapons in the political, strategic, and military-technological respect.

The coming of the new, younger leadership to decisive positions in the CPSU and Soviet government in 1985 signified the beginning of a fundamentally new era in the life of Soviet society, which influenced greatly Soviet-U.S. relations and international politics as a whole. The policy of the deep restructuring (*perestroika*) of the Soviet Union's economy and domestic policy, the development of socialist democracy and openness (*glasnost*), was inseparably linked with the reformulation of Soviet foreign policy, the development of new political thinking, and the concept of mutual and comprehensive security in international relations. Integral elements of this were the rapid revision of the Soviet negotiating position on the limitation and reduction of nuclear and space arms and the advancement of bold and radical ways of resolving these vitally important problems.

## The Theory and Practice of New Thinking: The First Steps

At the Geneva negotiations on nuclear and space weapons, which began in March 1985, the Soviet Union expressed its readiness for the most radical reductions of nuclear arms. In a conversation with U.S. congressmen on April 10, 1985, CPSU General Secretary Mikhail S. Gorbachev characterized the fundamental principles of the USSR's line at the Geneva negotiations in the following way:

We are satisfied that the U.S. has accepted our proposal on the negotiations. We have come to them in order to conduct them honestly, seriously, striving to reach an agreement on ponderable real results, on very major reductions of strategic and intermediate-range nuclear weapons. But achieving these goals is possible only if the American side gives up its provocative schemes for moving the arms race into space, where under the guise of "defensive" weapons it wants to guarantee for itself the capability to carry out a nuclear first strike with impunity. Therefore, it is precisely the resolution of issues of halting the nuclear arms race on Earth and banning it in space that is an indivisible problem which must be resolved comprehensively, just as was stipulated between the USSR and the USA in January of this year."[4]

Major recent landmarks in the struggle to curb the arms race include the Soviet proposals advanced during General Secretary Gorbachev's visit to France in October 1985, as well as during his meeting with the U.S. president in Geneva in November of the same year. The Soviet program for complete nuclear disarmament of January 15, 1986 formulated a major, long-term policy. The turning point came with the Reykjavik summit of Soviet and U.S. leaders in October 1986. A treaty to eliminate Soviet and U.S. intermediate- and shorter-range missiles on a global scale was subsequently worked out in 1987 and signed during Gorbachev's visit to the United States in December of that same year. All Soviet peace initiatives, ideas, and proposals received theoretical substantiation and further practical development in the documents of the 27th CPSU congress.[5] The most important provisions are the new principles, dictated by the realities of the nuclear-space age, of the Soviet approach to international affairs. First among them is the recognition of the impossibility of guaranteeing security in a military-technological way and the necessity of resolving this problem, a political one by its very nature, by political means (i.e., through negotiations). Fundamental as well are the unacceptability of attempts to guarantee one's security at the expense of the interests of other states, as well as the necessity of building Soviet-U.S. relations on the basis of mutual and equal security (and since this concerns international relations as a whole, on the basis of comprehensive security). Objectively, the United States and the Soviet Union have many areas of mutual interest, the main one being the requirement to live in peace, to cooperate on an equal and mutually advantageous basis. Yet another idea is that the world is in a state of dynamic and turbulent change, and that therefore no one can preserve by force an eternal status quo in it. In this world one must behave in the international arena with restraint and circumspection and live civilly in conditions of proper international reciprocity, cooperation and respect for international law. The great states must negotiate international problems point by point where they can cooperate to achieve solutions, and where they cannot, refrain from agreed-upon dangerous and destabilizing forms of involvement.

The realization of these principles requires, in the first place, breaking with ways of thinking and acting that since ancient times have been based on the permissibility of war, on power politics, and that do not correspond in any way to the realities of the nuclear age. One must first of all recognize that winning the arms race, as well as a nuclear war itself, is impossible. Also unthinkable and unwinnable is a conventional war between the United States and the USSR, or between alliances headed by the two great powers. Preparation for a nuclear war with the goal of achieving military superiority objectively cannot bring political gain to anyone. The present level of the nuclear balance—of equal danger to all states—is excessively high, and its further increase may push this danger to such limits that even the quantitative balance of forces, or parity, will no longer exert mutual military-political deterrence. Genuine and equal security may be based not on a maximally high but on a maximally low level of the strategic balance. The conventional forces of the most powerful states in this respect must also be reduced, redeployed, and limited—by way of negotiations and agreements—to levels of reasonable sufficiency and restructured in such a way that large-scale offensive operations will become unfeasible for either side.

Theoreticians may argue endlessly over whether this conceptual approach is new or old, realistic or naive, too binding or excessively broad. And on the theoretical level the polemics may never be finally resolved. Practice is the best measure of the substance of the new way of thinking, the only persuasive criterion of its value.

The Soviet Union's actions in practice, in accordance with the above philosophy, stipulate both unilateral measures to limit its military potential, as well as proposals to conclude agreements on the bilateral and multilateral limitation and reduction of arms. As a unilateral measure the USSR announced a moratorium on all nuclear explosions beginning with August 6, 1985, the symbolic date of the first atomic bombing, which wiped Hiroshima from the face of the earth and marked the beginning of the nuclear age. The unilateral Soviet moratorium was in effect for one-and-a-half years.

After the U.S.-Soviet summit in Reykjavik in October 1986, the parties managed in the course of 1987 to accomplish a fundamental breakthrough in the long-existing deadlock in the Geneva negotiations. This breakthrough took place on the issue of eliminating Soviet and U.S. missiles in Europe. A series of major Soviet initiatives helped to resolve this issue, one that had caused a deep crisis in the Soviet-U.S. arms control dialogue in the first half of the 1980s.

In February 1987 the Soviet Union agreed to decouple the INF issue from the Reykjavik package. The latter, as is known, stipulated the reduction of the two powers' INF forces to zero in Europe and their limitation outside of Europe to a ceiling of 100 nuclear warheads for each side. Meeting the West's position halfway, in the summer of 1987 Moscow agreed to also include in the treaty the elimination of the OTR-22 (SS-12) and OTR-23 (SS-23) operational-tactical (shorter-range) missiles with a range of 500–1,000 kilometers in Europe, and their limitation to equal levels outside Europe. Finally, in August 1987 the Soviet Union agreed to a "global double-zero option," that is, the complete elimination of Soviet and U.S. INF and operational-tactical missiles.

Issues of qualitative limitations, the elimination of the missiles' nuclear warheads, the elimination of U.S. nuclear warheads for the 72 West German Pershing-I operational-tactical missiles, and the nonmodification of U.S. GLCMs into SLCMs were resolved in the course of meetings of the two powers' foreign ministers in the United States in September 1987, and in the United States and the USSR in October 1987. Comprehensive verification measures were also agreed upon.

The treaty on intermediate- and shorter-range missiles was signed during the course of General Secretary Gorbachev's visit to the United States in December 1987. By all measures it was an important treaty, a big step forward in comparison to the SALT agreements of the 1970s. For the first time in history two entire classes of Soviet and U.S. nuclear weapons will be destroyed and prohibited—in all about 2,700 missiles and 2,200 nuclear warheads will be eliminated in the course of three years. Most of the missiles are brand new and will be dismantled without replacement by more sophisticated systems, as was so often the case in the past.

Many of the treaty's features are quite unprecedented. Not only deployed but also undeployed missiles will be destroyed. Not only launchers (as in SALT I and SALT II) but the missiles themselves, their warheads, transporter-erector vehicles, installations at the deployment areas, operational bases, and testing and training sites will be dismantled. The dismantling procedures have been worked out in great detail, including where to cut the missile stages, launchers, and other equipment, how they must be destroyed, crushed, and made inoperable. Of special importance are the verification provisions. They include national technical means, on-site inspections, permanent monitoring, and challenge inspections. The exchange of information on the location, numbers, status, and types of deployed and undeployed missiles is quite impressive. Intrusive measures for verifying this information, elimination procedures, and arrangements for monitoring deployment areas and production plants in the aftermath of the dismantling process are fixed in the treaty and its memorandums.

By the treaty the Soviet Union has accepted an obligation to eliminate twice as many missiles and three-and-a-half times as many warheads as the United States (respectively, 1,800:860 and 1,720:500). Some in the USSR are concerned that this is a unilateral concession. And some in the United States invoke this as a precedent in support of the U.S. "position of strength" policy embodied in the steady INF deployment since late 1983 and the tough negotiating tactics since 1981. In fact both assessments are wrong. The treaty is neither the former nor the latter. To build on these views prescriptions of what to do (or not to do) in negotiations on other arms control subjects in the future would be a deplorable mistake for both sides.

It is true that the Soviet Union in accordance with the treaty is obliged to get rid of many more missiles than the United States. But the first and simplest explanation is that the USSR has in its possession that many more of these weapons. Zero-zero is the ultimate level of parity, and if one side has to dismantle more weapons in order to reach it, it means that originally it had a corresponding advantage in this category of arms. That is why the differing scale of reductions is not a Soviet unilateral concession but the only reasonable and mutually acceptable compromise for agreeing on the radical reduction of nuclear capability. By definition disarmament agreements must always lead to equality on the lowest achievable levels. Let the side that has an advantage in a particular class of weapons pay for it by larger reductions. Moscow has accepted this principle of disarmament and this is an important breakthrough that the United States has yet to match in many other areas of arms control.

So why did the USSR build up to higher levels in the first place and what made Moscow agree to get rid of its advantage? Intermediate- and shorter-range missiles are not an isolated segment of the nuclear balance but an integral part of an overall picture of the global and regional strategic situation. In the past the USSR considered it necessary to have more intermediate- and operational-tactical missiles than the United States to compensate for British, French, and Chinese nuclear forces, for NATO advantages in strike aircraft and battlefield nuclear weapons, and to deter the openly declared Western strategy of using nuclear weapons first (a nuclear preemptive strike in Soviet eyes) and the "escalation dominance" strategy of the U.S. nuclear war-fighting doctrine. Certainly the geostrategic asymmetry (U.S. IRBMs and GLCMs can reach deep into Soviet territory while such Soviet missiles cannot reach the United States) biased in favor of overcompensating in numbers and providing for redundancy at the level of operational-tactical missiles. Finally, historical, organizational, and technical factors and peculiarities of the decision-making process all played some role. One must never pretend that force levels and capabilities always evolve on the basis of purely rational, precise calculations, of binding assumptions and conclusions.

What is important is the determination of the new Soviet leadership to cut through the tight knots of diplomatic experience, strategic calculations, and contradictory military and political perceptions of the two sides that had led to the negotiating failure in 1983 and produced a new deadlock in 1985–86.

The need to compensate at this time and in this particular agreement for third states' forces was revised first of all. At the present enormous levels of global nuclear potentials (including strategic), many individual asymmetries may be ignored or postponed for later solutions in order to proceed with nuclear arms reductions as quickly and radically as possible. That is why zero U.S. and Soviet intermediate-range nuclear forces in Europe was suggested by the USSR in Reykjavik in 1986. Not to create an impetus for the nuclear buildup on lower levels, Moscow agreed to include in the treaty shorter-range missiles on the same zero-zero principle. Taking into account the security interests of the Asian states, and in order to solve some verification complications and make the treaty more "leakproof," it was eventually decided to eliminate both classes of missiles on a global basis.

In fact these were not concessions to NATO, but rather concessions to the new way of thinking about security and nuclear weapons, to common sense, and finally, to the real security interests of the USSR itself. Quite obviously, much more fundamental, consistent, and positive reasons than Western "position of strength" diplomacy and missile deployments were needed for Soviet negotiating policy to acquire this attitude. The real reasons were the new way of thinking on national security matters and the deep restructuring of Soviet foreign and in particular arms control policy.

Actually, on many occasions in 1986–87 the USSR was not pressed into concessions by NATO but, on the contrary, was pulling the other side in the direction of more radical solutions. For instance, after Reykjavik it became apparent at the negotiations that the United States and its European allies were not at all enthusiastic about reducing intermediate-range missiles to a zero level in Europe. Not interested in the zero option, they preferred to build up to an equal level with the USSR. Washington wanted the right to modify the Pershing-II IRBM into the Pershing-Ib tactical missile system, to redeploy GLCMs on ships and submarines as SLCMs, to produce within the prohibited range limits conventionally armed ballistic and cruise missiles, and to develop and transfer the Pershing-Ib system to West Germany. These positions had to be rejected for the sake of a sensible agreement. On some occasions the Soviet position on verification issues was more advanced and radical than the U.S. stance.

Thus the real picture was very far from the caricature of "Soviet concessions under U.S. pressure." What really took place at the talks and in both capitals was a difficult and sometimes exhausting but determined search for a balance of interests and for a genuine compromise. These were eventually found not on the basis of the smallest common denominator (as was often the case in the past), but on the basis of the largest achievable denominator: the greatest possible scale and magnitude of reductions, the strictest dismantling procedures, the broadest extent of weapons and facilities included, and the most thorough verification rules. Obviously this joint effort brought great success.

From the military point of view the main significance of the treaty is that the most destabilizing element of the East-West strategic balance will be eliminated with a significant alleviation of the nuclear threat. The percentage of global nuclear arsenals destroyed (about 4–5 percent) is not the correct measure. This kind of assessment is proper for money-lending, but not for matters of nuclear security. Nuclear weapons are all different and play different roles in the strategic balance and in the probability of war. Politically it may signify the beginning of a new era in Soviet-U.S. relations and in East-West relations on the European continent, the strengthening of mutual trust and confidence, and a move away from 40 years of confrontation. For the arms control and disarmament process it may mean a great step forward, laying out many new approaches, precedents, and ways and means of reaching agreements.

What is of utmost importance now is whether the treaty will remain an isolated agreement or will become the first step of a new era in disarmament efforts and in strengthening the common security. For example, strategic offensive arms could undergo a first-stage 50 percent reduction, and the ABM Treaty, which prevents the arms race from moving into space, could be strengthened. WTO and NATO conventional arms and armed forces in Europe could also be substantially reduced, with the elimination of disproportions in offensive arms (such as tanks and tactical strike aviation) to provide for the restructuring of the two alliances' armed forces on purely defensive principles. A convention on the complete elimination of chemical arms and a treaty to reduce the yield threshold of nuclear tests and establish a low quota on their annual number should be concluded as well.

Should this momentum be capitalized on in future years, humanity will approach the end of the twentieth century under new conditions. The arms race will in serious measure have been brought under control, military arsenals radically reduced, and stability of the military balance strengthened at all levels. The threat of global war will have been far removed, and the general security of all, substantially strengthened.

## The Moscow Connection: The Interaction of Strategic Offensive and Defensive Systems

Three main points substantially complicated the search for a mutually acceptable "grand compromise" in this sphere in 1986–87. First of all, the Soviet and U.S. approaches deeply diverged concerning how the development of fundamentally new ballistic missile defense and space weapons systems and their influence on the ABM Treaty could affect the prospects for deep reductions of strategic offensive arms. Moreover, the parties did not reach a mutual understanding on what should be the ultimate goal of strategic arms reductions and the specific ways (qualitative and structural limits) for carrying out an initial 50 percent reduction of strategic potentials. Finally, Washington's refusal in Fall 1986 to observe the SALT I Interim Agreement and the SALT II Treaty complicated the situation in the most serious political and military-technical ways.

A key problem impeding deep reductions in Soviet and U.S. strategic offensive arms was created by the radical shift of U.S. policy in this area: the Reagan administration's rejection of the fundamental principle of the organic strategic and military-technical relationship between strict constraints on BMD systems and offensive arms limitations and reductions. This principle was accorded recognition by international law in the preamble of the 1972 ABM Treaty. The Soviet Union and the United States (during three administrations of both the Republican and Democratic parties) proceeded from this concept throughout more than a decade of SALT negotiations. And during the first years of the Reagan administration, while the START negotiations were being conducted (1982–83), in spite of Washington's unconcealed negative attitude toward arms control the notion of such an organic relationship did not come under doubt.

During 1986–87 the destabilizing consequences of a potential large-scale BMD system with space-based elements were examined in Soviet scholarly literature in sufficient detail according to the basic angles of this complex issue: with respect to the stability of the Soviet-U.S. military-strategic balance; from the point of view of preserving the ABM Treaty and prohibiting antisatellite weapons systems; for the prospect of reducing strategic offensive arms and prohibiting new third-generation nuclear weapons; for the goal of reducing the economic costs of the military competition; and concerning the security of the great powers' allies and the neutral and nonaligned countries.[6]

In the course of 1987 the prospects for preventing an arms race in space were determined by the interaction of tendencies in three fundamental and closely interconnected spheres. First was the course of the work in the realm of the SDI program itself, the results achieved and the prospects for developing its main technical projects and experiments, which in turn influenced notions of the possibility of creating a large-scale space-based BMD system and the formulation of its strategic goals and tasks. Second, of substantial importance was the further development of the SDI debate in the United States, of Congress's action in funding the program, and of ABM Treaty compliance issues. Third, and in a number of respects most important of all, was the evolution of the Soviet and U.S. positions on the issue of space and strategic defensive systems and their relationship to deep reductions in strategic offensive arsenals.

Despite the declarations of success by administration officials concerning the development of SDI technology, assessments by the majority of experts both in the United States and the Soviet Union testify to the

necessary, space-based configurations that would be intended not for de-
oying U.S. population and material assets but for intercepting probable
ace strike weapons;

veloping electronic warfare systems for disturbing the functioning of an
pponent's surveillance, battle management, and communications systems;

nsuring the adequate survivability of Soviet countermeasure systems and their
rveillance and C³I complex from U.S. offensive weapons and possible sys-
ems of counter-countermeasures.

Over the course of 1984–87 the true prospects for countermeasures
space-based BMD systems became increasingly clear to specialists, the
litary, and politicians in Congress, if not the U.S. public at large. Doubt
as also cast on the very feasibility of many of SDI's futuristic weapons
chnologies. The American Physical Society's extensive study *Science*
*d Technology of Directed Energy Weapons*, released in April 1987, made
gnificant contributions to the debate in this regard.⁹ On the basis of a
omprehensive professional analysis of DEW projects within the frame-
ork of SDI, these physicists offered quite pessimistic conclusions con-
erning certain strike weapons, SATKA systems, and the support,
ntegration, and defense systems of the proposed BMD. In particular,
he physicists pointed out that

lthough substantial progress has been made in many technologies of DEW over
he last two decades, the Study Group finds significant gaps in the scientific and
engineering understanding of many issues associated with the development of
these technologies.... Most crucial elements required for a DEW system need
improvements of several orders of magnitude.... We estimate that even in the
best of circumstances, a decade or more of intensive research would be required
to provide the technical knowledge needed for an informed decision about the
potential effectiveness and survivability of directed energy systems....

In contrast to the technical problems faced in developing DEWs capable of boost-phase kill for defense systems, the options available
to the offense, including direct attacks on DEW platforms, may be less difficult
and costly to develop and may require fewer orders-of-magnitude performance
improvements.¹⁰

The study's conclusions carried even greater weight by virtue of the
fact that by and large they were issued by experts not at all of a liberal
persuasion (as with the Federation of American Scientists or the Union
of Concerned Scientists) but by experts holding quite conservative views
and associated with major SDI contractors, such as Sandia National Laboratory, Lawrence Livermore Laboratory, the Air Force Weapons Lab-

fact that "even with consideration of the results of the developments and
experiments recently conducted in the U.S., the current technological
level of the kill systems being examined lags behind what is required.
Moreover, it still remains unclear whether it is possible to bring the
characteristics of the kill systems to the necessary level by way of incre-
mental improvement."⁷

The same conclusion in principle is justified with regard to the surveillance, acquisition, tracking, and kill assessment (SATKA) technologies being developed in the SDI framework, as well as to battle
management—especially if analyzed against the possible passive and active countermeasures available to the other side. In particular, Soviet
experts note that "many technical improvements whose application will
permit increasing the effectiveness of BMD weapons can be used anal-
ogously by the opposing side for improving the capability of its offensive
forces to penetrate a defensive system. This circumstance excludes in
practice the possibility of an absolutely effective defense, even in the
event that solutions to all the numerous technical problems of tracking,
guidance, and interception were found."⁸

The main problem of SDI is thus not that some laws of physics exclude
the possibility of a more or less effective global BMD system for the
defense of one's territory (although it is clear that its effectiveness will
be nowhere close to 100 percent, nor will its reliability ever be guaranteed
because of the impossibility of testing the enormously complex system
in conditions approximating a real war situation). In fact the essence of
the problem is quite different: using the very same laws of physics on
which the United States relies in its plans to develop a space-based BMD
system, the other side can effectively counter any of the possible versions
of such a system. The system's effectiveness at any point in the future
will therefore fluctuate depending on the state of the competition between BMD systems and anti-BMD systems, as well as on the particular
battle engagement scenario, much like the case between combat aircraft
and air defense systems. Whatever the effectiveness of air defense systems, the great absolute destructive power of nuclear weapons has always
ensured their dubious utility in a hypothetical nuclear war. There is no
fact or argument that BMD proponents may marshal that would give
the slightest grounds to expect that the situation will be different with
future large-scale space-based BMD systems. Space-based BMD is no
"magic weapon." Such a weapon never existed in the past and will never
emerge in the future. Rather, it will exist and develop in the context of
a prolonged arms race (as has always been the case) with all the traditional
uncertainties, costs, fears, and conflicting assessments, multiplied by the
vastness of outer space and the complexity of exotic technology.

The Reagan administration's stake on U.S. military-technical superiority in this respect is groundless, at a minimum, for two reasons. First,

there in no way exists an overwhelming U.S. advantage in the use of space and in the development of advanced technology in the framework of basic and applied research. In some areas the United States is ahead, in others, the Soviet Union, and nothing allows one to contend that this situation will radically change in either's favor in the future.

Second, one could logically justify hopes for U.S. military-technological superiority only in the event that the Soviet Union would blindly follow the U.S. example and allow itself to be pulled into an expensive competition in the development and deployment of an analogous space-based BMD system. However, the USSR's unambiguously formulated position is that it will provide an asymmetrical response—not with a BMD of its own, but with anti-BMD systems—with the use of less expensive and complex means, and not necessarily only space-based but also air- and ground-based. In such a context it is quite probable that SDI's fundamental paradox will be fully manifested: its development will carry the seeds of its demise.

The fact of the matter is that the majority of kill systems being developed within the framework of the "defense initiative" on the basis of kinetic or directed energy principles can be used not only from space against ballistic missiles in flight trajectories but also against the very same space-based BMD stations and satellites. These counter-systems can operate both from space and from earth. Thus the competition between space-based BMD systems and countermeasures to them will not be like a race between two riders on horses but rather like a competition between one horseman on a horse and the other sitting on the shoulders of the first. Should the USSR undertake the development of such weapons as a policy of counteracting a global U.S. BMD system, it will have a "head start" using a number of inherent advantages.

It is an axiom among specialists, for example, that all things being equal, a larger laser is more powerful than a smaller one, and that a larger laser is easier to build on the ground than in space. Ground construction allows for the capability to compensate for atmospheric distortions of the laser beam and a simpler task of ensuring high survivability. Many directed energy weapons (DEWs), including the X-ray laser, are more effective when irradiating from the stratosphere up into space than from space down to the atmosphere below, making them more effective weapons against spaced-based BMD systems than against ballistic missiles. In a counter-BMD mode all problems of launch platforms, positioning, time of detection and pop-up ascent, targeting, rate of fire, and so on, will be much easier to solve.

Because of the physical laws of objects in orbit and the rotation of the earth itself only a small portion of space battle stations can be present continually over a given area of the earth's surface. Therefore the majority of such stations will not be in position for interception, whereas

ground-based countermeasure systems will const destroy space-based objects passing over them a areas along predictable trajetories. The latter wo fewer targets and take advantage of the longer dw and destroying them than the orbital BMD sys ICBMs and SLBMs. The problems of detection quisition and tracking, battle management, energy and redundant elements, and ensuring adequate much more easily resolved for systems counteractin stations.

True, there are complications. For example, grou forces must themselves be defended from the enemy weapons (ballistic missiles, aviation, and cruise ground- and space-based anti-BMD systems can be survivable through hardening, dispersal, redundancy, cealment. Furthermore, certain fixed land-based inst protected by a limited ground-based BMD and air defe a direct nuclear strike. Its requirements for level of tainability in battle, and degree of survivability and co erations will be considerably relaxed. Such systems will less complex and expensive, and may become operation scale U.S. global BMD system.

Thus the main technical-strategic factor that tangib plans for creating on the basis of SDI a large-scale BM space-based elements is the probability of the other side sures. The Soviet Union in this respect has adopted an policy, having declared that its response will be asymmetr program, less costly, and require less time to implement. fective measures of this kind may be the following:

—improving and modernizing, but not necessarily proliferating fensive forces in order to complicate their interception by a mul (through, for example, reducing the boost phase of the traje time of warhead dispersal, improving decoys, and other means of ing BMD, such as MARV, and so on);

—diversifying strategic offensive arms by weapon class and type provide the USSR with a multitude of available azimuths and tr retaliatory strikes;

—increasing the survivability of strategic offensive arms and their v $C^3I$ systems in order to deprive the opponent of the capability, vi attack, of substantially weakening and disorganizing a Soviet retali in order to facilitate the damage limitation tasks of a U.S. BMD;

—developing systems of direct attack against the opponent's space-b using nuclear, kinetic, and directed energy weapons in land-, sea-

oratory, the U.S. Military Academy, AT & T Bell Laboratories, Stanford University, and others.

Influenced by the increasingly deeper and more detailed critique of the strategic concept of and program for a comprehensive defense from ballistic missiles, sentiments in U.S. political circles have recently undergone a quite radical shift. The essence of this turning point is that the idea of a leak-proof ("astrodome") space-based BMD system—to which President Reagan continues to cling and that still attracts a broad spectrum of average Americans—has been completely discredited on strategic, operational, and technical grounds in the eyes of informed people. Their ranks now include both liberal and conservative representatives of the U.S. political elite, the overwhelming majority of the military-academic "strategic community," and even the Pentagon bureaucracy, with the exception of some high officials (most notably Secretary of Defense Weinberger until his recent retirement) and the Strategic Defense Initiative Organization itself.

The shift in sentiments in the United States was reflected in the composition of Congress. Following both the 1984 and 1986 elections the Democratic party emerged with a solid majority in both houses of Congress. Accordingly, Congress began to throw down an open and unambiguous challenge to the administration's desired thrust of the SDI program. In particular, in one of the budget decisions for FY 1987, it was pointed out that "the major emphasis within SDI should be dedicated to developing survivable and cost effective defensive options for enhancing the survivability of U.S. retaliatory forces and command, control, and communications systems."[11] SDI appropriations in the FY 1988 budget were cut by Congress from $5.7 billion to $4.5 billion, that is, by 34 percent.[12] (Previously SDI funds had been cut from $1.8 to $1.4 billion in FY 1985, from $3.7 to $2.8 billion in FY 1986, and in FY 1987 from $5.3 to $3.5 billion.)

In fact, as a result of domestic and external obstacles confronting SDI in the late 1980s (including the Soviet position toward it and the ABM Treaty), the program's decision-makers are faced with a choice. As several Soviet experts observed, it consisted of the following dichotomy: "Either continue financing and developing on a reduced scale all the projects that had been planned earlier, which would most likely mean pushing back the date for making a deployment decision from the early 1990s to a later time, or develop a more detailed and strict system of priorities, that is, accelerate some (through greater funding) and decelerate or halt other projects in order to keep within the scaled-back appropriations and achieve the results (that is, a deployment decision) by the set date."[13]

Judging by available information, the second option has been chosen for the present. Almost half the SDI projects have slowed their devel-

opment, been reoriented toward more modest tasks, or cancelled altogether. For example, a system of orbiting chemical laser stations is no
longer considered as promising in the long-term. The Talon Gold system
(a space-based infrared tracking telescope) was cancelled completely.
Expectations of the nuclear-pumped X-ray laser's level of effectiveness
have been lowered. Its primary purpose in the foreseeable future, as well
as that of the charged particle beam system, is not destroying missiles
but discriminating real warheads from decoys. Enthusiasm for the space-
based electromagnetic mass accelerator (rail-gun) has withered significantly. Other futuristic DEW projects, such as the free-election laser and
the ground-based excimer laser with space-based reflective mirrors, are
being developed with an eye toward obtaining more or less tangible
results for a decision on their feasibility only by the late 1990s.[14]

At the same time the emphasis on technologies that are more feasible
at the moment and are not associated with such great uncertainty has
grown in the SDI program. In particular, according to the budget request
for FY 1988, appropriations to kinetic energy weapons (KEWs) have
almost doubled.[15] But such systems, although simpler than the exotic
DEW types in and of themselves, have a quite limited capability to intercept ballistic missiles.

## Limited Options of Ballistic Missile Defense

The unceasing debates, diplomatic negotiations, and scientific discussions of the past five years on SDI within the United States, the USSR,
and other countries have crystallized at the present moment several of
the most important theoretical positions, at which converges the opinion
of the overwhelming majority of the international community's specialists. First, a multilayered territorial and global space-based BMD system,
independent of the amount of money poured into research and development, cannot be tested and deployed on any scale significant for the
strategic balance before the year 2000. Second, the USSR's potential
countermeasures against such a system can significantly decrease its relative effectiveness, which, in the context of the great absolute destructive
power of even a small number of nuclear weapons and the concentration
of developed countries' population and industry in a few vulnerable
areas, would in practice mean the absence of protection from nuclear
destruction. Third, only the deep reduction of offensive nuclear arms,
the prohibition of potential countermeasures to BMD systems, and the
agreed deployment and modernization of such multilayered asymmetrical systems could reduce the nuclear threat below a level of unacceptable
damage. Finally, the conclusion of agreements (and verification of their
compliance) on such complex problems would require such a degree of
good will and mutual trust between states, such a restructuring of re-

lations between adversaries and allies, as to be more than sufficient for reducing the nuclear threat to comparatively lower levels even without a ballistic missile defense.

These conclusions undermine the Reagan administration's official policy justifying SDI and perceptibly weaken support for the program in the West with each passing year. However, the improbability of an "astrodome" defense does not imply the impossibility of various other BMD options with or without space-based elements. The broad front of SDI research and development guarantees the prospect of creating diverse military-technical systems with all kinds of applications, including ASAT systems; third-generation nuclear weapons with selectively enhanced kill effects; qualitatively new technology for surveillance and $C^3I$ systems for space, nuclear, and conventional armed forces; and fundamentally new means of war on the basis of DEW and KEW kill systems. Here lies the enormous momentum, the powerful destabilizing and unpredictable potential of the SDI program, however it may be revised, renamed, or redefined in the future.

The question of the possibility, consequences, and desirability of a limited ballistic missile defense has become a central one in today's debate. The U.S. Congress's resolution on the FY 1987 budget, as noted above, recommended an emphasis on the development of a BMD system for the defense of U.S. strategic forces and their $C^3I$ complex from a hypothetical nuclear counterforce strike.[16] However, the president and other leaders of the Republican administration (although disagreement existed even among them) stubbornly continued to proclaim that SDI's purpose is to create a defense for urban-industrial centers, "to destroy, not defend missiles," and "to defend people, not missiles."[17]

A limited defense of cities modeled on a modernized version of the Safeguard and Sentinel ABM systems (for example, using land-based endoatmospheric and exoatmospheric intercepters, new land-based radars and laser radars (ladars), and air- and space-based infrared means of target acquisition) could hardly be a cost-effective defense of urban-industrial areas given the current levels and qualitative characteristics of offensive nuclear arms. At the same time such systems would exert a destabilizing effect on the strategic balance, in that they would stimulate a further buildup of nuclear arms in order to counter the BMD and would increase the attractiveness of a preemptive strike in a crisis situation with the hope of weakening the enemy's retaliatory power and facilitating the effectiveness of one's own BMD.

In this sense the state and logic of the strategic balance have essentially remained unchanged since the early 1970s. New land-based ABM systems, suitable for deployment in the 1990s, are superior to the Safeguard-Sentinel and Moscow ABM systems along a number of lines, but modern offensive nuclear forces are even more superior to those of almost two decades ago. Even in a purely quantitative respect each power's strategic offensive arms in the 1990s will surpass by three to five times in warheads their forces of the early 1970s. Consequently, all considerations that at that time biased in favor of severely limiting such systems through negotiating the ABM Treaty to the same or even greater degree will remain in force for the foreseeable future.

Also inconsistent is the administration's idea of the feasibility of defending cities with a limited area or territorial BMD in the 1990s as the first or transition phase to the subsequent deployment of space-based echelons when their technology "ripens" by the year 2000. Not to mention that in view of the technical problems and potential countermeasures to a BMD such a system may never become sufficiently effective to justify its enormous cost, the first stage of deployment of a limited BMD would in and of itself seriously undermine strategic and political stability. In the event that additional space-based systems were deployed later, the introduction by the other side of countermeasures, themselves met in turn by counter-countermeasures, would finally and irrevocably destroy stability.

A more serious and complicated question is that of a BMD optimized for defense of strategic forces (point defense) but not having the capability to protect separate regions (area defense) or the country's entire territory. It is now more and more widely argued that hard-point limited BMD systems will, first, be technically more reliable, and second, will strengthen military-political stability.

The first thesis is justified as such: it is much easier to protect hard targets (e.g., ICBM silos, underground command bunkers) from nuclear attack than cities. Indeed, the requirements here are not so high. For example, a 50 percent effective BMD would not prevent catastrophic losses to population and industry but would be quite suitable for preserving a certain retaliatory capability in the event of a nuclear attack. Stability by means of point defense is promised to be enhanced by way of reducing the capability for a disarming first strike, which in turn would save the attacker from retaliation. And supporters allege that one side's BMD system would not undermine the other's confidence in the potential of its own retaliatory strike, since it would be of little effectiveness for the defense of large urban-industrial areas, much less the entire territory of its owner.

Such an approach, its proponents believe, would also help the negotiations to reduce strategic offensive arms. Both powers now possess great surpluses of strategic forces, knowing that in the event of a surprise attack only the surviving share of these forces will be available for retaliation. If these same strategic forces were reliably protected with a BMD system, such surpluses could be reduced.

This argument, in contrast to others concerning SDI, addresses some quite serious issues. It is no accident that it now attracts quite broad circles in the United States and the West as a whole, including as well certain opponents of the militarization of space and dedicated supporters of arms control. However, under close examination this approach reveals substantial flaws. The components of a point defense are relatively less complex and expensive, but one can also quickly create means of penetration against them (for example, MARVs). The offense-defense competition would soon invite a supplement to the hard-point terminal BMD consisting of exoatmospheric interception systems and eventually space-based echelons. The point defense would have to be broadened to an area defense, and then to a territorial and global BMD system—with all the above-mentioned destabilizing consequences for the strategic balance and second-strike deterrent capabilities.

To look at the issue from a different angle, the targets to be protected by a terminal point defense (silo-based ICBMs and launch control centers) account for only about 20 percent of the U.S. deployed strategic potential. Other forces—SSBNs at sea and bombers in the air—are not threatened by the other side's ballistic missiles and can neither be protected by a BMD nor require such protection. As for submarines in port and bombers on the ground, they, like the major elements of the $C^3I$ infrastructure, are not hard and numerous targets (like ICBMs) and can be protected only by a much more sophisticated multilayered BMD system with inherent area and perhaps even territorial defense capabilities (including exoatmospheric, mid-course, and probably boost-phase interception requirements). The development and deployment of such a system would usher in all the consequences characteristic of a territorial defense and inimical to stability.

Deployment of a BMD system for protecting strategic forces would hardly facilitate Soviet-U.S. negotiations. On the contrary, it would require renegotiating the ABM Treaty, which permits each side to have only one complex apiece of not more than 100 interceptors. Obviously, such a small number of interceptors is insufficient for protecting 1,000–2,000 strategic targets from many thousands of nuclear warheads.

But, for the sake of Soviet-U.S. strategic stability, could there perhaps be an agreement to revise the treaty in order to allow broadening a point defense system? Many in the West are raising precisely such an issue. But they have probably ill-considered the consequences of opening this Pandora's box, which was safely locked in 1972.

First, all the complications now being created for the Geneva negotiations by the asymmetry in the two powers' offensive strategic forces would grow geometrically if the disproportions in ABM systems were added to the existing picture. If the defense of all ICBM bases were to be allowed, the United States could protect about 20 percent of its strategic arsenal, while the USSR, more than 60 percent. If BMD were to be permitted for protection of the same number of ICBM fields, then the USSR could defend a much smaller portion of its land-based missiles than the United States.

The location of both powers' missile fields with respect to their urban-industrial areas is very different. The composition of threatening nuclear forces is dissimilar as well, which presents unequal demands even for a hard-point defense. Many problems would also be created by the inter-action of BMD systems with air defense systems. And all of this is a sideline to the powerful mechanism of BMD expansion that is built into the inevitable competition between point defenses and the offensive forces able to overwhelm them. In a word, point defense will create many more problems than it is alleged to be able to solve. Rather than being a more benign alternative to an SDI-type system, it is much more an insidious "foot in the door" for proponents of a large-scale space-based BMD and a bait for many sincere proponents of the traditional notion of stability and arms control.

Second, it is incorrect at the present stage to portray hard-point BMD as a necessary guarantee of a retaliatory strike potential. The oft-mentioned enormous surplus of destructive capability that has been accu-mulated by both sides beyond any reasonable sufficiency allows for a decisive reduction of U.S. and Soviet strategic forces without putting in doubt their retaliatory strike capabilities. No BMD system is needed for this. To the contrary, a point defense in the context of existing nuclear arsenals and strategic concepts would accelerate the trend toward de-veloping arms and operational plans for "limited" and "protracted" nu-clear war. BMD is not needed to ensure simple countervalue finite deterrent forces. However, it may become quite instrumental in much more sophisticated counterforce exchange scenarios, protecting forces and $C^3I$ specifically designed for such a strategy and operations.

Reducing Soviet and U.S. strategic forces, initially by 50 percent, and later to a still lower level, is the only effective, reasonable, and direct way to stability and equal security. In the context of such reductions, of course, the survivability of all strategic force components must not be degraded, so as not to increase the possibility of a first strike either relatively or absolutely. In other words, the arms that pose the greatest first-strike danger should be subjected on a mutual basis to a propor-tionately greater reduction, limitation, and eventual elimination.

Not a revision but, to the contrary, a strengthening of the regime limiting ABM systems on the basis of the existing treaty is the necessary condition. And in the future it may be necessary to supplement it by limitations on ASW, air defense, and other forces that affect the strategic balance, including nonstrategic nuclear arms and the forces of third countries.

## Issues in Preserving the ABM Treaty

In late July 1987 in the course of the eighth round of the nuclear and space arms negotiations, the Soviet delegation presented a draft proposal on certain measures to strengthen the ABM Treaty and prevent an arms race in space. In particular it was proposed to agree on the limitation of parameters and characteristics of objects launched into outer space or placed in an earth orbit. This step was an important landmark in the development of Soviet policy on this issue. It reflected the fact that broad military and civilian advances in technology, impossible to have predicted at the beginning of the 1970s, necessitate special supplementary agreements to clarify the ABM Treaty's provisions as well as the methods of verifying compliance with them.

At the Washington summit in December 1987 both sides agreed that their goal is to achieve an accord in compliance with the ABM Treaty as it was signed in 1972 so that it will not be endangered in the course of permitted research, development, and testing. Both sides will obligate themselves not to withdraw from the treaty for an agreed period of time. Three years before its expiration the two powers will begin intensive negotiations on future ways to strengthen stability. But if they cannot come to an agreement, each side will be free to choose a course of action for itself. An accord on the nonwithdrawal from the ABM Treaty as it was signed in 1972 for a set period of time is viewed as a necessary condition for the deep reductions of strategic offensive weapons. A nonwithdrawal agreement, the ABM Treaty, and a 50 percent strategic offensive arms reduction treaty will all be linked together and have a similar legal status.

It is important to keep in mind that the ABM Treaty has an unlimited duration. According to Article XV either side may withdraw only if some threat to its national security (not simply the technical success of SDI projects) makes compliance with the treaty inconsistent with the supreme interests of the state. A supplementary nonwithdrawal agreement should by no means be interpreted as imposing limited-duration status on an unlimited-duration treaty. If such an understanding gains acceptance in the United States (and some SDI partisans are presently trying to achieve such an effect), then a nonwithdrawal accord will be totally counterproductive. In fact this accord means only that during the agreed nonwithdrawal period, withdrawal from the treaty will automatically and legally invalidate the strategic offensive arms reduction treaty—with all the consequences being the responsibility of the side that withdrew from the ABM Treaty. The meaning of the principle that after a determined period each side will be free to choose its own course of action is that if both sides do not agree on something else after the expiration of the nonwithdrawal period, Article XV of the ABM Treaty will again come into full effect. The chosen course of action may include a unilateral announcement that one party's withdrawal from the ABM Treaty will be a threat to the other's interests, making compliance with the offensive arms reduction treaty inconsistent with its national security.

A nonwithdrawal agreement gives both parties a certain amount of time to reach a number of compromises on limiting permitted research, development, and testing in the field of BMD systems and space exploitation. This is what "intensive negotiations on stability" should focus on primarily, although it would be worthwhile to begin negotiations on the subject without much delay. In the draft protocol and common understandings to this agreement presented by the USSR in Geneva in July 1987 are defined objects, mechanisms, and characteristics of their operations that would be prohibited from being deployed in space if their qualitative parameters and actions exceeded the stipulated thresholds. Thus tests of missile interceptors would be limited in the permitted speed of approach of one object to another in space; electromagnetic rail guns, in the magnitude of the accelerated mass and its acceleration; lasers, in their brightness (joules per steradian); particle beam accelerators, in their energy (million electron volts); and space mirrors for redirecting laser beams, in area. Systems for acquiring and tracking ballistic missiles and their elements in flight would be included as well. The Soviet proposal also provided a definition for the notion of *research work* as that which is carried out on the ground, that is, in institutes, in research and development centers, on testing ranges, and in factories and plants. Deployment in space was understood as putting an object into orbit or into space in other ways and also as putting an object on a ballistic trajectory. For purposes of verification the USSR proposed, in addition to national technical means, an exchange of data on objects deployed in space and, most important, a challenge on-site inspection (i.e., at space vehicle assembly buildings on the ground) of objects scheduled to be put into space and their lift vehicles at the launching sites, if the other side's concern cannot be alleviated by other means.

The role of an agreement on the limits and thresholds of permitted research, development, and testing is crucially important in the overall framework of strategic offensive, defensive, and space-based arms issues, though it is still widely interpreted as simply a sort of secondary supplement to the ABM Treaty. However, agreement here appears to be more important than agreement on any kind of nonwithdrawal accord. In fact without threshold agreements the very concept of the organic relationship between the reduction of strategic offensive arms and compliance with the ABM Treaty would be quite pointless. Since nontraditional BMD and space technology is at issue, only a definition of thresholds of permitted work can serve as the basis for either a mutual obligation to observe the ABM Treaty (in connection with the reduction of strategic offensive arms), or as an indicator of the violation of the treaty by one of the parties (for justifying the other side's corresponding countermeasures, including those related to offensive strategic forces).

As is known, the so-called broad interpretation of the ABM Treaty, which SDI proponents persistently tried to push through in 1985–87, begins its departure from the authentic interpretation in Article II, where an ABM system is defined as "currently consisting of" ABM interceptors, their launchers, and radars constructed and developed for an ABM role. The "broad" interpretation contends that the phrase "currently consisting of" implies that only the enumerated components comprise an ABM system and that only they are the subject of the treaty. The authentic understanding of this phrase holds that it merely specifies the concept of an "ABM system" and its "components" that existed at the moment of the signing of the treaty but in no measure denies that all other potential and future ABM systems must be the subject of the treaty. Such an understanding is affirmed by other provisions of the treaty included in the preamble, by Article I, Article III, and others.

Depending on whether the "broad" or the authentic interpretation is used, Article V, which obliges the parties "not to develop, test, or deploy ABM systems or components which are sea-based, air-based, space-based, or mobile land-based," relates either exclusively to traditional ABM components or to any qualitatively new kinds as well. In this connection Agreed Statement D, which addresses itself to future ABM systems based on new physical principles, is also distorted by advocates of SDI. According to the "broad interpretation," since Agreed Statement D obliges the parties to discuss the specific limitations on the deployment (not development and testing) of new and exotic systems and components in order to comply with the limitations on deployment of Article III, any development and testing of new systems is supposedly allowed. Such "experiments" with systems based on new physical principles in space-based and air-based modes make up the majority of SDI projects through the mid-1990s.

According to the original understanding, Agreed Statement D hardly means that Article V does not relate to it. It does not restrict the sphere of operation of this article (such a restriction would contradict the supplemental documents to the treaty) but, to the contrary, gives meaning to and clarifies it. This statement naturally permits the development and testing of systems based on new physical principles only in a fixed ground-based mode, since Article V prohibits the development and testing of ABM systems or components in any other basing modes. The meaning and essence of Agreed Statement D is that even the deployment of exotic, fixed ground-based systems cannot be undertaken unilaterally according to one's own interpretation of how the limits of Article III apply to new BMD components. A special agreement of both parties is required for such a deployment, since the provisions of this article are specified only in conformity with the traditional ABM components that existed in the early 1970s.

It is obvious that the "broad interpretation" of the treaty contradicts its letter and spirit, a conclusion reaffirmed by Senator Sam Nunn's report in early 1987. To carry out the development and testing of BMD systems within the framework of the "broad interpretation" would be incompatible with the principle of the inviolability of the ABM Treaty regime. It would destroy the treaty and make strategic offensive arms reductions impossible. Fortunately this understanding was reflected as well in the U.S. Congress's resolution on FY 1988 SDI appropriations. Indeed, this approach to the ABM Treaty was fixed in the joint Soviet-U.S. declaration at the Washington summit in December 1987, at which the participants expressed their goal to reach an agreement during a certain period not to withdraw from the ABM Treaty "as it was signed in 1972."

The problem, however, is that even with the preservation of the authentic understanding of the treaty without supplementary agreements, serious complications for strategic stability and the disarmament process may arise. Three basic points may serve as the source of the great problems in preserving the ABM Treaty. They are:

—the uncertainty involved in differentiating the permitted research and the prohibited development, testing, and deployment of systems based on new physical principles;

—the erosion of boundaries between the development of fundamentally new BMD systems and the improvement of technology in other non-BMD military and civilian spheres using directed energy systems, the exploration of space, electronic-optical means, next-generation computers, improved energy sources, and so forth;

—the difficulty of verifying activities in these spheres, which could complicate for a power not only the physical discovery of a certain activity of the other side but also the identification of its character and purpose, and the exposure and proof of the fact of a violation of the ABM Treaty.

These circumstances can interact with each other in various combinations, catalyzing uncertainty, mutual suspicions, and political and military-technical instability. Article II of the treaty defines components of ABM systems: ABM interceptor missiles are "constructed and deployed for an ABM role, or of a type tested in an ABM mode"; ABM launchers are "launchers constructed and deployed for launching ABM interceptor missiles"; and ABM radars are "radars constructed and deployed for an ABM role, or of a type tested in an ABM mode." It is obvious that the most undeniable evidence of prohibited work on systems based on new physical principles (capable, as is mentioned in Agreed Statement D, "of substituting for ABM interceptor missiles, ABM launchers, or ABM radars") in violation of the treaty would be the testing of such systems against strategic ballistic missiles or their elements in a flight trajectory.

But the very fact of testing a BMD against a ballistic missile could be quite reliably verified only with respect to the interception or kill system, and only then if the target were destroyed or subjected to some noticeable influence (for example, deflection from trajectory). The testing of many passive or even interactive SATKA systems would be significantly more difficult for the other side to verify with the assistance of only national technical means. At the same time, it is precisely these systems and functions, substituting in a certain sense for traditional ABM radars, which are now considered the most crucial part of the SDI program and more difficult to develop than direct means of interception. Once perfected, it would be comparatively simple and require less time to match SATKA with corresponding kill systems. Thus progress on SATKA or SATKA-type projects may in the greatest degree push one of the sides forward toward the capability of acquiring a large-scale space-based BMD.

But even with BMD strike weapons as such, including space-based interception systems whose testing would be relatively easy to verify, the stage of full-scale testing would be too advanced toward a "breakout" deployment of a large-scale BMD for the other power to wait calmly to obtain this incontestable proof of the treaty's violation. Article V prohibits not only the deployment and testing, but also the development (*sozdanie*)[18] of space-based and other mobile ABM systems. The importance of this provision is that it allows each party to the treaty significantly greater time for taking political-legal and military-technical countermeasures against the transgressor. Legitimate grounds for such measures (and possibly, the renunciation of the corresponding treaties) must be the indisputable evidence of a violation of the ABM Treaty by the opponent. For that reason the treaty's limitations must as early as possible put verifiable barriers in the path of prohibited activity. Only then will countermeasures undertaken in advance have a greater chance of neutralizing the violator's attempts to acquire strategic superiority. And in this way the probability itself of attempts to break out of the treaty will be reliably deterred with respect to a potential transgressor by the certainty of early discovery of noncompliance and all its consequences, including military countermeasures by the other side.

However, the earlier the stage of work on new BMD components that is chosen as the threshold of the limitation, the more difficult it will be to discover the activities, to identify the character of activities as prohibited, and to prove their incompatibility with the treaty. Many systems under the SDI rubric, for example, are justified by arguments that they are supposedly incapable of fulfilling the functions of ABM components, since they have insufficient effectiveness and will not be tested in an ABM mode (that is, against ballistic missiles and their elements in flight trajectory). They are called, therefore, not "components" but "subcomponents," "prototypes," and "adjuncts." Development is defined as "research," and testing, as a "demonstration." The most complex task is, therefore, to find an optimal balance between the requirement to stop potentially destabilizing programs as early as possible and the capability to reliably verify the nonviolation of such limitations among the many technologies capable of playing a role in ABM components.

The matter is complicated as well by the fact that the work on many technical projects may serve the purposes of developing prohibited BMD components but not be captured directly by the treaty, since it has a broad application in other civilian and military spheres. For example, lasers have such tremendous prospects as communications, intelligence, and target discrimination and identification systems, and in tracking objects in and from space. Infrared and other electro-optical sensors in space can be used both for BMD as well as for early warning, intelligence, and other tasks. Space-based radars, including phased-array, can fulfill functions of both prohibited BMD components as well as systems for tracking objects in space, national technical means of verification, peaceful scientific research, communications, and for remote probing of the earth. Space-based energy systems (including nuclear reactors or power storage cells), various communication and navigation satellites, and next-generation supercomputers have multiple applications but are indispensible as support and battle management subsystems for a space-based BMD.

Certain space strike weapons capable in one way or another of fulfilling BMD functions pose a serious threat in and of themselves. For that reason they are an obligatory subject of special negotiations (in particular ASAT weapons and probable "space-to-ground" class strike systems). But they do not fall directly under the limitations of the ABM Treaty if they are not tested against ballistic missiles. The development of these systems, should they not be halted or limited by a subsequent agreement, apart from all their destabilizing consequences as such will inexorably begin to intrude from space ("from above") into the sphere of the ABM Treaty and gradually erode it.

Simultaneously, there is the danger of an analogous process "from below," through the improvement of systems for countering tactical ballistic missiles (ATBM systems) with nuclear or conventional warheads, the development of new high-acceleration air defense missiles against the new generation of SLCMs and ALCMs for strategic and tactical supersonic attack. These weapons may be developed since the ABM Treaty covers only systems for countering "strategic ballistic missiles." And at the same time they may be capable of serving as a terminal defense layer in a large-scale BMD for intercepting warheads in the terminal phase of flight. Many systems of that kind can be mobile and redeployed quickly in order to shift to functions of a terminal defense from strategic missiles.

Even within the framework of activities permitted by the treaty some potential components of a large-scale BMD may undergo significant development. For example, there may be attempts to justify land-based, air-based, and space-based infrared pointing and tracking systems, or laser and particle beam means of target acquisition and discrimination, as "accessory" equipment for increasing the effectiveness of the one ABM complex permitted each side by the treaty, to which allegedly the established limitations do not apply.

Another example is the constructing and testing of powerful fixed ground-based lasers (excimer or free electron) on agreed test sites, which is permitted by Agreed Statement D covering systems based on other physical principles. Theoretically, several such lasers under the guise of test models, should their irradiation power and the ability to compensate for atmospheric distortion be high enough, could in and of themselves provide an effective antisatellite capability and major component to a large-scale BMD.

In the latter case, it is true, the deployment of space-based reflective mirrors would be required. In order to prevent such a course of events an understanding is necessary on the fact that orbiting mirrors would be prohibited as "space-based ABM components," even though they themselves are incapable of replacing either radars or launchers in ABM functions. It will be necessary to separate according to certain parameters such objects from laser mirrors for communication, tracking space objects, and so forth. In order to limit their testing at an earlier stage the capability of determining the presence or absence of unpermitted mirror systems on corresponding space objects, and in general the ability to detect experiments with the laser illumination of space objects "in an ABM mode," will be required.

These examples show how serious are the tasks that must be resolved in the interests of preserving the ABM Treaty. That is why it seems prudent not to waste time but to use the nonwithdrawal period to begin negotiations on permitted activities as soon as possible. With a mutual Soviet and U.S. understanding and interest in strengthening the regime that limits BMD, the sides would first of all have to agree on which systems based on new physical principles and which technical developments in adjacent areas represent the greatest threat as potential components of a large-scale BMD system.

It then would be required to define in each case a threshold of effectiveness beyond which a given system would have a substantial capability to fulfill functions of ABM components or integral parts of ABM components and which would delimit the use of this system in an ABM mode from permitted civilian and military tasks.

The next logical step would be the identification of parameters in the construction or operation of the object that most adequately reflect its effectiveness according to the chosen criteria. Finally, an understanding is needed on the means and methods of verification that correspond to the selected parameters, including measures for cooperative verification, on-site inspections, and counting and assessment rules.

Along these lines it would be useful to establish such parameters both for the testing of new systems and for their deployment, which is most important if testing poorly lends itself to verification. Ultimately the expediency of one threshold or another for strengthening the ABM regime would be determined by an aggregate of factors: by the degree of the importance of a given system or object for the purposes of a large-scale BMD; by the appropriateness of the parameter according to which the threshold is being established as an indicator of a system's effectiveness; by the ability to distinguish with sufficient accuracy the use of a system at a near-threshold level in an ABM mode from other modes and tasks; by the degree of reliability in verifying thresholds with the use of national technical means and supplemental cooperative verification measures, on-site inspections, and so forth.

It is obvious that in a number of cases reliably guaranteeing the inviolability of the ABM Treaty is possible only with a simultaneous ban on ASAT systems and weapons of the "space-to-ground" (space-strike) class. In view of the technical uncertainty and futuristic nature of the latter's prospects, ASAT presently appears as the most important issue in negotiations both to strengthen the ABM regime and prevent an arms race in space.[19] This relationship has all the more significance in that many BMD systems in the process of development will inevitably pass through a stage in which they possess powerful ASAT capabilities even at levels of effectiveness significantly below those that are required for BMD purposes.

Many space systems, in particular charged-particle beam accelerators, kinetic interceptor missiles, electromagnetic rail guns, and nuclear-pumped X-ray lasers, would simply have no use in space if an understanding were reached on the prohibition of ASATs. The Soviet leadership and influential forces in the United States have proposed banning ASAT weapons. This desire is reflected in the moratoria on ASAT testing adopted unilaterally by both the Soviet Union and the United States since 1983 and 1985, respectively (in the U.S. case by Congress's amendments to the FY 1986, 1987, and 1988 military budgets). "Space-to-ground" strike systems enjoy even less popularity. The United States officially rejects plans to create them, and even their military rationale with a few exceptions (such as some counter-$C^3I$ space-based systems) remains quite questionable. Therefore a whole array of potential space weapons, in the event of an ASAT ban, would be halted completely at an early stage of development without need for establishing the many complementary thresholds on permitted research and development and testing. Inspection in space vehicle assembly buildings prior to launch, verification of space-lift vehicles on launch pads, and national technical means for verifying compliance in space (with some cooperative provisions) would offer a reliable guarantee against experimenting with such objects in space, thereby in parallel substantially strengthening the inviolability of the ABM Treaty.

An exceptionally important element of the Soviet draft agreement was the proposal to provide for, if necessary, on-site inspections of objects scheduled to be sent into space and their launchers. By way of inspecting space launchers and their payloads at the launch sites before or after loading, one may verify with a significant degree of certainty the presence or absence of explosives (besides those necessary for stage separation and a charge for emergency self-destruction); fuel and a motor for maneuvering in space (apart from those needed for reaching the programmed orbit and correcting orbital anomalies); objects of self-navigation; shrapnel-type materials for destroying targets in space; powerful radio transmitters and large antennae (beyond the requirements of communication) for guiding radio interference and generating microwave radiation in space; nuclear fuel for reactors beyond the requirements of providing energy for permitted activities; interceptor missiles; nuclear weapons; directed energy systems; and so on. Both visual as well as X-ray and gamma ray examination, Geiger counters, computerized tomography, and so on, can be used as methods of verification.[20] An examination utilizing several physical principles would make the use of camouflage, insulation, or protective cover quite ineffective for concealment. Moreover, their very presence would serve as grounds for suspicion.

Inspections could be conducted by representatives of a special international agency for verifying compliance with limitations, in particular under the aegis of the UN. In such a way certain truly secret details of space payloads not connected with prohibited activities could be spared from inspection, such as computer program security, electronic wiring diagrams, design and material features, and so forth. In any event, certain aspects of secrecy in military and commercial activities in space would best be sacrificed for the sake of a much more important goal—the reliable prevention of an arms race in space, with the strengthening of strategic stability, preservation of the ABM Treaty, and progress toward deep reductions of offensive nuclear weapons.

## In Search of a Compromise on Offensive Arms Reductions and Stability

In the post-Reykjavik period of Soviet-U.S. negotiations both sides, while diverging in the vision of the ultimate goals of strategic arms reductions, did create an important zone of overlapping interests concerning the desirability and feasibility of a major first step on this path, a 50 percent reduction of launchers and warheads over a five-year period.

As for future follow-on measures, the Soviet approach has at least some advantages over the U.S. one. Having in view a fully defined ultimate goal—the complete elimination of strategic arms—however difficult to attain this may now seem, the USSR is able to plan a long-term policy with consecutive steps for moving toward this goal, all the while preparing in advance the necessary attendant measures of disarmament. Such a course obviously puts disarmament negotiations at the apex of national security strategy and subordinates weapons programs to the goal of preserving parity and stability with the decreasing levels of the nuclear balance.

The U.S. approach first of all suffers from uncertainty about the ultimate goal of the strategic offensive arms reduction process. If it envisages halting this process after implementing 50 percent reductions or at some other (which?) lower level, then it is thereby doomed to undermine the officially proclaimed goal of "strengthening the stability of the strategic balance." Indeed, at whatever level the process of strategic offensive arms reductions would stop, however stable would be the balance set by the treaty from the beginning, technical progress in the sphere of strategic offensive arms and in adjacent areas will inevitably erode this stability over time and will create new means and methods of initiating and conducting nuclear war. The uncertainty of an ultimate goal dooms U.S. policy in arms limitations and reductions to following the tail of strategic offensive arms modernization programs. The U.S. negotiating position will thus be forced much more to accommodate itself to strategic programs than the other way around. This tendency was manifested quite graphically during the negotiations following the Reykjavik summit, when the greatest attention was concentrated on elaborating the first, 50 percent, stage of strategic offensive arms reductions.

The draft treaties for a 50 percent reduction of strategic offensive arms, introduced by the United States on May 8, 1987 and by the Soviet Union on July 31, 1987, were an important stage in the nuclear and space arms negotiations. A comparison of the two draft treaties allows one to clearly highlight the similarities and differences in the two sides' initial negotiating positions.

Concerning the general provisions, the similarity of Soviet and U.S.

approaches was reflected in both sides' expression of the opinion that nuclear war would have devastating consequences for all mankind; that measures for reducing and limiting strategic offensive arms will facilitate reducing the danger of the outbreak of war and strengthening international peace and security; that the interests of both sides and of international security require strengthening strategic stability. Both powers proceeded from a consideration of their obligations under Article VI of the Treaty on the Non-Proliferation of Nuclear Weapons.

The fundamental differences in the general provisions were that in the USSR's draft, in contrast with the U.S. document, it was pointed out that measures for reducing and limiting strategic offensive arms represent an important step in the direction of the ultimate complete elimination of nuclear weapons everywhere. The Soviet Union's draft observed that the interests of international security require an immediate cessation of the arms race on earth and its prevention in space. The USSR put special emphasis on the inseparable organic relationship between strategic offensive arms reductions and limitations in the area of BMD systems.

Also stressed in the Soviet document was the adherence of both sides to the 1972 ABM Treaty and the necessity of measures to strengthen it. Finally, it was observed that the draft treaty embodies the understandings reached at the Soviet-U.S. summit at Reykjavik on October 11 and 12, 1986, and that the parties are being guided by the principle of equality and equal security.

In defining the concepts and terms of the treaty, on which in turn largely depends the essence of its provisions, the positions of both sides basically coincided in the definition of an ICBM (a land-based ballistic missile with a range greater than 5,500 kilometers) and an SLBM. There were differences, however, in interpreting many terms. Certain concepts were contained in one side's draft treaty but were absent in the other's. They included: "launcher," "deployed ICBM," "deployed SLBM," "nondeployed ICBM," "nondeployed SLBM," "heavy ICBM," "heavy SLBM," "launch weight," "throw-weight," "launcher intended for testing," "warhead," "rapid reload," "installation for the production of ballistic missiles," "test site," "means for launching space-traversing objects," "space launch center," and others.

Both sides substantially diverged in what was understood to be within the category of "heavy bombers." For the Soviet Union, this meant presently the inclusion of the Soviet Tupolev-95 and Tupolev-160 and the U.S. B-52 and B-1B, and in the future, bomber types for each side that can fulfill tasks of heavy bombers in an analogous or better way. For the United States, the Soviet Tupolev-95 (Bear), Miasishchev (Bison), Tupolev-22M (Backfire), and Tupolev-160 (Blackjack) and the U.S. B-52 and B-1B were included in the heavy bomber category.

In quantitative limits, equal ceilings on the overall number of ICBM and SLBM launchers and heavy bombers as a result of the reductions were set at 1,600 in both side's draft treaties. The number of nuclear warheads on these systems was set at 6,000. Counting rules for heavy bombers equipped with bombs and short-range missiles also coincided: one such aircraft is counted as one launcher and one warhead.

The main differences were that the U.S. document included a sublimit of 4,800 warheads on deployed ICBMs and SLBMs, a sublimit of 3,300 warheads on deployed ICBMs, and an additional sublimit of 1,650 warheads for deployed ICBMs, excluding warheads on nonheavy silo-based ICBMs equipped with six or fewer warheads. Furthermore, in accordance with the earlier U.S. position, the new U.S. draft also included a limit on total ICBM and SLBM throw-weight at a level comprising 50 percent of the greater of the two sides' levels possessed as of December 31, 1986. The United States also introduced a provision on equal intermediate maximum levels in the course of reductions by the agreed dates.

The Soviet Union proceeded from the principle of allowing each side the right to determine the structure of its weapons remaining after the reductions according to its own discretion (freedom to mix). The only sublimit mentioned in the Soviet draft stipulated reducing deployed Soviet heavy ICBM launchers by 50 percent, that is, to a level not exceeding 154 missiles. At the same time the USSR included a provision to limit, apart from the 1,600–6,000 overall levels, long-range (greater than 600 kilometers) sea-launched cruise missiles at a ceiling of 400, with the stipulation that they be deployed only on certain types of submarines whose number in turn would be limited.

Qualitative limitations in both documents coincided concerning the obligation not to test ICBMs with more than ten warheads per missile. Both versions contained a provision on the exchange of data on the strategic offensive arms structure and on prohibiting the encryption of telemetry information during missile testing. The possibility of on-site inspection was envisaged, including as well at production enterprises for strategic arms.

Differences in this area included the Soviet proposal to undertake an obligation not to deploy long-range SLCMs on surface ships. The United States for its part introduced a provision that neither side produce new or modernized types of heavy ICBMs, flight-test them, or deploy them. The United States also stipulated that both sides refrain from deploying additional heavy ICBMs of existing types and that test launchers of such ICBMs be banned. This related as well to heavy SLBMs and the modernization and reconfiguration of their launchers. The U.S. document contained a ban on the production, testing, and deployment of mobile ICBMs and called for the destruction of mobile ICBM launchers and auxiliary installations and equipment within one year after the ratifica-

tion of the treaty. The United States also included in its draft a ban on
the flight testing of SLBMs with more than 14 warheads, whereas the
USSR proposed a limit of ten.

The nature of these divergences in the draft treaties is rooted in the
differences of the Soviet and U.S. approaches to the nature of the military-strategic balance and strategic stability. Based on its understanding
of stability, the United States is striving to change significantly the structure, operational planning, and military capabilities of the Soviet Union's
strategic forces. Arbitrarily defining ICBMs as the most "destabilizing"
weapons, the United States has insisted on including sublimits (4,900–
3,300–1,650) in the treaty that would entail breaking up the traditional
composition of Soviet strategic forces, conditioned by the specifics of the
USSR's geostrategic position, technological development, organizational
structure, and military doctrine and strategy.

As of 1987 the USSR had approximately 60 percent of its nuclear
warheads deployed on ICBMs, more than 30 percent on SLBMs, and
about 5 percent on heavy bombers.[21] If the Soviet Union had accepted
the U.S. sublimits, no more than 55 percent of its warheads could have
remained on land-based missiles, 25 percent on SLBMs, and 20 percent
on heavy bombers. In particular the 4,800 ballistic missile warhead sublimit would quite perceptibly affect Soviet strategic forces. Keeping 3,300
(55 percent) of its warheads on ICBMs, the Soviet Union would have
the right to only 1,500 warheads on SLBMs, which (considering the
distribution of various types of launchers on submarines) would entail
an almost five-fold reduction of the number of SSBNs, including the
dismantling of more than half of the relatively new submarines with
MIRVed missiles brought into the force since the late 1970s.[22]

The U.S. 1,650-warhead subceiling along with the provision to reduce
Soviet heavy ICBMs by 50 percent (to 1,540 warheads) would in practice
force the Soviet Union to cancel the RS-22 (SS-24) missile system, since
only 11 such ICBMs could be deployed within this limit. Similarly strict
limitations would be imposed on heavy ICBMs–traditionally the key
element of Soviet strategic forces—since producing, testing, or deploying
them in modernized versions and modifying or re-equipping their
launchers would be prohibited. In practice this would mean the gradual
"atrophication" of this system. The provision to prohibit and dismantle
mobile ICBMs would kill two Soviet programs at once: the RS-22 (SS-
24) MIRVed ICBM system and the RS-12M (SS-25) modernized single-
warhead ICBM.[23]

As for U.S. strategic forces, they would be affected less deeply according to the provisions of the U.S. draft treaty. With the retiring of
obsolete submarines (built in 1962–67) carrying Poseidon and Trident-I
SLBMs, old B-52 bombers (produced in the late 1950s and early 1960s),
and the Minuteman-II and some Minuteman-III ICBMs (1965–75), the

United States could in practice completely reconfigure its strategic forces with the latest systems. Specifically, within the limits of its subceilings it could deploy, for example, 17 *Ohio*-class submarines with Trident-II SLBMs, 70 B-1B heavy bombers with cruise missiles,[24] and 130 Stealth penetrating bombers, in addition to 100 new MX ICBMs, while retaining more than 200 Minuteman-III missiles with new Mk-12A warheads. Alternatively the United States could have 50 MX missiles and 380 Minuteman-III missiles (or 50 MX, 200 Minuteman-III, and 500 new single-warhead Midgetman missiles), provided that mobile land-based missiles are allowed.

As has been shown in the preceding chapters, the U.S. version of strategic stability, the basis of the U.S. approach to arms control arouses the most serious objections, both in its very essence and in relation to the principle of the equality and equal security of both sides. Notable, however, is the circumstance that Washington's position in reducing strategic offensive arms in a number of important respects contradicted even its own concept of stability, which according to official U.S. statements supposedly dictates U.S. military programs as well as its negotiating positions, and which is allegedly directed at strengthening the security of both sides through reducing each one's capability for a first strike.

This contradiction is manifested especially in the provision that prohibits mobile ICBMs. During the SALT II negotiations in the late 1970s, at a certain stage the prohibition of such systems was discussed. At that time the United States refused, since it was developing a mobile basing system for the MX missile. Later, in early 1983, the Scowcroft Commission recommended in favor of developing the Midgetman mobile single-warhead ICBM system. The shift to mobile basing was championed by a group of the most authoritative U.S. experts as a key factor for increasing the invulnerability of strategic forces, enhancing their retaliatory capability, and strengthening strategic stability.

Now the U.S. side has proposed banning such systems. While the fate of the Midgetman system is still a subject for debate within the U.S. Congress, the strategic community, and the Pentagon bureaucracy, the Soviet Union, in case of such a limitation, would immediately be deprived of the opportunity to increase the survivability of its strategic missile forces in the face of the growing counterforce threat of the new U.S. systems (MX, Trident II, cruise missiles), which possess a great capability for striking fixed hard targets, such as ICBM silos.

The U.S. provision to prohibit mobile ICBMs was officially justified by the difficulties of verification, in particular verification of the ban on the capability for the rapid reload of ICBM launchers. It is obvious, however, that with the comprehensive methods of verification being discussed now by the two sides, including on-site inspection based on the experience of the intermediate- and shorter-range missile treaty (having to do mainly with land-based mobile missiles), it would be possible to ensure reliable guarantees against a reload capability for mobile ICBM launchers. Symptomatic in this connection is the serious criticism this proposal has provoked both on the part of the strategic community, including its conservative representatives, and the opposition in the U.S. Congress.[25]

The administration has demonstrated precisely the opposite attitude toward verification issues affecting U.S. military programs. The U.S. draft treaty neglected any kind of limitations on long-range SLCMs, despite the understanding in principle reached in this regard at Reykjavik. SLCMs are a clearly pronounced destabilizing weapons system. They are highly accurate and have hard-target-kill capability. Their launch and flight are difficult to detect with the assistance of space- and land-based early warning means, which creates a threat both to the other side's strategic forces and to its $C^3I$ systems.

The United States plans to deploy around 4,000 *Tomahawk*-class cruise missiles in various modifications with nuclear and conventional warheads on the multipurpose *Los Angeles*- and *Sturgeon*-class nuclear submarines (in sum, on 93 SSNs by the mid-1990s), as well as on about 100 existing and planned surface vessels of the *New Jersey, Virginia, California, Ticonderoga,* and *Burke* class.[26] It is characteristic that the problem of verification therefore did not disturb the United States. In its May 1987 draft proposal it refused to discuss limitations on SLCMs, apart from nuclear-armed ones, although in practice the various versions of this system cannot be differentiated by functionally related observable differences, that is, visible external features.

The construction of new ICBM launchers was permitted in the U.S. document, since a new basing system for the MX may be required. Such a stipulation, however, goes contrary to the provision forbidding the construction of new fixed launchers that was enshrined in SALT I and SALT II—and at the insistence of the United States itself. This provision has traditionally been considered a most important parameter of limiting the buildup of strategic missiles.

Despite the official U.S. line, in accordance with which sea-based missile forces in view of their high survivability are considered "stabilizing," the subceiling at 4,800 ICBM and SLBM warheads in the U.S. draft treaty would entail, as was observed above, a manifold reduction in the number of Soviet SSBNs. This reduction would substantially broaden the effectiveness of the U.S. ASW mission, whose main task, according to the "Maritime Strategy" of former Secretary of the Navy John Lehman and Chief of Naval Operations James Watkins, is to search for and destroy the other side's strategic missile-carrying submarines. In this case as well the publicly proclaimed principle of strategic stability is given quite cavalier treatment.

One cannot help but observe that the Soviet draft in no way pursued the goal of accommodating the agreement to the USSR's deployed strategic forces and ongoing programs. Even with the preservation of the traditional structure of Soviet strategic forces, the Soviet Union over a period of five years would have to remove from its force structure more than 50 of its 62 strategic submarines. With the deployment of a certain number of RS-22 (SS-24) and RS-12M (SS-25) mobile land-based ICBMs and the reduction of the RS-20 (SS-18) heavy ICBMs to a level of 154 missiles there would simultaneously be dismantled, as one possible option, around 1,020 ICBMs of various types, and also a significant number of Tu-95 and Miasishchev bombers. The strategic forces of the USSR would be reduced by approximately 5,000 nuclear warheads.

Even without any sublimits, the 50 percent reductions would more perceptibly affect the strategic offensive arms of the Soviet Union than those of the United States. This is true for two main reasons. First, as is known, historically the United States has had a more or less balanced strategic triad. According to counting rules, as measured by warheads 21 percent of its forces are found on ICBMs (53 percent by launchers), on SLBMs, 52 percent (34 percent), and on heavy bombers, 27 percent (13 percent), respectively. By virtue of its geostrategic position and organizational-technical development the Soviet Union has had the following distribution of warheads: more than 60 percent on ICBMs (56 percent as measured by launchers), more than 30 percent on SLBMs (37 percent), and on heavy bombers, about 5 percent (7 percent).[27] This means that with 50 percent reductions, should the parties strive for preservation of their existing structures and reduce each component on an equal percentage basis, the U.S. reductions would be spread out more or less evenly, whereas the USSR would have to reduce the relative share of air- and sea-based components to quite low levels of forces in absolute numbers.

A second factor is connected with the fact that, because of the unevenness of the development of the two powers' strategic forces (the Soviet Union historically has basically responded to U.S. actions with an average five-year delay in the deployment of systems[28]), there are significantly more single-warhead delivery vehicles in Soviet strategic forces than in U.S. forces. In 1987 single-warhead missiles and bombers without ALCMs comprised 51 percent of Soviet delivery vehicles, and for the United States, 40 percent.[29] At the same time Soviet MIRVed ICBMs and SSBNs and ALCM-carrying heavy bombers are approximately 5–7 years "younger" than the U.S. ones. Moreover, the most expensive weapons systems (in terms of per-unit cost)—nuclear-powered submarines carrying MIRVed missiles—concede by age an average of 15 years to U.S. SSBNs. All of this means that reducing strategic forces by 50 percent will require the Soviet Union to dismantle much newer and less obsolete systems, especially submarines. The retiring of the older single-warhead missiles and aircraft provides a significant reduction in launchers (more than 50 percent), but a very small one in warheads (13 percent). The United States could in theory relatively painlessly reduce its strategic offensive arms by 60 percent in launchers and 65 percent in warheads (according to counting rules) at the expense of obsolete single-warhead and multiple-warhead delivery vehicles and old submarines.[30] This would be more or less sufficient for the 50 percent reductions and in addition would create a reserve for the introduction of new-generation strategic forces.

From the above calculations it becomes clear why the USSR would want to preserve a certain freedom of hand for carrying out reductions in order not to incur additional economic and technological costs. Nevertheless, manifesting a sincere desire to reach a compromise, the Soviet Union has taken a number of substantial steps to meet the U.S. position. In the course of the Washington summit the sides drew noticeably closer together on positions for preparing joint formulations of key parameters of the 50 percent strategic force reductions. Not only was the previous principle of a 50 percent reduction of strategic forces to a level of 6,000 nuclear warheads and 1,600 delivery vehicles for each side confirmed, but limits on heavy ICBMs—154 missiles with 1,540 nuclear warheads on them—were also agreed upon. An understanding was reached that the total throw-weight of Soviet ICBMs and SLBMs would be reduced by 50 percent to a level not to be exceeded by either side. The establishment of a sublevel of 4,900 ICBM and SLBM warheads was also a new feature. An agreement on ICBM and SLBM warhead counting rules was also reflected in the statement. A decision was made to concentrate attention on counting rules for ALCMs and on limiting long-range nuclear-armed SLCMs with a separate ceiling above the 6,000/1,600 limits. Based on the experience of the treaty on intermediate- and shorter-range missiles, measures for verifying the implementation of the future strategic arms agreement were developed significantly further.[31]

In light of such developments, the additional limitations on the structure and qualitative characteristics of both sides' weapons systems in the 50 percent reduction stage acquire much greater significance. In fact, on them will depend the stability of the strategic balance, the possibility and probability of a nuclear first strike. The introduction of sublimits (in particular, 1,540 delivery vehicles and 4,900 warheads) poses a question about a whole number of other limitations in order to assure strategic stability after the reduction of strategic forces by 50 percent. By the counting rules, the sublimit of 4,900 ICBM and SLBM warheads, in the event of the deployment of up to 3,300 warheads on ICBMs, would permit the Soviet Union to have five *Typhoon*-class submarines with SS-N-20 (*Typhoon*) missiles and 9–10 boats with SS-N-23 SLBMs (or alternatively, only eight *Typhoon* boats or any combination of submarines with the consideration that three boats of the latter type (called Delta-IV in the West) equal a single *Typhoon*-class SSBN). The number of remaining SSBNs may be increased, for example, at the expense of limiting ICBM deployment to a level of 3,000 warheads. As a result more SSBNs would remain on duty and would provide a more invulnerable sea-based deterrent potential (approximately five more boats with SS-N-23 missiles). But in such an event less than 1,460 warheads (3,000 minus the 1,540 on heavy ICBMs) would be spread among other types of land-based ballistic missiles. This would mean—even with the removal of the U.S. provision to ban mobile missiles—either 146 RS-22 (SS-24) mobile missiles, or a combination of MIRVed and single-warhead ICBMs (considering one RS-22 equal to ten single-warhead ICBMs). And the more RS-22 missiles (analogous to the MX system) deployed, the fewer the number of RS-12M-class (SS-25) single-warhead missiles there may be and the lower still the number of launchers in the land-based component.

The subceilings and other limitations proposed by Washington are based on a meticulously elaborated concept of "strategic stability." This concept has been formulated and widely discussed in the United States over the course of two decades among experts, politicians, and representatives of the mass media. Although the concept is not monolithic and has a number of differing versions, both the U.S. negotiating line and its strategic programs are justified by its general provisions.

In fact this concept has many vulnerable points and has come under serious criticism in the Soviet academic literature.[32] As has been shown above, U.S. military programs and negotiating proposals often contradict its own concept of stability. But since the strengthening of strategic stability is today assigned such an important place in Soviet-U.S. negotiations, it is obvious that at an official level the two sides' approaches to strategic stability require a more detailed and comprehensive explanation, discussion, and direct agreement. In those areas where U.S. forces can be limited by way of agreements, the necessity for certain Soviet nuclear arms and programs is eliminated, the elimination of which can in turn become part of the agreements. The decisions of the 27th CPSU congress, which gave highest accord to the political means of strengthening security, prescribe in precisely this way the ordering of priorities.

Disclosing and achieving a mutual understanding of military concepts would better permit the powers to understand in what way the strategy of the inadmissibility of war and orientation toward a retaliatory strike predetermines the existing and future structure and quantitative and qualitative characteristics of each other's strategic forces. Simply speaking, it would be useful to elucidate which potential nuclear war scenarios are considered to be the most probable and dangerous, what kinds of actions are assumed to be anticipated from the adversary in such a situation, and in what way strategic forces are called upon to implement a retaliatory strike in these conditions.

The disclosure of these issues in the context of publicizing and discussing military doctrines, as proposed by the Soviet Union, cannot weaken security. Indeed, the main goal of Soviet military doctrine (and in turn, of strategy, operational art, and force structuring) is to prevent nuclear war, not to "surprise" the opponent, if it has nevertheless decided to attack. The United States for its part also officially declares its exclusive adherence to the policy of deterrence and rejects plans for a first strike and capability for fighting and winning a nuclear war. The goal to prevent nuclear war, as well as its conviction that such a war cannot be won, have been repeatedly affirmed in the joint documents of the two countries.

Of course, some amount of military uncertainty can facilitate deterrence. The specific details of operational planning, the functioning of the $C^3I$ and warning system, to be sure, must be kept secret (and they are kept secret not only by the Soviet Union but by the United States as well) so that the other side will not attempt to take advantage of particular information for acquiring a "decapitating" or "disarming" strike capability. But uncertainty is quite counterproductive when it serves as the source of mutual distrust and suspicion, when it feeds new rounds in the arms race or is used for justifying them, and finally, when it encourages attempts to impose unequal agreements on the other side. And to the contrary, the elimination of excessive uncertainty would remove the grounds for speculation in this respect and facilitate reaching mutually acceptable agreements in the Geneva negotiations.

The political approach to guaranteeing security assumes major reductions of arms, both old and new. In this connection it is unnecessary to decry the impending removal from the arsenal of submarines, missiles, and aircraft. Such is, after all, the real process of disarmament. But the stability of the strategic balance must not be shaken in the course of this process. Since the sublimits now being discussed, as was shown above, would perceptibly limit the number of Soviet ICBMs and SLBMs (and SSBMs), it is, of course, not unimportant for the USSR which new systems the United States will be deploying in the late 1980s and 1990s under the agreed overall limits and sublimits. The reduction of strategic forces must lead to the strengthening of stability and the limitation of the counterforce potential of both sides (including as one of its elements hard-target-kill capability and the ability to barrage the deployment areas of land-mobile missiles). In this connection there are grounds for certain additional structural quotas on the strategic forces remaining after the reductions either under a 50 percent reduction or in the context of a follow-on strategic arms reduction agreement.

For instance, concerning sublimits for certain classes of ICBMs, it would be sensible to include certain subceilings within other components of the strategic triad as well. It would be useful to limit the deployment of the most destabilizing systems at sea and in the air. This concerns the new Trident-II SLBM and cruise missiles on heavy bombers (to be sure, along with their technical analogues in the USSR). So, rather than on the 17 boats planned, the United States might be limited to deploying Trident-II missiles on a much smaller number of *Ohio*-class submarines. The number of ALCMs deployed might too be limited. As a result, the number of powerful and accurate counterforce weapons that undermine stability and increase the threat of a nuclear first strike could be reduced.

Following the principle of guaranteeing security by political means, it would be possible to propose still more far-reaching measures. For example, the number of warheads on those systems that both sides consider destabilizing and posing the greatest danger for a disarming first strike could be limited by low and equal subceilings within each component. These sublimits would capture on the U.S. side the MX, Trident-II, and ALCM systems, and on the Soviet side the analogous weapons plus heavy missiles. Of course, in this event it would be necessary to seriously limit an additional number of Soviet weapons, but in return the new and dangerous U.S. systems would be sharply limited, with a substantial gain for the stability and security of both sides. More radical steps are possible as well, especially in light of the USSR's intentions not to stop with 50 percent reductions.

Proceeding from considerations of increasing the survivability of strategic forces, a ban on land-mobile ICBMs in the course of reductions is hardly justified, as long as there is the guarantee for adequate verification opportunities. To be sure, SLCMs, as one of the most destabilizing types of strategic weapons, must be limited. If the United States is prepared to discuss the limitation of only nuclear-armed SLCMs, they must themselves render assistance in guaranteeing reliable verification. If it is too difficult to limit and verify SLCMs as they are currently produced and deployed in the United States, then it would be necessary to make them verifiable, for example by changing their production and deployment pattern or perhaps even their technical features. It may also be necessary to apply complementary verification and control procedures, including permanent monitoring, onsite challenge inspections, and new technical detection means. Regarding land-mobile ICBMs and other Soviet systems, they pose precisely the same such issues. There is no reason whatsoever to treat sea-launched cruise missiles as a sacred cow. If verification measures and military programs come into contradiction, then for the sake of concluding more substantial agreements the second should be sacrificed, not the first. The political approach to guaranteeing security must be manifested in this area as well.

Moreover, a sharp reduction in the number of SSBNs will again urgently raise the problem of an agreement to limit ASW activities and forces. Radical measures conforming to ALCMs and SLCMs could in turn be accompanied by limitations on strategic air defense elements.

A serious approach to the strengthening of strategic stability at reduced levels of the nuclear balance—and the U.S. military-political leadership, one would like to hope, regards this problem seriously—is incompatible with attempts to "squeeze" unilaterally one's negotiating partner as much as possible while giving up as little as feasible, as well as with impulses to mask the buildup of its counterforce potential (i.e., the capability for a disarming strike), with considerations of "stability." The reduction of strategic arsenals, the lowering of the possibility and probability of nuclear war, is not a "zero-sum game." As the almost 20 years of negotiating experience on this problem (in some ways successful, in some ways not) show, the search for mutually acceptable agreements must proceed only from the common interests of both sides. Attempts to obtain unilateral advantages ultimately always turn against their initiator. Negotiations between governments and wide-ranging discussions among experts are necessary to broaden and deepen in every possible way the sphere of these mutual or overlapping interests of the USSR, the United States, and their allies, with the goal of reducing the physical size of the destructive arsenals and narrowing the probability of their use.

## Notes

1. Strobe Talbott, *Deadly Gambits* (New York: Vintage Books, 1985), xii.

2. *Pravda*, January 9, 1985.

3. U.S. Information Agency, "Realism, Strength, Dialogue" (Washington, D.C.: U.S. Government Printing Office, 1985), 7, 13–14, 23.

4. *Pravda*, April 11, 1985.

5. *Pravda*, February 26, 1986.

6 See Evgenii P. Velikhov, Roald Z. Sagdeev, and Andrei A. Kokoshin, eds., *Kosmicheskoe oruzhie: dilemma bezopasnosti* (Moscow: Mir, 1986); *SOI: amerikanskaia programma "zvezdnykh voin"* (Moscow: Voenizdat, 1987); "SOI: opasnosti, illiuzii, al'ternativa," *Novoe Vremia* [special supplement], 1987.

7. *SOI*, 66.

8. *SOI*, 113.

9. *Science and Technology of Directed Energy Weapons: Report of the American Physical Society Study Group* (Washington, D.C.: American Physical Society, April 1987).

10. *Science and Technology of Directed Energy Weapons*, 2–3.

11. Joseph Kruzel, ed., *American Defense Annual, 1987–1988* (Lexington, Ky.: Lexington Books, 1987), 76.

12. Evgenii M. Primakov, ed., *Razoruzhenie i bezopasnost', 1986, Volume 1* (Moscow: Novosti, 1987), 78.

13. *SOI*, 337.

14. *SOI*, 30–44.

15. *Otsenki dinamiki i perspektiv realizatsii programmy SOI* (Moscow: ISKAN, 1987), 23.

16. Kruzel, *American Defense Annual, 1987–1988*, 76.

17. Union of Concerned Scientists, *Empty Promise: The Growing Case against Star Wars* (Boston, 1986), pp. 149–56.

18. Translator's note: The precise translation of the Russian noun *sozdanie* (and its verb form *sozdavat'/sozdat'*) has been a point of contention in some quarters in the ABM Treaty interpretation dispute. Some argue that rather than translating as "development" (or "to develop"), as it is in the official English-language version of the ABM Treaty, it in fact means "creation" (or "to create"). The implication is that this latter translation would produce a more restrictive Article V. These same persons also argue that *razrabotka* and its corresponding verb form more closely approximate the English word *development*. In any event, it has been chosen here to adopt translations as they appear in the official English-language version of the treaty with the hope that this will be most familiar to the reader.

19. For more detail see *Razoruzhenie i bezopasnost', 1986. Volume 2* (Moscow: Novosti Press Agency, 1987).

20. Robert Bowman, *The Potential Role of On-Site Inspection in Preventing an Arms Race in Space* (Chesapeake Beach, Md.: Institute for Space and Security Studies, 1987).

22. The lifetime of an SSBN is usually 25–30 years.

23. *Razoruzhenie i bezopasnost', 1986, Volume 1*, 26; *Izvestiia*, August 12, 1987.

24. Or more, depending on the resolution of the counting rules question regarding ALCM bombers, which involves the number of ALCMs per bomber, any ALCM range limitations, and verification procedures.

25. Kruzel, *American Defense Annuals, 1987–1988*, 79.

26. Thomas B. Cochran, William M. Arkin, and Milton M. Hoenig, *Nuclear Weapons Databook: Volume 1, U.S. Nuclear Forces and Capabilities* (Cambridge, Mass.: Ballinger, 1984), 185, 247–60.

27. *Razoruzhenie i bezopasnost', 1986, Volume 1*, 39.

28. *Otkuda iskhodit ugroza miru* (Moscow: Voenizdat, 1987), 9.

29. *Pravda*, March 17, 1987.

30. *Pravda*, March 17, 1987.

31. *Pravda*, December 12, 1987.

32. See: "Strategicheskaia stabil'nost' v usloviiakh radikal'nykh sokrashchenii iagernykh vooruzhenii," Moscow: IMEMO, April 1987; also Alexei G. Arbatov, A. A. Vasil'ev, and Andrei A. Kokoshin, "Iadernoe oruzhie i strategicheskaia stabil'nost'," pt. 1, *SShA*, 9 (September 1987): 3–13; and Alexei G. Arbatov, A. A. Vasil'ev, and Andrei A. Kokoshin, "Iadernoe oruzhie i strategicheskaia stabil'-nost'," pt. 2; *SShA*, 12 (December 1987): 17–24.

# Conclusion

Writing on the strategic balance, the nuclear and space arms race, and on the current arms control negotiations is a bit like shooting at a moving target. It is probably the most dynamic area of contemporary international relations and domestic politics within the major countries, as well as of technological development. As for the negotiations, this rapid tempo of events in the current situation is an auspicious feature, a fortunate departure from the practice of the preceding 20 years of the Soviet-U.S. dialogue.

Owing to this rapid change, the state of the talks on strategic offensive, defensive, and space weapons will most likely again be different (hopefully in a positive sense) from the circumstances in which this book is being completed.

Still, the U.S.-Soviet summit in Washington in December 1987 seems to be a good point to complete the historic analysis, an analysis that has covered more than a quarter century of political events, weapons systems, strategic doctrines, and arms control negotiations. The Washington summit and the treaty on intermediate- and shorter-range missiles have underscored a distinct historical period of Soviet-U.S. relations, of strategic parity, deterrence strategy, and a new philosophy of stability, national security, and disarmament efforts.

Hopefully, perhaps, it will become clear in retrospect that the third Reagan-Gorbachev summit was a watershed in the 40-plus years of the nuclear-space era. Let us not make our bets now but note only that contemporaries have seldom realized it when they lived through crucial turning points in history. In any case, the events of this long period, crowned by the summit in 1987, lend themselves to certain generalizations and conclusions.

The approximate equality, or parity, of Soviet and U.S. strategic nuclear forces in the early 1970s marked the coming of a new period in the history of postwar international relations. The main effect of parity was not military but rather political. To the extent that in the postwar period the United States strove to build its relations with the surrounding world on the basis of military superiority over the socialist countries and of economic and political hegemony in the nonsocialist world, the major changes that took place in the course of the 1960s and were glaringly evident by the early 1970s have set the greatest problems squarely before U.S. policy.

U.S. ruling circles have tried to solve this problem in various ways over the past years, devoting in this respect primary attention to the correlation of nuclear forces between the USSR and the United States— one of the central issues in contemporary world politics. And here contradiction and inconsistency have distinguished Washington's policy, around which has taken place the most acute and persistent struggle of various alignments of the U.S. political elite and that has ultimately drawn in the broad U.S. public and spilled over beyond its borders. The complex processes and changes in the realm of the global nuclear balance over the past years, on the one hand, have been expressed in the steady broadening of the military-strategic equilibrium, which served as the basis for the first Soviet-U.S. treaties and agreements to curb the arms race. But on the other hand, the buildup of the arsenals of global destruction has continued in many directions, dangerous doctrines and concepts for using these forces have been advanced one after another, and not just once has the arms control dialogue led to a dead end or have attempts been undertaken to torpedo already existing agreements. As a result, if one looks at the state of affairs from Washington's perspective, then in comparison, for example, with the late 1960s, and even more so with any previous period, the strategic situation for the United States at the present time has become noticeably more complicated.

Indeed, over the security of the United States, just as over that of all other countries of the world, hangs the terrible threat created by the probability of putting into action the colossal modern destructive potentials, the accumulation of which the United States itself commenced 40 years ago. But to approach the matter objectively, one can see that in the perspective of the 1980s and beyond, two kinds of problems, essentially, stand before the United States. First, there are circumstances of a more or less objective character conditioned by the specifics of the current tendencies of the military balance. This concerns the existing structural and technical asymmetries in the Soviet and U.S. nuclear arsenals, which are the result of the peculiarities of their geostrategic positions and technological development. This also has to do with the complexity of undertaking long-term decisions on military programs whose implementation requires many years and enormous appropriations. Also involved are issues of the growing obsolescence of various strategic arms, issues that become more or less acute depending on how rapidly the weapons were introduced in the past. Finally, the intensive development of military technology periodically leads to the deployment of still more effective and refined arms able to introduce qualitative changes in the global military balance and pose new problems for strategy and policy.

Earlier, when it possessed nuclear superiority or significant unilateral advantages, the United States found it much easier, to be sure, to resolve these problems than at present, when the strategic balance places both sides at an equal position. At the same time, sufficiently rapid movement forward in the dialogue on arms limitations and reductions could in principle eliminate or significantly alleviate these difficulties. In this respect it is obvious that some of the problems (still being exploited by alarmists in the United States) were in large degree conditioned by U.S. attempts to achieve unilateral strategic advantages during the 1970s and 1980s, which instead urged on the strategic nuclear arms race and ultimately complicated the situation for the United States itself, such as was demonstrated by the MIRV experience.

Second, the situation of strategic parity has sharply reduced the United States' ability to use the nuclear threat in foreign policy. Meanwhile, the doctrine to use nuclear weapons first (and subsequently to escalate strikes to the intercontinental level) has been and remains the cornerstone of U.S. commitments to NATO and other blocs, the implicit and sometimes explicit instrument of political pressure covering direct military intervention in the Near and Middle East and other faraway regions. In this respect, arms control negotiations indeed cannot help the United States. Since the strengthening of parity and stability can be the only possible basis for arms control, such negotiations invariably only increase these "problems" in U.S. policy and strategy, for strategic equilibrium and stability fundamentally contradict the most important element of U.S. foreign policy: namely, the threat to unleash and conduct thermonuclear war, which in turn demands unilateral advantages or overall U.S. nuclear superiority in offensive, defensive, and space weaponry.

U.S. claims to a "special right" in this respect—the most glaring manifestation of the philosophy of "American exceptionism," of the inability to see itself as others see it—no doubt will never be allowed by other nations. But U.S. attempts to ensure for itself such capabilities by means of still newer weapons and strategic concepts only urge forward the strategic competition, increase the threat of global war, and complicate the arms control dialogue. Consequently, in the present situation the security of the United States itself is thus also being undermined to a growing degree. The past decade has been quite significant, for during the two terms of the Reagan administration the fundamental contradiction that lies at the heart of the dialectics of U.S. strategic policy has been vividly revealed. The contradiction is Washington's unwillingness to resign itself to strategic nuclear parity while being unable to change it in its favor in any significant way; its unwillingness to accept an equitable arms control dialogue with the Soviet Union while being unable to guarantee U.S. predominance in an unlimited military competition and bear the costs of an uncontrolled arms race.

There does exist a possibility to ease or eliminate the problems arising in U.S. strategic policy in the conditions of strategic equilibrium. But it exists not on the futile and dangerous path of upsetting parity and achieving superiority, but on the path of fundamentally restructuring Washington's relations with the surrounding world, of peacefully resolving international conflicts, of promoting policies of restraint and cooperation among the great powers and all interested states, and of pursuing broad and radical disarmament agreements. Thus the roots of the current problems lie in the manifest unwillingness of the West's ruling circles in the first half of the 1970s to move significantly further along the path of decreasing tensions, international cooperation, and arms control. Another chance to do that may present itself in the late 1980s and the 1990s. It would be wise for the West's responsible leaders and concerned public to try not to miss it again.

For the Soviet Union, adjusting to the state of the strategic equilibrium also raises complex problems, although of quite a different order than for the United States. First of all, there is the problem of finding the concrete criteria of reasonable sufficiency, which involves finding the most rational asymmetric responses to U.S. strategic and military space programs. These responses should be oriented not toward competing with the other side in analogous weapons systems, but toward developing different arms suited to the specific character of the Soviet geostrategic situation and technical capabilities, and to more simple and realistic strategic goals and operational requirements. This policy will not only render the other side's attempts to gain strategic advantages militarily and technologically futile, but also counterproductive and not cost-effective economically.

Second, the preservation of reliable deterrence at the highest and most important military level (strategic nuclear) means that less-stringent requirements are acceptable for the security of the USSR and its allies at the lower, theater nuclear and conventional force levels. This applies to, among other things, considerations of third powers' nuclear forces, opposing tactical nuclear systems, and so on. It also creates better prospects for reorienting conventional and dual-purpose weapons and forces on principles of defensive strategy and defensive sufficiency. This provides an opportunity for substantially reducing in Europe the Warsaw Treaty Organization and NATO force levels, and rearranging force structures (that is, the complement of offensive and defensive arms) and deployment.

There is also the important task of further integrating arms control and defense posture into the overall grand policy and strategy of international security, emphasizing the political ways of strengthening the security of the USSR and its allies, most of all through disarmament agreements. Their political effect sometimes outweighs the military effect of certain disproportions in arms reductions and limitations, which may be accepted for the sake of promoting arms control and alleviating political tension and the threat of war.

Finally, the expansion of openness (*glasnost*) in all aspects of the life of Soviet society is inseparable from and applies to the area of Soviet military policy-making and the formulation of principal arms control positions as well. The recent disclosure of Soviet and Warsaw Pact military doctrine initiated a follow-on process of broader information on strategic and operational concepts, force levels, and weapons programs as well. The tradition of secrecy dating from the period of Soviet strategic inferiority (and from even much earlier times) in many cases has become counterproductive in the present situation. As Soviet Foreign Minister Eduard Shevardnadze said, there should be no topics closed for discussion. Openness in the field of military strategy, programs, and arms control—without compromising the truly delicate aspects of security— will facilitate a much broader discussion among politicians, experts and in public circles in the USSR with the goal to examine thoroughly alternatives in national security policy and avoid miscalculations, excessive costs and problems in the future. This will also increase confidence between the USSR and other states, and alleviate suspicions and uncertainty, providing a firmer basis for stability and arms reductions and limitations. (And in addition this may make future books of this kind more balanced in their analysis of both sides' decision-making policies and programs.)

The above-mentioned ways of adjusting to the fundamentally new situation have already found expression in the "global double-zero" treaty, the Soviet approach to SDI, a nuclear test ban, a 50 percent strategic arms reduction, and proposals for substantially reducing conventional forces in Europe. This policy, based on principles of reasonable sufficiency, defensive defense, and a political emphasis in security strategy, proved to be successful in 1985–87, and there is good reason to further develop and refine it in the years to come.

In the West, most of all in the United States, it is widely believed that the U.S. and NATO "position of strength policy" in the 1980s eventually obliged Moscow to make concessions, which led to the "global double-zero" treaty and brought a 50 percent strategic forces reduction treaty within reach. Nevertheless, this "conventional wisdom" seems deeply flawed and, what is worse, may lead to wrong conclusions prone to many complications for East-West relations, including especially U.S.-Soviet arms control negotiations.

The first half of the 1980s was a difficult time for international relations in general and Soviet foreign policy in particular: the consequences of the breakdown of negotiations by late 1983, the stalemate of the Geneva talks in 1985–86, the acceleration of the arms race, the growth of world tension, and the continuing tragic war in Afghanistan with no hope for the end of hostilities all figured importantly among the considerations that served as the basis for a major revision of the attitude toward security problems in Moscow in the second half of the decade. But it was not the U.S. "position of strength policy" that caused this change in the Soviet position.

Actually, in purely military terms there was no U.S. or Western superiority that could have served as a foundation for such a policy. The USSR does not and will not in the foreseeable future lag behind the United States in strategic offensive forces and programs. The USSR, until the provisions of the 1987 Washington Treaty have been carried out, will possess larger intermediate-range and operational-tactical nuclear missile forces than does the United States and NATO. Neither is there a Warsaw Treaty inferiority in the conventional military balance in Europe. On the contrary, most Western sources ascribe to the WTO differing degrees of advantage or even superiority over NATO. And SDI, though very destabilizing, remains a quite dubious project in its potential for providing the United States with a strategic preponderance.

Also, from the economic and technological point of view, there is no doubt that the Soviet Union is able to sustain a high rate of the arms race indefinitely if arms control is unsuccessful in the future. Though the arms race is a heavy burden on the Soviet budget, virtually all specialists agree that the main source of Soviet economic problems lies elsewhere. It is the internal inefficiency of its traditional economic system, namely the inadequate incentives for high productivity, technological innovation, preservation and delivery of products to consumers, efficient use of resources, and quality control. Savings due to arms reductions, though potentially beneficial, are in no way a panacea in this respect. And radical economic reforms can drastically improve the economic situation in spite of the continuation of the arms race.

The fact is that the revision of Soviet negotiating positions after 1985 was part and parcel of the policy of general reconstruction of the Soviet economy, sociopolitical conditions inside the country, and its relations with the outside world. Most of all it was the revised attitude toward the realities of the nuclear-space age and the requirements for national security. There is a growing realization that under the existing state of the nuclear balance an advantage in numbers and destructive power of certain weapons and military forces may be not a blessing but a liability in arms control negotiations. Attempts to preserve advantage block the search for compromise at the negotiating table and provoke countermeasures from the opponent, which lead to counter-countermeasures and fuel the arms race to the detriment of the security of all sides. This is one of the most important new realities of the present situation.

Radical Soviet steps in the search for mutually acceptable solutions in the arms control talks, the readiness to do away with more weapons and forces as a result of agreements, are not concessions made under the political and military pressure of the West. They are the reflection of new political thinking in matters of security, a changed assessment of Soviet and WTO military requirements, a new attitude toward the various asymmetries of the military balance. They reflect the influence of reorganizing the decision-making process and introducing innovative ways to conduct disarmament negotiations. All these are also an integral part of the general *perestroika* of Soviet foreign policy. Its most important watershed was the great act of statesmanship in signing the Geneva agreement in April 1988, a prudent although very difficult decision to end the war in Afghanistan and begin the withdrawal of Soviet troops.

Most of the Soviet concessions in arms control talks since 1985 were concessions to common sense, and ultimately to its own security interests interpreted in much broader terms than the arithmetic calculations of missiles, aircraft, and nuclear warheads. Relative advantage in the number of nuclear weapons does not strengthen security if the absolute level of the nuclear threat to both sides is rapidly growing. Dismantling more warheads and missiles than the other side is not detrimental to one's own security if the nuclear threat to all parties is being reduced and in certain categories totally eliminated. Decommissioning relatively more missiles, submarines, and bombers, belonging either to the United States or the USSR, does not equal a corresponding gain or loss from a treaty if as a result the capability for both sides to deliver a disarming strike is substantially reduced and strategic stability enhanced.

Foregoing certain dubious options for new orbital weapons and systems is quite worth preventing the arms race from expanding into the vastness of outer space, avoiding dismemberment of the arms control process and existing regimes, and averting the squandering of astronomical amounts of resources on a space competition instead of mutually beneficial economic and scientific cooperation. Thorough and intrusive arms control verification is no less in the interest of the East than in that of the West, especially considering the recent U.S. record on different interpretations of the ABM Treaty, and actions with regard to SALT I and SALT II.

On the agenda of the negotiations to limit and reduce nuclear arms arise increasingly more complex problems. The only possible basis for these negotiations is military-strategic parity, and their goal has been and remains strengthening strategic stability at lower and lower levels of parity with the strict observation of the principle of the equal security of both sides. At the same time the very notion of the military-strategic balance is acquiring a new content by virtue of the creation of increasingly newer arms accompanied by increasingly more dangerous strategic concepts. The most important task in maintaining the military-strategic balance becomes the adoption of those measures that deprive a potential aggressor of the possibility of counting on a disarming or damage-limiting first strike. The future dialogue to limit and prohibit new kinds and types of weapons that increase the threat of a first strike and undermine the stability of the military balance is possible only on this basis. Deep reductions and stringent limitations on strategic offensive, defensive, and space systems are the only available ways to put under mutual control the military-technological race to higher and higher lethal frontiers.

Problems of the military correlation of forces, military strategy, military programs, and arms control are the most important, although quite specific as well, area of individual states' foreign policy and of international relations as a whole. The objective situation today is such that with the accumulated thermonuclear potentials that threaten the very existence of biological life on the planet, strategic concepts and plans not only determine how war would be conducted should it suddenly break out—and in fact many of these plans are utterly divorced from reality—but condition the very probability of nuclear conflict. It is the greatest international political issue of our time. Questions of the rate, scale, and directions of the arms race, intimately linked with strategic concepts, have also become a most important factor in the international situation that largely defines the degree of political tension in the world arena and the prospects for arms control and disarmament agreements.

The past decade has been a severe test for the matter of peace and disarmament, and not a few new difficulties and threats have been erected in their way. This has shown how carefully must be treated the first sprouts of mutual understanding and cooperation between states with different social systems, agreements on limiting military rivalry, and the first steps toward renouncing the policy of force. Events of the past years have demonstrated how strong still are the opponents of détente, how durable are archaic approaches to fundamentally new problems, and how easy it is to revive the spirit of chauvinism and militarism, to urge the world on toward the slide into the abyss of thermonuclear war.

But it is precisely in these difficult conditions, as never before, where the great "margin of safety" of the strategic equilibrium between the USSR and the United States has become obvious, just as has the futility of attempts to upset it and attain some kind of credible superiority.

The contemporary situation in many respects provides vivid testimony to the insurmountability of the new realities. They are the realities of the nuclear-space age, of the interdependence and indivisibility of the world, of the narrowing limits on the threat or use of force as an effective instrument of policy. Also they are the will of Soviet, American, and other peoples for peace, broad contacts, and the exchange of goods, political ideas, and cultural values. And these include the expanding pluralism of the global correlation of forces, ideologies, and national aspirations, which make international cooperation the only way to deal with most of the world's problems.

Not only the United States and the Soviet Union, but also the European states, Japan, China, and other countries must do much to adjust to the new situation. They should change significantly their attitude toward each other and toward the role of military power in their policies. They have to learn to limit their military, political, economic, and ideological interests and aspirations. They have no other rational choice but to find ways to work together to build a world of common security, based on mutually acceptable compromises and peaceful solutions of complicated and potentially explosive problems.

New realities render the present world much more complicated than in previous years, much more difficult and even dangerous to live in, especially with traditional views, perceptions, and policies. At the same time the new realities may serve as a good foundation for the *perestroika* of international relations on more reasonable principles.

# Bibliography

Abramov, Yurii K., and Andrei A. Kokoshkin. "Sostav verkhnego eshelona administratsii Reagana." *SShA: ekonomika, politika, ideologiia* 11 (November 1982): 117–27.

Andropov, Yuri V. *Shest'desiat let SSSR.* Moscow: Politizdat, 1982.

Arbatov, Alexei G. *Bezopasnost' v iadernyi vek i politika Vashingtona.* Moscow: Politizdat, 1980.

Arbatov, Alexei G., A. A. Vasil'ev, and Andrei A. Kokoshin. "Iadernoe oruzhie i strategicheskaia stabil'nost'," pt. 1. *SShA* 9 (September 1987): 3–13.

———. "Iadernoe oruzhie i strategicheskaia stabili'nost'," pt. 2. *SShA* 12 (December 1987): 17–24.

Ball, Desmond. "The Strategic Missile Programme of the Kennedy Administration." Ph.D. thesis. Canberra: University of Australia, 1972.

———. *Deja-Vu: The Return to Counterforce in the Nixon Administration.* Los Angeles, 1974.

———. *Developments in U.S. Strategic Nuclear Policy under the Carter Administration.* ACIS Working Paper no. 21. Los Angeles: University of California, 1980.

——— "Counterforce Targeting: How New? How Viable?" *Arms Control Today* 2: 2 (February 1981).

Bell, Coral. *President Carter and Foreign Policy: The Costs of Virtue?* Canberra: 1980.

Bobrakov, Yurii I. "Ob ekonomicheskoi programme administratsii Reagana." *SShA* 5 (May 1981): 45–51.

Bogdanov, R. G., ed. *SShA: voenno-strategicheskie konseptsii.* Moscow: Nauka, 1980.

Bogdanov, V. and A. Podberezkin. "Podlinnyi istochnik ugrozy miru." *Kommunist* 10 (July 1983): 94–104.

Bowman, Robert. *The Potential Role of On-site Inspection in Preventing an Arms Race in Space*. Chesapeake Beach, Md.: Institute for Space and Security Studies, 1987.

Brandon, Henry. *The Retreat of American Power*. New York: Doubleday, 1973.

Brown, Harold. "Statement in the USA Institute." Unpublished report from the Institute for the Study of the USA and Canada of the USSR Academy of Sciences, Moscow, March 1975.

————. "Speech at Naval War College: Official Text," August 20, 1980. Washington, D.C.: U.S. Government Printing Office, 1980.

————. *Thinking about National Security*. Boulder, Col.: Westview, 1983.

Brownstein, Ronald, and Nina Easton. *Reagan's Ruling Class*. Washington, D.C.: The Presidential Accountability Group, 1982.

————. *Reagan's Ruling Class*. New York: Pantheon, 1983.

Brzezinski, Zbigniew. "How the Cold War Was Played." *Foreign Affairs* 51: 1 (Fall 1972): 181–209.

————. *Between Two Ages: America's Role in the Technetronic Era*. New York: Viking Press, 1978.

Bundy, McGeorge, George F. Kennan, Robert S. McNamara, and Gerard Smith. "Nuclear Weapons and the Atlantic Alliance." *Foreign Affairs* 60: 4 (Spring 1982): 753–68.

Burt, Richard. "The Relevance of Arms Control in the 1980s." *Daedalus* 110:1 (Winter 1981): 159–77.

Carter, Ashton. "Assessing Command System Vulnerability," in Ashton Carter, John Steinbruner, and Charles Zraket, eds. *Managing Nuclear Operations*. Washington, D.C.: The Brookings Institution, 1987, 577.

Cochran, Thomas B., William M. Arkin, and Milton M. Hoenig. *Nuclear Weapons Databook: Volume 1, U.S. Nuclear Forces and Capabilities*. Cambridge: Ballinger, 1984.

Collins, John M. *U.S.-Soviet Military Balance: 1960-1980, Conflicts and Capabilities*. New York: McGraw-Hill, 1980.

Committee on Appropriations. U.S. House of Representatives. "Defense Appropriations, FY 1980, Part 3." *Hearings*. 96th Congress, first session. Washington, D.C.: U.S. Government Printing Office, 1979.

Committee on Appropriations. U.S. Senate. "Department of Defense Appropriations for FY 1965, Part 1." *Hearings*. Washington, D.C.: U.S. Government Printing Office, 1964.

Committee on Armed Services. U.S. House of Representatives. "Military Posture." *Hearings*. Washington, D.C.: U.S. Government Printing Office, 1962.

————. "Military Posture, Part 1." *Hearings*. 95th Congress, first session, March 2-3, 1977. Washington, D.C.: U.S. Government Printing Office, 1977.

Committee on Armed Services. U.S. Senate. "Fiscal Year 1973 Amended Military Authorization Request Related to SALT Agreements." *Hearings*. Washington, D.C.: U.S. Government Printing Office, 1972.

————. U.S. Senate. "Defense Authorization for Appropriations, FY 1980, Part 6." *Hearings*. 96th Congress, first session. Washington, D.C.: U.S. Government Printing Office, 1979.

————. "Nomination of Caspar Weinberger to be Secretary of Defense." *Hear-*

*ings.* 97th Congress, first session, January 6, 1981. Washington, D.C.: U.S. Government Printing Office, 1981.

————. "Nomination of Frank C. Carlucci to be Deputy Secretary of Defense." *Hearings.* 97th Congress, first session, January 13, 1981. Washington, D.C.: U.S. Government Printing Office, 1981.

————. U.S. Senate. "Department of Defense Authorization for Appropriations for Fiscal Year 1982, Part 1, Posture Statement." *Hearings.* 97th Congress, first session, March 4, 1981. Washington, D.C.: U.S. Government Printing Office, 1981.

————. U.S. Senate. "Modernization of the U.S. Strategic Deterrent." *Hearings.* 97th Congress, first session, October 5, November 5, 1981. Washington, D.C.: U.S. Government Printing Office, 1982.

————. U.S. Senate. "Arms Control Policy, Planning, and Negotiation." *Hearings.* 97th Congress, first session, July 21, 24, December 1, 1981. Washington, D.C.: U.S. Government Printing Office, 1982.

————. U.S. Strategic Doctrine. "Strategic Force Modernization Programs." *Hearings.* 97th Congress, first session, October 1981. Washington, D.C.: U.S. Government Printing Office, 1982.

Committee on Foreign Relations. U.S. Senate. "U.S.-USSR Strategic Policies." *Hearings.* Washington, D.C.: U.S. Government Printing Office, 1974.

————. "The SALT II Treaty." *Hearings.* 96th Congress, first session. Washington, D.C.: U.S. Government Printing Office, 1979.

————. "Nomination of Alexander M. Haig, Jr., Part 2." *Hearings.* 97th Congress, first session, January 14, 1981. Washington, D.C.: U.S. Government Printing Office, 1981.

————. "U.S. Strategic Doctrine." *Hearings.* 97th Congress, second session, December 14, 1982. Washington, D.C.: U.S. Government Printing Office, 1983.

Committees on Foreign Relations and Foreign Affairs. U.S. Senate and House of Representatives. *Fiscal Year 1979 Arms Control Impact Statements.* Washington, D.C.: U.S. Government Printing Office, 1978.

————. *Fiscal Year 1980 Arms Control Impact Statements.* Washington, D.C.: U.S. Government Printing Office, 1979.

————. *Fiscal Year 1981 Arms Control Impact Statements.* Washington, D.C.: U.S. Government Printing Office, 1980.

Congressional Budget Office. *Counterforce Issues for U.S. Strategic Nuclear Forces.* Washington, D.C.: U.S. Government Printing Office, 1978.

————. *The MX Missile and Multiple Protective Structure Basing: Long-Term Budgetary Implications.* Washington, D.C.: U.S. Government Printing Office, 1979.

————. *SALT II and the Costs of Modernizing U.S. Strategic Forces.* Washington, D.C.: U.S. Government Printing Office, 1979.

————. *Baseline Budget Projections: Fiscal Years 1983–1987 (CBO Annual Report, Part II).* Washington, D.C.: U.S. Government Printing Office, 1982.

————. *Modernizing U.S. Strategic Offensive Forces: The Administration's Program and Alternatives.* Washington, D.C.: U.S. Government Printing Office, 1983.

*Congressional Policy.* Washington, D.C., 1982.

Cox, Arthur Macy. *Russian Roulette: The Superpower Game.* New York: Times Books, 1982.

*Department of Defense Annual Report, Fiscal Year 1975.* Washington, D.C.: U.S. Government Printing Office, 1974.

*Department of Defense Annual Report, Fiscal Year 1976 and 1977.* Washington, D.C.: U.S. Government Printing Office, 1975.

*Department of Defense Annual Report, Fiscal Year 1978.* Washington, D.C.: U.S. Government Printing Office, 1977.

*Department of Defense Annual Report, Fiscal Year 1979.* Washington, D.C.: U.S. Government Printing Office, 1978.

*Department of Defense Annual Report, Fiscal Year 1980.* Washington, D.C.: U.S. Government Printing Office, 1979.

*Department of Defense Annual Report, Fiscal Year 1981.* Washington, D.C.: U.S. Government Printing Office, 1980.

*Department of Defense Annual Report, Fiscal Year 1983.* Washington, D.C.: U.S. Government Printing Office, 1981.

*Department of Defense Budget, Fiscal Year 1968.* Washington, D.C.: U.S. Government Printing Office, 1967.

*Department of Defense Budget, Fiscal Year 1972.* Washington, D.C.: U.S. Government Printing Office, 1971.

Fallows, James. "The Trap of Rearmament." *The New York Review of Books*, December 17, 1981.

Fedorenko, S. P. "Ideologicheskie aspekty sovremennoi voennoi politiki i strategii SShA," in V. I. Gantman, ed. *Razriadka mezhdunarodnoi napriazhennosti i ideologicheskaia bor'ba.* Moscow: Nauka, 1981, 106–142.

*Final Environmental Impact Statement: MX, Milestone II.* Washington, D.C.: Department of the Air Force, 1981.

"First Strike: An Interview with Daniel Ellsberg," *Inquiry Magazine*, April 13, 1981, 13–18.

Freedman, Lawrence. *U.S. Intelligence and Soviet Strategic Threat.* London: 1977.

Frolov, V. S. "Chto skryvaetsia za modernizatsiei SUS." *SShA: ekonomika, politika, ideologiia* 6 (June 1983): 116.

*From Weakness to Strength.* San Francisco, 1980.

Frye, Alton. "Strategic Build-down: A Context for Restraint." *Foreign Affairs* 62: 2 (Winter 1983/1984): 293–317.

Galbraith, John Kenneth. "The Conservative Onslaught." *The New York Review of Books*, January 22, 1981.

Gorshkov, Sergei G. *Morskaia moshch' gosudarstva.* Moscow: Voenizdat, 1976.

Gray, Colin S. "Presidential Directive 59: Flawed, but Useful." *Parameters* 11, no. 1 (March 1981): 29–37.

Greenwood, Ted. "Qualitative Improvements in Offensive Strategic Arms: The Case of MIRV." Ph.D. diss. Cambridge: The Massachusetts Institute of Technology, 1973.

Hoffmann, Stanley. "Requiem." *Foreign Policy* 42 (Spring 1981): 3–26.

———. "Reagan Abroad." *The New York Review of Books*, February 4, 1982.

Huntington, Samuel P., ed. *Strategic Imperative.* Cambridge, MA: Ballinger, 1982.

Hyland, William G. "U.S.-Soviet Relations: The Long Road Back." *Foreign Affairs* 60:3 (1982): 525–50.

Iakovlev, Aleksandr N. *Ideologiia amerikanskoi "imperii": problemy voiny, mira i mezh-dunarodnykh otnoshenii v poslevoennoi amerikanskoi burzhuaznoi politicheskoi literature.* Moscow: Mysl', 1967.

Joint Economic Committee. U.S. Congress. *Defense Buildup and the Economy.* Washington, D.C.: U.S. Government Printing Office, 1982.

Jones, David C. "United States Military Posture for FY 1981," in Committee on Appropriations. U.S. Senate. "Department of Defense Appropriations for Fiscal Year 1981, Part 1, Posture Statements." *Hearings.* 96th Congress, second session. Washington, D.C.: U.S. Government Printing Office, 1980.

Kahan, Jerome. *Security in the Nuclear Age.* Washington: Brookings Institution, 1975.

Kaplan, Fred. *The Wizards of Armageddon.* New York: Simon and Schuster, 1983.

Khalosha, B. M. *Voenno-politicheskie soiuzy imperializma.* Moscow: Nauka, 1982.

Kincade, William H., and Jeffery D. Porro, eds. *Negotiating Security: An Arms Control Reader.* Washington, D.C.: Carnegie Foundation for International Peace, 1978.

King, Anthony, ed. *The New American Political System.* Washington, D.C.: American Enterprise Institute, 1978.

Kir'an, M. M. *Voenno-tekhnicheskii progress i Vooruzhennye Sily SSSR.* Moscow: Voenizdat, 1982.

Kissinger, Henry A. *American Foreign Policy: Three Essays.* New York: Norton, 1969.

Klimovich, E. and S. Bukharov. "Strategicheskie rakety." *Voennye znaniia,* January 1980.

Kokoshin, Andrei A. *Prognozirovanye i politika.* Moscow: Mezhdunarodnye Otnoshenii, 1975.

Korb, Lawrence. *National Security Organization and Process in the Carter Administration.* Washington, D.C.: American Enterprise Institute, 1978.

————. *The FY 1981–1985 Defense Program: Issues and Trends.* Washington, D.C.: American Enterprise Institute, 1980.

Kronenberg, Philip S. *Planning U.S. Security: Defense Policy in the Eighties.* New York: Pergamon Press, 1981.

Kruzel, Joseph, ed. *American Defense Annual, 1987–1988.* Lexington, Ky.: Lexington Books, 1987.

Labrie, Roger P. *SALT Handbook: Key Documents and Issues 1972–1979.* Washington, D.C.: American Enterprise Institute, 1979.

Leitenberg, Milton. "Presidential Directive 59." *Journal of Peace Research* 18:4 (1981): 312

Lenin, V. I. *Polnoe sobranie sochinenii.* Moscow: Politizdat, 1966.

Lomov, N. A., ed. *Nauchno-tekhnicheskii progress i revoliutsiia v voennom dele.* Moscow: Voenizdat, 1973.

*Materialy Plenuma Tsentral'nogo Komiteta KPSS, November 22, 1982.* Moscow: Politizdat, 1982.

*Materialy XXV s'ezda KPSS.* Moscow: Politizdat, 1977.

*Materialy XXVI s'ezda KPSS.* Moscow: Politizdat, 1981.

McNamara, Robert. *The Essence of Security: Reflections in Office.* New York: Harper and Row, 1968.

Mel'nikov, Yurii M. *Ot Potsdama k Guamu: ocherki amerikanskoi diplomatii.* Moscow: Nauka, 1974.

Myers, Keith A., ed. *NATO: The Next Thirty Years.* Boulder, Col.: Westview, 1980.

Newhouse, John. *Cold Dawn: The Story of SALT.* New York: Holt, Rinehart and Winston, 1973.

Odean, P. *American Security in the 1980s: The Domestic Context.* Williamsburg: IISS, September 10, 1981.

Office of Technology Assessment. *MX Missile Basing.* Washington, D.C.: U.S. Government Printing Office, 1981.

Ogarkov, Nikolai V. *Vsegda v gotovnosti k zashchite Otechestva.* Moscow: Voenizdat, 1982.

Osgood, Robert E. "The Revitalization of Containment." *Foreign Affairs* 60:3 (1982): 465–502.

*Otkuda iskhodit ugroza miru,* 2d ed. Moscow: Voenizdat, 1982.

*Otkuda iskhodit ugroza miru.* Moscow: Voenizdat, 1987, 9.

*Otsenki dinamiki i perspektiv realizatsii programmy SOI.* Moscow: ISKAN, 1987.

Payne, Keith. *The BMD Debate: Ten Years After.* Washington, D.C.: Hudson Institute, 1980.

———. *Nuclear Deterrence in U.S.-Soviet Relations.* Boulder, Col.: Westview, 1982.

Pechatnov, Vladimir O. "Promezhutochnye vybory: itogi, perspektivy." *SShA: ekonomika, politika, ideologiia,* 1 (January 1983): 29–37.

Petrov, N., et al. *SShA i NATO: istochniki voennoi ugrozy.* Moscow, 1979.

Petrovskii, Vladimir F. "Politicheskii realizm i Evropa." *SShA: ekonomika, politika, ideologiia* 7 (July 1983): 7–19.

*The Presidential Campaign 1976, Volume 1, Part 1, Jimmy Carter.* Washington D.C.: U.S. Government Printing Office, 1978.

Primakov, Evgenii M., ed. *Razoruzhenie i bezopasnost', 1986* (vols. 1 and 2). Moscow: Novosti, 1987.

*Public Papers of the Presidents of the United States, John F. Kennedy, 1961.* Washington, D.C.: U.S. Government Printing Office, 1962.

*Public Papers of the Presidents of the United States, Richard M. Nixon, 1969.* Washington, D.C.: U.S. Government Printing Office, 1971.

*Public Papers of the Presidents of the United States, Richard M. Nixon, 1970.* Washington, D.C.: U.S. Government Printing Office, 1971.

*Public Papers of the Presidents of the United States, Richard M. Nixon, 1971.* Washington, D.C.: U.S. Government Printing Office, 1972.

*Public Papers of the Presidents of the United States, Richard M. Nixon, 1972.* Washington, D.C.: U.S. Government Printing Office, 1974.

*Radi mira na zemle: sovetskaia programma mira dlia 80-kh godov v deistvii, materialy i dokumenty.* Moscow: Politizdat, 1983.

"Report of the President's Commission on Strategic Forces." April 6, 1983. Washington, D.C.: U.S. Government Printing Office, 1983.

Roberts, Chalmers M. *The Nuclear Years: The Arms Race and Arms Control, 1945–70.* New York: Praeger, 1970.

Romm, Jeff, and Kosta Tsipis. "Analysis of Dense Pack Vulnerabilities." Report no. 8. Cambridge, Mass.: The MIT Press, 1982.

Savkin, Vasilii E. *Osnovnye printsipy operativnogo iskusstva i taktiki.* Moscow: Voenizdat, 1972.

Scheer, Robert. *With Enough Shovels: Reagan, Bush and Nuclear War.* New York: Random House, 1982.

*Science and Technology of Directed Energy Weapons: Report of the American Physical Society Study Group.* Washington, D.C.: American Physical Society, April 1987.

Scoville, Herbert Jr. *MX: Prescription for Disaster.* Cambridge, Mass.: The MIT Press, 1981.

*Setting National Priorities: The 1983 Budget.* Washington, D.C.: The Brookings Institution, 1982.

Shamberg, V. M. "Ob ekonomicheskikh kontseptsiiakh republikanskoi administratsii." *SShA: ekonomika, politika, ideologiia* 5 (May 1982): 36.

Simonian, Rair. "Kontseptsiia 'vybora tselei.' " *Krasnaia zvezda,* September 28, 1976.

————. *Voennye bloki imperializma.* Moscow: Voenizdat, 1976.

SIPRI. *World Armaments and Disarmament: SIPRI Yearbook 1983.* London: Francis and Taylor, 1983.

*SOI: amerikanskaia programma "zvezdnykh voin."* Moscow: Voenizdat, 1987.

Sokolovskii, V. D., ed. *Voennaia Stategiia.* Moscow: Voenizdat, 1968.

*Strategicheskaia stabil'nost' v usloviiakh radikal'nykh sokrashchenii iadernykh vooruzhenii.* Moscow: IMEMO, April 1987.

Stromseth, Jane E. *The SALT Process.* Geneva, 1981.

Trofimenko, Genrikh. *SShA: politika, voina, ekonomika.* Moscow: Mysl, 1976.

Tucker, Robert. W. *The Purposes of American Power.* New York: Praeger, 1981.

Tucker, Robert W., and William Watts, eds. *Beyond Containment: U.S. Foreign Policy in Transition.* Washington, D.C.: Potomac Associates, 1973.

Union of Concerned Scientists. *Empty Promise: The Growing Case against Star Wars.* Boston: Union of Concerned Scientists, 1986.

*U.S. Defense Policy: Weapons, Strategy and Commitments,* 2d ed. Washington, D.C.: Congressional Quarterly, Inc., 1980.

U.S. Information Agency. "Realism, Strength, Dialogue." Washington, D.C.: U.S. Government Printing Office, 1985.

Ustinov, Dmitrii F. *Sluzhim rodine, delu kommunizma.* Moscow: Voenizdat, 1982.

Van Cleave, William, ed. *Strategic Options for the Early 1980s: What Can Be Done?* White Plains, Md.: Automated Graphic Systems, 1979.

Velikhov, Evgenii P., Roald Z. Sagdeev, and Andrei A. Kokoshin, eds. *Kosmicheskoe oruzhie: dilemma bezopasnosti.* Moscow: Mir, 1986.

*Vneshniaia politika Sovietskogo Soiuza i mezhdunarodnye otnosheniia: 1979, sbornik dokumentov.* Moscow: Mezhdunarodnye Otnoshenie, 1980.

Vorontsov, G. A. *SShA i Zapadnaia Evropa: novyi etap otnoshenii.* Moscow: Mezhdunarodnye Otnoshenii, 1979.

White, Theodore H. "Weinberger on the Ramparts." *The New York Times Magazine,* February 6, 1983.

Zav'ialov, I. "Novoe oruzhie i voennoe iskusstvo." *Krasnaia zvezda,* October 30, 1970.

Zhurkin, Vitalii V. *SShA i mezhdunarodno-politicheskie krizisy.* Moscow: Nauka, 1975.


## Periodicals

*Arms Control Today*
*Aviation Week and Space Technology*
*The Baltimore Sun*
*The Christian Science Monitor*
*Daedalus*
*The Defense Monitor*
*Department of State Bulletin*
*FAS Public Interest Report*
*Foreign Affairs*
*Foreign Policy*
*Inquiry Magazine*
*Izvestiia*
*The Journal of Peace Research*
*Kommunist*
*Krasnaia zvezda*
*The New York Review of Books*
*The New York Times*
*The New Yorker*
*Newsweek*
*Novoe vremia*
*Parameters*
*Pravda*
*Public Opinion*
*SShA: ekonomika, politika, ideologiia*
*The Sunday Times*
*Survival*
*Time*
*U.S. News and World Report*
*Voennye znaniia*

# Index

# About the Author

ALEXEI G. ARBATOV was born in Moscow in 1951. In 1968 he graduated from high school with a specialization in physics. In 1973 he graduated from the Moscow State Institute of International Relations, having majored in world politics and history. In 1976 Arbatov defended his Ph.D. dissertation, which dealt with the subject of systems analysis and its application to decision-making on strategic weapons programs. In 1982 he received his postdoctorate degree in political science, having written on strategic arms negotiations, weapons systems, and nuclear strategy. He has published a large number of articles and three books dealing with problems of disarmament negotiations, the military balance, and military strategy, some of which have been translated and published abroad.

Since 1976 Arbatov has worked in the Institute for World Economy and International Relations (IMEMO) of the USSR Academy of Sciences. He is the head of the Department of Disarmament and Security Affairs, which consists of several dozen researchers and a support staff, including political scientists, economists, engineers, and military professionals. One of the products of the department's work is the *Disarmament and Security* yearbook, a nongovernmental publication assembled by a large group of experts in arms control, military, and political issues, and which is the Soviet equivalent of the SIPRI *Yearbook* and the IISS *Strategic Survey*.

Arbatov is a member of the Scientific Advisory Council to the Soviet Foreign Ministry and has participated as an expert in some of its official delegations and working groups. He is also a member of the Council of

Soviet Scientists for Peace against the Nuclear Threat, as well as other scientific and public organizations. He frequently participates in the Dartmouth conferences, Pugwash and UN Association sessions, and many other exchanges between Soviet and Western scholars.

Arbatov presently lives in Moscow with his wife and ten-year-old daughter.